Cycles
of
Opportunity

A student of the ageless wisdom and the teachings of Carl Jung, the author is managing editor of the *Journal of Esoteric Psychology*. She has four years of undergraduate work in anthropology and English, with an emphasis on mythology, and three years of graduate work in esoteric psychology, which is continuing.

Meditation Qualifier—The meditations in this book are intended to be used in groups. People using these meditations should be experienced at meditation or use these meditations with guidance; in any case, they should use their own judgment and accept full responsibility for the results.

Published by:
Source Publications
P.O. Box 1160, Mariposa, California 95338
source@yosemite.net
http://www.yosemite.net/sources/books/

Cover by:
Todd Eckhoff
Teck Design, Visalia, California 209-732-6235

Printed and bound in the United States of America

Library of Congress Cataloging-in-Publication Data
    Beckham, Carole, 1943-
        Cycles of opportunity / Carole Beckham.
                p.   cm.
        Includes bibliographical references and index.
        ISBN 0-9635766-3-1 (alk. paper)
        1. Theosophy. 2. Meditation.   I. Title.
    BP567.B43   1998
    299'.93--dc21   97-32068
                                        CIP

Cycles
of
Opportunity

Carole Beckham

Source Publications — Mariposa, California

And I gave my heart to seek and search out by wisdom
concerning all things that are done under heaven:
this sore travail hath God given
to the sons of man to be exercised therewith.

—Ecclesiasties 1:13

Contents

List of Tables and Figures

Tables

Figures

To every thing there is a season,
and a time to every purpose under the heaven:
A time to be born, and a time to die;
a time to plant, and a time to pluck up that which is planted;
A time to kill, and a time to heal;
a time to break down, and a time to build up;
A time to weep, and a time to laugh;
a time to mourn, and a time to dance;
A time to cast away stones, and a time to gather stones together;
a time to embrace, and a time to refrain from embracing;
A time to get, and a time to lose;
a time to keep, and a time to cast away;
A time to rend, and a time to sew;
a time to keep silence, and a time to speak;
A time to love, and a time to hate;
a time of war, and a time of peace.

—Ecclesiastes 3:1-8

Preface

The teachings of all mystery schools, including both eastern and western esoteric traditions, come from the same basic ageless wisdom, seeded at the beginning of our evolution and drawn upon over the ages by humanity through our collective consciousness. One of the most exciting revelations a student of philosophy and psychology has is the deepening of understanding that comes with linking the teachings of the various systems with each other, for often one tradition gives clues to help us solve the mysteries of another tradition.

This book draws primarily upon the Trans-Himalayan Yoga system, as presented for western humanity by the Tibetan Master Djwhal Khul through Alice A. Bailey, for these books contain teachings that I have not found elsewhere, especially within the fields of esoteric astrology, telepathy, and the subtle planes. I have integrated the concepts from the Tibetan's work with ideas that were stimulated by a study of the works of Carl Jung; also the western mystery tradition, as presented by Dion Fortune, Paul Foster Case, and others. Personally, I have found the philosophical systems I use to be in basic agreement, once one penetrates to the foundations of these teachings.

I have attempted to present this information in a clear fashion that will make it useful to anyone who is concerned with the upliftment of human consciousness and thinks that meditation might be a way to contribute. Vast numbers of people in all walks of life are already meditating with the intention of helping the world and promoting the cause of increased consciousness and accelerated evolution on Earth. Meditation groups often meet at the full moon, a time when more energies are available and also a symbolic time when we know that others are meeting around the globe, which lends force to what we seek to accomplish. This book seeks to show how we can make best use of the energies available to the planet at a given time.

What's In This Book

The first two chapters are a brief foundational overview of the ageless wisdom teachings. Chapter 1, "Life in the Universe," gives an interpretation of some of the basic philosophical tenets, including the very important Law of Correspondences ("as above, so below," in ancient Hermeticism) and presents thoughts on the processes of evolution of consciousness in the universe. Spirituality is defined as a quest for higher consciousness and a desire for ultimate perfection, and telepathy is shown as a process that naturally occurs in group living. This leads to a discussion of how we can deliberately focus the mind to create thoughtforms that can later manifest into concretion.

Chapter 2, "Levels of Consciousness," presents an overview of some rather technical material that maps the streams of energy that flow into our solar system and eventually into our planetary life. It describes the planes and subplanes upon which these energies manifest and indicates what the effects of these energies could be upon human consciousness. Then it describes the concept and processes of initiation into higher forms of consciousness. This material provides a structure but is not necessary for the understanding of the rest of the book.

Chapter 3, "Mind and Telepathy," expands upon the concepts of the conscious and unconscious mind, particularly from the standpoint of the universal consciousness and the collective unconscious, as presented by Carl Jung. We explore the possible attributes of a collective consciousness. Next we examine the basis for telepathy, which surveys the ideas of both metaphysical and scientific thinkers and shows their commonality. Then we present the concepts of telepathy by the Tibetan and describe the various levels of telepathic communication. We end with a list of ways to develop psychic capacities for constructive work in the world.

Chapter 4, "Astrology, The Science of Relations," discusses relationships: the relationships between astronomy and esoteric astrology and the relationships between traditional astrology and esoteric astrology. This chapter further provides some foundational material on esoteric astrology.

Chapter 5, "The Seven Rays," gives the cosmic sources of energies that come into our system and primarily talks about the seven streams of consciousness called the seven rays. It shows how the rays interact with zodiacal constellations and planets to provide the qualities and characteristics we work with in our lives.

Chapter 6, "The Zodiacal Constellations," is a study of the attributes of the twelve constellations of the zodiac and shows how these constellations interrelate with the rays and planets to further qualify and adapt the cosmic energies for our use. Esoteric astrology, the basis for this chapter, encompasses all that we have learned in traditional astrology, plus it gives us two additional planetary rulerships. So instead of having just one planet associated with a zodiacal sign, we have three, a triangle (or trinity) of signs—we learn throughout the book that threeness is a basic energetic force in the universe. The energies that we discuss in this and the following chapter are from an esoteric and global, rather than an individual, point of view.

Chapter 7, "Solar and Planetary Energy," tells about our Sun and the planets and their roles in advancing the state of consciousness and the evolution of life upon the spiritual Path. We discuss the process of veiling, where the Sun and the Moon stand in for other planets when consciousness on Earth is not advanced enough to handle the greater energies. We also show how the planets work in triangles for certain purposes and describe some of these triangular interactions.

Chapter 8, "Earth Energy," describes what happens to cosmic and zodiacal energies after they reach Earth. It discusses the great centers of the world, Shamballa, Hierarchy, and Humanity, and the work performed by each group. It tells about the activities of the New Group of World Servers, a name given to describe people of all philosophical persuasions and walks of life around the planet whose work and goals are to improve the state of culture and civilization.

Chapter 9, "Timing, Relationships, and Karmic Opportunity," starts with a general discussion of timing and cycles and sets the stage for the study of geometrical forms and aspects. It shows how constellations and planets in various geometrical configurations work with the Law of Periodicity to influence people and civilizations and uplift the consciousness of humanity on Earth. We finally discuss karmic opportunities, how they are managed, the causes and effects of group karma, and how we can understand the karmic parameters of our work.

Chapter 10, "What Energies are Available Now?," tells us how we can analyze an astrological chart of a full-moon event from a spiritual standpoint. This chapter also covers interpretative information not discussed elsewhere in the book, such as the effects of conjunctions, planetary nodes, retrograde planetary movement, and sacred versus non-sacred planets. It discusses the pros and cons of using sidereal or tropical charts, leaving the choice up to you.

This chapter presents further geometrical information that can be used directly for interpretations and introduces the idea of the "complete triangle," which seems to make sense of all the studies of trinities, triangles, and configurations of three. Finally, we have the example configurations, which are four sample full-moon charts, each with unique configurations. These show how we can use the concepts of the complete triangle and crosses of manifestation in actual work.

Chapter 11, "Meditation," discusses meditation and tells us how we can bring in spiritual energies that will elevate our consciousness and, as a result, that of humanity. It presents meditations we can use in our daily practices (some of which are quite practical), at the time of the full moon, and during special spiritual festivals. Most of this information is drawn from or based upon the teachings of the Tibetan and Alice A. Bailey.

Chapter 12, "The Living Commitment," contains my closing comments.

Appendix A is an ephemeris of all the full moons between 1998 and the year 2007. Appendix B give the locations of fixed stars most pertinent to this work.

The Glossary defines and clarifies some of the terminology.

The research for this book was rather extensive, so I have provided ample references and a bibliography for those who would like to continue exploring some of the concepts presented in this book.

Finally I have provided a brief list of groups who can provide further resources.

It is my sincere hope that others will take these ideas, work with them, and carry on with this line of research, for there is much understanding that is yet to be gained on the very deep and profound teachings of the ageless wisdom with regard to the use of energy.

Acknowledgements

In addition to heartfelt thanks to everyone in my study and meditation groups, I express special gratitude to my friends and colleagues, William Meader and David Kesten, for taking the time to review this material and provide ideas and comments.

For inspiring me to study esoteric astrology in the first place, I give special thanks to Maureen Temple Richmond, whose presentation at a seminar many years ago sparked my interest and stimulated me to long periods of research. Her book, *Sirius*, motivated me to complete this one.

For being a constant source of inspiration, I thank my friend, co-worker, and co-meditator, Avon Mattison, of Pathways to Peace.

I appreciate Michael Robbins for sharing his in-depth knowledge of the Tibetan's work with me and many others, and especially for the Astro-Rayology seminar he gave in early 1994, which inspired my work on this book.

Most of all, I thank my husband, business partner, and best friend, Rick Prater, for his enthusiastic supportiveness, his editing help, and for many wonderful discussions of the ideas and concepts that eventually wove their way into this book.

Carole Beckham
December 29, 1997

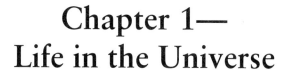

Chapter 1—
Life in the Universe

"All beauty, all goodness, all that makes for the eradication of sorrow and ignorance upon the Earth must be devoted to the Great Consummation. Then when the Lords of Compassion shall have spiritually civilised the Earth and made of it a Heaven, there shall be revealed to the Pilgrims the Endless Path which reaches to the Heart of the Universe. Man, then no longer man, will transcend nature and impersonally, yet consciously, in at-one-ment with all Enlightened Ones, help to fulfill the Law of the Higher Evolution, of which Nirvana is but the beginning."—Evans-Wentz[1]

One of our primary assumptions is the sentience of all life, that everything—rocks, plants, animals, humans, planets, stars, and the Earth itself—is imbued with some form of consciousness. This is taught by the mystery schools that have custody of the ageless wisdom teachings and can be found in books pertaining to both eastern and western mystery traditions (see bibliography). These teachings have a common underlying truth and help us to understand our place in the spiral of evolution.

Other assumptions based on these teachings are that the universe is continually evolving and that we evolve as well through many lifetimes of experience and improvement. In the next stage open to us, we develop superhuman characteristics and thus join those who have gone before us, the sages and masters who unobtrusively work behind the scenes and, with respect for the free will of humanity, guide our civilization. We then continue our evolution in more advanced systems depending upon the choices we make and the opportunities we have prepared ourselves for.

The fact of the unity and interconnectedness of all life in the universe is generally accepted by leading thinkers of today, as well as a growing recognition of our ability to draw upon the wisdom and energies accessible to all life. How we invoke these energies depends entirely upon our own interpretations of the cosmos, our own approach to life, and our own conception of God, nature, and the universe. These concepts of ours depend upon the uniqueness of our own experiences in the universe. All experience is valid; it is the combination of all experience and the totality of consciousness that makes up the universe and continues to create it—for it is always going in and out of manifestation, just as our physical bodies die and we reincarnate.

We could say that everyone's concept of God is generally correct, for God represents everything in the universe. Thus, as the wise ones who gave us the ageless wisdom teachings suggest, we should accept and work with ourselves as we are at any point of time and interpret the teachings for ourselves, accepting only the parts with which we can truly identify and using other parts as working hypotheses until we can develop our own conception of the cosmos and acquire an internal realization of truth—what is sometimes called spiritual intuition or straight knowledge. These concepts also should not be static but should always improve, just as evolution itself improves us all, our sages, the universe, and probably even God.

Starting with these principles, then, we talk about life from the standpoint of the macrocosm and then compare it, via the law of analogy, to the microcosm—ourselves. The macrocosmic universe consists of great beings who physically manifest their lives through galaxies, stupendous suns, and planets. Can we even imagine the consciousness of such beings? Yet the teachings of all ages tell us that our consciousness—through millennia—will also expand to this degree, where the expression of our lives will encompass such total richness. Through endless civilizations, these great beings have experiences of such a totality that we can only experience minute portions of their consciousness and, thus, their energy. However, as we develop, we can very gradually share in more of this cosmic wealth of energy and consciousness, just as we are warmed by the rays of the Sun.

The energy of the universe is neutral; there is no such thing as beneficent energies and malefic energies, just as there is not good or bad electricity. It is the common usage of the various types of energies by humankind today that causes people to state that the energies themselves are imbued with these qualities. However, different cosmic and planetary beings do decidedly have their own specialized energies, many of which have become common knowledge to humanity today through the science of astrology.

We will explore an overview of the various types of energies that we know about with an esoteric interpretation based on the ageless wisdom teachings and the arcane knowledge found in ancient and modern mystery schools. But most of all, we will discuss how these energies interweave with each other and how we can use them more scientifically in our lives. The hypothesis is that as heavenly beings come into conjunction or aspect with each other, they are performing some type of group work together, admittedly on a vast scale. Although we cannot even imagine what this work could be, or even sense most of the energies they are generating to do this work, still we can hypothesize on some of the energies involved and, if it is appropriate for the group work that we are doing, we can tap into some of these energies.

At other times our purposes require access to energies that do not seem to be readily available from the cosmos. However, we should know that all energies are always available somewhere and just trust that we can invoke through meditation the energies that we need, as long as we approach the invocation with the spirit of helpfulness to the cause of evolution and increased consciousness.

During our normal course of work for the upliftment of consciousness, we can look to see what energies might be available at a particular time and attempt to use them, for they provide the course of least resistance for the spiritual work we are trying to accomplish.

If we are working as individuals, we should know that it is not as effective (and perhaps even dangerous) to invoke large-scale energies from cosmic sources. What we can do, however, is to focus our consciousness at the highest level we can reach through meditation and then, through our creative imagination, place ourselves in the company of the people in our spiritual group. By linking in with others telepathically, through the etheric network of the collective consciousness of humanity, we can more effectively use the energies that the cosmos offers us.

The Law of Correspondences

"As above, so below; as below, so above."—The Kybalion[2]

One of the primary occult laws in all the mystery traditions is the Law of Correspondences, or "as above, so below," and its western sources were traced to the ancient Hermetic wisdom teachings. Ancient as it is, though, this law of analogy is a very basic tool that ever opens the door to the knowledge of the universe. We use this law in our daily lives every time we compare situations and objects and extrapolate other situations and objects from those comparisons.

The ageless wisdom teaches us to use the Law of Correspondences to compare human microcosmic life with those large planetary and stellar life forms. If we can correctly deduce a fact about our own life, we can then look for its parallel in higher life. Conversely, if we can deduce a fact about a planet or star, we can then look for its correspondence within ourselves. We already know this through comparing atomic life with large systems; this is nothing new to us. However, if we can incorporate this Law of Correspondences more consciously into our knowledge systems, we find that we can fit the pieces of the great puzzle together more accurately—even if we are still just working on the outer edge pieces, we at least have this as a starting point. That is, in essence, how basic this great law is to the type of study we're engaged in. The material in this book assumes this law as a working hypothesis.

Our universe is based on the number seven, as is the constitution of the human. It is also interesting to note that one-seventh of the life in our universe is in visible manifestation at any particular time.[3] Seven great rays of energy—also called seven streams of consciousness—pour into the universe. Seven planes of manifestation form the material of consciousness. The rays and planes circulate and interweave, and where they intersect they form energy centers, called chakras. These energy centers exist in the body of an atom, a person, a planet, a solar system—in all forms of life. And everything is alive and has some form of innate consciousness, whether we recognize it or not.

Higher levels of life include in their forms and existences the inner and outer forms of the lower levels of life, just as our bodies contain atoms and our Earth includes humanity. Each level of life transcends but includes its predecessors; the higher levels contain functions, capacities, or structures not found on lower levels while yet being comprised of the lower levels. Ken Wilber states, "...life transcends but includes matter; mind transcends but includes life; soul transcends but includes mind; and spirit transcends but includes soul." This is what establishes and constitutes hierarchy.[4]

Richard M. Restak, M.D. in his book on the brain tells us that "The number of neurons in the human brain is almost equal to the number of stars in our Milky Way—over fifteen billion."[5] Carl Jung discusses the alchemical view of microcosmic man being a complete miniature equivalent of the macrocosmic world and relates it to levels of human consciousness involving the existence of a common consciousness and intuition.[6] The Tibetan Master Djwhal Khul says: "The microcosm, when known, holds ever the clue to the Macrocosm. The Macrocosm eternally reflects itself in man, the microcosm, and hence man has within himself the possibility and the potentiality of total comprehension."[7]

Manly Palmer Hall compares the magnetic fields of the planets to the magnetic fields of the human body, indicating that they are invisible bodies, archetypes upon which physical bodies are built. The invisible magnetic fields develop the human embryo and also create the planets themselves. Each field is a sphere and they all revolve around greater fields of life. Accordingly, we can regard the Earth's magnetic field as a series of worlds, each containing life. Orders of life surround and interpenetrate us and are only separated from our conscious knowledge by rates of vibration. Thus, in the beginning, when we descended into manifestation, we came from the higher magnetic fields of our own system. The fall of man, spoken of in scripture, was in reality the "descent of these lives from their invisible magnetic fields into the visible, tangible world in which we find ourselves today."[8]

The Spiral of Evolution

"The greater Three, each with their seven lesser wheels, in spiral evolution, rotate within the timeless Now, and move as one. The cosmic Lords from Their high place, view the past, control the Now, and ponder on the Day be with us."—AAB[9]

The phrase, "on a higher turn of the spiral," is a familiar part of our modern language, yet all the mystery traditions of the world use this concept in their descriptions of the order of the universe. This is an example of just how pervasive the group mind is; how many of the ideas of the world's secret teachings are actually well known to us already, on an inner level.

Whether motion is the basis of change or whether change is the basis of motion is a debatable question in abstract philosophy, but the concrete effect is the same and that is our concern here, with the plane of manifestation. Nevertheless, here is a little esoteric background in change, motion, and spirallic activity.

In the ageless wisdom, the term involution describes the "involving" of spirit into matter, or the "fall" of man, where evolution is the development of life into more refined forms. Both processes are always occurring; the elemental kingdoms progress from spirit to form and the human kingdom progresses from form to spirit.

The processes of involution and evolution are the effects of the motion, or vibration, inherent in life itself; life as we know it and the life impulse that we share with the entire universe. Evolution occurs through a combination of forward-progressive, spiral-cyclic, and rotary motions from the three major sources of energy in the universe, the archetypal trinity. Forward-progressive motion represents synthesis, spiral-cyclic motion represents attraction, and rotary motion represents economy.[10] What do these aspects of energy mean to humanity? The Tibetan teacher explains in *A Treatise on Cosmic Fire* that:

- Forward-progressive motion represents our evolution—the unified consciousness of all groups.

- Spiral-cyclic motion represents opportunities that are made available to us repetitively, throughout cycles of time, but on a higher turn of the spiral each time, at a higher stage of evolution—group-consciousness.

- Rotary motion represents the purification of the atoms in the human body—individual consciousness.

The activity of the soul itself is rotary-spiral-cyclic.[11] More refined opportunities are available on each turn of the spiral because of our development and also because the planetary and constellational bodies that are emitting the cyclic energies are evolving and enriching the energies they are able to transmit. Every cycle originates from another cycle that is relatively complete and gives place to an ever higher spiral, resulting in periods of apparent relative perfection that lead to those that are still greater.[12]

The Great Bear, Sirius, and the Pleiades are of special importance in the spiral-cyclic activity of our own system, as they influence the incarnation, evolution, and progress of our own Solar Logos, the great being who manifests through our Sun. Our Solar Logos and six other great beings form seven energy centers in a Cosmic Logos. Through their united activity, they produce a motion of progress onward which propels us to an unknown point in the heavens.[13]

Incorporating the rotary motion of all atoms, our Solar Logos adds his own spiraling periodical movement and circulates along an orbit or spheroidal path around another central focal point in an ever-ascending spiral. Through this activity, he gathers the atoms into forms. By means of these forms, he gains the needed contact and develops full consciousness, gradually refining the forms as he proceeds onward toward his goal, the source from which he came. These forms are the total of all spheres and atoms within our solar system.[14]

The goal of our Solar Logos (as with all of us) is the expansion of consciousness and he builds forms to be his instruments of experience. The methods of expansion, vibratory stimulation, and magnetic interaction (the Law of Attraction and Repulsion) lead to cyclic progress, rotary repetition, and spiraling ascension. This develops the quality of love-wisdom through the active intelligent use of the form, leading to full consciousness and a relative perfection.[15]

The solar system is shaped by the motion of the constellations in conjunction with its own rotary motion in space. The Law of Relativity, or the relation between all atoms, produces light and forms the sphere of the solar system.

As Earth revolves around the Sun, it expresses its own rotary-spiral-cyclic action, held in place by the Sun's magnetism. Earth is under the constant impression of other planets, each of which produces its own effects upon our planet. Inflowing energy from the zodiacal constellations reaches Earth via the Sun. The force currents thus produced by the solar system are described as a "swirling tide of intermingling currents, with numerous focal points of energy demonstrating here and there, yet in no way static as to location."[16]

Seven of the planets in our solar system are considered to be sacred, meaning that they have achieved a high level of evolution and are major energy centers of the Solar Logos. They represent seven types of spiral-cyclic energy and produce seven types of humanity, as exemplified by seven rays of consciousness. These planetary distinctions account for the nature of cycles, which repeat in an ever-ascending spiral, in space, time, planes of existence, and forms.

Spiral-cyclic activity:

- Demonstrates in all forms as a tendency to repeat, owing to the backward pull of the rotating atoms, yet is offset by the strong progressive impulse of evolution.

- Gathers the rotating atoms of matter into definite types and forms, holding them there as long as necessary and sweeping them toward a stronger point of energy.

- Leads to expansion and our eventual enlightenment, linking our spirit, mind, and body and vitalizing the thoughtforms we fabricate.[17]

Therefore, everything in the universe has its own spiral movement. Creativeness proceeds according to the spiral and each attractive or repulsive energy creates its own spiral.[18] The great creative hierarchies who create the archetypes of our system manifest in a spiral. Streams of love energy cross streams of will and karmic energy, creating expansions of consciousness called initiations, enabling life to pass to a higher turn of the spiral.

In the words of the Tibetan teacher, "All these streams of energy form geometrical designs of great beauty to the eye of the initiated seer. We have the transverse and bisecting lines, the seven lines of force which form the planes, and the seven spiraling lines, thus forming lines of systemic latitude and longitude, and their interplay and interaction produce a whole of wondrous beauty and design. When these are visualised in colour, and seen in their true radiance, it will be realised that the point of attainment of our solar Logos is very high, for the beauty of the logoic Soul is expressed by that which is seen."[19]

Spirituality, An Evolutionary Impulse

"Under, and back of, the Universe of Time, Space and Change, is ever to be found The Substantial Reality—the Fundamental Truth."—The Kybalion[20]

The word "spiritual" is widely significant and encompasses a fundamental attitude, not restricted to religion or even philosophy. Spirituality is what lies beyond the point of our current achievement. It embodies vision and urges us onwards toward a higher goal.[21] The concept of sin threatens us and complicates our lives, giving human aspiration a self-protective undertone. Instead, we can meditate and pray as a means of cooperating with the divine Plan for our evolution and know that, in fact, our directed energies can contribute to the forces for good on our planet. Separative attitudes have held us back from understanding in the past. However, the time has now come when we, humanity, can make informed choices about how to approach our spirituality and divine truth. This transformation of thought is our immediate task.

We hear much of the laws of nature, the law of cause and effect, and so on, but instead of feeling ruled by law, we should consider that a law is but the spiritual impulse, incentive, and life manifestation of that greater being in which we "live and move and have our being." These laws, which are laws of nature, demonstrate the intelligent purpose of the universe, "wisely directed, and based on love."[22] We can identify ourselves with a higher purpose and align our thoughts and energies to those higher spiritual impulses—the goals of evolution.

In studies on comparative religion, Willis Harman and Huston Smith, among others,[23] found that all religious traditions contain public, exoteric versions and inner-circle, esoteric versions of the teachings, where the esoteric versions are more experiential and usually involve some kind of meditative discipline or yoga. Remarkably, these esoteric versions are essentially the same across all the teachings.

The perennial wisdom (as Huxley called it) "is to be found in every religion and can be owned exclusively by none. [It] is not merely an ancient system of belief and practice...It is, rather, a whole set of archetypical realities waiting to be discovered, at the highest reaches of the human consciousness, by all people."[24]

The perennial wisdom holds that "Nature is directed from within by a higher intelligence or mind; that all minds in the universe are linked together by participation in one universal mind or source; that because of this, various mental or physical rituals can sometimes effect what they symbolize, or set the proper conditions in motion for the desired events or result to occur; that all individuals have a powerful, if hidden, motivation to discover and identify with a higher Self which is, in turn, in immediate connection to the universal mind."[25]

Through our own expansions of consciousness and the greater scope of our vision, we can distribute ideas, life, and potential into the world.

Unity, Omnipresence and Telepathy

"Quantum theory forces us to see the universe not as a collection of physical objects, but rather as a complicated web of relations between the various parts of a unified whole."—Fritjof Capra[26]

The Biblical reference to the presence of God as "In Him we live and move and have our being" gives us the fundamental meaning of omnipresence. Omnipresence is based on the substance of the universe and what we call the ether, which denotes an ocean of energies that are all interrelated and constitute the unity of all that is.

Therefore, in a consideration of the subject of telepathy, we recognize that the etheric or energy body of every form in nature is an integral part of the universe, the One Life, or God Himself. Accordingly, the etheric body of every human being is an integral part of the etheric body of the planet, the solar system, and on, up to the greatest being that exists. Through this medium, each of us is related to every other expression of life, small or large.

The Tibetan tells us that the function of the etheric body is to receive energy from various streams of force from higher sources and to use it to energize our emotional and mental bodies and the soul. The etheric body is, in actuality, energy—myriads of tiny threads of force, coordinated and held in relationship to our various vehicles. These streams of energy affect the physical body, sweeping it into activity according to the nature and power of whatever type of energy may be dominating the etheric body at any particular time.

Relating to mind and consciousness, Carl Jung, in his alchemical studies, found that the realization of wholeness consists of three parts:[27]

- Mental union, which consists of reuniting the spirit/soul complex with the body. One's insights are now made an integral part of one's daily existence.

- Mind/body union, which signifies the return of the unified body/soul/spirit to its initial oneness with the universe.

- Mind/world unity, in which the unified psyche finally realizes its unity with all of existence.

And in his studies on archetypes and the collective unconscious, Jung states: "One can only conclude that the unconscious tends to regard spirit and matter not merely as equivalent but as actually identical, and this in flagrant contrast to the intellectual one-sidedness of consciousness, which would sometimes like to spiritualize matter and at other times to materialize spirit."[28]

Lama Anagarika Govinda sums up the idea of unity in the Tantric Buddhist tradition: "The Buddhist does not believe in an independent or separately existing external world, into whose dynamic forces he could insert himself. The external world and his inner world are for him only the two sides of the same fabric, in which the threads of all forces and of all events, of all forms of consciousness and of their objects, are woven into an inseparable net of endless, mutually conditioned relations."[29]

Thoughtforms and Creative Work

"The laws of thought are the laws of creation, and the entire creative work is carried forward on the etheric level."—AAB[30]

The matter of space responds to, or is attracted by, the potency of the four higher etheric vibrations, or planes, of existence. These four ethers are, in their turn, swept into activity by the dynamic impact of the divine thought of the universal mind. When we become thinkers and creators and can formulate our thoughts and desire their manifestations, we also energize the four higher ethers and a dense physical manifestation is inevitable. We thus attract as much of the responsive matter in space as we need to embody the form we are creating, using our pranic energy, colored by our desire and animated by the potency of our thought.

In creating forms, we need to have a recognition of the material we are building from, which, through our past association with it, is already colored by our thought and purpose and is, accordingly, capable of responding to our current thought. We then need the further recognition of our objective, which is a one-pointed focusing upon our goal and holding of our purpose through the vicissitudes of creative work and in spite of outside influences. This can be summarized as memory of the past, working out in the present, with the goal of the future purpose.[31]

We can best grasp the concept of the universal mind through our concrete mind, abstract mind, and our intuition. The concrete mind builds forms; "thoughts are things." The abstract mind builds patterns;

it works with the blueprints or archetypes upon which the forms are modeled. The intuition, or pure reason, links us into contact with the universal mind, and enables us to grasp a synthesis of divine ideas or to isolate some fundamental and pure truth. In terms of evolution, our goals are:

1. To learn to think and to discover the faculties and powers of our mind.

2. To discover the ideas that lie behind our thought processes and form-building propensities and learn to use them in collaboration with the divine plan.

3. To enter the realm of pure intuition where we can find truth at its source and express the resulting ideas and ideals.

4. To consciously build thoughtforms based upon these divine ideas, which emanate as intuitions from the universal mind. This goes forward through meditation.[32]

It takes concentration to focus or orient the lower aspects of the mind to the higher. Through meditation, which is the mind's power to hold itself in the light, we bring through the needed ideas. Through the contemplation stage of mediation, we enter into that silence which can enable us to align ourselves with the universal mind.

When we work in a group, we wield a mighty force. "Only through the steady strong right thinking of the people and the understanding of the correct use of mental energy can progressive evolution go forward along the desired lines." Right thinking involves:[33]

1. An ability to sense the vision. This involves a capacity to realize the archetype on which the Great Ones are endeavoring to fashion the race. Our intuition is involved here, which will enable us to touch sources of power that are not on the mental levels themselves, but on those levels from which the mental plane itself draws sustenance.

2. Having sensed the vision, grasp the opportunity to bring as much of it as possible down to the mental plane. It is difficult to hold this high consciousness for a long time, but the attempts will eventually lead to the ideas filtering through to the concrete levels of the mental plane, where they become a concrete thought and, thus, something that we can visualize and build upon.

3. Next is a period of gestation, wherein we build our thoughtforms of as much of the vision as we can bring into consciousness. This is done slowly, for we want a stable vibration and a well built form. As we build, we gradually develop a longing to see the vision brought down to earth and to share it with others.

4. As we continue to vitalize the thoughtform with the power of our will, we sense that the rhythm becomes heavier and slower, the material built into the form is coarser, and finally the thoughtform of the vision is clothed in matter of the mental and astral planes.

5. Finally, we bring the vision still nearer to humanity and work it into existence on the physical plane.

When we learn to do this effectively, we will have the wonderful joy of accomplishment and the knowledge that we are able to co-create with the masters to help lift consciousness a little higher on the ladder of evolution. The Tibetan teacher tells us that "This is the joy that is set before you all—and not so very far ahead it lies. So work, not for joy but toward it; not for reward, but from the inner need to help; not for gratitude, but from the urge that comes from having seen the vision and realisation of the part you have to play in bringing that vision down to earth."[34]

Chapter 2—
Levels of Consciousness

"Everything flows, out and in; everything has its tides; all things rise and fall; the pendulum-swing manifests in everything; the measure of the swing to the right is the measure of the swing to the left; rhythm compensates."
—The Kybalion[1]

Keeping the Law of Correspondences in mind, we will now look at an outline of the major entities in the universe that affect life on our planet and the planes of manifestation that their energies penetrate and work upon. We can see how these energies interact with human and global consciousness and how they can produce those expansions of consciousness called initiations. A major stream of energy begins with the seven rays; progresses to the three great constellations of the Great Bear, Sirius, and the Pleiades; pours through the twelve zodiacal constellations; and flows through three planets that are associated with each of the zodiacal constellations.

Other streams of energy include: forces from great stars, such as Betelguese, Antares, and others, which reach us indirectly at this time; and seven solar systems of which ours is one, which do not yet produce noticeable results upon humanity.[2]

Here and later in the book, we use the numbers three, four, and seven rather extensively; these same numbers are discussed thoroughly in traditions such as Qabalah and alchemy. Geometry indicates a resonance amongst the various energies and the planes of manifestation, with the spiritual goal of fusing spirit and form, thus increasing the vibration of matter and raising consciousness in the universe.

The numerical set of 7 + 5 = 12 is also prominent. There are seven forms of light and they are related to the substance of the seven planes. There are five kingdoms on Earth: the kingdom of souls (our sages), humanity, the animals, plants, and minerals. These are stimulated and enhanced by the twelve forms of light of twelve creative hierarchies, which create the archetypes of lives in our system and are related to the twelve lights of the zodiac.[3] Also, esoteric astrology refers to twelve planets, classified into seven sacred planets and five non-sacred planets, some of which are, so far, veiled or hidden to us.

Streams of Energy

"The goal of evolution for humanity is to become consciously and livingly aware of the nature of these energies and begin to know them and to use them."—AAB[4]

Energies that have direct bearing on our planet Earth come from seven streams of consciousness, called the seven rays, and pass through three great constellations: the Great Bear, Sirius, and the Pleiades. From these three great constellations, energies pass through seven groups of zodiacal constellations, in groups of three constellations for each ray. After the energies pass through the zodiacal constellational triangles, they are qualified by our Sun and pass through various planets, grouped in triangles of exoteric, esoteric, and hierarchical planets, one triangle of rulers per constellation, nine planetary energies per ray, as shown in the following table, which is adapted and modified from the Tibetan's *Esoteric Astrology*. "Exoteric" planets (the ones used in traditional astrology) condition the personality, "esoteric" planets condition the soul, and "hierarchical" planets condition the group life or monad.

Constellational and Planetary Triangles

Ray	Constellation	Exoteric Planets	Esoteric Planets	Hierarchical Planets
1	Aries	Mars	Mercury	Uranus
	Leo	Sun (Jupiter)	Sun (Neptune)	Sun (Uranus)
	Capricorn	Saturn	Saturn	Venus
2	Gemini	Mercury	Venus	Earth
	Virgo	Mercury	Moon (Vulcan)	Jupiter
	Pisces	Jupiter	Pluto / Neptune	Pluto
3	Cancer	Moon (Neptune)	Neptune	Neptune
	Libra	Venus	Uranus	Saturn
	Capricorn	Saturn	Saturn	Venus
4	Taurus	Venus	Vulcan	Vulcan
	Scorpio	Mars / Pluto	Mars / Pluto	Mercury
	Sagittarius	Jupiter	Earth	Mars
5	Leo	Sun (Jupiter)	Sun (Neptune)	Sun (Uranus)
	Sagittarius	Jupiter	Earth	Mars
	Aquarius	Uranus	Jupiter	Moon (Uranus)

6	Virgo	Mercury	Moon (Vulcan)	Jupiter
	Sagittarius	Jupiter	Earth	Mars
	Pisces	Jupiter	Pluto / Neptune	Pluto
7	Aries	Mars	Mercury	Uranus
	Cancer	Moon (Neptune)	Neptune	Neptune
	Capricorn	Saturn	Saturn	Venus

As we elaborate in Chapter 9, energies flow through triangles and manifest through crosses (the concept of the three and the four of the alchemist in the western mystery tradition). Triangles represent the potentiality of spirit and crosses (squares) represent the potentiality of matter. In the above diagram, we can see that it takes three cooperating constellations to handle the energy of one ray and then filter it through three levels of rulership for the eventual use of humanity.

Accordingly, we also have a triangle of planets acting as rulers of an astrological sign—unlike traditional astrology that usually assigns only one ruler to a planet. The traditional "exoteric" planet guides the activities of the personality life. The esoteric planet governs the soul and the hierarchical planet governs large groups of people and also the individual spirit once a high level of evolution has been achieved by that individual. We might justifiably ask, how can a planet "rule" a constellation or sign, when the constellation carries such a greater force? This is because a planet has a special rapport with the sign and acts as a ruler, or carrier, for the sign's qualities and energies.

I might also explain my usage of the term "constellation" rather than astrological "sign" throughout this book. According to the ageless wisdom teachings, the sign, which is related to seasonal activity, acts as a representative of the constellation by its same name and channels the constellation's energy. Since this book is intended for use by people who may not have a background in astrology, I am using the term "constellation" so as to avoid the confusion of using both terms, sign and constellation. If the sign does indeed stand in and act for the constellational energy, this is accurate. Chapter 10 contains a detailed discussion on tropical and sidereal astrology, leaving it to your individual preference as to how to handle it in your use of the information in this book.

We notice that some of the constellations in the above table work with two different rays, some work with three rays, and others work with only one ray. Also, planets are not evenly distributed along this table. Some patterns can be found, such as the similarity between Ray One constellations and Ray Seven constellations, and are discussed later in this book.

The Sun and the Moon "veil" other planets (usually Vulcan, Neptune, and Uranus), and I indicate the hypothetical veiling planet in parentheses. The process of veiling is explained in detail in Chapter 7, but briefly this concept means that the energies of the veiled planets are not completely integrated into our system at this time for all the levels of consciousness that humanity lives and acts upon. It is also an interesting speculation as to whether we can invoke the energies of the veiled planets at times other than when the Sun is in the constellations these planets are associated with—for example, at the time of the full moon.

Each zodiacal constellation joins with three other zodiacal constellations to form a cardinal, fixed, or mutable cross. In this manner, the potentiality of spirit represented by the triangle manifests into the potentiality of matter represented by the square. As indicated above, energies flow through triangles and manifest through crosses. The cross configuration is what gives the opposition and the right-angle, or square, in the horoscope their active potency.

Following are diagrams of the constellations on each of the three crosses. Chapter 9 gives a full description of the energies that each of the crosses represent.

Mutable Cross:

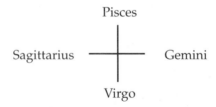

```
                    Pisces

       Sagittarius  ──┼──  Gemini

                    Virgo
```

Fixed Cross:

```
                   Aquarius

         Scorpio  ──┼──  Taurus

                    Leo
```

Cardinal Cross:

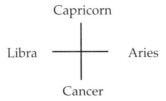

We should keep in mind that great beings, such as constellations, stars, and planets, can directly and indirectly access energies from each other. That way, when we discover an interplay of seemingly unrelated energies, we can understand that in a particular cycle those energies were necessary for evolution and thus were appropriated from cooperative sources.

Even though a study of esoteric astrology and rayology reveals an intricate interweaving and a great degree of interrelation amongst all the energies, we find that selected energies are more accessible at given times, providing us with an opportunity to take advantage of them. The Tibetan teacher gives us a directive to live more scientifically (and thus not waste any needless time in handling our evolution), so we should explore some of these concepts for ourselves and see what we can do. For example, in August we could try to intuit for ourselves what it might be like when the mystery schools are externalized; the month of August has special significance for drawing upon the energies of Sirius.[5]

When the energies reach our solar system, the Sun transforms these cosmic influences for our use and blocks other energies that we cannot handle or are not ready for at this time. It is implied that there are also energies of cosmic evil that the Sun blocks, which is a good reason for us not to arbitrarily pick a star in a night sky and meditate upon it; we have no way of knowing if its energies would be helpful or harmful to us.

Following is a figure that shows how the energies flow from the seven rays; through the three major constellations, the Great Bear, Sirius, and the Pleiades; through the zodiacal constellations; through the Sun; through the planets; and to the Earth. (The energy flow in the diagram is from top to bottom.)

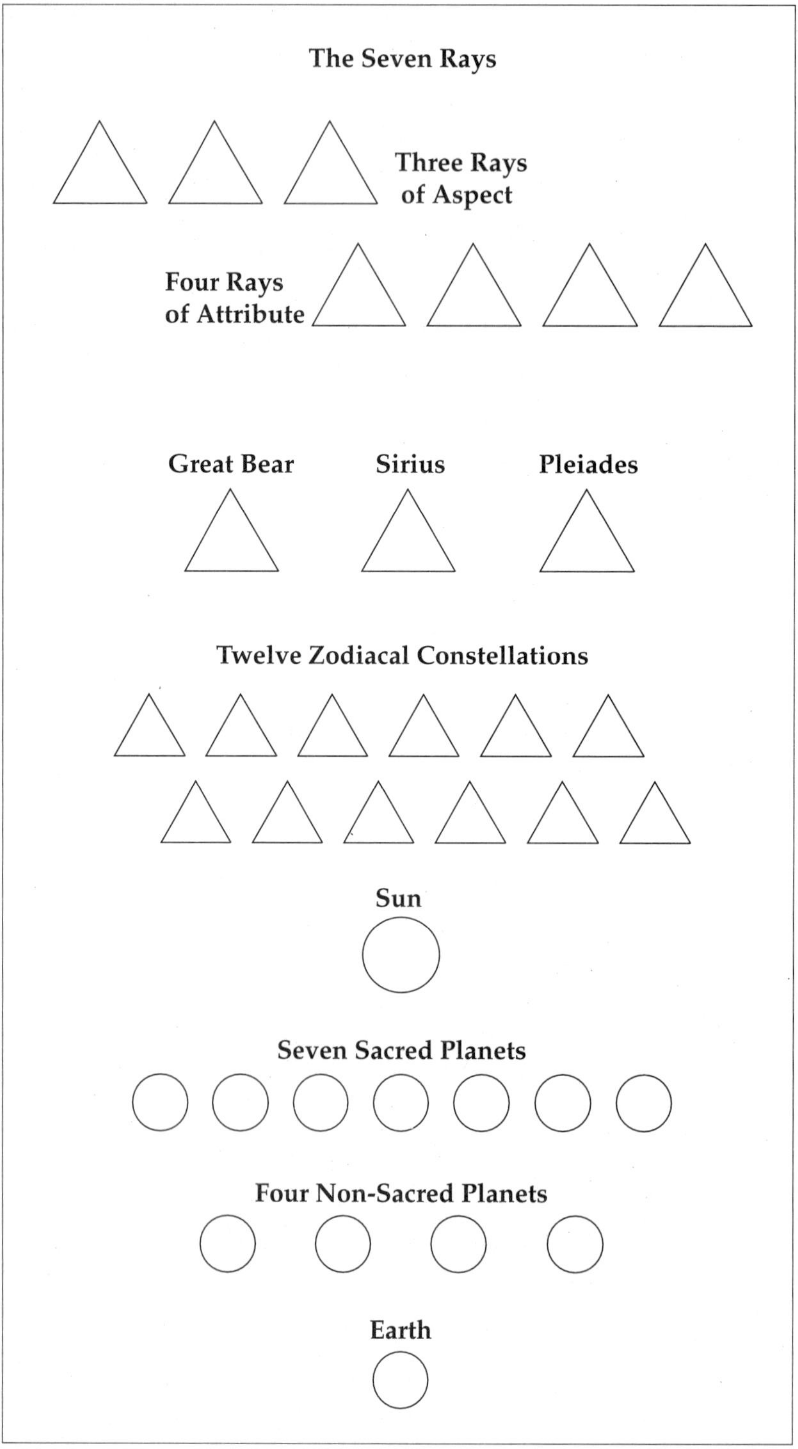

The Seven Rays

Three Rays of Aspect

Four Rays of Attribute

Great Bear   Sirius   Pleiades

Twelve Zodiacal Constellations

Sun

Seven Sacred Planets

Four Non-Sacred Planets

Earth

When these energies eventually reach Earth, they are filtered through three great centers on Earth—Shamballa, Hierarchy, and Humanity—and are manifested within fields or planes of consciousness. These planes comprise matter, whether dense physical matter or refined atomic matter. The subtlety or density of the matter of these planes depends on the perspective of the manifesting entity: atom, human, or Logos. For example, thoughts on the mental plane and emotions on the astral plane are considered as dense matter to the consciousness of the Solar Logos. The physical plane is where we are intended to express all that is within us.

Each unit of life, no matter how large or small, contains seven major energy centers where the rays and planes intersect. For example, seven highly evolved planets of our solar system are the seven energy centers of the Sun. On the microcosmic level, our seven energy centers are the head (crown), ajna, throat, heart, solar plexus, sacral, and base-of-spine centers. We know then, from the Law of Correspondences, that the seven highly evolved (sacred) planets form those centers for the Solar Logos, the entity who manifests through the Sun.

Planes of Manifestation

"In all things cosmic, perfect law and order are found, and the ramifications of the plan can be seen on all planes and all subplanes."—AAB[6]

We have seen that just as we have seven energy centers in our physical body, the larger lives in the universe that we are a part of—such as our solar system—all have seven energy centers as well. Each human and cosmic energy center is comprised of matter that has its own rate of vibration, which differentiates each center into planes of consciousness and manifestation.

The topic of planes and subplanes is very complex, but what we want to glean from this discussion is the concept that matter in vibration—even if that "matter" is thinner than air—can set up harmonic vibrations in grades of matter that are octaves higher and lower, just as a note from a pitch pipe will vibrate the corresponding string of a violin. However, what we are speaking of here are the very vibrations of the great universal mind.

Life on Earth is on what esotericists call the cosmic physical plane, which includes seven planes of consciousness and manifestation. The mind of God (the Logos), which is the universal mind on our cosmic physical plane, manifests in humanity as the threefold human mind— the lower concrete mind; the abstract mind related to the world of ideas; and the intuition or pure reason, which is for us the highest aspect of mentality.

The cosmic astral plane, which is the next great plane above the cosmic physical plane, generates the impulse that produces form existence and concrete expression, because all form-taking is the result of desire. The cosmic mental plane, above the cosmic astral plane, generates the will-to-be in time and space, which produces the seven groups of soul lives, each group affiliated with one of the seven rays. However, even initiates know practically nothing of the cosmic planes beyond the cosmic physical.[7] The value of us knowing about this at all is that it emphasizes the idea that energy is a life fluid circulating throughout the entire body of the Logos and vivifying even the tiniest atom in the whole.

Planes and Subplanes of the Cosmic Physical Plane

	First Etheric Subplane	Second Etheric Subplane	Third Etheric Subplane	Fourth Etheric Subplane	Gaseous Subplane	Liquid Subplane	Dense Subplane
Logoic Plane	1:1	1:2	1:3	1:4	1:5	1:6	1:7
Monadic Plan	2:1	2:2	2:3	2:4	2:5	2:6	2:7
Atmic Plane	3:1	3:2	3:3	3:4	3:5	3:6	3:7
Buddhic Plane	4:1	4:2	4:3	4:4	4:5	4:6	4:7
Mental Plane	5:1	5:2	5:3	5:4	5:5	5:6	5:7
Astral Plane	6:1	6:2	6:3	6:4	6:5	6:6	6:7
Physical/ Etheric Plane	7:1	7:2	7:3	7:4	7:5	7:6	7:7

While looking at the diagram of the planes and subplanes of the cosmic physical plane, we need to think of the planes of manifestation as interpenetrating and the corresponding subplanes as being directly related to each other, not separated from each other by intervening layers of denser matter.[8] In actuality, the boundaries of each plane and subplane overlap as they flow into the neighboring planes and subplanes.

As we can see from this diagram, there is a numerical resonance throughout as the energies of the various subplanes weave through those of the planes.

As evolution proceeds, we progress from the bottom upward and to the left, as depicted on this diagram. The logoic level is the borderland of the cosmic astral plane and is the level of operation for the Planetary Logos, that great entity in charge of our planet. Next down is the level of the monad, the ultimate point of human synthesis. Then, the realm of the spiritual triad, or trinity of energy, occupies the atmic, buddhic, and higher mental (manasic) planes. Our human goal is to contact this level as consciously as possible, though we may often only have access to it in states of concentration or meditation. The normal field of operations for humanity today is the personality level, which is the triad of lower mental, astral, and physical/etheric, and this personality level is a reflection of the spiritual triad.

The soul is located on the third subplane of the mental plane (5:3), within the influence of the spiritual triad. If a person has an astral vehicle composed largely of third subplane astral matter (6:3) and a mental vehicle mostly of fifth subplane (5:5) material, the soul will center its activity on the astral body. However, if the person has a mental body of fourth subplane matter (5:4) and an astral body of fifth subplane matter (6:5), the polarization will be mental. Thus, when we speak of the soul taking control of us, we are indicating that we have built into our vehicles matter of the higher subplanes and eliminated matter of the seventh, sixth, and fifth subplanes. The soul takes a certain amount of control when we have built in matter from the fourth subplane. A certain proportion of third subplane material indicates that we are on the path and a predominance of second subplane material means that we have taken initiation. We become masters when we have matter from only the first subplane.[9]

Underlying our physical body with its intricate system of nerves is a vital or etheric body, which is the counterpart of the outer physical form. The etheric body is likewise the medium for the transmission of energy to all parts of the physical body and to our consciousness. Our etheric body is linked with the etheric body, or aura, of humanity and the bodies of our planetary and solar systems; it is a part of the whole, of the universe itself. This is the scientific basis of astrological theory.

The following table shows the correspondences of relationships between each of the seven planes, the seven rays, and the seven planets. Vulcan and Pluto are usually associated with Ray One, however for this table I am using the Sun. We are also not certain where the Earth fits in, although we are told that it has connections with Rays Three and Four.

Correspondences of Planes, Rays, and Planets

Logoic plane	Life	Ray 1	The Sun
Monadic plane	Universal love	Ray 2	Jupiter
Atmic plane	Spiritual will	Ray 3	Saturn
Buddhic plane	Intuition	Ray 4	Mercury
Mental plane	Mind	Ray 5	Venus
Astral plane	Emotional body	Ray 6	Neptune, Mars
Physical/etheric plane	Etheric or energy body	Ray 7	Uranus

Spiritual work lifts our status on any plane of manifestation "for matter is but spirit on the lowest plane, and spirit, we are told, is but matter on the highest. All is spirit and these differentiations are but the products of the finite mind."[10]

The Effects of Energy Upon Consciousness

The unfoldment of consciousness is the goal of all evolutionary processes.

Through life in many incarnations, we experience countless combinations and permutations of energies from all the signs of the zodiac, and thus expand our consciousness. The energies of the seven rays, the constellations, the solar rays, and the planets all play upon the soul or consciousness aspect of humanity.

Our expansions of consciousness always result in initiation of some type; these available energies give us the opportunity to venture forth into a wider field of awareness, expression, and contact with the higher sources. Indeed, the unfoldment of consciousness is the purpose of our solar system itself and the goal of all evolutionary processes.

Dion Fortune explains that the correspondences between the soul of man and the universe are not arbitrary, but arise out of developmental identities, meaning that certain aspects of consciousness were developed in response to certain phases of evolution, and therefore embody the same principles and react to the same influences.[11]

Humanity functions within three levels of consciousness: mass-consciousness, self-consciousness, and group-consciousness. But as we evolve, we will also achieve an understanding of the larger purpose which motivates the higher levels of life in our solar system, and when we are thus initiated, we will be able to cooperate in great creative processes and purposes.

Right now, though, our consciousness is in a state of flux, as our energies shift from the Age of Pisces to the Age of Aquarius, and from Ray Six to Ray Seven. Great shifts of consciousness always create upheaval in the outer forms. How we relate to these shifts depends upon our ability to respond to the incoming energies, which depends upon the development of our own energy centers.

The Concept of Initiation

"All human beings evolve through a graded series of initiations, either self-induced or brought about on our planet with extraneous aid."—AAB[12]

Throughout world mythology, all the travels and travails of the heroes of antiquity represent the treading of the path of initiation. Initiation is a dynamic entering into a new state of consciousness by an act of the focused will, leading inevitably to a new realization of being.[13] Expansions of consciousness always culminate in an initiation of some sort. We can thus apply all our life experiences into an initiation of ourselves into a wider field of awareness, expression, and spiritual contact.

As we develop a consciousness and understanding of the larger purpose, we learn and cooperate with the creative plan for evolution. We manifest creatively in the world, rule our conduct wisely, control our impulses intellectually, and balance material and spiritual law. As we prepare ourselves to enter into new and deeper experiments and experiences as a participator in the divine plan and as a cooperator in the divine purpose, we become our own initiator and are thus ready to take initiation.[14] The process of initiation is actually one of self-initiation, because we initiate our own tests and trials.

An initiate has to be both a mystic and an occultist. As mystics, we must be capable of pure vision, motivated by spiritual intent, and be able to make the best use of our inherent sensitivity. As occultists, we must be trained, mentally polarized, and be aware of the realities, forces, and energies of existence. As both, we must be free from the glamours and illusions which influence the average person.[15] Some of the characteristics of initiation are:

- Synthesis and fusion
- Dynamic, creative will
- A focused purpose which expresses the will-to-good
- A sustained effort that brings fulfillment
- A process of developing inclusiveness
- An increase in the range of vibrations that we can respond to
- An infusion of the soul into the personality
- Responsiveness to group energies and eventually the consciousness of highly evolved lives
- A transmutation of the mind into intuition and intellect into wisdom
- A transmutation of emotion/desire into love/aspiration
- An orientation to the soul and dedication to the evolutionary plan for humanity
- The demonstration of intuitive understanding put to practical expression
- The evolution of the will implemented by love

Through each sign of the zodiac, we have to express the results of our earlier life experience and soul achievement. We have to transform selfishness into living active service, transmute desire into spiritual aspiration, and identify with the will of God. We incarnate in each of the signs to learn the needed lessons, broaden our horizons, integrate our personality, and eventually incorporate the energies of the soul. As we become initiated and near the end of the process, we undergo twelve final tests in the twelve signs.[16]

The forces of initiation produce their major effects upon the physical plane, for it is there that we have to demonstrate our liberation, understanding, and divinity.[17] Oftentimes the human way of achieving an expansion of consciousness is through crisis, when we are forced to make a change. Crises are tests of our strength, purpose, purity, motive, and the intent of the soul. Crises evoke confidence when surmounted and produce greatly expanded vision. "They foster compassion and understanding, for the pain and inner conflict they have engendered is never forgotten, for they draw upon the resources of the heart. They release the light of wisdom within the field of knowledge and the world is thereby enriched."[18]

There are nine possible initiations for humans upon Earth. They include five major planetary initiations, three solar-systemic initiations, and one cosmic initiation which relates the initiate to Sirius. It is more typical for an Earth dweller to take seven initiations and then move on to another system. Each of these seven initiations gives us entry into the state of divine consciousness on each of the seven planes of divine experience and expression.[19]

Under the Trans-Himalayan Yoga system, we are considered to be an initiate when we have taken the third initiation of transfiguration. This initiation embodies certain characteristics, abilities, and powers:[20]

- We become conscious of the monadic vibration and thus can note the effect of the three great constellations, the Great Bear, the Pleiades, and Sirius.

- We can respond consciously to the influences of:

  - The planets, affecting our personalities

  - The Sun sign, indicating our life trends

  - The ascendant, or rising sign, indicating the life goal for a particular life or for a period of seven lives

- We willingly and freely serve the plan of evolution, conscious of our intent and purpose on the physical plane.

- We respond to planetary, systemic, and certain cosmic influences and become a lens through which "the many lights which are energy itself" can stream and thus be focused upon Earth. To these energies, initiates tune their consciousness and thus become planetary servers.

- We relate the energies of all three crosses within ourselves, consciously and effectively.

- Our centers are ruled by the seven sacred planets, although initiates can and do work with the energies of all the planets.

As we approach the path of initiation, we are concerned with the effects of the cosmic influences upon Earth and with the study of the resultant changes that affect our evolution. As the evolutionary changes are brought about and as human, planetary, and solar consciousness progressively develop, the influences pouring from the constellations, via their intermediaries, the planets, will produce very diverse changes and significant happenings to which we will consciously or unconsciously respond according to our point of development.[21]

Today certain world disciples and initiates have reached the point in their unfoldment where they are ready to take some of the higher initiations. However, before they can do that, they must find others to take their place and fulfill their functions. This puts humanity in a state of flux, of increased activity before a great step forward in conscious unfoldment and expression of a sense of responsibility. The forces of Cancer, Leo, and Gemini are actively engaged in this process as it affects mass humanity. The forces of Taurus, Scorpio, Leo, Capricorn, and Pisces are affecting world disciples and initiates.[22] All these energies are giving us the responsibility of choice, evoking our free will toward fulfilling world need.

As we enter into the Age of Aquarius, the sign of the world server, the ranks of initiates will be greatly augmented. The bulk of the world initiates finalize their experience in Aquarius and become liberated world servers. They join the ranks of the Hierarchy. Those who achieve in Pisces and make the higher and further grade in their development pass into Shamballa.[23] Chapter 8, "Earth Energy," discusses these great centers of the Earth—Hierarchy and Shamballa.

Chapter 3—
Mind and Telepathy

"It is all one vast system of transmission and of interdependence within the system. All receive in order to give, and to pass on to that which is lesser or not so evolved. Upon every plane this process can be seen."—AAB[1]

One of the goals for humanity is what the Tibetan teacher calls "all knowledge" and what the Buddhists and others call "enlightenment." A way to achieve enlightenment is through "right-mindfulness."

Mindfulness is the process of paying attention to situations and events around us, to be aware of our surroundings, and to live a life that is in alignment with our internal and external environment. In essence, it means being alert to opportunities, which results in gaining knowledge and, eventually, enlightenment.

As we develop, we will be able to gain knowledge in many ways, including those ways related to telepathy. These involve higher senses—a higher degree of sensitivity—and these higher senses include etheric vision which, simply stated, is the ability to see auric energies and thus be able to find our coworkers, those with whom we share rapport in ideals and goals. Telepathy is also increased sensitivity but is involved after we find our coworkers; it is a method whereby we can communicate more easily with our coworkers when we are at the stage of doing meaningful work toward planetary enlightenment. It is also a method by which we can send positive thoughts and ideas out into the aura of the Earth, where they can help uplift the condition of humanity.

Telepathy, like any other extension of the senses, increases with knowledge and use. Telepathy cannot be forced or desired too strongly, for a strong energy field of personal desire tends to repel it; telepathy evolves in its own time. The best approach to developing telepathy is to be aware of how it manifests and then to simply form and act upon the intent to send out constructive energies telepathically to persons or trouble-spots on our planet that need them. As we act, we develop.

We can sensitize ourselves to telepathic communications from our spiritual teachers. These great ones have a vested interest in what we do, for they share the planet with us and their progress is dependent upon ours; they cannot advance themselves without some of us being trained to take their places. They can only guide us when we seek guidance. It is our job to manifest spiritual ideals on the physical plane, for we work in the world and are more equipped for this. In fact, we build upon the foundations laid by wise ones—such as Pythagoras, Plato, and Leonardo da Vinci—who were at our level many lifetimes ago and have subsequently moved on. As Einstein said, we stand on the shoulders of giants.

To communicate with us, the great ones plant ideals and ideas into the ethers, the universal mind or universal consciousness. These ideas penetrate into the intuitional plane of our planet, and we grasp them as we approach higher intuitional levels. This type of telepathy is spiritual telepathy and is the purest level we can reach at our current stage of evolution. Lower levels of telepathy are valid for other purposes, but more distortion occurs as the energies penetrate downward because they become colored by the network of thoughtforms on the mental plane and by human emotion on the astral plane. The intuitional telepathic energies do eventually have to penetrate downward into these planes and all the way to physical plane expression, but on the way down the original lofty ideals and ideas necessarily pick up the less refined material that is required for their eventual manifestation. This has to be: we need the thoughtforms on the mental plane to concretize the idea and we need the desire on the astral plane to act upon it. Then, for the idea to have any value at all, something needs to occur on the physical plane.

On a macrocosmic scale, stupendous consciousnesses that work through constellations and planets are in telepathic rapport with those other consciousnesses on their level that they have chosen to work with. They transmit their energies into our system via great entities including our Solar Logos and the Planetary Logos of Earth. Those energies are received by the highest levels of adepts on Earth—Shamballa and Hierarchy—and eventually transmitted on to us—Humanity.

Members of the spiritual Hierarchy of adepts know the most propitious moments for accessing these energies. We can infer these times by examining the seasons and cycles in which constellational and planetary entities are in aspect with each other. The Tibetan tells us that at each full moon it is as if a door opens giving us access to a greater degree of light. He gives us meditations enabling us to link in with him and increase our intuitive awareness of the Plan, the archetype for humanity in this era. Each full moon provides a specialized type of energy, which is then qualified by the planets that are in rapport (aspect) with each other. Three great spiritual festivals represent special full moon opportunities—the spiritual festivals of Easter during Aries in April, the Wesak during Taurus in May, and the Festival of Goodwill during Gemini in June. Special meditations are available for invoking these energies (see Chapter 11).

Components of Mind

"There is a larger Mind of which the individual mind is only a subsystem."—Gregory Bateson[2]

To explain the process of telepathy, we start by defining the components of mind, and then proceed with explanations of how thoughts might be shared amongst various levels of mind and groups of individuals. Recent scientific research, as noted below, lends support to these hypotheses.

Carl Jung defined mind as personal and collective, and further divided collective mind into what he called the collective unconscious and personal unconscious. The Tibetan addresses three forms of consciousness: (1) the anima mundi, or the soul of all things, which he refers to as the subconscious; (2) the human consciousness; and (3) the world of superconscious contact.[3]

The following discussion classifies mind as universal and individual. The universal mind permeates the entire human race and includes the collective unconscious and collective conscious aspects of mind. Individual mind is the property of the unique individual human and includes the personal unconscious and personal conscious aspects of mind.

All levels of mind interact and interrelate. For example, the unconscious aspects of mind are, in some degree, dependent upon and conditioned by conscious awareness, just as the conscious aspects of mind are influenced by the unconscious. Also, the content of collective thought blends with individual thought, and vice versa. All levels of mind grow dynamically, as each era and society contributes mental content and symbols, and as humanity evolves.

Following is an overview of the components of mind:

Collective Unconscious (subjective universal mind):

- Is universal and timeless and belongs to the entire human race.
- Exists in a hidden or enfolded form that is not normally accessible to active attention.
- Includes a record of all human events that have ever transpired.
- Is inherited, with pre-existent archetypal forms.
- Includes material that has never before attained consciousness in the mind of the individual or the conscious mind of the society.
- Contains mythological and dream images.

Collective Conscious (objective universal mind):

- Links our thoughts and minds together into a commonwealth of ideas and concepts. Influences public opinion and societal behavior.
- Is qualified by cultural considerations.
- Is the medium through which thoughts, feelings, and impressions are transmitted and received. In other words, telepathy occurs here before precipitating into the individual conscious mind.

Personal Unconscious (subjective individual mind):

The aspect of the collective unconscious that has been personalized by the individual and modified according to the experience of that individual. This includes material acquired during this lifetime, such as forgotten or repressed material, as well as material too weak to enter directly into consciousness.[4]

Personal Conscious (objective individual mind):

The waking consciousness of the individual and the concrete aspect of mind from which action takes place.

The following diagram depicts the components of mind as levels of universal mind and individual mind:

Collective Unconscious	Collective Conscious	=	Universal Mind
Personal Unconscious	Personal Conscious	=	Individual Mind

The Collective Unconscious

During his research on dreams and recurring archetypes, Carl Jung developed his famous theory of the collective unconscious. He defined this deeper, universal layer of mind as the "fundamental structure underlying every personality."[5] He stated that the contents of the collective unconscious are universal and timeless, mythological images from the source of the "inherited brain-structure itself, which shapes these images according to certain archetypal patterns."[6]

Jung called these patterns archetypal in so far as they represent universal ideas of world periods, critical transitions, and gods and half-gods who personify the eons. These images are not from conscious reflections, but from worldwide conceptions, such as "the world periods of the Parsees, the yugas and avatars of Hinduism, and the Platonic months of astrology with their bull and ram deities and the 'great' Fish of the Christian aeon."[7]

As Jung studied mandalas that were drawn and painted by his psychoanalytic patients, he was struck with the similarity of the symbols depicted. Since he did not influence his patients in the production of their mandalas, he concluded that there must be a general predisposition in all of us, during all time periods and in all places, to generate the same or similar symbols while we are in a deep state of reflection. He called the unconscious creative source of these symbols the "collective unconscious" and he called the symbolic products "archetypes." In our conscious minds, we are unaware of the common origin of these symbols and, in order to recover these historical layers of the collective mind and to understand our psyche, we have to search through old texts and investigate ancient cultures.[8]

One class of archetypes, Jung discovered, represents active personalities that appear in dreams; another class of archetypes represents what Jung called the "archetypes of transformation," or those which portray "situations, places, ways, and means that symbolize the kind of transformation in question."[9]

According to David Peat, "archetypes are essentially dynamic in nature and unfold their projections in time. The whole pattern of an individual's life, for example, may be the gesture of an archetype."[10] He further informs us that Jung suggested that each age contributes its own levels and structures to the collective unconscious, and that archetypes can unfold over hundreds or thousands of years and manifest themselves as historical events.[11]

However, Peat adds: "The collective mind contains levels that stretch back into the remote past of the human race, but at the same time, it is constantly being restructured by dynamic forces that lie below the level of mind. In this way the door is opened for the collective unconscious to change its contents and structures creatively. No single level in mind or matter can be taken as absolutely fundamental since it is always being conditioned by the levels above and below it. In a similar way, therefore, it becomes possible for the conscious mind, through its perceptions, insights, and reflections, to act back on the collective unconscious and change it. Inspiration wells up into the mind of an artist from its collective depths. In the light of consciousness this material is molded and worked on ... [and] becomes an act in the external world."[12]

The Collective Conscious

In its highest aspect, this is the omnipresent, omniscient, omnipotent conscious universal mind that exists, has always existed, and will always exist, even though humanity has not evolved to the point where we can perceive it directly. It is the mind of the universe and of nature (the mind of God). In its aspects that are more accessible to humanity at this time, the collective conscious includes portions of the collective unconscious that become known consciously to humanity as we evolve.

The Master KH states in *The Mahatma Letters* that it is a philosophical necessity that the universal mind, like the human finite mind, have two attributes or a dual power: the conscious and the unconscious. He says, "Did it ever strike you, ... did you ever suspect that Universal, like finite, human mind might have two attributes, or a dual power— one the voluntary and conscious, and the other the involuntary and unconscious or the mechanical power."[13]

Satprem, in his work on Aurobindo, tells us that many of the levels of being that modern psychology mixes together in its discussion on the collective unconscious are indeed very conscious forces, "definitely more so than we are."[14] States Aurobindo, "The gradations of consciousness are universal states not dependent on the outlook of the subjective personality; rather the outlook of the subjective personality is determined by the grade of consciousness in which it is organized according to its typal nature or its evolutionary stage."[15]

The collective conscious mind encompasses both impersonal, universal energy and human group-consciousness. In Aurobindo's yoga, the two are closely intermingled and he compares this with modern science where the movement of energy appears to be a wave on one side and a particle on the other.[16] In fact, an exploration of Aurobindo's concepts of the mind, what he called "Supramental consciousness" would provide much information for a discussion of the universal mind, but it is beyond the scope of this particular book.

The Metaphysical Basis for Telepathy

"The Universe is Mental—held in the Mind of THE ALL."—Kybalion[17]

Willis Harman indicates that throughout history there have been a number of streams of alternative knowledge, of which he mentions that the following schools of thought stand out as bridging the gap between metaphysics and modern scientific concepts of causality.[18]

- Western esoteric, which emphasizes the transformation of the person and the environment. This includes the fields of thought of Hermeticism, Alchemy, Rosicrucianism, Freemasony, and its "contemporary 'project,' modern science."[19]

- Eastern Vedantist, which emphasizes deep inner exploration. Harman tells us that the Church of Religious Science and Unity, as well as the so-called New Age subculture, have been directly influenced by this stream and the western esoteric.

- Buddhist esoteric, also pursuing the deep inner exploration, but with a more psychological emphasis.

- Native traditions around the world, which emphasize a discovery of reality through relationship with the natural environment and the creatures of the Earth.

- The esoteric elements of Islamic (Sufi), Persian, and Chinese traditions.

All these streams of alternative knowledge are open to the possibility of telepathic communication. Ernest Holmes, Manly P. Hall, and Dion Fortune, three great thinkers in the western mystery tradition, impart the following ideas about telepathy.

The Science of Mind

Ernest Holmes states that we are surrounded by a mind or intelligence that contains the potential knowledge of everything including ourselves. This mind of the universe holds the abstract essence of wisdom, truth, and beauty and we can draw from it. However, what we draw from it must be through the channel of our own conscious minds. We must establish a unity and make a conscious connection with this greater mind before we can derive the benefits that it can reveal or impart to us.[20]

Telepathy is no surprise if we consider ourselves surrounded by a universal mind, a medium through which streams of thoughts can flow. This universal medium is always present, allowing communication with others to be going on all the time, whether the conscious mind is aware of it or not. What is known in one place can be known in all places. Even if these impressions are subliminal and vague, they are nevertheless there and have an unconscious effect upon us.

"Telepathy is the act of reading subjective thought, or of receiving conscious thought from another without audible words being spoken."[21] However, we have to tune in selectively to the type of vibrations we want. Telepathy, the transmission of thought, can be compared to radio, where we are surrounded by all sorts of waves and often there is interference or static, preventing us from receiving the messages clearly or just producing noise. We can receive a clear message only when we tune the instrument properly.

The transmitter does not know if the message is being received or how many people are receiving it. In the teachings, we are often cautioned to guard our minds, lest our thoughts and the messages we are sending to our coworkers be picked up by people who are not entitled to have this information.

Since our minds are linked with the universal mind, which has no limits, we also have the possibility of endless creativity and expansion. When we create a mental image of something we would like to accomplish, the powers of the universal mind immediately set to work to produce the thing outlined. If we seek knowledge, we receive instruction from this center of all knowledge. Holmes states: "Science, invention, art, literature, philosophy and religion, have one common center from which, through experience, is drawn all knowledge."[22]

He further tells us: "Anything that has ever been thought at any time in the history of man, exists today in a subjective state in universal mind. When we get into the field of Mind, there is no past, present or future. They merge into one medium."[23] Thus, this collective mind contains a record of all human events that have ever transpired.

Planetary Memory

Manly Hall tells us that psychometry, or the facility of universal memory, is operative because of "the photographic nature of atmosphere or energy itself," and also because "energy has within it a retentive power, and any impression made upon energy remains locked within it, subject to be drawn forth by association, exactly as in the case of human nature."[24]

Human thought processes set up energy patterns, or vibrations that are released into the magnetic field of the Earth in much the same manner as radio and television broadcasts. We live in a field or sea of these vibratory forces, which bombard us from practically every part of the universe. To selectively receive the vibrations we want, we effectively "tune in" on a particular channel and, depending on our focus, the remainder of the innumerable channels are not noticeable to us.[25]

We respond most to those energy patterns or vibrations that resonate with our own vibrational level at the time. For example, if we emit vibrations of love, we magnetize more vibrations of love. Or, if we ask the universe a question, we receive an answer.

Each of us has an underlying energy keynote that is uniquely ours throughout life, and we respond in particular to energies in the universe that resonate with our keynote. Therefore, our thoughts and emotions set up energy fields that relate most particularly to us. The messages inherent in the thoughts and feelings we transmit result in the karmic records that apply to our lives. Thus, we create and modify activities and bring about their results, according to the great universal law of cause and effect.

Hall tells us that spiritual energies manifest as the power of will, mental energies as attention, emotional energies as interest, and physical energies as vitality. Psychic energies include the mental and emotional activities of attention and interest.[26]

It is obvious that if the universe is consciously intelligent and if it is evolving, the universe must also contain all the essentials of a universal memory.

Hall says, "We have no reason to doubt that its essential retentive function is similar to that of the human mind. It may be grander and more inclusive, but it must be essentially of the same principle, inasmuch as man's function also bears witness to this principle. Man did not create the pattern of his own retentive memory; he merely specialized it according to his needs. But the pattern itself, as an availability of specialization, has to exist in space, or man could not have gained access to it or energized it."

He adds, "A universal memory is essential if we assume evolution to be true, because evolution depends for its productivity upon certain perspectives...If the individual cannot learn from yesterday so that he will be better today, one of the most important prodding agencies of evolution is lost."[27]

Mental Images

Dion Fortune states that the Great Ones influenced the forerunners of humanity by telepathic suggestion, giving primitive mankind the images necessary to translate sensation into mentation. Thus, in the beginning, we were saved the lengthy and laborious process of having to build these images out of accumulated experiences.

Gradually, the concrete or objective mind of humanity was built up from the inspirations given us by these sages, who attained their development during the period immediately preceding ours. Their task was to forge a connecting chain of associated ideas from consciousness to subconsciousness, thereby giving us a link with the higher, more subjective spheres.

In this manner, the elder brethren of our race enabled, and still enable, our evolution to recapitulate stages that our forebears had to go through the hard way during their own evolution, through a process that took much longer because it was new to Earth.[28]

Dion Fortune indicates that telepathic communication is often at work between us and our guides on the inner planes, but also that this type of communication can come from other sources that we would not normally accept.[29] Accordingly, we want to be alert to ideas that come into our minds that we ordinarily would not originate ourselves and then judge the veracity of these ideas in the light of what we ourselves think is best. As developed humans, we look within to our own conscience and judgment rather than just blindly accepting something that pops into our minds. Although we want to be open to inspiration and higher guidance, we want to develop the ability to discern the sources of the information we receive.

The Scientific Basis for Telepathy

"Each object in the world is not merely itself but involves every other object, and in fact is every other object."—Marilyn Ferguson[30]

During the past several years, many philosophical books and articles on the ideas of God or consciousness have been written by professional scientists. Only a few of these are reviewed here.

Jeanne Achterberg tells us, "Evidence from several disciplines, including psychophysiology, parapsychology, the basic sciences, and thousands of case studies and self-reports, suggests not only that consciousness is capable of altering the physical world, but that consciousness is commingled with the emotions, images, thoughts, and experiences of others with whom we are in relationship. And even with others with whom we are not in relationship. For example, research has shown that EEG brain waves of couples in 'bonded' relationships tend to synchronize rapidly, providing some evidence of shared mental emotional experience. Researchers Robert Jahn and Brenda Dunn have also shown that when a couple in close relationship share intentions to alter the output of a random number generator, their success is significantly noteworthy."[31]

Quantum theory tells us that everything is, indeed, connected to everything else. The invention of the hologram and David Bohm's theory of the implicate order have created a revolution in modern thought about the nature of consciousness, especially from the standpoint of the interconnectedness of mind and matter.

The Implicate Order and Holography

Physicist David Bohm introduced the concept of the "implicate order," which is, essentially, the underlying connectedness of the universe. This is in contrast to the "explicate order," which is the world we experience in our daily life.

Bohm used the hologram as an analogy. As succinctly put by Willis Harman, "The hologram is a process which makes a photographic record of the interference patterns of light waves reflected from an object. Whereas the usual photograph displays a point-to-point correspondence between the image and the object photographed, the hologram enfolds the form and structure of the entire object within each region of the photographic record. Thus every portion of the hologram contains the information of the whole object." In like fashion, "in the implicate order the totality of existence is enfolded in each region of space (and time)."[32]

Bohm considered the brain to be a hologram—storing, decoding, and revealing images—participating in a holographic universe. Ken Wilber relates: "In the explicate or manifest realm of space and time, things and events are indeed separate and discrete. But beneath the surface, as it were, in the implicate or frequency realm, all things and events are spacelessly, timelessly, intrinsically, one and undivided."[33]

This bears out the sense of universal unity and helps explain the process of telepathy, since thoughts and impressions exist everywhere simultaneously.

The basic tenets of the holographic model, according to scientist Ken Dychtwald, are:[34]

- There is no such thing as pure energy or pure matter. Every aspect of the universe seems, instead, to exist as a kind of vibrational or energetic expression.

- Every aspect of the universe is itself a whole, a full being, a comprehensive system in its own right, containing within it a complete store of information about itself. This information may exist as energetic or vibrational information.

- Every aspect of the universe seems to be part of some larger whole, grander being, and more comprehensive system.

- Since each aspect of the universe expresses itself vibrationally, and all vibrational expressions intermingle within the master hologram, every aspect of the universe contains knowledge about the whole within which it exists.

Influenced by Bohm's ideas, neuroscientist Karl Pribram has proposed an implicate order model for memory. "Just as information in the holograph is both enfolded into each small region of the plate and distributed across the whole, so, too, are memories not specifically located in particular cells or regions of the brain but have a distributed quality. Pribram suggests that incoming sensations fold themselves over large regions and, when recalled, unfold into specific memories."[35]

Thoughts trigger other thoughts, seemingly unrelated, but associated by subtle connections and feelings. Similarly, individual minds are linked in the background of the collective mind, and act upon each other.

Bohm stated, "in some sense the individual has direct access to the cosmic totality. And therefore it is through the individual that the general consciousness has to get cleared up...The individual is an actuality which includes this manifestation of the consciousness of mankind, but he is more. Every individual is his own particular contact. Every individual is in total contact with the implicate order, with all that is around us. Therefore, in some sense he is part of the whole of mankind and in another sense he...is a focus for something beyond mankind."[36]

Bohm felt that it is possible for a number of individuals who are in close relation and who trust each other to be able to establish a united consciousness which could act as one. He said that even a group of ten people could profoundly affect the consciousness of humanity as a whole.[37]

Physicist David Peat indicates that the implicate order is an appropriate descriptor of society. He cites that "a crowd of people consists of individuals, each of which has his or her own motivations and beliefs. Nevertheless, in certain situations, the crowd also has a collective behavior, just as do the electrons in a plasma...In such a case the behavior of the crowd is enfolded in each individual and in turn each individual is unfolded within the whole crowd. In a more subtle way a society and its members are related through an implicate order of folding and unfolding."[38]

Distant Viewing

Physicist Russell Targ, a pioneer in the development of the laser, tells us that hundreds of remote viewing experiments were carried out at the Stanford Research Institute (now called SRI International) from 1972 through 1986 for their sponsor, the CIA. Targ worked with Harold

Puthoff, another laser researcher at SRI, on these experiments. Remote viewing is the cognitive ability to access information on events and situations that are remote in space and time. The process is not yet understood. A simple test of this ability would be to hide an object in a box and ask the subject to attempt to describe it.

The team designed some of the experiments to elucidate the physical and psychological properties of psi abilities. Other experiments were to provide information for the CIA about current events in remote places. They learned that the accuracy and reliability of remote viewing "was not in any way affected by distance, size, or electromagnetic shielding," and they discovered that the more exciting or demanding the task, the more likely they were to be successful. Above all, they became totally convinced of the reality of psi abilities.[39]

"One particular remote viewing experiment that we conducted with one of our most talented psychics, Pat Price, shows why we believe that remote viewing is an example of the near-omniscient ability of consciousness to transcend our ordinary awareness of space and time."[40]

In July 1995, the CIA declassified these remote viewing experiments. Harold Puthoff indicates that, even though details have not been released of their broad range of experiments, they have nevertheless been able to publish summaries of what was learned in these studies about the overall characteristics of remote viewing.[41]

Morphic Resonance

Biologist Rupert Sheldrake proposes that there are fields of information that influence the structure of matter. These morphogenetic fields have measurable physical effects and are responsible for the characteristic form and organization of systems at all levels of complexity. These fields affect events and impose patterned restrictions on the energetically possible outcomes of physical processes. Sheldrake suggests that these fields are derived from other morphogenetic fields from previous similar systems. "According to this hypothesis, systems are organized in the way they are because similar systems were organized that way in the past."[42]

Jung states, "In addition to our immediate consciousness, which is of a thoroughly personal nature and which we believe to be the only empirical psyche (even if we tack on the personal unconscious as an appendix) there exists a second psychic system of a collective, universal, and impersonal nature which is identical in all individuals. This collective unconscious does not develop individually but is inherited. It consists of pre-existent forms, the archetypes, which can only become conscious secondarily and which give definite form to certain psychic contents."[43]

David Peat tells us that the implication of Sheldrake's idea is that it extends the nature of matter by introducing a new level, that of "active information."[44] Peat further indicates that, in the absence of morphic fields, "there would simply be too many alternatives and contingencies for nature to exhibit the sort of unity in diversity that is seen in the structure of matter and living things."[45] Accordingly, this memory characteristic of matter gives a new material entity the advantage of being able to learn from the experiences of its predecessors.

Peat adds, "These morphic fields are a type of memory that acts like a formative pattern with regard to material structures and patterns of behavior. In this sense they are related to Jung's archetypes, which could be thought of as formative fields of the collective unconscious. Just as the whole evolutionary and developmental history of an organism is supposed to be enfolded within its hierarchy of morphic fields, so is the history of a people, and indeed of the whole human race, supposed to be enfolded within the archetypes. Is it possible therefore that the archetypes and the morphic fields have a universal aspect, being formative fields of information that have an active role within the processes of matter, thought, and behavior?"[46]

If, indeed, there is active information associated with matter, we could easily surmise that this would provide a link between our consciousness and the consciousness of others, including nature and the universe itself.

Synchronicity

Carl Jung developed the concept of synchronicity, "a meaningful coincidence of two or more events where something other than the probability of chance is involved. Chance is a statistical concept which 'explains' deviations within certain patterns of probability. Synchronicity elucidates meaningful arrangements and coincidence which somehow go beyond the calculations of probability. Pre-cognition, clairvoyance, telepathy, etc. are phenomena which are inexplicable through chance but become empirically intelligible through the employment of the principle of synchronicity, which suggests a kind of harmony at work in the interrelation of both psychic and physical events."⁴⁷

"Synchronicity," according to David Peat, "arises out of the underlying patterns of the universe rather than through a causality of pushes and pulls that we normally associate with events in nature."⁴⁸ Peat states that Jung called synchronicity an "acausal connecting principle" and that an acausal connection is exactly what Nobel Prize winner, Wolfgang Pauli (also a collaborator with Jung), proposed in his exclusion principle, Pauli's most famous contribution to physics. The exclusion principle is "an abstract pattern that lies hidden beneath the surface of atomic matter and determines its behavior in a noncausal way."⁴⁹

Throughout his book, *Synchronicity: The Bridge Between Matter and Mind*, Peat discusses how science attempts to reveal pattern, order, and symmetry in nature. He proposes that fundamental symmetries are the archetypes of all matter and the ground of material existence. Elementary particles are simply the material manifestations of these underlying symmetries.⁵⁰

Peat states that there is no ultimate distinction between the material and the mental, and that synchronicities represent the explicit unfolding of deeper, archetypal orders.⁵¹ "For Jung believed that it is only within the objective layers of the mind, deep below the levels of personal repressions, that the energies and patterns of synchronicity are to be found. Indeed the deeper we dig into the mind the more we discover that the distinction between mind and matter is dissolved and the operation of the objective intelligence begins to manifest its power."⁵²

Peat cautions us that "The analogy between archetype and fundamental symmetry is, of course, a loose one and must not be taken too far, but it does suggest that the origin of structures and patterns does not lie in mind or matter as such, but arises in some more subtle level. Synchronicities, which have been called the activation of the archetypes, therefore no longer imply just an occasional form of coincidence but the essential meaningful relationship between the mental and material aspects of the universe."⁵³

Marilyn Ferguson states that "We may now be experiencing the effects of a social hologram, a pattern of interconnectedness of individuals. Synchronicity, meaningful coincidence, makes sense in a meaningful, holographic universe."⁵⁴

Willis Harman indicates that it is more difficult to explain apparent separateness than it would be to explain meaningful coincidences, or synchronicities. He says, "the question is not 'How can we explain apparent telepathic communication?' but rather 'How can we explain why our minds are not cluttered by all that information in other minds.'"[55]

The Planetary Mind Field

In his book, *The Planetary Mind*, Professor Arne Wyller gives us a thorough review of molecular and cellular biology, leading to the rather startling conclusion that the processes of evolution, as we know of them, have simply not had time to evolve the complexity of life as we know it today on our planet. He suggests, "May we not consider the existence of an invisible intelligence field—a Mind Field—that right now exists on Earth along with the physicist's equally invisible vibrating quantum energy fields, which manifest their vibrations as material particles? And that this Planetary Mind Field continually manipulates the material energy field into evolving life forms?"[56]

Wyller then proposes that we explore the light field or photon field as a means by which the planetary mind field might manipulate the energy fields of matter to produce biological organisms. "In the physicist's world picture, light particles are embedded in the very structure of the atom, acting as intermediaries—gluons—for the electromagnetic force that holds the electron and the nucleus in the atom together."[57]

He continues to tell us that the light particle, at rest, has no mass, no weight, and carries no electric charge, yet can split itself into an electron-positron pair. "Finally, it is its own antiparticle: light that arises from fields of antimatter is indistinguishable from light given off by ordinary matter."[58]

This coincides with Sri Aurobindo's reference to "the light of the Thought that carries in it its own opposites."[59] In fact, in Satprem's discussion on Aurobindo's work, he stated, "It may be interesting here to draw a parallel with Einstein's theory of relativity…The supramental consciousness, which is Light itself, is also the conquest of time and distance. There is perhaps less difference than we might imagine between the physicist's light and the seer's."[60]

Dr. Wyller further shows that light is by far the most preponderant particle in the Universe. "After the Big Bang, which represented the beginning of history of our Universe, there now resides an afterglow of light so significant that for every one atom of ordinary matter in the Universe there exist 1 billion light particles. Matter is an utterly insignificant 'contaminant' in the particle Universe. Although most of the energy resides in matter, almost all particles in the Universe are those of light."[61]

He indicates how, within our modern scientific framework, the light particle might act as a mediator between the mind field and the matter fields. To further support his idea of the mind field, Wyller refers to David Bohm's later research[62] on the idea of active information carried by an invisible quantum field that accompanies an elementary particle. Wyller says, "His [Bohm's] basic idea is that a form having very little energy (the quantum field) enters into and directs a much greater energy (the motion of the elementary particle), much as a radio or TV wave containing very little energy can carry considerable amounts of information in the form of sound messages or visual images. Bohm also mentions the biological example of DNA, which carries large amounts of information in its structure."[63]

In the latter part of his book, Wyller discusses the ramifications of the mind field on cultural evolution and suggests that it must operate through individual mind channels. "Once a culturally influential idea appears in the brain of a single human individual, that individual can act to spread that idea into human society, thus affecting the cultural evolution of the human species. I believe that the Mind Field can move the individual through its manipulative channel: the subconscious part of the human brain, which is also called the unconscious."[64] He adds:

"Because it had to create the unconscious partly out of matter, the Mind Field is constrained by the relative material murkiness of that channel and by the cooperation of the individual in such communication. Thus, the Mind Field has to rely on the statistical properties of those individual communication channels. It must hope that as it sends 'waves of ideas' out to billions of individual channels, a very few individuals [at least] will be open to receiving the ideas. Humans will then be inspired to make intuitive leaps that fertilize their cultural fields. For example, the mystics occasionally have transparent channels through which total nonverbal communication is possible; the great scientists, on the other hand, have intuitive access to the Mind Field's scientific nature."[65]

Types of Telepathy and Communication

"One of the characteristics, distinguishing the group of world servers and knowers, is that the outer organisation which holds them integrated is practically non-existent. They are held together by an inner structure of thought and by a telepathic medium of inter-relation."—AAB[66]

In the system of the Tibetan Master Djwhal Khul, there are two laws of telepathic communication:[67]

1.   The power to communicate that lies within the ether and is thus a part of the very nature of substance itself. The significance of telepathy is to be found in the concept of omnipresence, based on the fact that the etheric bodies of all forms constitute the world etheric body.

2.   The interplay of many minds, which produces a unity of thought that is powerful enough to be recognized by the brain.

There are several types of telepathy and several vehicles that transmit and receive telepathic communication. Types of telepathy range from the empathy or emotional sensitivity that we have for one another through all levels up to the highest inspirations we can experience from divine sources. These energies go through our physical/etheric, emotional, mental, intuitional, and spiritual vehicles, or centers, according to our development and focus at the time.

Our centers correspond with the planes of consciousness (which, in the grand scheme, are subplanes on the cosmic physical plane). These planes, from the highest to the lowest, are: logoic (atomic), monadic, atmic, buddhic, mental, astral, and etheric. In addition, these seven planes are further subdivided into seven subplanes, thus giving Earth a total of 49 subplanes of manifestation. Humanity today typically operates on fewer than half of these subplanes, but we can access higher ones with practice and during particularly insightful meditations; group meditation facilitates reaching higher levels. The monadic plane is probably the highest level today's humanity can possibly reach.

Through the Law of Correspondence, we extrapolate that great entities, such as planets and constellations, have corresponding fields of activity on their own planes of consciousness.

In the following discussion on types of telepathy, we must remember that sometimes these distinctions are blurred and a telepathic communication might involve multiple levels. However, for the greatest success, we must select the appropriate levels for our communication and consciously direct our energy accordingly. To work telepathically, we should be aware of which of our vehicles (mental, astral, or etheric) are most active, which is essentially where our life energy is predominantly focused and most expressive.

Intuitional Telepathy

Intuitional telepathy involves the highest levels that humanity can work with under our current evolution. This form of telepathy involves the monadic, atmic, or buddhic planes and the head, heart, and ajna centers in the human body.

The head center is receptive to impression from higher sources and the ajna center receives idealistic intuitional impressions. The ajna center can then broadcast what is received, "using the throat center as the creative formulator of thought, and the factor which embodies the sensed or intuited idea."[68] Intuitional telepathy is "one of the fruits of true meditation."[69]

To do spiritual work, we attempt to focus our energies in our head center and, through meditation, bring in the power of the soul. This type of telepathy has been responsible for all the inspirational writings and speeches of real power, the world scriptures, and the language of symbolism; it is only possible when there is an integrated personality focused in the soul consciousness, with the mind and the brain in alignment.[70]

Mental Telepathy

Mental telepathy involves the mental plane and the mind or manasic vehicle. Both the transmission and reception processes involve the head, ajna, and throat centers.

The throat center is the medium of all creative work, but the heart and the throat must be used in synthesis, the Tibetan tells us. The lines of energy that link and bind together can only stream from the heart center. Because of this, the Tibetan assigned certain meditations to his disciples to stimulate the heart center into action and link the heart center (between the shoulder blades) to the head center through the medium of the thousand-petalled lotus in the head center, which is the higher correspondence of the heart center.

When the heart center, linked as described, is adequately radiatory and magnetic, it relates disciples to each other and to all the world. It also produces a telepathic interplay "which is so much to be desired and which is so constructively useful to the spiritual Hierarchy—provided it is established within a group of pledged disciples, dedicated to the service of humanity. They can then be trusted."[71]

Mental or mind-to-mind telepathy can occur only when emotion and strong feeling are eliminated from the telepathic communications. This type of telepathy demands detachment, else the emotional vehicles will interfere in the transmission and reception of the messages.

Empathic and Instinctual Telepathy

Empathic and instinctual telepathy involve the emotional and etheric vehicles, respectively. This is the level of desire and manifestation. The astral and physical/etheric planes are involved, along with various combinations of the heart, solar plexus, sacral, and base centers.

Instinctual telepathy concerns feelings in every case and invariably involves radiations from the solar plexus. One example of this type of telepathy is that existing between a mother and her child. Another example is when people nonverbally transmit to each other their anxieties, worries, sorrows, and desires.

Another level of instinctual telepathy is exhibited by modern mass psychology and public opinion, when it is predominantly emotional and unintelligent in its expression. However, when this shifts into the realm of intelligent public opinion, the throat and ajna centers are involved.

Where high levels of devotion, aspiration, and love are concerned, especially in groups, communication will be from heart to heart, from group heart to group heart.[72]

The Communication Channels

"Some groups of energy communicators and transmitters will carry
illumination between groups of thinkers. They are illuminators of group
thoughts. They transmit energy from one thought centre to another. They
transmit, above everything else, the energy of ideas."—AAB[73]

Telepathic communication occurs amongst all levels of manifestation in the universe. We can only speculate on the interactions of great cosmic beings, but the Tibetan gives us a lot of information about how members of Hierarchy communicate (telepathy is their main form of communication) and how humanity can (and often does) communicate.

The nature of the energies of the entities involved determine how they interact with each other.

Communications of Great Beings

We can safely assume that the Planetary Logoi of the planets in our solar system engage in telepathic communication with each other and with the Solar Logos. However, there must be certain cycles during which their communication is more active, and these cycles could be during conjunctions, oppositions, or when the planets are at an angle to each other. The Tibetan places a lot of importance upon triangles, but the triangles that he cites in his many volumes are not evident on the physical plane.

The type of telepathy must also depend on the development of the planets involved, for example, whether they are considered "sacred" or "nonsacred," in the Tibetan's terms. However, it certainly seems possible that the type of telepathy used between planets at a given time might depend on the work that needs to be done.

The energies involved might be extrapolated from research on radiation and magnetization levels, orbits, cosmic rays, the light spectrum, and other sorts of vibratory activity.

Communications of Adepts

Telepathy is the primary means by which members of the planetary Hierarchy of adepts and sages communicate with each other. The Tibetan tells us that members of Hierarchy are telepathically linked, "and can—at the slightest need and with the least expenditure of force—get en rapport with each other. They are all tuned to a particular vibration."[74]

They send suggestions to humanity as to what needs to be done to help the evolution on our planet but, in doing so, they must (and do) always respect our free will. A basic law of the universe is that we retain our free will and that Hierarchy can help us only when we invoke their assistance. The Tibetan gives the following description of how ideas flow from the Hierarchy to humanity:

"The Universal Mind is tapped by some member of the planetary Hierarchy according to His mental bias and equipment, and the immediate needs sensed by the working adepts. He then presents the new idea, new discovery, or the new revelation to the group of adepts (telepathically, of course, my brother) and, when it has been discussed by them, He later presents it to His group of disciples. Among them He will find one who responds more readily and intelligently than the others and this one, through his clear thinking and the power of his formulated thoughtforms, can then influence other minds. These others grasp the concept as theirs; they seize upon it and work it out into manifestation. Each regards it as his special privilege so to do and, because of this specialising faculty and his automatically engendered responsibility, he throws back of it all the energy which is his, and works and fights for his thoughtforms."[75]

Communications of Humanity

The Tibetan often talks about the New Group of World Servers, members of humanity who are a little farther along the spiritual path than average humanity, yet the members of this group include world workers who are not affiliated with any spiritual philosophy. The main criteria is that the workers be sincere in wanting to help better life on planet Earth. There is no overt organization, but generally members of the New Group of World Servers are people who are working in groups scattered around the Earth to improve the conditions of life.

The Tibetan tells us: "The New Group of World Servers includes selfless humanitarian workers, political leaders, economists, scientific workers, representatives from all the world religions, practical mystics, and occultists. Its members are linked telepathically or they recognize each other through the quality of the work they are doing in the outer world and the inclusiveness in which they work. It is inspired from above by the souls of its members and the Great Ones and is energized into activity by the need of humanity itself. It is composed of living conscious souls working through coordinated personalities."[76]

He further states: "In the new groups are collected together people who are very diverse in their nature, who are found upon differing rays, who are of different nationalities, and who are each of them the product of widely varying environments and heredity. Besides these obvious factors which immediately attract attention, there is also to be found an equal diversity in the life experience of the souls concerned. The complexity of the problem is also tremendously increased when one remembers the long road which each has traveled and the many factors (emerging out of a dim and distant past) which have contributed to make each person what he now is. When, therefore, one dwells on the barriers and difficulties supervening upon such diverse conditions, the question arises at once: What provides the common meeting ground, and what makes it possible to have an interplay between the minds involved?"[77]

From these statements, we can see clearly that, if it is our mission to help uplift humanity, we need to find groups of like-minded people that we can work with to accomplish these goals. Then, to further the work, we need to meditate, which is the quickest means by which we can start working telepathically toward our common goals. Chapter 11 provides some meditations that we can use, including an exercise for telepathic alignment.

The Messages

"They express, because of their state of expanded consciousness,
the Mind of God."[78]

Now that we have discussed the types of communication and the communicators, what of the message? For example, how do we know if our "intuition" is valid? Where is the message coming from? One test of whether a message is spiritually based is to analyze it and think of its results: does the personality have anything to gain from it? If we could possibly have any personal interest in the results of the communication, then we need to keep the possibility in mind that the message could be a result of wishful thinking or desire.

At some point in time, telepathy will be a natural aspect of living, thus we will have a definite need to know how to discriminate amongst the levels of messages we are receiving. In fact, our discriminative faculties are being greatly challenged now due to the wide variety of channeled material that is available today. According to the Tibetan, the source of most channeled information is the astral body of a well-meaning aspirant who has tuned into the emotional level of higher concepts and ideals. He goes on to say that the astral plane is where we have to learn to distinguish truth from error and that those who are misled are only learning a needed lesson. He says that the good effect is that the fact of the spiritual Hierarchy is being brought to the attention of the masses, even though the astral reflection is being confused with the reality.[79]

Even though the Tibetan wrote this many years ago, it still seems applicable today. However, just within the past few years, there seems to be a trend toward the type of mental approach to the development of higher consciousness that the Tibetan keeps telling us is the essential basis for the intuitive levels of spiritual development that is our goal and the accomplishment of adepthood.

Developing Psychic Powers

"We are today close to the time when the fact of there being modes of perception other than those of the physical senses will be recognised, and the attitude of medicine and of the psychiatric and neurological sciences will undergo definite changes —much to the assistance and aid of humanity."—AAB[80]

The Tibetan gives us a list of several capacities, inherent in the soul, that we must develop if we are to most effectively meet world need. These are:[81]

- Intuitional response to ideas.

- Sensitiveness to the impression which some member of the Hierarchy may seek to make upon our mind. Using the opportunity of contact at the time of the full moon enhances this sensitivity.

- Quick response to real need. This involves heart knowledge rather than a solar plexus reaction.

- Right observation of reality upon the soul plane. This leads to right mental perception, to freedom from illusion and glamour, and to the illumination of the brain.

- Correct manipulation of force, involving an understanding of the types and qualities of force and their right creative weaving into service upon the outer plane.

- A true comprehension of the time element, with its cyclic ebb and flow and the right seasons for action.

Chapter 4—
Astrology, The Science of Relations

"Stars and constellations have an occult and mysterious influence on, and connection with, individuals. And if with the latter, why not with nations, races and mankind as a whole? This again is a claim made on the authority of the Zodiacal records."—HPB[1]

We respond to impressions from many different sources, which include all the experiences we have built up ourselves from previous lives, plus the experiences of others in their previous lives since we are all interconnected telepathically. We respond to mass public opinion and world ideas of the current age and, most particularly, the opinions and ideals that we resonate with, generated by our culture, community, and the groups with whom we have come into incarnation. We respond to evolutionary forces and ideals seeded by great thinkers and sages: when we decide that we want to think for ourselves, rather than just responding, we become co-creators with these adepts and plant our own seeds of thought into that vast field of knowledge and wisdom that Patanjali referred to as the "Raincloud of Knowable Things" and that we think of as the universal consciousness.

However, we also know that besides these obvious sources of influence, we respond to planetary and cosmic energies, from our solar system and brought to our solar system from other places in the universe. We are now aware that it is commonly recognized by scientists, astrologers, philosophers, and thinking people of today that certain cosmic forces play upon and produce changes in our solar system, and consequently upon our planetary environment and all life within it.

We will specifically cover some of those concepts. Then, we will examine how the Tibetan's system of esoteric astrology can fit in with and enhance many of the principles and systems of astrology and cosmology that have been worked out by leading thinkers of our current age.

The Astrological Year

"Golden-haired Helios who wield the flame's untiring light, who drive in lofty turns around the great pole, ...from you come the elements arranged by your own laws which cause the whole world to rotate through its four yearly turning points."—Betz[2]

The zodiac represents the cycle of the year and its seasons, as seen from the northern hemisphere where western astrology originated. Astrologers used the stars as a background for the cycles of the Sun because the stars are "fixed" in the sky, thus ever there when early humanity needed to take measurements of the processes of time. As people became aware that they responded differently to various cycles, they developed a rich folklore of the personality types that would emerge from specific placements of the Sun and the planets in the sky. Some of this folklore could have been seeded by the wise men and sages of the time; those who had what esotericists call "straight-knowledge." Eventually, these characteristics became enfolded into a self-fulfilling prophecy—what we call a thoughtform—that became embedded in the collective unconscious and actually influenced and imprinted human qualities and behavior, as archetypes do. This is only one of the reasons that astrology "works." Another reason astrology works is that there are, in addition, real influences from the constellations and planets themselves.

The twelve zodiacal signs represent those constellations of the same names that are in a belt within eight or so degrees on either side of the ecliptic. The ecliptic is the apparent path of the Sun as the Earth revolves around the Sun during the course of the seasons. The Sun appears to move along this path by roughly one degree of arc per day, 30 degrees per sign, and 360 degrees per year.

The signs are measured from the spring or vernal equinox, which western astrologers call 0-degree Aries, the first sign of the zodiac. Due to the precession of the equinoxes, the Sun at the vernal equinox is no longer where the constellation of Aries is in the sky. Precession occurs due to a wobble in the Earth as it spins on its axis. When western astrology was invented, the astrological 0-degree Aries was in alignment with the constellation of Aries, but now at the vernal equinox, it has precessed through Pisces and is entering Aquarius, giving us the "Age of Aquarius." The entire process of precession through all of the signs of the zodiac takes around 26,000 years, with approximately 2,200 years spent in each sign, or "Age." The period of 26,000 is referred to as the Greater Zodiac.

The four cardinal signs of the zodiac define the relationship of the ecliptic to the celestial equator (the celestial equator is Earth's equator projected into space). Cancer and Capricorn mark the points of greatest separation between the ecliptic and the equator at the times of the summer and winter solstices. Aries and Libra mark the points where the lines of the ecliptic and the celestial equator join, at the times of the vernal and autumnal equinoxes.

The solstices and equinoxes have long been celebrated as spiritual festivals in the history of humanity.

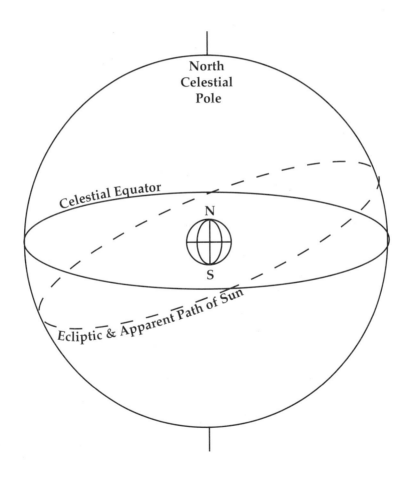

Relationships Between Astronomy and Esoteric Astrology

"Perhaps the new studies of cosmic radiation, the Sun's magnetic field and the inner structure of the planets will lead to a revival of astrology on a higher plane than it occupied in antiquity."—Nelson/Addey[3]

In Chapter 3 we surveyed many thoughts from recent science which support the concept of subtle influences that science at this time cannot explain. These studies point to the fact, known by students of the ageless wisdom, that consciousness is a definite force in the universe and, so far, physical science has no means of quantifying it.

Physicist Will Keepin relates that, according to the Dalai Lama, there are four steps to follow in the study of reality: first, study the obvious, the physical nature of things; second, go inward; third, attempt to find the relationship between the first two; and fourth, by drawing on the first three steps, we can come to know the deepest secrets of the universe. Keepin's impression was, "Wow, western science took the first step to be the whole enchilada."[4]

Keepin is one of many traditional scientists who are now exploring alternative theories of the universe with zest, considering such factors as the role that consciousness has to play. The work of others is reviewed in Chapter 3.

The following excerpts of articles from *Sky & Telescope* and *Astronomy* magazines are written by reputable scientists who are not associated with astrology, as far as I know; my review of their work is not meant to make that implication. Instead, I include these excerpts to give you an idea of some of the issues in astronomy today that I consider fascinating and relevant to the effects that the universe has upon life on Earth.

Sunspots and Solar Flares

Bradley E. Schaefer in *Sky & Telescope* tells us: "In March 1989 a large sunspot rotated onto the disk of the Sun and started emitting powerful flares. These explosions, caused by the magnetic field that formed the spot, involved a bright pulse of light (across all wavelengths) accompanied by an outpouring of high-energy particles. The energetic protons spiraled down the Earth's magnetic field and induced low-frequency currents in large loops of wire, such as those that form power grids."[5]

This event, and others similar, have been responsible for collapses of power systems and failures of communication and navigation systems. In addition, astronomers believe that these perturbations on the surface of the Sun are responsible for climactic changes on Earth,[6] resulting in events that included the "Little Ice Age" in the fourteenth century and the extinctions of certain life forms over the ages. This is to say nothing of all the social turmoil these phenomena have caused over the centuries.[7]

The sunspot cycle is around 11.5 years in length—similar to the 11.86-year Jupiter orbit—however the sunspot cycle actually varies in length from eight to fifteen years. Scientists Sallie Baliunas and Willie Soon tell us, "Other periods are also present, for instance the 80- to 90-year 'Gleissberg Cycle' and a 200-year cycle. A period of roughly 2,200 years is suggested by records of solar magnetism from the radiocarbon abundance in bristlecone-pine tree rings that can be traced over several millenniums."[8] (What a coincidence that the cycle of an astrological age is also approximately 2,200 years.)

There was a period in the seventeenth century, called the "Maunder Minimum," where there was a very low level of solar magnetic activity, resulting in cooler temperatures and long winters; conversely, periods of sunspot activity result in warmer temperatures. Minimal sunspot phases have been linked with an abundance of carbon-14 and beryllium-10 radioisotopes in Earth's atmosphere, which would normally be deflected by the solar wind but were not since the Sun was magnetically weak at the time. In addition, the Sun changes in brightness by about a half percent between minimal and maximum phases.[9]

As Schaefer concludes in his article: "As we have seen, our lives are indeed connected to the cosmos in numerous ways."[10]

Solar Winds

According to Kenneth R. Lang in *Sky & Telescope*, the expansion of the Sun's corona into interplanetary space fills the solar system with a thin, perpetual outflow of ionized matter called the solar wind. At a distance from the Sun, gas pressure from the million-degree corona overcomes the Sun's gravitational attraction, producing a wind that accelerates away to supersonic speeds. There are two components: a slow wind, with a speed of about 400 kilometers per second; and a wind that, for unknown reasons, travels almost twice as fast.

Lang states, "The Ulysses spacecraft conclusively demonstrated that the high-speed component of the solar wind escapes from holes in the corona near the Sun's poles (*S&T*: March 1996, page 24). At least this was the situation near the current minimum of the Sun's 11-year magnetic-activity cycle. Magnetic lines of force in the coronal holes stretch straight outward, providing a fast lane for the high-speed wind. …The slower wind originates near the solar equator (at least around activity minimum), but its exact source remains a mystery to be solved by future observations."[11]

Lang continues to tell us that the magnetic cocoon, or magnetosphere of the Earth is "constantly buffeted and reshaped by the variable solar wind, and the gusty interplanetary 'weather' can affect us significantly. By disturbing the Earth's magnetic field it can produce geomagnetic storms, create auroras, disrupt radio navigation and communication systems, endanger astronauts, destroy satellite electronics, and cause power blackouts on Earth."

In another issue of *Sky & Telescope*, Sun Kwok discusses stellar winds and planetary nebulae: "When a low-mass star like the Sun reaches the end of its hydrogen-burning life, it swells into a red giant that slowly ejects its atmosphere. A fast wind then emerges from the exposed stellar core. A planetary nebula is born when this fast wind plows into the previously ejected material, leaving behind a hot bubble of rarefied, X-ray-emitting gas."

Kwok further indicates that "Planetaries are also useful tracers of the most enigmatic component of galaxies: dark matter. Since they exist not only in a galaxy's plane but also in its halo, their orbital motions are affected by normal luminous matter (stars and interstellar gas) as well as by the large amount of invisible dark matter in a halo."[12]

Solar winds, which are undoubtedly mutating over time, reach out beyond the boundaries of the Sun's planetary orbits, constantly affecting all life forms in their path.

Dark Matter

"News Notes" in the November 1996 issue of *Sky & Telescope* states: "One of cosmology's long-standing problems is that the universe doesn't "weigh" enough. The matter visible to astronomers isn't sufficient, for example, to keep clusters of galaxies from flying apart. Consequently, there must be some 'dark matter' that has escaped detection. Now a Harvard astronomer has put forth tantalizing if tentative evidence that planet-size objects scattered throughout galaxies may constitute this hidden mass."

This astronomer, Rudolph E. Schild of the Harvard-Smithsonian Center for Astrophysics, bases his research on quasars that undergo gravitational lensing. The lensing galaxy "must be teeming with roughly a million planet-mass objects for each of its stars. If the objects are indeed planets, they presumably formed along with stars, only to somehow escape into the galaxy's interstellar reaches. And according to Schild, such abundance also suggests that all stars have as many planets as they can hold onto, and almost certainly every star has one habitable planet."[13]

Jeff Kanipe in the October 1996 issue of *Astronomy* informs us that "visible matter constitutes a small minority of the universe, making up anywhere between 1 and 10 percent of its total mass. That means that at least 90 and as much as 99 percent of the universe exists in some alternate form of matter that has yet to be directly detected. On galactic scales, then, each galaxy must be fixed in its own block of dark-matter resin, like a mosquito in amber, while on cosmological scales, galaxy clusters are to sea foam as dark matter is to the ocean."[14]

As we discussed in Chapter 2, the universe consists of seven major planes of manifestation, only one of which we can see—the physical subplane of the cosmic physical plane. The other six subplanes of the cosmic physical plane are considered material to the great being who manifests through our Sun, but these subplanes are subtle, rather than densely physical, to us. It is widely known to people who study esoteric philosophy that the etheric, emotional (astral), mental, intuitional (buddhic), plus the atmic, monadic, and logoic subplanes that are beyond the sensitivity of most of us today, do indeed exist.

We do not know the magnetic characteristics of subtle planes and subplanes but we do know that energy passes through them before it reaches us and that these planes definitely have an influence on our lives and our consciousness. In fact, the cohesiveness of our very existence depends upon them. Furthermore, according to the generally accepted Law of Correspondences, all entities in the universe would be influenced by subtler planes as well.

Thus, there is definitely more out there than we have discovered to date.

The Great Attractor

In 1987, astronomers discovered that hundreds of galaxies, including our own Milky Way, seem to be collectively swarming toward a super-massive center of attraction, said to exert the gravitational muscle of 100,000 Milky Ways. This center of attraction, called the "Great Attractor," is hidden by the Milky Way's opaque dust clouds, but its presence is theorized from a subtle distortion in the universe's otherwise steady expansion.

Then, in 1996, an international team of astronomers, led by Renée C. Kraan-Korteweg of Paris Observatory, pinpointed a galactic cluster known as Abell 3627 in the southern sky, some 200 million light-years away. Although the derived mass of Abell 3627 can account for only roughly 10 percent of the Great Attractor's gravitational grip, it remains to be seen whether the rest of the mass can be attributed to galaxies or whether "dark matter" needs to be invoked.[15]

The Agni Yoga teachings refer to an attractive center of the universe called the Cosmic Magnet. These teachings tell us that our creative striving to uplift our surroundings fulfills the higher will of the universe, which magnetizes and transforms us. This propels evolution and transforms the universe as well. Stages of evolution are guided to be in harmony with the laws of the universe, and the more highly evolved lives assist the lesser evolved.

The principle of the Cosmic Magnet abides upon the principle of Hierarchy, which means an ordered series of lives at all stages of evolution. The attraction to this great creative center of the universe is said to be immutable to such an extent that it is manifested as the quality called necessity, and that the whole universe is saturated with this principle.[16]

Magnetic Resonance and Plasma Streams

In a recent issue of *The Journal of Esoteric Psychology*, science writer Bo Rotan[17] presented a paper entitled "The Resonance Triad of Gravity, Magnetism and Plasma" in which he examines how long-distance resonance might occur in the solar system.

Rotan describes the structure of the octave, where harmonics establish the conditions of resonance. "When cycles, orbits, or processes resonate or vibrate together, there are unexpected exchanges of energy. These energy exchanges can create higher levels of cohesion."[18] Rotan further states that, although these processes are tangible and empirical, they remain largely unexplained in scientific terms.

He goes on to describe the features of the octave and then to describe comparative gravitational resonances. As just one of his many examples, Mercury's rotational day is the same as 59 Earth days (an Earth day is a standard measurement in astronomy) and Mercury's sidereal year is 88 Earth days. This 3:2 ratio is termed a "resonance."

In his discussion on the mathematics of plasma cosmology, Rotan tells us: "Plasma is ionized gas comprised of charged electrons and protons. This is the basic material of suns and as such is by far the most common form of matter in the Universe. When plasma is pushed into stellar, interstellar and galactic levels of Space in the form of filament structures, it is capable of exerting force on such cosmic scales. In fact, plasma becomes a candidate for the explanation of the dark matter problem.

"…When plasma is ejected from a sun or a galactic core, it carries self-sustaining magnetic field lines with it. This would be due to the electrical potential of ionized gas (plasma). These magnetic lines drawn from suns, groups of suns, or galactic cores allow plasma the cohesion of filamentary structures. These filaments start to resemble cosmic webbing and could play a role upon extremely large portions of Universal Space-Time"[19]

Rotan seeks to establish a cosmic feedback loop of a triadal nature, and summarizes the points, quoted as follows:[20]

1. Gravitational orbit resonances unlock solar magnetic cycles.

2. Solar magnetic cycles unlock solar plasma flare cycles.

3. Solar plasma falling under plasma cosmologies' dark matter description is capable of exerting huge amounts of cosmic cohesion.

Long-range resonance patterns fall under the category of such "cosmic cohesions."

4. Solar plasma is a candidate for the mechanism producing the original gravitational orbit resonances which unlocked the solar magnetic cycles in the first place.

5. The entire process is a cosmic feedback loop in which gravitational, magnetic, and plasma forces of the solar system are combined in a truly synthetic and triadal manner.

6. These synthetic triads bridge into the fourth dimension and we are forced to consider the solar system as an "electrical whole." The planets are fourth-dimensional coils which are extremely capable as electrical transmitters. These electrical potencies, building upon resonance triads and working upon higher dimensional levels, are comprehensive candidates for the long-distance resonance problems we have addressed in the paper.

Rotan suggests that we attempt to "link the outflow of immense amounts of solar plasma, which travels the solar system as solar wind," with the mysterious long-range resonances he described in his paper.[21] Our next logical step would then be to "consider ways in which nearby stars and star systems might 'extend their influence.' We are talking about subtle influences, whether the context is scientific or esoteric— the influences from nearby planets must be amplified through resonance upon the Sun and the Earth to begin to create patterns upon individual human beings. Most of the influence is exerted upon humanity as a whole. Once a kingdom at large has received an impulse or celestial nuance, then an electrical signal can be transferred to more 'cellular' units within a generalized species group. If this is true for the interactions of the solar system, it is even more necessary to 'visualize' star influences as being of the 'subtlest' of natures."[22]

He concludes that the cosmic effectivity of resonance feedback potentials would seem to require a triadal synthesis, such as between gravity, magnetism, and plasma.[23]

Relationships Between Traditional and Esoteric Astrology

"It is the chief characteristic of psychic and spiritual life that the whole is present in each part. We are therefore not merely cogs in a machine, we are the machine itself and the mind which directs it. But this is only fully true of the personality which has realised its own inner nature…The imperfect man is pulled and pushed by forces external to himself, just because he is still external to his true Being."—Dean Inge[24]

In its highest aspect, astrology enables us to expand our awareness, focus our understanding, and function in an appropriate manner. As we work with astrology, we can learn the values and the secrets of true coordination between soul and personality.

Astrology, at its most basic, is occupied with the positions of the Sun, the Moon, and the ascendant (rising sign) at the time of birth or origin—whether it be the birth of an individual, a place, or an event. According to esoteric astrology, the Sun sign influences the life of the personality, the ascendant reveals the purpose of the soul, and the Moon sign affects the emotions and the quality of the physical body.

The Sun sign represents the particular situations that we are to comprehend and solve in the present incarnation. It sets the tempo of the activity aspect of our current life. According to the Tibetan, the sign in which we incarnate also indicates the sign in which we passed out of incarnation in the previous life, for we pick up the thread of experience from where we left it before, starting again with the same type of energy and development we had previously.[25]

The ascendant indicates the line along which our energy as a whole can flow if we are to fulfill the purpose of any incarnation. It holds the secret of our future and indicates what we can be and what we can achieve. This energy, used correctly, produces harmony with the will of our soul during any particular incarnation.

The Moon indicates the limitations under which we have to work but it also provides us with a synthesis of all our experience from past incarnations. We might remember that, when we speak of the physical form, this includes the brain, which brings subtle-plane impressions and memories into waking consciousness.

The following table indicates a few of the major differences between the viewpoints of traditional astrology and esoteric astrology. As we can readily see, esoteric astrology does not replace traditional astrology, but instead takes it to new levels of awareness.

Traditional Astrology	*Esoteric Astrology*
Deals with effects	Deals with causes
Usually one ruler of a sign, acting on the personality level	Three rulers of a sign, acting on personality, soul, and monadic/group levels
Influence of zodiacal constellations	Influence of zodiacal constellations plus the seven rays
Twelve houses	Twelve arms of three crosses
Aspects: conjunctions, oppositions, trines, squares, sextiles (plus minor aspects)	Unity, polarities, triangles, crosses, stars

Causes and Effects

Many aspects of traditional astrology are focused on the qualities of personality and form, events, situations, and the conditioning environment that appear in the personal horoscope.

Esoteric astrology deals with the unfoldment of consciousness, our awakening to the particular gifts of a sign and ray endowment, and with our consequent enrichment as we proceed through the stages of humanitarian awareness through eventual initiation. Esoteric astrology concerns itself with the theme of initiation—both personal and especially group initiation.

The goal of esoteric astrology is for us to think in terms of our use of energies, lines of force, relationships, and qualities. Astrology is a study of the magnetic interplay that manifests the inner reality and is concerned with the creative response to the pull of energy and streams of force.

Three Rulers

The influences of the esoteric and hierarchical planetary rulers combine with the influences of the traditional planetary rulers and supplement them, without negating the influence of the traditional planets. We are thereby enriched, our experience is extended, and our consciousness is expanded by the additional energies, but all the time the effects and conditioning achieved and attained under the traditional influences are still a part of our consciousness.

As we progressively evolve and expand our consciousness to the point where we are more influenced by the light of the soul, the esoteric planets often have more bearing on our lives. However, as long as we are incarnated on Earth, we work with the energies of the traditional planets. We often use the traditional planetary energies to implement the goals that we perceive from the esoteric and hierarchical planets.

See Chapter 6 for a discussion of planetary rulerships and Chapter 7 for a detailed description of the planets.

The Zodiac and the Seven Rays

When we come into incarnation, we are endowed with specific ray energies for our various vehicles of manifestation; more specifically, we each have a soul ray, personality ray, mental ray, emotional ray, and physical/etheric ray. The combination of these rays has a profound influence on our qualities and determines how we will respond to life.

Thus, if we use the Tibetan's system of esoteric astrology to interpret a person's astrological chart, we need to try to discover the ray makeup of the individual concerned. This is a science in itself and is covered in great depth by Michael Robbins in his two-volume series on the rays, *Tapestry of the Gods*. Other authors, including Kurt Abraham and Zachary Landsdowne, have also given us valuable interpretive information on the seven rays.

Ray energies also affect places, cities, nations, and cultures over various cycles of time. Professor Charles DeMotte in his book, *The Inner Side of History*, distinguishes ray cycles from astrological cycles by telling us that ray cycles relate to space and astrological cycles relate to time. Ray cycles are manifested in the incarnation of groups of human egos over vast periods of time who "radiate the qualities of one ray or another across the broad landscape of history."

This could mean that the ray energies act as archetypes that humanity has manifested and built into the universal mind over eons. In other words, ray qualities are imprinted on life as it is seeded and then evolved on Earth.

DeMotte further states, "Astrological cycles, on the other hand, are planetary modifications of ray energy that have a direct magnetic impact upon the planet and thereby precipitate a specific quality of events at certain periods. Put another way, such cycles create a force field of potentialities by which certain conditions exist that will make it probable that one or more corresponding events will likely occur."

He continues, "Insofar as the rays and planetary influences on earth are essentially one and the same, it follows that astrological cycles are the result of energy that has been filtered through the solar system so as to reach earth in a modified form."

See Chapter 5 for a detailed discussion of the seven rays.

Aspects and Relationships

Traditional astrology offers much information on the aspects and relationships between planets and constellations; these contributions to human thought are invaluable. Most of this research by traditional astrological thinkers can apply to esoteric astrology as well, but esoteric astrology approaches it somewhat differently.

For example, two of the major aspects of traditional astrology are the trine and the square. Esoteric astrology speaks of triangles and crosses and a very elaborate system can be based upon these configurations. Oppositions in traditional astrology are thought of as polarities in esoteric astrology. Conjunctions (the most important aspect for astrologers and astronomers alike) are thought of as unities.

See Chapters 9 and 10 for a detailed discussion of aspects and relationships.

Houses and Crosses

Houses are the division of the 360-degree wheel of the zodiac into twelve portions, and each house is related to an astrological sign. Houses represent the field of activity for the energies of the planets within the houses. When a horoscope is cast, the ascendant is at the beginning of the first house, but if the ascendant is not known, Aries, the natural ruler of the first house, is often used.

Crosses form when four zodiacal constellations are linked together into two pairs of opposites. As we mentioned in Chapter 2, Pisces, Gemini, Virgo, and Sagittarius comprise the mutable cross; Aquarius, Taurus, Leo, and Scorpio make up the fixed cross; and Capricorn, Aries, Cancer, and Libra form the cardinal cross.

Houses are a main component of traditional astrology. Crosses are a unique contribution of esoteric astrology; the Tibetan indicates throughout his work that crosses will play a key role in the astrology of the future.

When we look at astrology within a cycle of a year, houses are important in both systems of astrology. The following table gives a few of the keywords for a comparison of traditional and esoteric features for each of the twelve houses. Esoteric astrologers work with both the traditional and esoteric characteristics of the houses because they represent a synthesis of the life of the personality and the soul.

Traditional and Esoteric Characteristics of Houses

House	Traditional	Esoteric
First	self, body, personality, outlook on life	emergence of soul expression, ray types and qualities
Second	material resources, earning ability, possessions	values, control of form, use of energy, acquisition of spiritual powers, prana
Third	communication, concrete mind, early education	telepathy, control of the mind, inner spiritual messages, omnipresence
Fourth	home, parents, security	foundations, spiritual group
Fifth	creativity, love and romance, entertainment	spiritual creativity, joy of being, soul expression
Sixth	health, work, habits	healing, service, self-improvement
Seventh	relationships, marriage, partnership	right group relations, union of soul and personality
Eighth	sex, death, partner's resources, taxes, sacrifice	shared values and energies, spiritual resources, tests leading to regeneration
Ninth	philosophy, religion, foreign travel	wisdom, continuity of consciousness, higher dharma

Traditional and Esoteric Characteristics of Houses, continued

House	Traditional	Esoteric
Tenth	profession, career, status	spiritual vocation, higher karma
Eleventh	friends, hopes, and wishes	group creativity, circulation of energies, ashramic connection
Twelfth	limitations, self-undoing, hidden enemies, subconscious mind	hidden strength, transcendent idealism, collective unconscious

The position of the planets in the twelve houses are conditioned by karmic influences. However, as we evolve, we start to overcome karmic influences and become sensitive to a wider range of vibrations, including the soul ray and the influences of the crosses. For example, if the Sun sign is Sagittarius, we have ready access to the energies from Gemini, the polar opposite, and then Virgo and Pisces—the four arms of the mutable cross. We are told that all the four influences of the three crosses are present in the chart of a master.[26]

On the spiritual path, we start off on the mutable cross, where we are focused on the personality life. When we achieve soul-consciousness, we step upon the fixed cross and, finally, initiate-consciousness places us upon the cardinal cross. The realms of the mutable and fixed crosses are most applicable to the life of humanity today.

However, these associations of the crosses relate to the path of consciousness expansion and initiation; the signs that we are working with in our current incarnations are a separate matter and do not indicate our level of development. For example, an initiate can have a predominance of signs of the mutable cross in his or her makeup and, conversely, a person on the probationary path can have a predominance of signs of the cardinal cross.

Traditional astrologers can readily see how crosses are related to oppositions and squares, which could help explain why oppositions and squares are so dynamic in our lives. Chapter 9 discusses this in more detail. These crosses involve change, then direction, and finally initiation.

Foundations of Esoteric Astrology

*"…these attitudes will serve as stepping stones to a new life and a better
and more simple way of living; new values will be released and
comprehended among men and new goals will be revealed."*—AAB[27]

Esoteric astrology is called the Science of Relations—interrelation,
interdependence, intercommunication, and interplay. This Science of
Relations includes the sciences of:

- The seven rays
- Triangles
- Energy centers, or chakras
- Destiny

The science of destiny is founded upon the others and is an
interpretation of the future based upon an understanding of personality
and soul rays and the influence of the triangles—zodiacal, planetary,
racial, and human. A knowledge of the human triangles is revealed by
a study of the individual human centers or chakras.

When we can work all this out into a new style of horoscope, we
can begin to apply the science of destiny. The Tibetan indicates that the
personal progressed horoscope is the embryonic seed for the science
of destiny.

Our goal would be to actively focus within ourselves the various
energies that are available to us from sources such as the twelve
constellations as they distribute their energies through the ruling
esoteric planets. As the Sun and Earth cycle through the seasons of the
year, we could make a special effort to gain certain aspects of control
over the factors that each sign represents, along with the energies of
the other three signs on the same cross.

Twelve Premises of Esoteric Astrology

The Tibetan makes twelve points that relate to the lines along which
astrological investigation can run.[28] Most of these points are explained
in detail in subsequent chapters of this book.

Some of these points relate to the charts of individuals, which I do
not cover in this book because my focus is upon working with energies
that are available at a particular time. However, these points should
give a general idea about what esoteric astrology covers.

We can extrapolate from individual to group considerations as our work deems it appropriate to do so.

1. Each of the centers (corresponding to the chakras of the human body) are governed by one of the seven rays.[29]

   In alignment with the Law of Correspondences, three rays influence a center but one ray "governs" or exerts more control over that center, depending upon the stage of evolution reached by the entity whose body incorporates that center.

   In *The Destiny of the Nations*, the Tibetan speaks of five major centers in the body of the entity, Earth—the five cities of London, New York, Tokyo, Geneva, and Darjeeling. He assigns rays and astrological signs to these cities, as follows:[30]

City	Soul Ray	Personality Ray	Astrological Sign
London	Five	Seven	Gemini
New York	Two	Three	Cancer
Tokyo	Six	Four	Cancer
Geneva	One	Two	Leo
Darjeeling	Two	Five	Scorpio

   It is interesting to note that the astrological signs given above do not necessarily correspond with the constellations given for the rays in the table on page 16, "Constellational and Planetary Triangles." This is just one example in the Tibetan's work that supports the idea that ray energies and astrological energies are discrete from each other, and further compels us to believe that the interactions and interrelationships of rays and signs are more vast than our knowledge about them today.

2. The planets transmit the ray energies, as follows:[31]

Sacred Planets	Ray	Non-Sacred Planets	Ray
Vulcan	One	Mars	Six
Mercury	Four	The Earth	Three
Venus	Five	Pluto	One
Jupiter	Two	The Moon	Four
Saturn	Three	The Sun	Two
Neptune	Six	(veiling a planet)	
Uranus	Seven		

These are the primary rays that the Tibetan assigns to the planets. Chapters 5 and 6 discuss these relationships in more detail.

3.   Ordinary humanity is ruled by the traditional planets; advanced humanity by the esoteric planets.[32]

The highest goal for all of humanity is to be able to use the energies of both the traditional and esoteric planets. As we evolve, we are anchored less to planetary influences and develop more sensitivity to the influences of the cosmos.

4.   The Sun sign with the traditional planetary ruler rules the personality, indicates heredity and equipment, and is a summation of that which has been, thus providing the background.[33]

The goal of the Sun sign is the well integrated personality, ready to perform with competence in the world of manifestation. This well integrated personality is a powerful tool for the soul.

5.   The horoscope, interpreted around the Sun sign, is appropriate for ordinary humanity. The traditional planets rule and the twelve houses apply.[34]

This type of horoscope is relevant for people who are soul-oriented because all of us need to access these energies for our effectiveness in the world of manifestation.

6.   The ascendant, with the esoteric planetary rulers, indicates soul purpose and points the way to the future, offering opportunity. Horoscope interpretation focused upon the ascendant with the esoteric planets indicates the way of the soul and conveys the destiny of the advanced person.[35]

The emphasis of the astrological charts in this book is on global events rather than specific locations, thus a discussion of the very important ascendant is beyond the scope I offer here. Other authors, both traditional and esoteric, provide valuable details about the ascendant.

7.   The Sun sign indicates the nature of the person and holds the secret of right use of the personality ray. The ascendant indicates the remoter possibilities, the spiritual goal, the purpose of the present incarnation, and holds the clue to the right use of the soul ray.[36]

This is usually interpreted to mean that the ray of the exoteric (traditional) ruler of the Sun sign would be the personality ray and the ray of the esoteric ruler of the ascendant would be the soul ray. For example, if the Sun sign is Sagittarius and the ascendant is Gemini, the exoteric ruler would be Jupiter and the esoteric ruler would be Venus. Thus, the personality ray would be Ray Two and the soul ray would be Ray Five.

However, it may be that this formula, in actual practice, is too simplistic, though it does provide a hint.

Before working with the horoscope, it is first necessary to intuit the soul and personality rays.

8. The planets which are exalted, in detriment, or which fall in any particular sign can sometimes indicate the three phases of the Path: (1) the involutionary cycle of becoming increasingly involved in matter, or life upon the mutable cross; (2) the interlude of readjustment or struggle for liberation which leads to the mounting of the fixed cross; and (3) the period of liberation with the final mounting of the cardinal cross.[37]

   As we discuss in Chapter 6, the exaltations, detriments, and falls of planets in particular signs can modify our use of planetary energies at a particular time.

9. The twelve arms of the three crosses—cardinal, fixed, and mutable—pour their influences through the esoteric planetary rulers via the twelve houses.[38] The crosses encompass the interplay between a sign and its polar opposite.

   The particular cross that is applicable to our level of development is not necessarily the cross that is prominent in the horoscope because our progress upon the crosses on the initiatory path proceeds over many lifetimes. More information about crosses is included in Chapter 9.

10. The Sun sign, governed by the ruling esoteric planets, and the rising sign, governed also by the esoteric planets, can both be used in interpreting the horoscope of an initiate; when these charts are superimposed upon each other, they show the outer life and the subjective inner life.[39]

    Several good astrology computer programs offer bi-wheels and tri-wheels, which is a way of comparing charts. We can apply these techniques and gain useful information from them, regardless of the level of our spiritual advancement.

11. When the Sun sign with the traditional rulers is worked out in a chart, the rising sign with the esoteric rulers is also worked out, and the two are superimposed upon each other, the problem of any one incarnation will appear.[40]

This reinforces the fact that, in order to be effective in the world of manifestation (which is our dharma), we need to work with the energies from both personality and soul levels.

12. The Science of Triangles, which will emphasize the idea of synthesis, is the esoteric basis of astrology and will be developed as the result of the growth of initiate understanding.[41]

The Science of Triangles encompasses zodiacal, planetary, racial, and human triangular configurations, each triangle linking various macro- or microcosmic centers (or chakras) together. Triangles affect the realm of ideas and the world of consciousness and its expansion.[42] More information about triangles is included in Chapters 7 and 9.

Chapter 5—
The Seven Rays

"Each of the great rays has a form of teaching truth to humanity which is its unique contribution, and in this way develops man by a system or technique which is qualified by the ray quality and is therefore specific and unique."—AAB[1]

As mentioned earlier, Sirius, the Great Bear, and the Pleiades are the three major sources of energies that pour into our zodiacal constellations and eventually into our own system. Through telepathic rapport, these three great constellations influence the spiral-cyclic activity of our solar system and are in relationship to the spiritual triad of our Solar Logos.[2] The spiritual triad, or trinity of energy, consists of atma, buddhi, and manas, representing the planes they are named after. Every life—macrocosmic and microcosmic—has its own spiritual triad, the influence of which affects its incarnation, evolution, and progress.

Gemini, the Great Bear, and the Pleiades form a cosmic triangle which is the symbol of the archetypal Cosmic Christ. Gemini forms a point of entrance for cosmic energy from Sirius, Libra is related to and transmits the potencies of the Pleiades, and Aquarius expresses the universal consciousness of the Great Bear.[3] The three constellations, Gemini, Libra, and Aquarius, represent the element of air, which symbolizes mind, thus through them flows the energy of mind or manas from Sirius into our system, where it is received telepathically by our Solar Logos.

The seven stars of the Great Bear are the prototypes for the seven sacred planets in our solar system, thus there is a telepathic alignment between each planet and its respective star. These stars emit great waves of energy that sweep cyclically through our entire solar system. The strength of these vibrations depends upon the closeness of the connection and the accuracy of the alignment between the planets and their respective stars.[4] Finally, all energies that come into our solar system are transformed and conditioned by the Sun.

The energies that directly affect our solar system and Earth are seven streams of consciousness called the seven rays. As we contemplate the seven rays, we must ever bear in mind that these are great Beings who are fully conscious and entirely aware of the purpose and the divine plan; they are awake, active, self-conscious, group-conscious. and intimately related to the universal mind. In turn, our ability to understand these energies that are coming in to us depends upon our own telepathic rapport with the vibrations or thoughtforms radiating from the universal mind through the evolved lives on our planet and through the ethers that surround us.

The first three rays of the seven—Rays One, Two, and Three—incorporate all of the seven in an original, archetypal triangle, in which Ray Three also holds the qualities of Rays Four, Five, Six, and Seven. This triangle, whose outposts are the atmic, buddhic, and manasic planes, is then differentiated into the seven rays, or seven types of soul energy. These seven energies are further subdivided into forty-nine groups of forces, which direct the manifestation of form in the physical world as we know it.[5]

The energies of the seven rays originate from the seven stars of the Great Bear, which are the prototypes for the seven sacred planets in our solar system.[6] A triangle of zodiacal constellations then transmits each of the seven rays into our system, as shown in the following table, which is adapted and modified from *Esoteric Astrology*.[7] The planets listed are those that are associated with those particular constellations, so we can assume that a modified form of the ray energy, as directed through these triangles, is reaching these planets.

The ray of our solar system itself is Ray Two and all the other ray energies that reach us are qualified and adapted by Ray Two. This means that the energy of love, expressed with wisdom, is the line of least resistance for us in this solar system. This is very encouraging to us for, as the Tibetan teacher says, "Each human being, as a whole, therefore, lives in a universe and on a planet which is constantly the objective of God's love and desire, and which constantly (as a result of this love) is itself attracted and attractive. For this we do not make adequate allowance. Teachers, parents and educators would do well to recognise the potency of this ray force, and trust to the Law to make all things good."[8]

The Sun and the Moon "veil" other planets, and the planets veiled or hidden are indicated in parentheses (Vulcan, Neptune, and Uranus). The process of veiling is explained in detail in Chapter 7, but briefly it means that the energies of the veiled planets are not completely integrated into our system at this time for all levels of consciousness that humanity lives and acts upon.

Constellational and Planetary Triangles

Ray	Constellation	Exoteric Planets	Esoteric Planets	Hierarchical Planets
1	Aries	Mars	Mercury	Uranus
	Leo	Sun (Jupiter)	Sun (Neptune)	Sun (Uranus)
	Capricorn	Saturn	Saturn	Venus
2	Gemini	Mercury	Venus	Earth
	Virgo	Mercury	Moon (Vulcan)	Jupiter
	Pisces	Jupiter	Pluto / Neptune	Pluto
3	Cancer	Moon (Neptune)	Neptune	Neptune
	Libra	Venus	Uranus	Saturn
	Capricorn	Saturn	Saturn	Venus
4	Taurus	Venus	Vulcan	Vulcan
	Scorpio	Mars / Pluto	Mars / Pluto	Mercury
	Sagittarius	Jupiter	Earth	Mars
5	Leo	Sun (Jupiter)	Sun (Neptune)	Sun (Uranus)
	Sagittarius	Jupiter	Earth	Mars
	Aquarius	Uranus	Jupiter	Moon (Uranus)
6	Virgo	Mercury	Moon (Vulcan)	Jupiter
	Sagittarius	Jupiter	Earth	Mars
	Pisces	Jupiter	Pluto / Neptune	Pluto
7	Aries	Mars	Mercury	Uranus
	Cancer	Moon (Neptune)	Neptune	Neptune
	Capricorn	Saturn	Saturn	Venus

For example, Ray One energy flows into Aries, Leo, and Capricorn, and these constellations, working in this triangular configuration, further distribute the energies into the planetary lives associated with them. Aries directs the ray energy into the three planets that are considered to "rule" Aries energy: Mars, Mercury and Uranus. Leo and Capricorn do the same with their associated planets. All energies flow through triangular formations such as this for, as we remember, energies flow through triangles and manifest through crosses.

Independently, the planets each possess a major ray coloring, just as we people receive light from all the rays but yet have our own predominant ray characteristics. "Each planet is the embodiment of some one ray aspect, and its quality is marked predominantly on all its evolution."[9]

The following table lists the rays associated with the planets.[10]

Rays of the Planets

Ray	Planet	Planetary Symbol
1	Vulcan	♈
4	Mercury	☿
5	Venus	♀
3	Earth	⊕
6	Mars	♂
2	Jupiter	♃
3	Saturn	♄
7	Uranus	♅
6	Neptune	♆
1	Pluto	♇

There is no planetary symbol for Vulcan that I know of, so I am using a stylized 𝒱.

Rays Three and Seven govern our vital physical life and our physical body. Rays Two and Four govern our emotional life and determine the type of our emotional body. Rays One, Four, and Five predominate in the life of humanity and govern our mind nature and mental body. Rays Four and Five in particular sweep through humanity in the current cycle of activity. Ray Four gives us intuition and Ray Five gives us intellect. These rays guarantee our attainment, but they also present turmoil. We gain harmony, beauty, and creative power through battle, stress, and strain. We gain knowledge, expressing itself eventually through wisdom, through the agony of successive choices. Thus, during the life experience, we learn discrimination, true values, the vision of the ideal, and the capacity to distinguish reality.[11]

The rays, in time, produce the world patterns and planetary forms that facilitate evolution. The emotional pattern embodies the aspiration of humanity and is the sum total of the desire tendency. The mental pattern governs the thought processes of humanity and eventually controls the personality or form life. The soul pattern is our eventual destiny and eventually supersedes the emotional and mental patterns.[12]

Rays One, Two, and Three are the rays of aspect and produce, primarily, the unfolding of purpose. Rays Four, Five, Six, and Seven are the rays of attribute and produce the development of character and quality. Thus, when a major ray of aspect is in manifestation, the divine intent, the universal purpose, and the Plan emerge with greater clarity and we can look for great happenings in racial development. When a minor ray of attribute is manifesting, we see the growth of psychic sensitivity and the emergence of a form life that can express the divine nature more potently than it can express the divine plan.[13]

We are currently in an important period of time when Ray Six is passing out of manifestation and Ray Seven is coming in. The overlapping of two rays comes only at rare and long intervals of time and ushers in a particularly significant period of divine activity; "old things pass entirely away, yet the ancient landmarks are restored."[14] Ray Seven will express the visions and the ideals of the Ray Six cycle, for one ray prepares the way for the next. The numerical succession gives us a rapid following of effect upon cause (this is a rare opportunity for us).

Next, we discuss the individual qualities of each of the seven rays and present figures that depict the flows of energy, as indicated in the table on page 79. In addition to the symbols of the constellations and the planets associated with the constellations, the diagrams show numbers that indicate which ray energizes the planets involved. However, we recognize that, according to the Law of Correspondences, each planet has a spirit, soul, and personality body, as we humans do, and thus would have a ray governing each of these three bodies. The rays we indicate are the rays for the soul bodies; there are speculations outside the context of this book as to what the other rays might be for each planet.

Each ray has special virtues associated with it, as well as virtues to be acquired. The ones indicated are taken from *Esoteric Psychology*, Volume I. The ray methods of activity and of teaching truth are from the same source.[15] The words of power for each ray are seed thoughts we can use while doing antahkarana meditations.[16] See Chapter 11 for details about building the antahkarana, or rainbow bridge between spirit and form.

Ray One: Will and Power

"I assert the fact."

Ray One brings in the dynamic energy of the life force and includes a strong sense of purpose. This ray of governance, will, and power enables humanity to manifest leadership, one-pointed focus, and to differentiate between the essential and the nonessential—to see the whole. Ray One gives us courage, independence, and detachment. With it comes the ability to initiate action and gain an understanding of the principles and priorities involved. This ray also enables us to repulse what is no longer needed for our evolution, and thus it controls the processes of death and rebirth.

Ray One is the first aspect of deity, with the theme, "Will, dynamically applied, emerges into manifestation as power."[17] This ray expresses the aspect of the will that stimulates and produces initiation.[18]

Ray One energy flows into the constellational triangle of Aries, Leo, and Capricorn, and from there into the planets associated with these constellations, as shown in the following figure. Aries is currently the "source of the initial [Ray One] energy, producing the New Age."[19]

Ray One Triangles

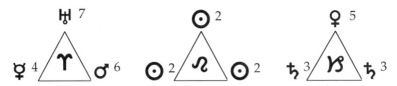

The planets Vulcan and Pluto are associated with Ray One, as indicated in the table on page 80. Vulcan is the esoteric and hierarchical ruler of Taurus and could perhaps be the planet that the Moon veils in Virgo (see "The Process of Veiling" in Chapter 7). Pluto is the esoteric and hierarchical ruler of Pisces and an esoteric ruler of Scorpio. Ray One energy, as transmitted through Vulcan and Pluto in the signs of Taurus and Pisces, transmutes desire into sacrifice and the individual will into the divine will.[20]

Ray One is not in full expression at this time, except insofar as it brings cycles to an end and causes destruction that leads to liberation.

We move forward on Ray One through sheer force of will. This is a ray of power, but united with wisdom and love, it becomes a creative and governing ray.

Special Virtues

Strength, courage, steadfastness, truthfulness arising from absolute fearlessness, power of ruling, capacity to grasp great questions in a large-minded way, and ability to handle people and measures.

Virtues to be Acquired

Tenderness, humility, sympathy, tolerance, patience.

Ray Methods of Activity

Destruction of forms through group interplay.
Stimulation of the self, the egoic (soul) principle.
Spiritual impulse or energy.

Ray Methods of Teaching Truth

Higher expression: The science of statesmanship and of government.
Lower expression: Modern diplomacy and politics.

Words of Power

"I assert the fact."

Ray Two: Love-Wisdom

"I see the greatest light."

Ray Two brings in loving wisdom, magnetism, attractive love, the power to understand, empathy, sympathy and compassion, sensitivity, receptivity and impressionability, intuition, inclusiveness, tolerance, the ability to redeem, the ability to teach and illumine, patience, and serenity. It is the great teaching ray for humanity and is also associated with religion (structured or not).

Ray Two is the second aspect of deity, with the theme, "Love, magnetically functioning, produces wisdom."[21] This ray expresses the aspect of the will that causes vision or the power to see.[22]

Ray Two energy flows into the constellational triangle of Gemini, Virgo, and Pisces, and from there into the planets associated with these constellations, as shown in the following figure. Virgo is currently the controlling factor for Ray Two energy, producing the "increased activity of the Christ principle in the heart of humanity."[23]

Ray Two Triangles

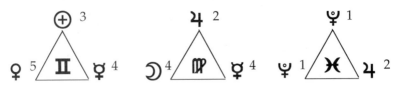

The Sun and Jupiter are associated with Ray Two. The Sun is the exoteric, esoteric, and hierarchical ruler of Leo. Jupiter is the exoteric ruler of Sagittarius and Pisces, the esoteric ruler of Aquarius, and the hierarchical ruler of Virgo. I also hypothesize that the Sun veils Jupiter as the exoteric ruler of Leo (see rationale in Chapter 7). Our solar system is a Ray Two system, thus all the other rays coming into our system are qualified by the Ray Two energy of our Sun.

The wisdom aspect of Ray Two gives us a desire for pure knowledge and absolute truth. When mixed with power and love, this is the great teaching ray of humanity where those, like the Buddha, attain wisdom for the sake of others.

We move forward on Ray Two through close and sincere study of the teachings until they become such a part of our consciousness that they are no longer merely intellectual knowledge, but a spiritual way of living, thus bringing in intuition and true wisdom.

Special Virtues

Calm, strength, patience and endurance, love of truth, faithfulness, intuition, clear intelligence, and serene temper.

Virtues to be Acquired

Love, compassion, unselfishness, energy.

Ray Methods of Activity

Construction of forms through group intercourse.
Stimulation of desire, the love principle.
Soul impulse or energy.

Ray Methods of Teaching Truth

Higher expression: The process of initiation as taught by the Hierarchy of masters.
Lower expression: Religion.

Words of Power

"I see the greatest light."

Ray Three: Active Intelligence and Adaptability

"Purpose itself am I."

Ray Three brings in the energies of activity and adaptability, including the ability to manipulate, plan, and strategize. It gives us the ability to understand economy and to relate effectively to our environment. It heightens executive and business aptitudes. Ray Three is also associated with philosophy—the capacity for abstract thinking and the ability to theorize and speculate. It provides an understanding of relativity and inspires mental fertility and creativity.

Ray Three is the third aspect of deity, with the theme, "Intelligence, potentially found in substance, causes activity."[24] This ray expresses the aspect of the will that develops sensory perception into knowledge, knowledge into wisdom, and wisdom into omniscience.[25]

Ray Three energy flows into the constellational triangle of Cancer, Libra, and Capricorn, and from there into the planets associated with these constellations, as shown in the following figure. Cancer is currently the controlling factor for Ray Three energy, giving its energy to "the mass movement towards liberty, release, and light."[26]

Ray Three Triangles

Saturn and the Earth are associated with Ray Three. Saturn is the exoteric and esoteric ruler of Capricorn and the hierarchical ruler of Libra. The Earth is the esoteric ruler of Sagittarius and the hierarchical ruler of Gemini. Sagittarius and Capricorn, via the Earth and Saturn, cause the one-pointed disciple to become the initiate.[27]

We move forward on Ray Three by deep thinking on philosophic or metaphysical lines until we can bring our results down to practical use.

Special Virtues

Wide views on all abstract questions, sincerity of purpose, clear intellect, capacity for concentration on philosophic studies, patience, caution, absence of the tendency to worry oneself or others over trifles.

Virtues to be Acquired

Sympathy, tolerance, devotion, accuracy, energy, and common sense.

Ray Methods of Activity

Vitalizing of forms through group work.
Stimulation of forms, the etheric or pranic principle.
Material impulse or energy.

Ray Methods of Teaching Truth

Higher expression: Means of communication or interaction, including travel.
Lower expression: The use and spread of money and gold.

Words of Power

"Purpose itself am I."

Ray Four: Harmony, Beauty, and Art

"Two merge with one."

Ray Four energies develop the capacity to reconcile and produce harmony out of conflict. This ray brings in refined artistic and aesthetic sensibilities, provides mathematical exactitude, and lends a sense of proportion. Ray Four gives us the facility for compromise, mediation, and bridging, as well as a love of beauty and a sense of drama. It inspires intuition, creative imagination, spontaneity, and improvisation.

Ray Four energy flows into the constellational triangle of Taurus, Scorpio, and Sagittarius, and from there into the planets associated with these constellations, as shown in the following figure (the V stands for the planet Vulcan). Ray Four expresses the aspect of the will which is the illumined will, the basis of buddhi or the intuition.[28] Scorpio is currently the controlling factor for Ray Four energy, and "through this constellation comes the testing of humanity, the world disciple."[29]

Ray Four Triangles

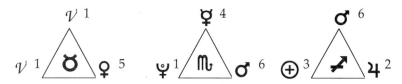

The planets Mercury and the Moon are associated with Ray Four. Mercury is the exoteric ruler of Gemini and Virgo, the esoteric ruler of Aries, and the hierarchical ruler of Scorpio. The Moon (which can veil Vulcan, Neptune, or Uranus),[30] is the exoteric ruler of Cancer, the esoteric ruler of Virgo, and the hierarchical ruler of Aquarius. Aries and Virgo, through Mercury and the Moon, harmonize "the cosmos and the individual through conflict, producing unity and beauty."[31] Ray Four energy is expected to come into fuller manifestation around the year 2025.

We move forward on Ray Four through self-control and by gaining equilibrium over the conflicting forces of our nature.

Special Virtues

Strong affections, sympathy, physical courage, generosity, devotion, quickness of intellect, and perception.

Virtues to be Acquired

Serenity, confidence, self-control, purity, unselfishness, accuracy, mental and moral balance.

Ray Methods of Activity

Perfecting of forms through group interplay.
Stimulation of the solar angels or the manasic (mental) principle.
Intuitional or buddhic energy.

Ray Methods of Teaching Truth

Higher expression: The Masonic work, based on the formation of the Hierarchy and related to Ray Two.
Lower expression: Architectural construction, modern city planning.

Words of Power

"Two merge with one."

Ray Five: Concrete Knowledge and Science

"Three minds unite."

Ray Five gives us the capacity to think and act scientifically and provides a keen and focused intellect leading to the power to know. We associate Ray Five with the power to define, the power to create thoughtforms, and with highly developed powers of analysis and discrimination. This ray provides detached objectivity, the power to discover through investigation and research and to verify through experimentation, the discrimination of truth from error, practical inventiveness, mechanical ability, technical expertise, common sense, lucidity of explanation, accuracy, and precision in thought and action.

Ray Five energy flows into the constellational triangle of Leo, Sagittarius, and Aquarius, and from there into the planets associated with these constellations, as shown in the following figure. Ray Five expresses the aspect of the will that is the cosmic seed of liberation; this is an aspect of destruction.[32] Leo is currently the controlling factor for Ray Five energy and "produces the growth of individualism and of self-consciousness, so prevalent today on a world scale."[33]

Ray Five Triangles

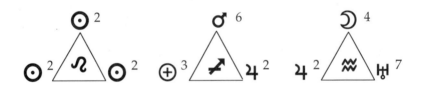

Venus is associated with Ray Five—the only planet that is. Venus is the exoteric ruler of Taurus and Libra, the esoteric ruler of Gemini, and the hierarchical ruler of Capricorn.[34]

In its current cycle, Ray Five energy has accomplished more on Earth than originally expected, thus this energy might have to be held in abeyance or withdrawn for a time.[35] (We discuss this under "Timing and Cycles" in Chapter 9.)

We move forward on Ray Five by scientific research, pushed to ultimate conclusions, and by accepting the inferences that follow these.

Special Virtues

Strictly accurate statements, justice (without mercy), perseverance, common sense, uprightness, independence, keen intellect.

Virtues to be Acquired

Reverence, devotion, sympathy, love, wide-mindedness.

Ray Methods of Activity

Correspondence of forms to type, through group influence.
Stimulation of the Logoic dense physical body (Earth), the three worlds (mental, emotional, and physical).
Mental energy or impulse, universal manas (mind).

Ray Methods of Teaching Truth

Higher expression: The science of the soul. Esoteric psychology.
Lower expression: Modern educational systems.

Words of Power

"Three minds unite."

The Ray Five words of power assert the fact that the universal mind, the higher mind, and the lower concrete mind are blended through the projected antahkarana.

Ray Six: Devotion and Idealism

"The highest light controls."

Ray Six brings in transcendent idealism, the power of abstraction, intense devotion, self-sacrificial ardor, unshakable faith, and undimmed optimism. It provides one-pointedness; single-mindedness; loyalty; earnestness and sincerity; humility; persistence; the power to arouse, inspire and persuade; the ability to achieve ecstasy and rapture; purity; goodness; and sainthood.

Ray Six energy flows into the constellational triangle of Virgo, Sagittarius, and Pisces, and from there into the planets associated with these constellations, as shown in the following figure. Sagittarius is currently the controlling factor for Ray Six energy and "produces the focused one-pointed effort of the world aspirant."[36] Ray Six expresses the aspect of the will that is the cause of the thoughtform-building faculty, related to the creative urge.[37]

Ray Six Triangles

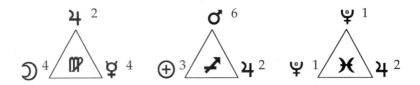

The planets Neptune and Mars are associated with Ray Six. Neptune, veiled by the Moon, is the exoteric ruler of Cancer. Unveiled, Neptune is the esoteric and hierarchical ruler of Cancer. Neptune (along with Pluto) is an esoteric ruler of Pisces. Mars is the exoteric ruler of Aries and Scorpio, the esoteric ruler of Scorpio, and the hierarchical ruler of Sagittarius. Neptune and Mars, through Cancer and Scorpio, transform the "mass consciousness into the inclusive consciousness of the disciple."[38]

Ray Six is associated with Christianity and came into influence around the time of Christ's work on Earth. This ray is now withdrawing its energy for the shorter term and more Ray Seven energy is coming into manifestation during the emergence of the Aquarian age.

We move forward on Ray Six through prayer and meditation, aiming at union with God.

Special Virtues

Devotion, single-mindedness, love, tenderness, intuition, loyalty, reverence.

Virtues to be Acquired

Strength, self-sacrifice, purity, truth, tolerance, serenity, balance, and common sense.

Ray Methods of Activity

Reflection of reality through group work.
Stimulation of humanity through desire.
Desire energy, instinct, or aspiration.

Ray Methods of Teaching Truth

Higher expression: Christianity and diversified religions (related to Ray Two).
Lower expression: Churches and religious organizations.

Words of Power

"The highest light controls."

Ray Seven: Ceremonial Order, Magic, and Organization

"The highest and the lowest meet."

Ray Seven gives us the power to plan and organize, to create order, and to manifest and perfect the objects of our work (form) upon the material plane. This ray relates spirit and matter on the physical plane. It provides a keen sense of timing and rhythm; the ability to manage detail; the power to coordinate groups; and the capacity to understand and implement the law, to build, renovate and transform, and to synthesize. Ray Seven also controls magical power, ritualism, and ceremonialism, which is the ability to work with the devic and elemental forces.

Ray Seven energy flows into the constellational triangle of Aries, Cancer, and Capricorn and from there into the planets associated with these constellations, as shown in the following figure. Capricorn is currently the controlling factor for Ray Seven energy and "produces initiation and the overcoming of materialism."[39] This ray expresses the aspect of the will which is the principle of order.[40]

Ray Seven Triangles

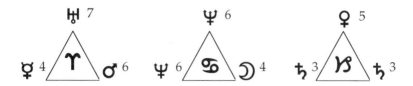

Uranus is associated with Ray Seven—the only planet that is. Uranus is the exoteric ruler of Aquarius, the esoteric ruler of Libra, and the hierarchical ruler of Aries. Veiled by the Sun and Moon, Uranus is also the hierarchical ruler of Leo and Aquarius.[41] Now, during the beginnings of the Aquarian age, more Ray Seven energy is flowing into Earth life.

We move forward on Ray Seven through observance of rules and practice of ritual.

Special Virtues

Strength, perseverance, courage, courtesy, extreme care in details, self-reliance.

Virtues to be Acquired

Realization of unity, wide-mindedness, tolerance, humility, gentleness, and love.

Ray Methods of Activity

Union of energy and substance through group activity.
Stimulation of etheric forms.
Vital energy.

Ray Methods of Teaching Truth

Higher expression: All forms of white magic.
Lower expression: Spiritualism in its lower aspects.

Words of Power

"The highest and the lowest meet."

Ray Energies, Keywords, and Relationships

Following is a summary of the seven ray energies and some of the keywords associated with them, as well as the planets and constellations through which they transmit their energies:

Ray	Type of Energy	Constellations	Planets
I	Will and Power: leadership, focus, courage, action, detachment, death and rebirth	Aries, Leo, and Capricorn	Vulcan, Pluto
II	Love-Wisdom: understanding, receptivity, intuition, inclusiveness, patience	Gemini, Virgo, and Pisces	Jupiter, Sun
III	Active Intelligence and Adaptability: abstract thinking, mental fertility, creativity	Cancer, Libra, and Capricorn	Saturn, Earth
IV	Harmony, Beauty, and Art: conflict, mediation, aesthetics, mathematical exactitude, bridging	Taurus, Scorpio, and Sagittarius	Mercury, Moon
V	Concrete Knowledge and Science: focused intellect, discrimination, truth, analysis, research	Leo, Sagittarius, and Aquarius	Venus
VI	Devotion and Idealism: faith, optimism, sincerity, purity, persuasiveness, persistence	Virgo, Sagittarius, and Pisces	Neptune, Mars
VII	Ceremonial Magic and Organization: ritualism, order, management, synthesis, law	Aries, Cancer, and Capricorn	Uranus

Major Ray Cycles

In his book, *The Inner Side of History*, Charles DeMotte has made a study of the cycles of the seven rays as they have manifested through historical events. Drawing on some of the work of Dane Rudhyar, Charles has provided us with the following table:[42]

Ray	Entry	Peak	Completion
1	2100 CE	——	——
2	1575 CE	1825	2075
3	1425 CE	1875	4425
4	2025 CE	——	——
5	1775 CE	——	2000 (estimated)
6	100 BCE	1625	2062
7	1675 CE	3425	3775

As you can see, Rays Two, Three, Five, Six, and Seven are currently in manifestation and Rays One and Four will come into manifestation within the next one-hundred years.

Of the rays currently in manifestation, DeMotte tells us that Rays Two and Six have stimulated the astral plane, and thus the emotional life of humanity, and Rays Three and Seven, which govern the physical body, condition us to our environment.[43] Ray Five has stimulated science and discovery and, according to the Tibetan, has actually had more of an influence than originally projected. For example, the planetary Hierarchy did not anticipate that humanity would discover the processes of atomic energy until a hundred or more years later than actually occurred.

The influences of Rays One and Four coming into manifestation during the next one-hundred years does not mean that their effects have not already been felt. For example, Ray One is having a definite effect on the mental plane. Its forces have also been invoked throughout history to put the evolutionary processes back into order after major disturbances, such as the world war.

Ray Four energies are already giving humanity a greater sense of values and the synthesis of order that can also be called beauty. The Tibetan tells us that Ray Four, in collaboration with the developing Saturnian influence, will lead many people onto the spiritual path.[44]

Chapter 6—
The Zodiacal Constellations

"In the understanding of the significance of the distinction between constellations as galaxies of stars, and signs as concentrated influences will come fresh light upon the science of astrology. This is fundamentally connected with the difference between the relation of a ray energy to the triangle of constellations and the human relation."—AAB[1]

In our consideration of the twelve signs of the zodiac, we bear in mind that these signs represent the seasonal cycles of Earth, and draw their energies from the constellations of the same name. These constellations, in turn, receive many streams of energy from various sources before transmitting them into our solar system. In our discussion here, we often use the term "constellation" rather than "sign," in respect to the original sources of these energies, but we think of the usage of their energies in terms of our annual earthly cycles.

Our purpose in this study is to act as recipients for the energies generated during the windows of time represented by full moons and then as distributors of these energies to humanity and other kingdoms of nature. Accordingly, we focus on the global and group, rather than individual, nature of the signs and highlight the esoteric mottoes, meditation seed thoughts, and keywords for each of them, for use when their energies are prominent.

When we study the attributes of the constellations and planets, we become very much aware that not only are they tremendously influenced by the seven rays, but also that many of the constellations and planets have more rapport with certain of their peers than others. When the seasonal cycles and the periods of the full moon bring certain of these great beings into stronger focus, this focus is further strengthened if other great beings they are in rapport with are also playing an active role, through aspect, in the cyclical pattern. For that reason, we are providing information on the significant relationships of each of these great beings in the following pages.

A very significant relationship for constellations to have is a configuration with three others in a cross formation, keeping in mind that the number four represents materialization of energy. The placement of constellations upon the vertical or horizontal arm is extrapolated from a statement by the Tibetan that Aquarius and Leo are always on the vertical arm.[2] Although he does not specifically state what arms the constellations of the other crosses are on, I nevertheless draw conclusions based on his other statements that Pisces, Aquarius, and Capricorn are all three exit points from their corresponding crosses, leading the pilgrim onto the next cross.[3]

A planet in one of the signs of a cross magnetizes energies into the arm of the cross for that particular sign. This magnetizing also draws energies in along the other four arms of the cross, starting with the sign opposite the planet and then through the signs on the other axis. (Crosses are discussed in detail in Chapter 9.)

Other significant relationships occur when constellations hold ray energies in common with each other, when constellations have planetary rulers in common, and when the planets have ray energies in common with the constellations.

We might justifiably ask, how can a planet "rule" a constellation or sign when the constellation carries such a greater force? This is because a planet has a special rapport with the sign and acts as a ruler, or carrier, for the sign's qualities and energies.

In esoteric astrology, each constellation (or sign) has three planets, rather than one, associated with it: the traditional "exoteric" planet, an esoteric planet, and a hierarchical planet. These planets transform the energies of the constellations, stepping them down for more practical use by us. The traditional exoteric planet deals with the personality life, the esoteric planet deals with the soul life, and the hierarchical planet deals with the group life of a particular race or civilization. The hierarchical planet also comes into play in the life of a very advanced individual, and perhaps subliminally in the life of an ordinary person. As an elaboration:

1. The traditional planetary rulers influence the personality life (as do the twelve houses governed by the planets).

2. The esoteric planetary rulers influence the soul, and bring in planetary and ray energy in a more dynamic manner.

3. The hierarchical planetary rulers influence the spirit or monad, and bring in energies to group and planetary levels.

The influence of the constellations, signs, and planets work out upon three levels of awareness, and are felt first of all upon the mental plane, then upon the astral plane, and finally upon the physical plane. This triple interpretation relates to the exoteric, esoteric, and hierarchical planets and the rays that they express.[4] All these planetary energies work together; the esoteric and hierarchical forces do not replace the exoteric forces, but instead supplement and dominate them. These additional energies, thereby, enrich us, extend our experience, and expand our consciousness, but do not alter the energy or aliveness of what we achieve and attain under the exoteric influences. As we evolve, we can respond to the additional influences more.[5]

The powers of planets in particular signs—their exaltations, detriments, and falls—can modify our use of planetary energies at a given time. Monique Pommier has written a series of articles for the *Journal of Esoteric Psychology* discussing planetary exaltations. She tells us that "It [exaltation] reveals a planet's identity in its plenitude of being. The sign in which the planet is exalted indicates the particular energy field which galvanizes this revelation by eliciting the very purpose at the root of the planet's qualities and functions. Thus the exalting sign gives fundamental insights into the planet's energy."[6] David Kesten tells us that exaltations smooth out the less desirable qualities of the planet and also give something to the sign which the sign is in need of. Falls and detriments indicate the circumstances under which planetary energy is less effective.

All systems of astrology assign the elements fire, air, water, and earth to zodiacal constellations. In esoteric astrology, fire represents the planes of higher spiritual intuition, air represents the mental plane, water represents the emotional plane, and earth represents the physical plane. The following chart shows the constellations in their various elements.

Fire	*Air*	*Water*	*Earth*
Aries	Gemini	Cancer	Taurus
Leo	Libra	Scorpio	Virgo
Sagittarius	Aquarius	Pisces	Capricorn

The table on the next page summarizes the zodiacal constellations, their rulers, the approximate dates they are in force on the tropical zodiac, and some of the energetic principles associated with them:

Signs With Rulers, Dates, and Energetic Principles

Sign	*Rulers*	*Dates*	*Energetic Principles*
Aries	Mars, Mercury, Uranus	Mar 20 - Apr 19	Beginnings, creativity, identity, activity, pioneering
Taurus	Venus, Vulcan, Vulcan	Apr 19 - May 20	Values, refinement, resources, building, illumination
Gemini	Mercury, Venus, Earth	May 20 - Jun 21	Communication, understanding, versatility, truth
Cancer	Moon, Neptune, Neptune	Jun 21 - Jul 22	Nurturance, sensitivity, mass-consciousness
Leo	Sun (Jupiter[7]), Sun (Neptune), Sun (Uranus)	Jul 22 - Aug 22	Individuality, individual-consciousness, creativity, magnanimity
Virgo	Mercury, Moon (Vulcan), Jupiter	Aug 22 - Sep 22	Analysis, discrimination, service, germination
Libra	Venus, Uranus, Saturn	Sep 22 - Oct 23	Balance, choice, relationship, justice, judgment
Scorpio	Mars, Pluto, Mercury	Oct 23 - Nov 21	Intensity, transformation, power, testing, triumph
Sagittarius	Jupiter, Earth, Mars	Nov 21 - Dec 21	Direction, intuition, idealism, aspiration, achievement
Capricorn	Saturn, Saturn, Venus	Dec 21 - Jan 19	Authority, accomplishment, crystallization, synthesis, initiation
Aquarius	Uranus, Jupiter, Moon (Uranus)	Jan 19 - Feb 18	Group-consciousness, idealism, inventiveness, humanitarianism
Pisces	Jupiter, Neptune, Pluto	Feb 18 - Mar 20	Inspiration, spirituality, sacrifice, release, liberation

Aries

"I come forth and from the plane of mind, I rule."

The Sun is often thought of as having been in the sidereal constellation of Aries at the beginning of our current astrological cycle.[8] Aries, the first sign, holds the secret of beginnings, cycles, and emerging opportunity. The birthplace of ideas, Aries awakens the first impulse to initiate a cycle of activity and manifestation. The act of initiation is an entrance into a state of increased self-realization and spiritual illumination; the ideational power of Aries helps us to know and master ourselves and the universe. Thus, Aries gives us the capacity to set forces into motion and thereby bring something new into existence.[9]

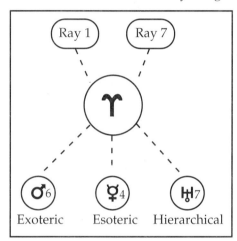

Exoteric   Esoteric   Hierarchical

Creation, being, activity, strife, and synthesis are Aries energies. On the personality level, Aries helps us create activities, conditions, and processes that enable us to manifest the soul through the medium of form. On the soul level, Aries helps us express the creative energies that lead to the manifestation of spirit through the soul. Both these processes demonstrate the true nature of life, quality, and appearance—the three basic energies of the spirit, soul, and personality.

Aries begins the creative processes of the first step of the soul toward incarnation, the recurring cycles of experience, and the period when the soul aligns itself with its purpose.

Experience leads to mastery, and Aries energies help us develop the power of organization and control over our circumstances so that we can cooperate with the Plan and practice will in correctly guiding and directing planetary affairs. Aries represents the dynamic nature of God, with the qualities of will, power, and action, the archetypes of the creation of the universe.

Aries' Relationships With Rays and Constellations

Aries forms a point of two constellational triangles that bring through the energies of Rays One and Seven from the Great Bear, Sirius, and the Pleiades (see the table on page 79). Since Rays One and Seven are at opposite ends, a point of balance is provided in Libra, the polar opposite of Aries.

Aries, Leo, and Capricorn form the Ray One constellational triangle that brings through the Ray One energies of will and power. Aries is the primary agent of this Ray One energy, which comes from the divine prototype in the Great Bear. This energy becomes transmuted into the force and activity of the Ray One Planetary Logos (whichever planet he might embody) and works out as his triple activity under the focus of the planets associated with Aries—Mars, Mercury, and Uranus.

Aries, Cancer, and Capricorn form the Ray Seven constellational triangle that brings through the energies of ceremonial order, magic, and organization.

Through its planetary rulers, Mars, Mercury, and Uranus, Aries is associated with the energies of Rays Six, Four, and Seven respectively. These ray energies relate Aries to other signs that have planetary rulers on Rays Six, Four, and Seven: Gemini, Cancer, Virgo, Libra, Scorpio, Sagittarius, and Aquarius.

Aries and its polar opposite Libra make up the horizontal arm of the cardinal cross. Cancer and its polar opposite Capricorn make up the vertical arm. Indirectly, Aries has access to the energies of the planets of the signs on the other arms of the cardinal cross: Venus, Uranus, Saturn, the Moon, and Neptune, which embody the energies of Rays Five, Seven, Three, Four, and Six, respectively. In the cycle of consciousness expansion and initiation, Aries represents the culmination and synthesis of experience upon the cardinal cross. After this, "the ONE proceeds upon the higher Way and passes on to realms unknown e'en to the highest of the Sons of God upon our Earth."[10]

To sum up, Aries has direct access to the energies of Rays One, Four, Six, and Seven, with a double influence of Ray Seven from the Ray Seven constellational triangle and from the planet Uranus. Through its position on the cardinal cross, Aries has indirect access to all the energies of that cross, especially its own and the energies from Libra.

Three planets act as rulers, or transformers, for Arian energy: Mars, Mercury, and Uranus. As exoteric ruler, Mars rules the personality level;

as esoteric ruler, Mercury rules the soul level; and as hierarchical ruler, Uranus rules the group level of human life.

Personality Ruler—Mars

Mars, the exoteric or personality ruler of Aries, is associated with the Ray Six energies of devotion and idealism. The god of war and strife, Mars produces the fiery processes that purify. Mars embodies Ray Six force, which leads to idealism, destructive fanaticism, struggle, strife, war, effort, and eventual evolution. Mars rules and controls our physical bodies. In Aries, Mars makes the first move toward objective manifestation, or physical incarnation.

Mars relates Aries to Scorpio, where Mars also rules on the personality level.

Soul Ruler—Mercury

Mercury, the esoteric or soul ruler of Aries, is associated with the Ray Four energies of harmony, beauty, and art. Mercury, the star of the intuition, illumines the mind and directs our way through life, giving us vision and helping us to become aware of the divine plan. As the Messenger of the Gods, Mercury mediates between soul and personality. This mediatorship produces opposition and a long drawn out conflict, but finally works out into victory and the dispelling of illusion through the illumination of the lower mind.

Group Ruler—Uranus

Uranus, the hierarchical or group ruler, is associated with the Ray Seven energies of ceremonial order, magic, and organization. The work of Uranus is analogous to that of Mercury, for the Ray Four influence of Mercury and the Ray Seven influence of Uranus both relate the pair of opposites, spirit and matter, to produce manifestation. Uranus is sometimes said to be a higher harmonic of Mercury.

In its role of group rulership, Uranus, the hierophant, rules the occult way and is connected with the mysteries of initiation. The path of initiation is begun by the free choice of the initiate, made under the influence of Libra, the polar opposite of Aries.

Uranus relates Aries to Aquarius and Leo, where Uranus (veiled by the Moon and the Sun) also rules on the group level.

Exaltations, Falls, and Detriments

The Sun is exalted in Aries, the power of Venus is lessened, and Saturn falls. The Sun is exalted because it represents the life of the spirit which comes into full expression as the result of the evolutionary process initiated in Aries. Monique Pommier says, "Aries reveals the spirit of the Sun—the spirit of selfhood—as emergence."[11] The power of Venus is lessened in Aries because lesser luminaries fade out when the Sun is exalted and blazes forth in all its glory. Saturn falls in Aries because, as the Lord of Karma, Saturn demands full payment of all debts from the form side and the soul side. When we incarnate and "fall" into generation (form), Saturn falls also. Later, when we free ourselves from karma (soul), Saturn's work will be accomplished and his power ended.[12]

Meditation Seed Thoughts

The keywords and phrases associated with Aries are:

- Express the will to be and do

- Unfold the power to manifest

- Enter into battle for the Lord

- Arrive at unity through effort

When we achieve the objectives underlying these phrases, we can truthfully say: "I come forth and from the plane of mind, I rule." All events and circumstances have their origin in the mind because knowledge and understanding must be present before action is possible. The creation of the universe itself is a product of divine mind and the result of the Creator's archetypes of life.

The key phrase for the personality level during an Aries cycle is: "And the Word said: Let form again be sought." This represents the evolutionary urge of reincarnation, which begins in Aries, and also represents the human focus on giving birth to new forms and ideas, experienced particularly in Aries. Aries cycles inspire the following trends of development:[13]

- Blind, undirected experience, leading to directed personality effort, leading to recognition and work with the Plan

- Instinctual reaction, leading to desire, leading to will

Keynote on the Path: Aries turns toward Capricorn

Taurus

"I see and when the Eye is opened, all is illumined."

Taurus, a constellation in a brightly lit part of the heavens, guards the secret of light and brings us illumination. Taurus is the sign of major life incentive and governs desire in all its phases. It tests us on the astral plane and, as we succeed, we uplift our desire sensitivity from form to sensitive perception on the intuitional plane. Desire thus becomes aspiration, darkness gives place to light and illumination, and our attention becomes focused upon spiritual attainment.

Taurus represents the urge for beauty, truer values, refinement, and synthesis. In Taurus, synthesis expresses upon the physical plane because its basic quality is desire in the average person and will or directed purpose in the more advanced person. This quality's best manifestation is as intelligently expressed will, actuated by the impulse of love, representing adherence to soul purpose.

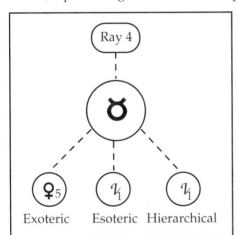

Exoteric   Esoteric   Hierarchical

Because Taurus is an earth sign, the working out of the Plan or the fulfillment of desire must be carried out upon the outer plane of living. This will or desire expresses itself in our environment as Taurus forges the instruments of constructive living or destruction—the chains that bind or the key that unlocks the mystery of life. Vulcan controls the anvil-like processes of time and strikes the blow that shapes the metal into what is desired.[14]

Liberated Taurian energy is a constructive, planning, creative, forward-moving force. In Taurus there is a constant emphasis upon struggle—a cosmic, planetary and individual struggle, for desire/will underlies all manifested activities. It is the struggle from darkness to light, the struggle of the soul to dominate the outer form, the struggle to transmute desire into aspiration and aspiration into the will to achieve, and the struggle to attain the goal that an increasing light reveals.[15]

In Taurus, we possess the creative potential to build and develop a better mechanism of reception that can enable us to respond to all impacts and every type of divine energy. When we grasp the nature of the will, the Tibetan says, we will grasp the significance of Taurian influence.[16]

Taurus' Relationships With Rays and Constellations

Taurus forms a point of one constellational triangle that brings through the Ray Four energies of harmony, beauty, and art from the Great Bear, Sirius, and the Pleiades (see the table on page 79). The other two constellations that form this triangle are Scorpio and Sagittarius.

Through its planetary rulers, Taurus is associated with the energies of Rays Five and One. These two rays, viewed in combination with the Earth (Ray Three), are a difficult combination of rays, for all are along the Ray One line of energy and involve the will aspect. Taurus, Pisces, and Scorpio through Vulcan and Pluto, are related to Ray One and deal with the transmutation of individual will into divine will and of desire into sacrifice. Taurus is related to Libra, Gemini, and Capricorn through Venus, which is associated with the Ray Five energies for all these signs. Taurus is related to Virgo through the Moon, since the Moon veils Vulcan in Virgo for particular levels of evolution.

Taurus and its polar opposite Scorpio make up the horizontal arm of the fixed cross. Aquarius and its polar opposite Leo make up the vertical arm. Indirectly, Taurus has access to the energies of the planets of the signs on the other arms of the fixed cross: Mars, Pluto, Mercury, the Sun (veiling Jupiter, Neptune, and Uranus), Jupiter, and the Moon, which embody the energies of Rays Six, One, Four, Two, Two, Six, Seven, Two, and Four, respectively. The spiritual side of Venus and Ray Two energies from Taurus's companion signs on the fixed cross can help with the Taurian task of transmuting intelligence and knowledge into wisdom, personal focus into spiritual aspiration, and desire into love.

Thus, Taurus is associated with the influence of all the rays except for Ray Three, and that is present because it is the ray of Earth. It is especially difficult for us to deal with all these energies, but working with them successfully brings special opportunities toward illuminating and solving the problems of humanity. These problems mostly stem from the misuse of desire, proper usage of which can be a strong force for aspiration and eventual enlightenment.

Although Taurus constitutes a complex aggregation of forces, it is simple in its expression because it is governed directly by only two planets, Venus and Vulcan. As exoteric ruler, Venus rules the personality level; as esoteric and hierarchical ruler, Vulcan rules the soul level and the group level of human life.

Personality Ruler—Venus

Venus, the exoteric or personality ruler of Taurus, is associated with the Ray Five energies of concrete knowledge and science, the mental energy of humanity which establishes relationships between people and nations. As the source of the intelligent mind, Venus can act either through desire or love, depending upon our point in evolution. Venus represents the relation of the lower self to the higher self and an inner fusion and harmony between the two, a transcendence in consciousness when the two become unified.

Venus holds a unique relation to Earth, causing a closer relation between Taurus and the Earth than perhaps exists in any other zodiacal relation where Earth is concerned. Today, Taurus, Venus, and the Earth have a close karmic relation and a definite dharma to work out, expressed by the words, will, desire, light, and plan.[17]

Venus relates Taurus to Libra, where Venus also rules on the personality level.

Soul and Group Ruler—Vulcan

Vulcan, the esoteric or soul ruler of Taurus, is associated with the Ray One energies of will and power. Vulcan is also the hierarchical or group ruler of Taurus. Vulcan links the first ray with the first kingdom of nature, the mineral kingdom, through numerical resonance. This forms a triangular rapport between Shamballa, humanity, and the mineral kingdom which works out from the angle of the Plan, but also from the expression of materiality.

As the forger of metals, Vulcan symbolizes the densest, most concrete expression of the natural world. He goes into the depths to find the material from which to fashion what is beautiful and useful, thereby representing our delving into the depths of our consciousness to evolve our spiritual expression.

The energy of Vulcan is the strength and potency that sets the world evolutionary process in motion; it embodies the energy of Ray One, which initiates and which also destroys, bringing about the death of the form so that the soul may be set free.

Exaltations, Falls, and Detriments

The Moon is exalted in Taurus, meaning that the form side of life can exert powerful control over us. Monique Pommier says, "Taurus exposes in the Moon the all-vehicle of Being, the battleground of duality, between the receptive function of all forms and the opaque will of their constituent matters."[18] When we translate desire into aspiration and spiritual will, the form is exalted on a higher level as we use the creative energies of Vulcan to materialize the Plan on Earth. The Moon, the mother of the form, veils Vulcan, the shaper of the form, bringing in both feminine and masculine aspects of form-building, the creative functions of mother-father.[19]

Uranus, the planet of the hidden mystery and one of the most occult of the planets, falls in Taurus, producing an accentuation and sharp division between body and soul. While in the cycle of Taurus, the task of Uranus, hidden in the depths, is to awaken and evoke our intuitive response to an ever-increasing light until full illumination and the development of spiritual consciousness is achieved and higher soul aspects are substituted for lower form reactions. The exaltation of Uranus in Scorpio, the polar opposite of Taurus, encourages us to think that Uranus will complete its job in Taurus successfully.

Mars is in detriment in Scorpio and that influence can give a warlike nature to Taurus, but the potency of the Taurian struggle is so great that the effect of Mars is lost in the larger whole. It "adds to the glamour and confusion and yet holds within itself hope for the struggling man."[20]

Meditation Seed Thoughts

The keywords and phrases associated with Taurus are:

- Incentive behind evolution (impulse), intense struggle
- Desire for experience, for satisfaction
- Intelligent activity, illumination, the light of knowledge
- Will to liberation, the will to be, the will to live
- Ambition and power
- Motive, aspiration, plan, and purpose

The following qualities or aspects are in juxtaposition:

- Desire, leading to aspiration
- Blindness, leading to sight
- Darkness, leading to light
- Death, leading to liberation

When we achieve the objectives underlying these phrases, we can truthfully say: "I see and when the Eye is opened, all is illumined." The eye refers to the "third eye" of the initiate which, when opened, illumines the mind. According to the eastern tradition, Buddha achieved enlightenment during the full moon of Taurus. On a cosmic level, the "eye...of God is open and from it light pours radiantly...Hence victory is inevitable for the potency of cosmic energy will unfailingly and in time subdue and re-orient the energy of humanity."[21]

The key phrase for the personality level during a Taurus cycle is: "And the Word said: Let struggle be undismayed." This is the evolutionary urge that we express during the stages where it is appropriate for us to go courageously after what we desire. Taurus cycles inspire the following trends of development:[22]

- Selfish desire, leading to aspiration, leading to illumined living
- The light of Earth, leading to the light of Love, leading to the light of Life

Keynote on the Path: Taurus rushes blindly until Sagittarius directs

Gemini

"I recognise my other self and in the waning of that self I grow and glow."

Gemini deals with polarities, not only those within its own range of influence, but Gemini also provides a third, mediating point of a triangle in the activities of all the pairs of signs in the zodiac that are polar opposites. In its role of divine messenger for the many opposites in manifestation, Gemini comprehends extremes and relates them to each other. Gemini is sometimes called the "constellation of the resolution of duality into a fluid synthesis."[23] Accordingly, through the ages, Gemini has produced many of the messengers of God, the revealers of new divine truths, intermediaries between Hierarchy and humanity, and mediators within the realm of humanity itself.

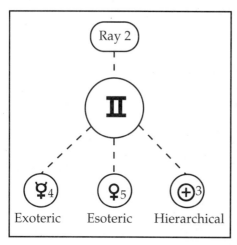

Exoteric   Esoteric   Hierarchical

Gemini brings us intuitive sensitivity and quick reaction, a fluid versatility and an equally fluid but analytical understanding of people and situations. Under the Gemini influence, we develop insights from the constant activity, ceaseless movement, and changing conditions inherent in Gemini. Gemini influences and determines the principle of change itself and assumes responsibility for its rate of progression.

Through Gemini, we recognize reality and we seek stability, ordered changes, and unity with the truth. The relation between the duality of soul and body emerges, in which the body or form serves the soul. We respond to soul impression and, consequently, stabilize life on the physical plane. The mystical vision emerges into consciousness and we become aware of the higher self through the faint flickerings of the intuition.

Through conflict in the evolutionary process, we progress to conflict upon the Path. The goal of the first conflict is to harmonize the personality and achieve personality integration; the goal upon the final stages of the Path is to attain harmony between soul and form.

Gemini, working through the etheric body of the planet, transmits psychic and soul energy and leads to the fusion of the pairs of opposites, the intelligent work of synthesis. The opposites of attraction and repulsion condition our life on Earth and these energies reach us through Gemini. This conditioning is the effect of a cosmic energy at present unknown to humanity.

The waxing and waning light of Gemini energies, produced by the interplay of the twins that are symbolically associated with this constellation, distinguishes soul experience from Earth experience, influences the rise and fall of civilization, and promotes the growth and unfoldment of all cyclic manifestations.[24]

Gemini's Relationships With Rays and Constellations

Gemini forms a point of one constellational triangle that brings through the Ray Two energies of love-wisdom from the Great Bear, Sirius, and the Pleiades (see the table on page 79). The other two constellations that form this triangle are Virgo and Pisces.

Through its planetary rulers, Mercury, Venus, and Earth, Gemini is associated with the energies of Rays Four, Five, and Three. These rays relate Gemini to the other signs that have planetary rulers on these rays: Aries, Taurus, Cancer, Libra, Virgo, Scorpio, Sagittarius, Capricorn, and Aquarius. Rays Three, Four, and Five produce a synthesis of activity and potencies essential for the development of humanity:

- Ray Three, active intelligence, under the influence of this third sign, Gemini, conditions the etheric body.

- Ray Four, harmony through conflict, under the influence of Gemini-Sagittarius, stages situations upon the astral plane that will produce conflict in the astral body which will lead us to eventual liberation.

- Ray Five, concrete knowledge and science, under the influence of Capricorn focused through Venus, enables us to take initiation.

Gemini and its polar opposite Sagittarius make up the horizontal arm of the mutable cross. Virgo and its polar opposite Pisces make up the vertical arm. Indirectly, Gemini has access to the energies of the planets of the signs on the other arms of the mutable cross: Jupiter, the Earth, Mars, Mercury, Moon/Vulcan, Neptune, and Pluto, which embody the energies of Rays Two, Three, Six, Four, Four/One, Six, and One, respectively. The energy of one ray is lacking in Gemini—Ray Seven of ceremonial order, magic, and organization, which fixates experience and anchors the ray forces into form. The lack of Ray Seven lends an instability and fluidity to Gemini, but provides versatility.

The three planets that transform Geminian energy, Mercury, Venus, and the Earth, also form the personality vehicle of the Planetary Logos of Earth. This gives these energies a particular focus toward the development of humanity and the unfoldment of the consciousness of universality. Earth, which is related to the material aspect of divinity, assumes the role of releasing sorrow and purifying pain, while Mercury and Venus focus the energies to provide the release. The Earth is an intermediary planet because it rules both Gemini and Sagittarius and is potent in the relationship between this pair of opposites, balancing the two great streams of cosmic energy emanating from Sagittarius and Gemini. Mercury and Venus aid and influence this condition, which produces a unique situation on Earth.

Personality Ruler—Mercury

Mercury, the exoteric or personality ruler of Gemini, is associated with the Ray Four energies of harmony, beauty, and art. Mercury expresses the dual aspect of the mind as it mediates between the higher and lower aspects of our personality life and our relationships between personality and its environment. By carrying messages between the soul and brain, Mercury establishes right relations between the lower and higher self. In this aspect, Mercury is illumined mind. Later, Mercury is the abstract mind, removed from form contact and relating soul and spirit.

Mercury increases the latent sense of duality in its various stages and the sense of distinction, leading to mental agility. Mercury governs Gemini until we establish a balanced relationship between the personality and the soul and can function as either at any moment with equal facility. In its messenger role, Mercury helps Gemini find points of contact with people on nearly every ray.

Mercury relates Gemini to Virgo, where Mercury also rules on the personality level.

Soul Ruler—Venus

Venus, the esoteric or soul ruler of Gemini, is associated with the Ray Five energies of concrete knowledge and science. Venus relates humanity in a unique way to Gemini. The Tibetan tells us that in the coming world religion, this fact will be noted and in the month of June, in which the influences of Gemini are especially strong, due advantage will be taken to bring us nearer to the spiritual realities. Meditation groups will recognize the potency of Venus in relating such pairs of opposites as Hierarchy and the animal kingdom (the animal kingdom represents the synthesis of the subhuman kingdoms) leading to a great approach between soul and form. Appeal will be made to the Forces that can utilize this planetary potency to work out the divine plan upon the Earth.[25] This shows the power of the mind, exemplified in Venus, in connection with the process of the initiation of life into higher kingdoms of nature.

Group Ruler—Earth

Earth, the hierarchical or group ruler of Gemini, is associated with the Ray Three energies of active intelligence and adaptability. This ray, under Gemini's influence, conditions the etheric body. The hierarchical ruler of Gemini, Earth, is a non-sacred planet and is also the esoteric ruler of Sagittarius. These are the only two constellations ruled by the Earth, which is of major significance, creating an unusual situation in the solar system and a relationship that is unique to this pair of opposites. The cosmic line of force between Gemini and Sagittarius is subjectively and esoterically related to Earth, thus guaranteeing our soul development, the unfoldment of form as an expression of that soul, and leading humanity to initiation in Capricorn. The three energies of Rays Three, Four and Five, focused through the three planetary rulers of Gemini, are polarized in the Earth and dedicated to our development.[26]

Exaltations, Falls, and Detriments

In Gemini, no planet either falls or is exalted, and this is also the situation in Sagittarius, Gemini's polar opposite. This is because the interchange between Gemini and Sagittarius promotes equilibrium, balance, harmony, and an avoidance of extremes. The influence of Mercury, however, is lessened in Sagittarius until Mercury's lower-higher mind dualism is transcended by the universal or spiritual mind.

In Gemini, the influence of Jupiter is lessened on the personality level until the body-soul dualism of Gemini is transmuted into the soul-spirit dualism of Jupiter.

Meditation Seed Thoughts

The keywords and phrases associated with Gemini are:

- Fluidity and versatility
- Understanding
- Mediation and communication
- Mental discrimination
- Recognition of duality
- Soul control
- Synthesis

When we achieve the objectives underlying these phrases, we can truthfully say: "I recognise my other self and in the waning of that self I grow and glow." This statement represents our recognition of our higher self and, under the influence of the soul, the waning of the lower self.

The key phrase for the personality level during a Gemini cycle is: "And the Word said: Let instability do its work." This statement represents our desire for evolution after our fluctuation between lower and higher consciousness for so long. Gemini cycles inspire the following trends of development:[27]

- Mutation of relation, leading to orientation of relation, leading to right relation

- "I serve myself," leading to "I serve my brother," leading to "I serve the One"

Keynote on the Path: Gemini moves toward Libra

Cancer

"I build a lighted house and therein dwell."

In Cancer, the gateway of mass-consciousness, we can invoke the cosmic mother principle which nurtures, protects, and is sometimes able to heal. We develop sensitivity and an intuitive awareness of the

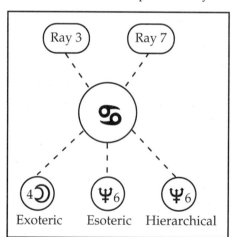

Ray 3   Ray 7

Exoteric   Esoteric   Hierarchical

realms of feeling and sentiment. Cancer is the door into the physical incarnation of humanity. As we incarnate in form, we learn how to transform the servitude of form into the service of the Plan. Reincarnation is implicit in the universe and is a basic and fundamental theme underlying the rhythm of cyclic manifestation.

The energies of Cancer, concerned with the world of causes, are vague and subtle to ordinary people because they manifest in spirit more than in soul or body.

Psychologically, Cancer is the polar opposite of the state of group-consciousness toward which humanity is tending. Today we are at a midway point between mass-consciousness and group-consciousness. Many of us are becoming group-conscious, while others are emerging out of the mass-conscious stage and becoming self-conscious individuals. This accounts for much of the world difficulty and the clash of idealisms because the two groups bring a different approach to world problems.

Seasonally, the sign of Cancer brings the summer and the turning point in the annual cycle when the Sun begins its apparent path southward; the peak of light is reached in the highly populated northern hemisphere of Earth, for which Capricorn, Cancer's polar opposite, is the lightbearer. Cancer is the lightbearer in the southern hemisphere. Esoterically, Cancer and Capricorn are both considered gateways of light to humanity.

Cancer's Relationships With Rays and Constellations

Cancer forms a point of two constellational triangles that bring through the energies of Rays Three and Seven from the Great Bear, Sirius, and the Pleiades (see the table on page 79). Cancer, Libra, and Capricorn form the Ray Three triangle of active intelligence and adaptability. Cancer, Aries, and Capricorn form the Ray Seven triangle of ceremonial order, magic, and organization. The force of Ray Seven (producing a synthesis of expression upon the physical plane) combined with Ray Three (producing intense activity in matter) brings about experience and human expression.

Through its planetary rulers, the Moon and Neptune, Cancer is associated with the energies of Rays Four and Six. These ray energies relate Cancer to other signs that have planetary rulers on Rays Four and Six: Aries, Gemini, Leo, Virgo, Scorpio, Sagittarius, and Aquarius.

Cancer and its polar opposite Capricorn make up the vertical arm of the cardinal cross. Aries and its polar opposite Libra make up the horizontal arm. Indirectly, Cancer has access to the energies of the planets of the signs on the other arms of the cardinal cross: Saturn, Venus, Mars, Mercury, and Uranus, which embody the energies of Rays Three, Five, Six, Four, and Seven, respectively. In Cancer, we respond to the uses of conflict through Mars, to the light of intuition through Mercury, to the cosmic pull of Uranus, the intellect of Venus, and the presentation of opportunity through Saturn.

Because the light of Cancer is diffused, the Ray One influences of focused intention and purposeful will and the Ray Two influences of love-wisdom (recognized duality and gained experience) are not focused in Cancer. Ray forces affect Cancer from the angle of mass mind and reaction rather than that of the individual.

Personality Ruler—Moon Veiling Neptune

The Moon and Neptune, transmitting the energies of the psychic nature and form, plus the tendency to achieve through conflict, rule Cancer directly and indirectly. They control the form and the lower psychic nature.

The Moon, as exoteric or personality ruler of Cancer, is associated with the Ray Four energies of harmony, beauty, and art. The Moon itself veils Vulcan for the physical body, Neptune for the astral body, and Uranus for the mental body, thus forming the creative triangle of the personality.

In Cancer, the Moon, in its own right of ancient thoughtform control and as veiling both Vulcan and Neptune, connects the force of Cancer with the energies of Taurus, Virgo, and Aquarius. This relates the form-building aspect with the consciousness aspect.

As stated by two esoteric astrologers: "The difference between the Moon and Neptune is the difference between change for its own sake and change as a means of progress toward a more inclusive state of being. Neptune is imbued with the sense of cosmic purpose which the Moon ordinarily lacks, and therefore its effects are more permanently stamped upon the psyche."[28]

Soul and Group Ruler—Neptune

Neptune, the esoteric or soul ruler of Cancer, is associated with the Ray Six energies of devotion and idealism. Neptune is also the hierarchical or group ruler of Cancer and, in that role, helps us develop group-consciousness. Sagittarius also is associated with the Ray Six energies for the group level through Mars.

Neptune, ruler of the ocean, whose trident and astrological symbol signifies the Trinity in manifestation, rules the Piscean age.[29] Neptune introduces the water of life into the ocean of substance and thus brings light to the world. This demonstrates the control of the fluidic astral plane.

Neptune relates Cancer to Leo, where Neptune (veiled by the Sun) also rules on the soul level.

Exaltations, Falls, and Detriments

Jupiter and Neptune are exalted in Cancer, the sign of rebirth, because these two planets indicate the successful development and eventual use of the form aspect and the development of psychic sensitivity, both in the higher and lower senses.

Jupiter, embodying Ray Two, ensures that love as relationship to divinity and wisdom as relationship to form lie behind the soul's intent. In space and time, for long eons, form controls and hides the soul. This is equally true in regard to the fluidic psychic nature, as governed by Neptune. The form aspect and psychic nature reach an eventual concrete perfection in Capricorn to become again in Cancer the perfect instrument of service which we wield when we seek to render mass service instead of being involved and lost in the mass.

Saturn is in detriment in Cancer, which produces difficult conditions and situations that lead to struggle and amplifies Cancer's inherent energies of harmony through conflict brought in via the Moon. This can lead to Cancer being a place of symbolic imprisonment through wrong orientation. The conflict of the soul with its environment, carried on consciously or unconsciously, provides conditions of suffering that our souls willingly accepted when choosing life on Earth, with all its consequent sacrifices and pains.[30]

Meditation Seed Thoughts

The keywords and phrases associated with Cancer are:

- Sensitivity
- Gateway of mass-consciousness
- Nurturance
- Shelter and protection
- Bearer of light

When we achieve the objectives underlying these phrases, we can truthfully say: "I build a lighted house and therein dwell." The lighted house concerns the forms we are building. In Cancer, we attempt to build forms that will embody the light and warmth of the magnetic, attractive soul nature to shelter and support our fellow people.

The key phrase for the personality level during a Cancer cycle is: "And the Word said: Let isolation be the rule and yet the crowd exists." This represents the evolutionary pull of Cancer, which is to vanquish the illusion of isolation and loneliness in preparation for the unity and liberation of humanity. Cancer cycles inspire the following trends of development:[31]

- The blind unit is lost (leading to) the unit awakes to that which is around (leading to) the whole is seen as one

- The mass (leading to) the house (leading to) humanity

Keynote on the Path: Cancer visions life in Leo

Leo

"I am That and That am I."

Leo represents the integration of consciousness. It gives us the opportunity to attain individuality and true self-consciousness (which is different from self-centeredness). Being truly self-conscious means being aware of purpose, living self-directed lives, and having developed definite life plans—all of which are a result of mental perception and integration.

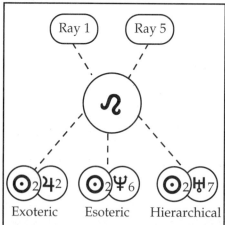

Exoteric   Esoteric   Hierarchical

In Leo, we can use the energies of the soul to focus on the spiritual goal of selflessness. We learn awareness; we know ourselves, and we know our group. We can enhance our creativity in Leo and become co-creators with each other and with the Hierarchy. The influence of Leo prizes originality and instills in us a genuine pride of accomplishment. We learn how to demonstrate a new way of life and acquire the courage to act on our convictions.

We learn from life in Leo rather than from teachings and disciplines that are imposed. We distinguish ourselves by our aura of confidence and freedom from external coercion. We act rather than react. Our behavior is voluntary and not forced on us by circumstances. We assume the right to determine our own destiny. We vitalize what we identify with while retaining our own center of consciousness.

Leo is one of the most important signs for humanity today because it reflects the individual need to pull away from mass-consciousness and public opinion and to think for ourselves. This is happening increasingly as people begin to take stock of and responsibility for their own lives. The pull in this direction is the result of our entering the Age of Aquarius. Leo, being the polar opposite of the sign of Aquarius, is also having a profound effect on our life and culture.

Leo is a part of the Sphinx, a great mystery which relates to the higher and lower mind and their relation to each other. We are told that when the nature of the world is revealed, the mystery of the Sphinx will be solved.[32]

Leo's Relationships With Rays and Constellations

Leo forms a point of two constellational triangles that bring through the energies of Rays One and Five from the Great Bear, Sirius, and the Pleiades (see the table on page 79). Leo, Aries, and Capricorn form the Ray One triangle of will and power. Leo, Sagittarius, and Aquarius form the Ray Five triangle of concrete knowledge and science.

Through its planetary ruler, the Sun, Leo is associated with the energies of Ray Two. The Sun veils other planets; in the case of Leo, the Sun veils Jupiter as the exoteric ruler, Neptune as the esoteric ruler, and Uranus as the hierarchical ruler. These planets are associated with Ray Two, Six, and Seven energies.

Leo and Aquarius, through the Sun and Jupiter, are related to Ray Two and develop individual consciousness into world-consciousness, leading to world service. Ray Two potencies pour into Earth via the Sun (veiling a hidden planet) and Jupiter. These sweep the forces of Leo, Sagittarius, Pisces, Aquarius, and Virgo into and through our entire planet and all its kingdoms in nature.

Leo and its polar opposite Aquarius make up the vertical arm of the fixed cross. Taurus and its polar opposite Scorpio make up the horizontal arm. Indirectly, Leo has access to the energies of the planets of the signs on the other arms of the fixed cross: Uranus, Jupiter, Moon/Uranus, Venus, Vulcan, Mars, Pluto, and Mercury, which embody the energies of Rays Seven, Two, Four/Seven, Five, One, Six, One, and Four, respectively.

In summary, we see that Rays One, Two, Four, Five, Six, and Seven have direct or indirect influence in Leo, and that Ray Two influence is particularly strong due to the rulership of the Sun, regardless of the veiling process. Ray Three energy is obtainable from the Earth so, in this manner, we have access to the energies of all the rays in Leo.

The Sun rules all the three conditions of Leo—exoteric, esoteric and hierarchical. The purpose of this solar system is the unfoldment of consciousness and since Leo's theme is the stimulation of consciousness, the Sun is the source of physical consciousness (exoteric and symbolic of the personality), soul awareness (esoteric), and spiritual life (hierarchical). This intense influence of the Sun eventually develops sensitivity to the universal mind and to the divine plan and purpose.

Personality Ruler—Sun Veiling Jupiter[33]

The Sun, the exoteric or personality ruler, is associated with the Ray Two energies of love-wisdom. For the personality, the Tibetan seems to indicate that the Sun veils Jupiter: "Jupiter is the agent of the second ray which the Sun expresses—cosmically and systemically. Hence the triple relation of the Sun to Leo which is unique in our solar system, and hence the importance of the triangle which controls the man born under Leo—the Sun, Uranus and Neptune. The energy of Leo is focused through the Sun, and is distributed to our planet via the Sun and the two planets which it veils."[34]

Jupiter relates Leo to Sagittarius and Pisces, where Jupiter also rules on the personality level.

Soul Ruler—Sun Veiling Neptune

The Sun, the esoteric or soul ruler, is associated with the Ray Two energies of love-wisdom. For the soul level of Leo, the Sun veils Neptune, which is associated with the Ray Six energy of devotion and idealism. The relation of Leo to Cancer through Neptune concerns the consciousness aspect of evolution. There is mass-consciousness; then consciousness of the dramatic, isolated self; and finally group-consciousness, the highest forms of group and individual consciousness combined in the service of the Plan.

Group Ruler—Sun Veiling Uranus

The Sun, the hierarchical or group ruler, is associated with the Ray Two energies of love-wisdom. For the group level of Leo, the Sun veils Uranus, which is associated with the Ray Seven energy of ceremonial order, magic, and organization. When Uranus controls, we become the true observer in Leo, detached from the material side of life but utilizing it as we please. Our spiritual consciousness is capable of great expression and we can become dynamic leaders, pioneers in new fields of endeavor, and the magnetic center of a group.

Uranus relates Leo to Aquarius and Aries, where Uranus also rules on the group level (veiled by the Moon in Aquarius).

Exaltations, Falls, and Detriments

No planet falls in Leo and no planet is exalted in Leo, but the powers of both Uranus and Saturn are somewhat lessened, except in the case of advanced people who respond powerfully to the esoteric influence of Uranus.

Leo people, in their consciousness, are self-aware and therefore maintain control and remain uninfluenced. This fact will be increasingly understood as advanced Leo people make their appearance. They are distinguished by their personal freedom from outside control and their ability to rule their own lives; therefore, no planet is exalted and likewise no planet falls.

The power of the mind, symbolized by Uranus, is lessened, for it is not the mind that controls but the self, or soul, using and controlling the mind. Then, we are not conditioned by our surroundings or life events, but rule them with deliberation, bringing what we require out of our circumstances and environment. Therefore, Saturn, the Lord of Karma, has his power lessened in Leo.[35]

Meditation Seed Thoughts

The keywords and phrases associated with Leo are:

- The will to illumine
- Self-knowledge, self-perception, and intellectual positivity
- The will to rule and dominate
- Self-mastery and control of the personality, leading to control of groups

- Self-discipline leading to perfection
- Intellect governing ambition
- Individuality, individual-consciousness, true self-consciousness
- "I know"

When we achieve the objectives underlying these phrases, we can truthfully say: "I am That and That am I." We achieve the truth of this statement when, after initial conflict, we rule ourselves, gain higher consciousness, and prepare for fresh and universal expression in Aquarius, the polar opposite of Leo.

The key phrase for the personality level during a Leo cycle is: "And the Word said: Let other forms exist, I rule." This is the evolutionary urge we express in the earlier stages when we are conscious of our powers but before we put them to use for humanity. Leo cycles inspire the following trends of development:[36]

- The lower self, leading to the higher self, leading to the one self
- The hidden point, leading to the revealing point, leading to the relinquished point

Keynote on the Path: Leo seeks release in Scorpio

Virgo

"I am the Mother and the Child, I God, I matter am."

We can use the energies of Virgo when we feel the need for analytical intellect and hard work on the concrete plane and when we want the material world to serve the purposes of a greater cause. In Virgo, we tend to the forms, nurture them, and then release the hidden soul of all things.

Like Cancer, Virgo is a sign of service and responsiveness to the needs of others. However, Virgo, the sixth sign, represents involution and evolution, as depicted by its ancient symbol, the six-pointed star. Virgo carries these processes to the point of balance, expressed in the next sign, Libra.

The pairs of opposites—soul and body—are blended in Virgo and are of great importance to each other; mother-matter guards, cherishes and nurtures the hidden soul. Soul and substance each serves the other.

The integrated personality results from the functioning form nature, the developed and qualified expression of the third aspect of divinity, the active intelligent and nurturing principle of the universe.

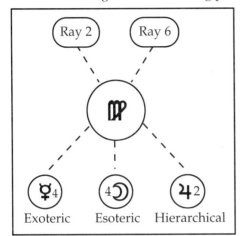

Ray 2   Ray 6

♍

☿₄   ₄☽   ♃₂

Exoteric   Esoteric   Hierarchical

Virgo symbolizes depths, darkness, quiet, and warmth. She represents the valley of deep experience where secrets are discovered and eventually brought to light—the place of slow, gentle, yet powerful crises and periodic developments that take place in the dark and yet which lead to light.

The Eve aspect of Virgo symbolizes the mental nature and our mind attracted by the lure of knowledge to be gained through the experience of incarnation. Eve took the apple of knowledge from the serpent of matter and started the long human undertaking of experiment, experience, and expression, which was initiated from the mental angle in our cycle of time. Isis stands for this same expression on the emotional or astral plane. Virgo, the cosmic mother, provides what we need for the mental, emotional, and physical expression of the hidden but ever present divinity.

Virgo stands for the "womb of time" wherein God's plan (the mystery and the secret of the ages) is slowly matured and, with pain and discomfort and through struggle and conflict, is brought into manifestation at the end of the appointed time.[37]

Virgo's Relationships With Rays and Constellations

Virgo forms a point in two constellational triangles that bring through the energies of Rays Two and Six from the Great Bear, Sirius, and the Pleiades (see the table on page 79). Virgo, Gemini, and Pisces form the Ray Two triangle of love-wisdom. Virgo, Sagittarius, and Pisces form the Ray Six triangle of idealism and devotion.

Through its planetary rulers, Virgo is associated with the energies of Rays Two and Four and is related to eight other signs of the zodiac that are associated with these rays: Aries, Gemini, Cancer, Leo, Scorpio,

Sagittarius, Aquarius, and Pisces. These eight signs, plus Virgo, produce an interrelated numerical synthesis of nine signs through which creative energies pour that produce changes needed in the progress of the soul and inspire the process of divine manifestation.

Ray Four relates Virgo to Aries and Cancer through Mercury and the Moon, harmonizing the cosmos and the individual through conflict, producing unity and beauty. Jupiter relates Virgo to Sagittarius and Pisces. This is an exoteric impact but produces a constant stimulation of the life of the indwelling soul. Sagittarius rules and conditions the activity of the lunar lords who build our bodies out of their own substance.

Virgo and its polar opposite Pisces make up the vertical arm of the mutable cross. Gemini and its polar opposite Sagittarius make up the horizontal arm. Indirectly, Virgo has access to the energies of the planets of the signs on the other arms of the mutable cross: Jupiter, Neptune, Pluto, Mercury, Venus, Earth, Jupiter, and Mars, which embody the energies of Rays Two, Six, One, Four, Five, Three, Two, and Six, respectively.

The fact that all four energies of the mutable cross, three of the fixed cross and two of the cardinal cross pour into Virgo indicates the importance of this "sign of reception." All nine energies are required to bring us to the point where the world and influence of the solar system have done their task in:[38]

- Preparing the vehicle of reception and protection, the personality

- Bringing into manifestation the group-conscious soul

Mercury, the Moon (veiling Vulcan), and Jupiter are the three rulers of Virgo. The Moon and Mercury indicate the activity of the lower and higher mind and are, therefore, related to Ray Three, active intelligence. Ray One influence through Vulcan, the planet veiled by the Moon, begins the process of will and control of the self-conscious person that was unfolded in Leo.

Personality Ruler—Mercury

Mercury, the exoteric or personality ruler, is associated with the Ray Four energies of harmony, beauty, and art. Mercury represents the versatile energy of the soul, the mediator between spirit and matter in Virgo, and also the result of the union between these two. Mercury, which is the esoteric ruler of Aries, achieves concrete manifestation through its exoteric rulership of Virgo. In Virgo, intelligence is brought down to earth and made productive.[39]

Mercury relates Virgo to Gemini, where Mercury also rules on the personality level.

Soul Ruler—Moon Veiling Vulcan

The Moon, the esoteric or soul ruler, is associated with the Ray Four energies of harmony, beauty, and art. The Moon, in the case of Virgo, veils Vulcan, an expression of Ray One energy. "The Moon rules the form and it is the will of God to manifest through the medium of form."[40] The energy of Vulcan is currently making its presence felt through the struggles going on upon Earth between people of selfish and ambitious will and people of goodwill who are trying to achieve the good of the whole.

Vulcan relates Virgo to Taurus, where Vulcan also rules on the soul level.

Group Ruler—Jupiter

Jupiter, the hierarchical or group ruler, is associated with the Ray Two energies of love-wisdom. Jupiter is the conveyor of expansive love. When humanity is fully awakened to spiritual and not simply material possibilities, the work of Jupiter will immediately intensify and this beneficent ruler will lead the human family into the ways of peace and progress.

Exaltations, Falls, and Detriments

Mercury is exalted in Virgo because mother-matter is ruled by her son, the "Son of Mind who is also the Son of God." The mother protects this son and is responsible for his development and acquired experience. In Virgo, Mercury reaches his full power, for Virgo is intelligence and the hidden Christ is wisdom or pure reason. Monique Pommier says, "In the exaltation of Mercury, Virgo disclosed the 'great work' of the mental nature—the alchemical work of transmutation and redemption."[41]

Mercury, the Messenger of the Gods, is the agent of the third aspect, active intelligence and adaptability, from one point of view and of the second aspect, love-wisdom, from another. Ruler of the antahkarana,

Mercury embodies both these aspects of the mental principle, the expression of the concrete and the abstract mind. The concrete mind was developed in the first solar system and the higher abstract intuitional mind, pure reason, is unfolding in this system.

Venus, pure love-wisdom, falls into generation in Virgo, occultly "descends to earth" and stands (as *The Secret Doctrine* has pointed out) for the gift of mind and of divinity, and thus for the descent of the Christ principle into generation or into matter. Virgo and Venus are two aspects of intelligence. The symbolism of the descent of spirit into the womb of the virgin mother is preserved for us in the astrological fact that Venus falls in this sign; esoterically, she disappears from view and vanishes into the darkness.

Neptune, which expresses Ray Six, devotion and idealism, is less powerful in Virgo because the drive of devotion and desire give place in Virgo to the natural processes of form production and the silent activity that is going on within the womb of time and space.

Jupiter, in spite of its latent power, is "lessened" in influence during the Virgo cycle of time because the second aspect of divinity, the Christ principle, descends into the depths and is temporarily veiled or hidden.[42]

Meditation Seed Thoughts

The keywords and phrases associated with Virgo are:

- Opportunity to bring the form more under soul influence

- Incentive behind the goal

- The cherishing of an idea

- Material life

- Gestation

- Desire for expression leading to spiritual desire

- The hidden light of God

- The mother of the Christ child

- "Christ in us, the hope of glory"

When we achieve the objectives underlying these phrases, we can truthfully say: "I am the mother and the child. I, God, I, matter am." This represents the unity of the dualities of self. We are both cause and effect, spirit and matter, God and human.

The key phrase for the personality level during a Virgo cycle is: "And the Word said: Let matter reign." This expression of materiality is the appropriate evolutionary urge before a higher stage of development. Virgo cycles inspire the following trends of development:[43]

- The germinating energy, leading to the creative force, leading to the Christ activity

- The Mother, leading to the Protector, leading to the Light

Keynote on the Path: Virgo hides the light which irradiates the world in Aquarius

Libra

"I choose the Way that leads between the two great lines of force."

Libra demonstrates the balance of spirit and matter, the self-direction and point of equilibrium between soul and form. It signifies the emergence of free choice. It represents consciousness of duality and the effort to balance the two.

Libra is a sign of balancing—of carefully weighing values and

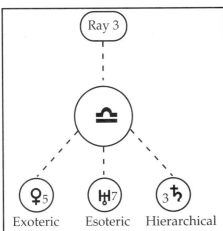

achieving the right equilibrium between the pairs of opposites. It is often the sign in which the first real vision of the Path appears and of the goal toward which we must ultimately direct our steps. Running between the pairs of opposites, the Path requires a sense of values and the power to rightly use the balancing, analytical faculty of our minds.

Libra helps by giving us, also, the intuitive perception we need to do this. Libra represents contemplation, the balance of soul and personality, equilibrium, and an interlude between two activities. Libra is the place of judgment, where decisions are made.

The Tibetan tells us that at the end of this century the influence of

Libra will steadily come into pronounced control and occupy a position of power in the planetary horoscope.[44]

Because of Libra's balancing quality, it is associated with relationships and sex. This balancing of the pairs of opposites and establishing of a point of equilibrium between the male and female principles is a mental drive and reaches its solution and unification on that level. Advanced Libran energy can influence men and women coming together in marriages to be less concerned about their individual rights and privileges from the contractual agreement and to be more focused on the energies they can generate as they move toward a common goal.

Opposites that can be balanced in Libra are:

Fickleness and variability	A secure position
Imbalance	Balance
Bias, prejudice	Justice, judgment
Dull stupidity	Enthusiastic wisdom
Untrue, showy outer form life	True correct expression
Intrigue	Straightforward conduct
Materialistic attitude	Spiritual attitude

Libra is considered to be a unique point in intermediate space where the twelve zodiacal energies meet and cross, called the "hub of the wheel."[45] Thus, it presides over a moment in a cycle of lives where a point of balance is reached and we can step up onto a higher turn of the spiral.

Libra's Relationships With Rays and Constellations

Libra forms a point in one constellational triangle that brings through the Ray Three energies of intelligent activity and adaptability from the Great Bear, Sirius, and the Pleiades (see the table on page 79). The other two constellations that form this triangle are Cancer and Capricorn.

Through its planetary rulers, Libra is associated with the energies of Rays Five, Seven, and Three. These ray energies relate Libra to other signs that have planetary rulers on Rays Five, Seven, and Three: Aries, Taurus, Gemini, Sagittarius, Capricorn, and Aquarius.

Libra and its polar opposite Aries make up the horizontal arm of the cardinal cross. Cancer and its polar opposite Capricorn make up the vertical arm. Indirectly, Libra has access to the energies of the planets of the signs on the other arms of the cardinal cross: Mars, Mercury, Uranus, Saturn, Venus, the Moon, and Neptune, which embody the energies of Rays Six, Four, Seven, Three, Five, Four, and Six, respectively.

Ray Three, Five, and Seven energies, which Libra has an abundance of, predispose Libra to concrete understanding, intelligent will, and knowledge, making Libra effective upon the physical plane and giving developed people in Libra the power to project inner spiritual purpose or intended will into physical expression. These rays would seem to give Libra an impersonal, intellectual quality, but this is mitigated by Rays Four and Six that come in through the cardinal cross. Also, in spite of its Ray Five energy, Venus is the planet of love and relationship, and Libra's energies seem to strongly follow that direction.

Venus, Uranus, and Saturn are the three rulers of Libra. We could affirm that "the love of Venus and the laws of Saturn support the Uranian drive to fashion something new and original out of preexistent materials."[46]

Libra, through Ray Three, is closely connected with the third aspect of divinity and is a major conditioning constellation where law, sex, and money are concerned. Law expresses itself as justice, sex is the relationship between the pairs of opposites, and money represents "concretized energy." The Tibetan tells us that if we study law, sex, and money as they express themselves today and as they can express themselves in the future, we can gain insight into physical human achievement and future spiritual expression, and that through a study of Libra, light upon the third aspect of active intelligence will come.[47]

Personality Ruler—Venus

Venus, the exoteric or personality ruler, is associated with the Ray Five energies of concrete knowledge and science. Venus rules in Taurus, Libra, and Capricorn, and is the source of the intelligent mind, acting through desire in the early stages or love in the later stages. In Libra, we can attain the point of equilibrium between material personal desire and intelligent spiritual love, for the two qualities of cosmic desire are brought to the fore in the consciousness in Libra and are balanced one against the other.[48]

Venus especially relates Libra to Taurus, where Venus also rules on the personality level.

Soul Ruler—Uranus

Uranus, the esoteric or soul ruler, is associated with the Ray Seven energies of ceremonial order, magic, and organization. Uranus is of particular importance in Libra for Ray Seven works through Uranus and embodies the principle of concretion and materializing what is in need of objective manifestation by bringing together spirit and matter. In Libra, Uranus evokes the will to rise above the fatalistic interplay of action and reaction to liberate us from our bondage to materiality. Uranus helps us weigh alternatives from a more objective standpoint.

Group Ruler—Saturn

Saturn, the group ruler, is associated with the Ray Three energies of active intelligence and adaptability. As one of the most potent of the four Lords of Karma, Saturn controls the experiences and processes of evolution, of which the path is built as we work out karma on a daily basis. Saturn compels us to face up to the past and learn from it and, in the present, find and use available opportunities to prepare for the future.

Exaltations, Falls, and Detriments

In Libra, Saturn is exalted because, at the point of balance, opportunity comes, bringing situations that make choice and determination inevitable. This choice has to be made intelligently and upon the physical plane, in the waking brain consciousness. Only now can the full purpose and work of Saturn for humanity reach a point of group usefulness, for only now has humanity reached a point of general and widespread intelligence that can make any choice a definite conscious act, entailing responsibility.[49] Hence the intense activity of Saturn as we enter into the Age of Aquarius, because humanity itself now is at this stage of choice. Through Saturn, Libra governs choice.

The power of Mars is lessened in Libra for Libra controls interlude, forcing the active energies of Mars to be temporarily quiescent.

The Sun's influence falls in Libra because neither the personality nor the soul dominates in Libra. Instead a balance is achieved and they esoterically "tune each other out." As the *Old Commentary* puts it, "a gentle oscillation now proceeds. No strident note is heard; no violent colouring of the life affects and no upsetting of the chariot of the soul."[50]

Meditation Seed Thoughts

The keywords and phrases associated with Libra are:

- The interlude between two activities; contemplation

- Balance and equilibrium

- Judgment

- Choice

- The dispensation of karmic law

When we achieve the objectives underlying these phrases, we can truthfully say: "I choose the Way that leads between the two great lines of force." This phrase releases the initiate from the power of the Lords of Karma. Upon achieving balance and equilibrium, we are freed from the imbalances of lower life.

The key phrase for the personality level during a Libra cycle is: "And the Word said: Let choice be made." Libra gives us many opportunities to choose during our evolution until we reach the point where we can accurately choose our way. Libra cycles inspire the following trends of development:[51]

- Unbalanced fiery passion, leading to the weighing of the opposites, leading to balance attained

- Human love, leading to devotion and aspiration, leading to understanding

Keynote on the Path: Libra relates the two in Gemini

Scorpio

"Warrior I am, and from the battle I emerge triumphant."

Scorpio is the sign of testing for individuals and humanity, where we learn how to overcome desire and bring the personality under the control of the soul. Scorpio's tests involve physical plane life, and our solutions involve the use of the reasoning mind. In Scorpio, we learn to work with the fundamental creative forces in the universe, which are often in the guise of sex or money.

Experience through the Scorpio cycle involves a confrontation with the past and the two factors of recapitulation and reorientation. The recapitulation of past events (and incarnations) involves memory, leading to reorientation as a consequence of memory.

Memory, an aspect of thought, coupled with imagination is a creative agent because thoughts are pre-material things. When we evolve to the point where we can use memory in a conscious and creative manner, we can then bring clarity to the struggles of humanity and, as a result, victorious accomplishment.

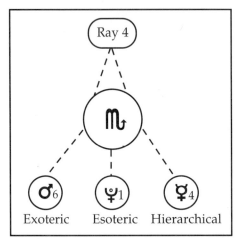

Exoteric   Esoteric   Hierarchical

In Scorpio, we must overcome all of the unsubdued characteristics of the lower self that are holding us back. In each life, we make progress, but the unconquered residue and ancient liabilities are numerous and potent. When finally we establish soul contact, then we have to contend with all the illusions we built during the process of forming our highly developed and powerful personalities. We enter a conflict that we somehow have to resolve; the glory of the soul has to eventually win out and supersede the glory of the personality, while still keeping the features of the personality life that we need to function in the world and do the work of improving the world.

Thus, we have tests. These tests are self-initiated; we put ourselves into an environment where trials and discipline are unavoidable and inevitable. As a result of our struggle and victory, we anchor ourselves upon the physical plane with such accuracy and clarity that there is no doubt of our spirituality, and then we learn the meaning of what it is to set an example to others.

In Scorpio, we finally demonstrate the creativity that works under inspiration and vision. We constructively attempt to express the beauty that all forms veil, revealing the underlying purpose that motivates all events and forms. We manifest all these aspects of basic change in purpose, interest, and orientation in Scorpio. Desire in Taurus becomes spiritual aspiration in Scorpio.

Scorpio's Relationships With Rays and Constellations

Scorpio forms a point of one constellational triangle that brings through the Ray Four energies of harmony, beauty, and art from the Great Bear, Sirius, and the Pleiades (see the table on page 79). The other two constellations that form this triangle are Taurus and Sagittarius.

Through its planetary rulers, Scorpio is associated with the energies of Rays Four, Six, and One. These ray energies relate Scorpio to other signs that have planetary rulers on Rays Four, Six, and One: Aries, Taurus, Gemini, Cancer, Virgo, Sagittarius, Aquarius, and Pisces. Cancer and Scorpio, which are related to Ray Six through Neptune and Mars, deal with the transformation of mass-consciousness into an inclusive consciousness. Scorpio and Pisces, which are related to Ray One through Pluto, impel the process of transformation.

Scorpio and its polar opposite Taurus make up the horizontal arm of the fixed cross. Aquarius and its polar opposite Leo make up the vertical arm. Indirectly, Scorpio has access to the energies of the planets of the signs on the other arms of the fixed cross: Venus, Vulcan, the Sun (veiling Jupiter, Neptune, and Uranus), Uranus, Jupiter, and Moon/ Uranus, which embody the energies of Rays Five, One, Two (Two, Six, and Seven), Seven, Two, and Four/Seven, respectively.

From this, only Ray Three of active intelligence and adaptability is missing. All the other rays pour through into our nature and environment. In Scorpio, where we learn to solve our problems in the light of the soul and the intuition and through the stimulation of the intellect, a focus of attention upon the material world is not desirable, thus Ray Three is "occultly deflected."

Through Scorpio's rulers, Mars and Mercury, two rays are brought into a potent controlling position in Scorpio; Ray Six of devotion and idealism and Ray Four of harmony through conflict, beauty, and art. Ray Six relates to the passing Piscean age and Ray Four relates to human development.

Mars, the planet associated with Ray Six, is especially active because, according to the Tibetan's system, it controls both the personality and soul life in Scorpio. Mercury, associated with Ray Four, is more active in the group life of humanity.

Scorpio's other ruler, Pluto, transmits the Ray One energy of major separations and death. In this connection, however, the death is brought about by the soul.[52]

Personality and Soul Ruler—Mars and Pluto

Mars is associated with the Ray Six energies of devotion and idealism and Pluto is associated with the Ray One energies of will and power. The warlike nature of Mars provides the testing that we experience in Scorpio, and gives us the fortitude by which we can pass through our ordeals triumphantly and emerge into the light of the soul. The lower prideful and separative nature of Mars becomes transformed into a total commitment to an ideal, which then controls the physical instinctual drive and confers spiritual power. We then demonstrate the strength, character, and quality we have developed through life's pilgrimage.

Pluto's influence in Scorpio provides energies that deal with death and rebirth and the transformation of our consciousness from a lower to a higher level—and not always without pain. We are all familiar with these liberating energies in our lives and in this era have actually experienced the transit of Pluto through the astrological sign of Scorpio. Much contemporary research has been done on this topic and many fine descriptions exist on the energies of Pluto in Scorpio.

Mars relates Scorpio to Aries, where Mars rules on the personality level. Pluto relates Scorpio to Pisces, where Pluto rules the soul level.

Group Ruler—Mercury

Mercury, the hierarchical or group ruler, is associated with the Ray Four energies of harmony through conflict, beauty, and art. Mercury helps develop group-consciousness in Scorpio so that the challenges we undergo in the Scorpio cycle transmute us for world service. Humanity itself, through Mercury's hierarchical placement in Scorpio, is the divine messenger to the world of form, bringing light and life to the other kingdoms of nature.

Exaltations, Falls, and Detriments

In Scorpio, Uranus is exalted, the power of Venus is lessened, and the Moon falls. Uranus characterizes the stage where occult knowledge takes the place of the mystic way of feeling, which leads to the transmutation of knowledge into wisdom. Uranus initiates a new order of life and conditions, producing an understanding of causes and the desire to change the old orientation into the new. This can be seen happening today in connection with humanity and with world processes. Carried forward to its logical conclusion, the influence of Uranus finally produces an unfolded spiritual consciousness, which is why Uranus is exalted and assumes a position of power and directed influence in Scorpio.

Venus, the intelligent mind, has its power lessened in Scorpio because the intellect, having been developed and used, must now be subordinated to a higher power of the soul, the spiritual intuition. The Moon in Scorpio stands for the personality. In our final victory during the Scorpio cycle, personality desire is sublimated into the light of the soul. Thus, the influence of the Moon fades out.

Meditation Seed Thoughts

The keywords and phrases associated with Scorpio are:

- Testing and trial
- Consummation of experience
- Dissipation of astral glamour
- Triumph on the physical plane
- Strength
- Illumination
- Triumph of the soul
- The path of discipleship

When we achieve the objectives underlying these phrases, we can truthfully say: "Warrior I am, and from the battle I emerge triumphant." The key phrase for the personality level during a Scorpio cycle is: "And the Word said: Let Maya flourish and deception rule." This portrays a necessary evolutionary step expressed by people before they are ready to face up to the battles that must ensue in the Scorpio cycle.

Both the soul and personality key phrases are significant and illuminating, depicting deception leading to the triumph of the soul, control by illusion leading to soul control, and conflict leading to peace. Scorpio cycles inspire the following trends of development:[53]

- Unity of selfishness, leading to conflict with duality, leading to higher unity

Keynote on the Path: Scorpio stages the release of Leo

Sagittarius

"I see the goal. I reach the goal and see another."

In the Sagittarius cycle, we orient ourselves to new objectives, focus toward higher goals, and unfold some basic and directing purpose. These purposes can range from simple desire and selfish human ambition to the objectives of higher spiritual evolutionary attainment.

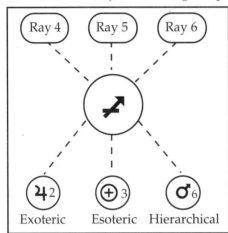

Exoteric   Esoteric   Hierarchical

In Sagittarius, the developed intellect becomes sensitive to the higher mental experience of intuitive perception. We are better able to solve problems and achieve rapid progress. We establish a balanced relationship between the personality and the soul and can function as either with equal facility at any moment we choose.

In Sagittarius, direction is one of the major themes: aiming at some specific goal. A sense of guidance is characteristic of an enlightened consciousness. When we can develop a faculty of sensitive direction, we can use it to align soul and personality activity with God's Plan, the ordered direction of God's thought in the universe. There is no true direction apart from thought; thought is power. To comprehend the direction of God's Plan, we first work with a phase in our own lives that is subject to our own mental direction.

From the standpoint of the polarized personality, we are identified with desire-mind in Sagittarius, which influences our lives with its focus upon personal satisfaction. In the later stages of personality development, the focus is upon control of desire by the mind, with the objective of intelligently using all our powers to satisfy desire, often manifesting in the ambition to attain some objective. Then, when we become aligned with the soul, our goal is the expression of love-wisdom, selflessly developed and consecrated to the good of the whole.

The hallmarks of Sagittarius are directed activity, the development of higher rational faculties, and the aspiration toward more and more inclusive states of consciousness, as well as a definitely expanded consciousness. Our purposefulness gives expression to an all-encompassing global outlook. In Sagittarius, we have a proclivity to plan for the future, but also an immediate urge to express our goals in concrete actions to materialize what we envision in practical terms. We can combine the best attributes of management and application to give substance to our spiritual objectives.

Sagittarius' Relationships With Rays and Constellations

Sagittarius forms a point of three constellational triangles that bring through the energies of Rays Four, Five, and Six from the Great Bear, Sirius, and the Pleiades (see the table on page 79). Sagittarius, Taurus, and Scorpio form the Ray Four triangle of harmony through conflict, beauty, and art. Sagittarius, Leo, and Aquarius form the Ray Five triangle of concrete knowledge and science. Sagittarius, Virgo, and Pisces form the Ray Six triangle of devotion and idealism.

Through its planetary rulers, Jupiter, Earth, and Mars, Sagittarius is associated with the energies of Rays Two, Three, and Six. These ray energies relate Sagittarius to other signs that have planetary rulers on Rays Two, Three, and Six: Aries, Gemini, Cancer, Leo, Virgo, Libra, Scorpio, Capricorn, Aquarius, and Pisces. Jupiter, in particular, relates Sagittarius to three of these constellations:

- Pisces, which exoterically indicates the final goal for humanity

- Aquarius, which esoterically indicates the purpose of all material evolution and the objective of all incarnating processes

- Virgo, which hierarchically indicates the purpose of the archetypal Cosmic Christ[54]

Sagittarius and its polar opposite Gemini make up the horizontal arm of the mutable cross. Virgo and its polar opposite Pisces make up the vertical arm. Indirectly, Sagittarius has access to the energies of the planets of the signs on the other arms of the mutable cross: Mercury, Venus, Earth, Moon/Vulcan, Jupiter, Neptune, and Pluto, which embody the energies of Rays Four, Five, Three, Four/One, Two, Six, and One, respectively.

What the Tibetan calls the "forces of conflict" are powerful in Sagittarius, especially when we decide to take control over our evolution. The Ray Four energies of harmony through conflict are active at the personality and the soul levels. The Ray One power, focused in Pluto, brings change, darkness, and death. To this intensity and potency of Pluto is added the forceful and dynamic energy of Mars. This brings us under the law of strife, based in this cycle of time upon Ray Six devotion to an ideal, high or low.

Sagittarius and Capricorn are related through the Ray Three energies of the Earth and Saturn, which give us a focused field of energy where we can achieve the consummation of initiation. As with its polar opposite Gemini, only the energy of Ray Seven is left out of the Sagittarian repertoire.

Three planets act as rulers, or transformers, for Sagittarian energy: Jupiter, the Earth, and Mars. Jupiter gives expansion, which the Earth diverts to practical considerations, and Mars provides the idealism that inspires the aspiration toward higher goals.

Personality Ruler—Jupiter

Jupiter, the exoteric or personality ruler of Sagittarius, is associated with the Ray Two energies of love-wisdom. In Sagittarius, Jupiter represents the expression of the personality life as it expands itself to fulfill desire and satisfy demand. The expansiveness of Jupiter then transmutes these energies into the higher values of generosity toward others and eventually into the attributes of love-wisdom.

Jupiter relates Sagittarius to Pisces and Leo, where Jupiter also rules on the personality level (veiled by the Sun in Leo).

Soul Ruler—Earth

Earth, the esoteric or soul ruler of Sagittarius, is associated with the Ray Three energies of active intelligence and adaptability. As esoteric ruler of Sagittarius, the Earth is a state of mind more than a place. It represents the impact of planetary experience which expands personal self-awareness into group-consciousness. In the Sagittarian cycle, we must realize that in our journey through life on the terrestrial plane we are following a path that leads upward. Above all, the Earth is a school for souls as we progress from grade to grade in order to learn the laws of life and to coordinate our activities in line with a growing sense of direction.

Earth is the hierarchical ruler of Gemini, the polar opposite of Sagittarius. The relationship of these two constellations with the Earth and the cosmic line of force produced through their opposition will eventually ensure that Earth becomes a sacred planet.

Group Ruler—Mars

Mars, the hierarchical or group ruler, is associated with the Ray Six energies of devotion and idealism. Mars produces great struggles, leading to great revelation, disclosing the nature of knowledge and the purpose of incarnation. In Sagittarius, Mars gives us the power to see the vision and to direct our course toward it. In Sagittarius, Mars also reveals the purpose of soul control over the lower kingdoms in nature, via the human center of energy.[55] This reinforces the concept of humanity's responsibility for the animal, plant, and mineral kingdoms.

Exaltations, Falls, and Detriments

No planet is exalted and no planet falls in Sagittarius and this is the same in Gemini, Sagittarius' polar opposite. Accordingly, Sagittarius is esoterically regarded as a sign of balance and of no extremes, meaning that in Sagittarius we have to tread a path between the pairs of opposites, uninfluenced by either the "power of exaltation or the potency of that which falls."[56] However, the power of Mercury is definitely lessened, insofar as it works with lower-higher mind dualism rather than with the energies of the universal or spiritual mind.

Meditation Seed Thoughts

The keywords and phrases associated with Sagittarius are:

- The returning arrow of the intuition; the shaft of the arrow of aspiration returns to the sender as the arrow of the intuition
- Human ambition leading to spiritual aspiration
- Freedom and one-pointedness—the bow and arrow
- Idealism, the power to see the vision and to direct our course toward it
- A clear shaft of light representing an intuitive and focused attitude
- Inspiration; soul inspires the personality
- Preparation for initiation

When we achieve the objectives underlying these phrases, we can truthfully say: "I see the goal. I reach the goal and see another." This represents visionary aspiration which is never satisfied because higher goals keep appearing, a result of the evolution and growth of the soul. The Sagittarian sense of direction and one-pointed focus enable this achievement.

The key phrase for the personality level during a Sagittarius cycle is: "And the Word said: Let food be sought." This phrase expresses the evolutionary desire and ambition to acquire the necessary sustenance for the personality life. Sagittarius cycles inspire the following trends of development:[57]

- Self-centeredness, leading to one-pointedness, leading to the directorship of people
- Experimental approach, leading to directed approach, leading to control of the gate

Keynote on the Path: Sagittarius, the disciple, becomes the Savior in Pisces

Capricorn

"Lost am I in light supernal, yet on that light I turn my back."

Ancient traditions tells us that the secret of evolution can only be understood when we understand (and experience) Capricorn.[58] Capricorn, an earth sign, represents immersion into materiality to the densest point of concrete manifestation of which we are capable until our ways of life are finally so crystallized that they can be easily

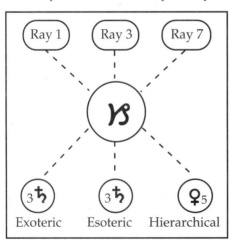

Exoteric   Esoteric   Hierarchical

shattered and destroyed. We then have the opportunity to rebuild these structures and initiate new cycles of effort.

Throughout this process, the energies of Capricorn leads us to struggle and fight with lower forces and undergo the strenuous conditions entailed by spiritual tests until the eventual triumph of spirit over matter.

Capricorn can represent

the best and the worst of what humanity is capable; it is a sign of extremes. We learn that further progress becomes impossible under outgrown old forms and that we have to give up what was once dear to us and build for the future.

In an ideal use of Capricorn influence, we learn to perfectly balance head and heart. Capricorn ultimately represents the crisis of initiation, signifying the emergence of the Christ-consciousness, which means higher synthesis and group-consciousness.

Capricorn, in the natural tenth house of the horoscope, is at the peak of the mountain, either of materiality or spirituality, or perhaps both if we show spiritual competence through the mastery and upgrading of the material world.

Seasonally, the sign of Capricorn is the turning point in the annual cycle when the apparent path of the Sun moves northward, thus bringing in more light to the highly populated northern hemisphere of Earth. Cancer, Capricorn's polar opposite, is the lightbearer in the southern hemisphere. Esoterically, Capricorn and Cancer both are considered gateways of light to humanity.

The Capricorn time of year is a time for reflection on what has occurred during the outgoing yearly cycle and a time to plan for the new year. For many, it is also a time for sociability during the first third of its cycle and then, after the first of the year, a time for going back into our work life with vigor and a desire for accomplishment. As often occurs, satiation leads to cutting back and renewed discipline.

Capricorn is a sign of conclusion and the inauguration of a new cycle of effort.

The Capricornian Avatar

From time to time, great beings incarnate on Earth to bring in more light and opportunity for new cycles of evolution so that we might elevate our consciousness to the degree necessary to carry forth the work for the development of human culture at a given time. These beings, who are messengers with a specific goal, are called avatars and they are known of, often as heroes in myth, throughout the history of all civilizations.

Once in the history of each scheme, an avatar from the constellation Capricorn appears on mental levels, the lowest level on which interplanetary deities can appear. This avatar arrives in the third round of the third chain, and leaves in the fifth round of the fourth chain. We are currently in the fourth round of the fourth chain, so this avatar is currently with us.

The products of much earlier kalpas or ages, these interplanetary avatars come in when systemic conditions are refined enough to permit their appearance. They are very advanced beings of an earlier solar cycle who again take the opportunity to finish (in an active sense and through physical manifestation) certain uncompleted work.[59]

Capricorn's Relationships With Rays and Constellations

Capricorn forms a point of three constellational triangles that bring through the energies of Rays One, Three, and Seven from the Great Bear, Sirius, and the Pleiades (see the table on page 79).

Capricorn, Aries, and Leo form the Ray One constellational triangle that brings through the Ray One energies of will and power. Capricorn, Cancer, and Libra form the Ray Three triangle of active intelligence and adaptability. Capricorn, Aries, and Cancer form the Ray Seven triangle of ceremonial order, magic, and organization.

Interestingly, these constellational triangles in which Capricorn is a participant also include those constellations that are on the other arms of the cardinal cross with Capricorn—in addition to Leo, which is a fixed-cross constellation of Ray One energy.

Through its planetary rulers, Saturn and Venus, Capricorn is associated with the energies of Rays Three and Five. These ray energies relate Capricorn to other signs that have planetary rulers on Rays Three and Five: Taurus, Gemini, Libra, and Sagittarius. These relationships give Capricorn direct access to the energies of Rays One, Three, Five, and Seven, with a double influence of Ray Three from a constellational triangle and from a planet.

Capricorn and its polar opposite Cancer make up the vertical arm of the cardinal cross. Aries and its polar opposite Libra make up the horizontal arm. Indirectly, Capricorn has access to the energies of the planets of the signs on the other arms of the cardinal cross: the Moon, Neptune, Mars, Mercury, Uranus, Venus, and Saturn, which embody the energies of Rays Four, Six, Six, Four, Seven, Five, and Three, respectively.

We also note that Saturn provides extra energy in its role as the hierarchical ruler of Libra, and Venus provides extra energy in its role as the exoteric ruler of Libra.

These two planets, Saturn and Venus, also act as rulers, or transformers, for Capricornian energy: Saturn rules the personality and soul levels and Venus rules the group level of human life.

Personality and Soul Ruler—Saturn

Saturn, the exoteric or personality ruler of Capricorn, is associated with the Ray Three energies of active intelligence and adaptability. Saturn is also the esoteric or soul ruler of Capricorn.

Saturn imposes structures and restrictions on life that immature people consider oppressive but that more advanced people use as the basis for a discipline that eventually leads to freedom. Saturn designs a structure and sets limits and boundaries within which we can build. As the Lord of Time, Saturn controls the process of healing as well as disintegration and decay.

Moses, the Lawgiver on Mount Sinai, represents Saturn in Capricorn, imposing the Law of Karma upon the people.[60]

Group Ruler—Venus

Venus, the hierarchical or group ruler of Capricorn, is associated with the Ray Five energies of concrete knowledge and science, or of the mind. These Venusian energies in the sign of Capricorn represent the merging of love and mind. This reveals to us the concept of the whole and the universal, which is the true expression of the spiritual life. In its highest aspect in Capricorn, Venus is the mental energy of humanity and establishes human group relationships on a local and global scale.

Exaltations, Falls, and Detriments

Mars is exalted in Capricorn, the power of the Moon is lessened, and Jupiter and Neptune both fall. Mars, the god of war and the producer of conflicts, triumphs in Capricorn during the early stages of human evolution. Materialism, the fight for the satisfaction of personal ambitions, and the conflict with higher spiritual tendencies goes steadily forward and Capricorn, the most material of all signs, is the battleground of the old established order and habits and the new and higher inclinations and tendencies.[61]

Monique Pommier says, "To consider the exaltation of Mars is to contemplate the human adventure as a slow exaltation of the instinctual impulses of animal-man into the courage of a responsible human being, then further on, the exaltation of man's striving-to-collaborate into the silent activity of a Master wielding the purpose of the time."[62]

As evolution proceeds, the power of the Moon, the symbol and ruler of form, grows less and less, and humanity steadily frees itself from the control of matter.

Jupiter, as the ruler of Pisces and Aquarius, falls in Capricorn. In its lowest aspect, Jupiter encourages us to fulfill our personal desires, and in its highest aspect, Jupiter is the outgoing expression of love and a desire for the good of the whole. In Capricorn, therefore, Jupiter reaches its lowest point of expression in the densest material aspect, and then, as love and selflessness triumph, this lowest aspect vanishes. It is to the "fall" of the highest aspect that the symbolism refers, and then later to the fall or disappearance of all that is base and low. Love is fallen and blinded when desire is rampant; desire vanishes when love triumphs.

Neptune falls in Capricorn for the same reasons. Neptune, the god of the waters, is esoterically related to Pisces. Both Neptune and Jupiter are exalted in Cancer wherein the desire for incarnation finds its fulfillment; the power of both is lessened in Virgo, wherein the first signs of the Christ-consciousness are felt; both fall in Capricorn, when the Christ life and consciousness come to full fruition.[63]

Meditation Seed Thoughts

The keywords and phrases associated with Capricorn are:

- Illumination governing intuition
- Soul-consciousness in later stages ("I realize" and "the secret of the hidden glory")
- Service, the incentive behind initiation
- Desire for liberation
- The light of life

When we achieve the objectives underlying these phrases, we can truthfully say: "Lost am I in light supernal, yet on that light I turn my back." We finally ascend the mountain top that was so hard to climb, and find ourselves in the rarefied upper atmosphere. Then, having reached illumination ourselves, we think of still-struggling humanity and how we can help illumine them as well. Thus, we turn our backs on the very light we have sought for so long and reach back to help the rest of humanity so that we can all progress together. We hold the gateway open for that "last weary pilgrim."

The key phrase for the personality level during a Capricorn cycle is: "Let ambition rule and let the door stand wide." This is the evolutionary urge experienced by people before spiritual ambition and a desire for liberation supersedes worldly ambition and, finally, a true sense of reality supersedes both. Capricorn cycles inspire the following trends of development:[64]

- The earthbound soul, leading to the one who crosses the water, leading to the conqueror of death

- Fluid, leading to initiated

Keynote on the Path: Capricorn consummates the work of Scorpio

Aquarius

"Water of life am I, poured forth for thirsty men."

Aquarius provides a unique opportunity for us to contact the energies that will be setting the pace for the planet during the next age. By aligning with these energies and working with them, we find our highest goals and objectives empowered by the forces of evolution.

The energies of Aquarius motivate us, on the personality level, to

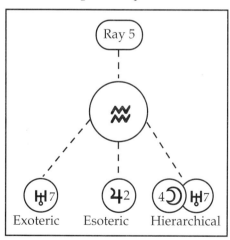

be group-conscious workers in activities in which we have a vested interest. This could represent loyalty to our jobs or to our families.

When we incorporate Aquarian energies on the soul level, we experience group life, assume responsibility within our communities, and then eventually expand our motivation to improving the world.

In Aquarius, an air sign, we can move and change activity, but are always vital and unique. With these energies, we put our individuality to work for the good of the whole. We know the exaltation of the soul and touch the sense of spiritual power that soul control gives us.

Interplay, action, and reaction are necessary for our growth and understanding and, as we begin to analyze these causes and effects, we start to understand the significance of the cycles they represent and learn how to master them.

In Aquarius, the self-conscious, self-aware life we experienced in its polar opposite, Leo, is supplemented by the group-consciousness of the humanitarian and the universalist. Then, as we progress in Aquarius, we contact the universal consciousness. We progressively recognize that knowledge brings responsibility and apply our Uranian inventiveness toward promoting our causes and the unity of humankind, perhaps through the linkage of science and religion.

Aquarius is of particular importance to us at this time because we are beginning to enter the Age of Aquarius, a cycle of approximately 2200 years. The beginning of a new cycle and the ending of the previous one, the Age of Pisces, are largely responsible for the accelerated changes we, and all the kingdoms of nature, are experiencing now. We are moving out of an age of idealism, devotion, and (often) fanaticism into an era of opportunity, illumination, and brotherhood, represented by Aquarius.

As the Sun moves into the Age of Aquarius, these energies gain momentum and increase their potency, effecting many changes in Earth life and in all of nature. These energies are particularly interpenetrating because Aquarius is an air sign, and is thus more subtle and pervasive.

Aquarius' Relationships With Rays and Constellations

Aquarius forms a point of one constellational triangle that brings through the Ray Five energies of concrete knowledge and science from the Great Bear, Sirius, and the Pleiades (see the table on page 79). The other two constellations that form this triangle are Leo and Sagittarius.

Through its planetary rulers, Aquarius is associated with the energies of Rays Seven, Two, and Four. These ray energies relate Aquarius to other signs that have planetary rulers on Rays Seven, Two, and Four: Aries, Gemini, Cancer, Leo, Virgo, Libra, Scorpio, and Pisces.

These rays determine the final stages of our progress as well as the initial stages, being more potent at the beginning of the involutionary path and the end of the evolutionary path than in the middle period.[65]

Ray Seven expresses spirit and matter upon the physical plane and relates them to each other, producing an efficient, functioning whole. Ray Two expresses the soul and spiritual consciousness, pouring out love and wisdom upon Earth. And Ray Four indicates the field of service and the mode of attaining the goal, which is that of struggle in order to reach harmony and truth, a particular attribute of the human kingdom.

Ray Seven is the focused differentiated energy of Ray One as it expresses the power to relate and manifest (by an act of will) both spirit and matter. It brings this about through the activity of Ray Three, expressing through humanity and combining with the energy of Rays Seven, Two, and Four released through the ruling planets. Ray Three expresses through Aquarius, reaching us through Uranus through the activity of Alcyone (one of the Pleiades).[66] There is, therefore, a double influence of Uranus, bringing in energies of both Ray Seven and Ray Three.

Aquarius and its polar opposite Leo make up the vertical arm of the fixed cross. Taurus and its polar opposite Scorpio make up the horizontal arm. In the cycle of consciousness expansion and initiation, Aquarius represents the culmination and synthesis of experience upon the fixed cross prior to moving on to the cardinal cross. Indirectly, Aquarius has access to the energies of the planets of the signs on the other arms of the fixed cross: the Sun (veiling Jupiter, Neptune, and Uranus), Venus, Vulcan, Mars, Pluto, and Mercury, which embody the energies of Rays Two (Two, Six, and Seven), Five, One, Six, One, and Four, respectively. Through its position on the fixed cross, Aquarius has access to all the energies of the seven rays except for Ray Three. However, since Earth is a Ray Three planet, we automatically have access to Ray Three in the Aquarian cycle.

Uranus and Jupiter transform Aquarian energies on the personality and soul levels. On the group or hierarchical level, the Moon rules, but veils Uranus, giving us an abundance of Uranian energy while we are in Aquarius. The rulers of Aquarius and their rays are of special interest:

- Uranus and Ray Seven provide the will to be and to know simultaneously on all planes of manifestation.

- Jupiter and Ray Two fuse the heart and mind, which is the subjective purpose of manifestation, brought about through Rays Three and Seven, as noted above.

- The Moon and Ray Four provide the will to be and to know plus the fusion of heart and mind, which is the result of the work carried forward by humanity under the influence of energy that produces harmony through conflict.

Personality Ruler—Uranus

Uranus, the exoteric or personality ruler of Aquarius, is associated with the Ray Seven energies of ceremonial order, magic, and organization. Uranus generates innate spontaneous activity, producing both natural and spiritual evolutionary development and the urge to better conditions. The Uranian side of Aquarius manifests in the production of scientific devices that have put us in touch with the ideas of others around the world. Uranus in Aquarius extends our base of awareness.

Soul Ruler—Jupiter

Jupiter, the esoteric or soul ruler of Aquarius, is associated with the Ray Two energies of love-wisdom. Jupiter gives fusion and promotes the ultimate achievement of synthesis. In Aquarius, Jupiter helps promote a concern with human rights and altruism. Aquarius, the sign of distribution, makes Jupiter's managerial talent more effective in a far-reaching way. Jupiter enlarges the sphere within which Aquarian energies can circulate. Together these influences show that we must be free (Aquarius) to grow (Jupiter), and that all growth leads, in turn, to greater freedom in cooperation with the guiding principles of the universe.[67]

Group Ruler—Moon Veiling Uranus

The Moon, the hierarchical or group ruler of Aquarius, is associated with the Ray Four energies of harmony through conflict, beauty, and art. The Moon veils Uranus in Aquarius, which is associated with the Ray Seven energies of ceremonial order, magic, and organization. The influence of Uranus is doubled since it also rules the personality level of Aquarius.

The Moon helps bring about the conditions that transform our instinct into intellect, but Uranus causes us to transfer our consciousness from intellectual perception to intuitive knowledge. Using the Uranian energies, we can learn to focus our will and develop into leaders who can bring about the changes and new conditions that help the soul of humanity express itself more freely.

Uranus relates Aquarius to Aries and Leo, where Uranus (veiled by the Sun in Leo) also rules on the group level.

Exaltations, Falls, and Detriments

No planet is exalted and no planet falls in Aquarius because Aquarian energy represents a point of balance. Aquarius is not affected by the pairs of opposites, but uses each polarity for spiritual ends. Thus, Aquarius stands free, distributing energy and life, symbolized by its two wavy lines.

The Sun's influence is lessened in Aquarius because everything achieved in Leo (the polar opposite of Aquarius) through the Sun's influence there is consummated in Aquarius. At this stage of activity, the light of the personality is dimmed by the light of the subjective Sun that influences the soul.

Meditation Seed Thoughts

The keywords and phrases associated with Aquarius are:

- Service of the personality transmuting into service of humanity

- Superficial activity changing into activity on behalf of Hierarchy

- Self-conscious living changing into sensitive humanitarian awareness

- "I go forth," representing inspiration, governing group-consciousness and service

When we achieve the objectives underlying these phrases, we can truthfully say: "Water of life am I, poured forth for thirsty men." During the Age of Aquarius, the words spoken will be: "I am the server, and I the dispenser am of living water."[68]

The key phrase for the personality level during an Aquarius cycle is: "And the Word said: Let desire in form be ruler." This is the evolutionary effect of desire becoming gained knowledge, and the knowledge of what is hidden at any stage upon the path of evolution relates us to Uranus.

Aquarius cycles inspire the following trends of development:[69]

- All things to all men, leading to dedication to the soul, leading to the server of all men

- The burden of the self, leading to the burden of humanity, leading to the burden of the world

Keynote on the Path: Aquarius releases Virgo from her load

Pisces

"I leave the Father's home and turning back, I save."

Pisces carries our development into the mental processes where we can merge our self-will with divine will, resulting in inspiration and the emergence of world saviorship. What we began in earlier cycles, we consummate and complete in Pisces.

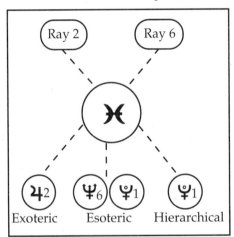

Pisces produces the fusion of soul and form, manifesting the perfected individual soul. The greater and the lesser polar opposites (human and God, microcosm and Macrocosm) are brought to destined expression and manifestation in Pisces, thus its symbol of two fishes linked together by a band. One fish stands for the soul and the other for the personality or form nature. Between them is the thread, or sutratma, the silver cord that keeps them bound throughout the cycle of manifested life.

In the first cycle of experience, the soul is in captivity to substance; it has come down into the prison house of matter and linked itself to form. We have the potencies and characteristics of the indwelling Christ, but they are not manifesting and are only latent possibilities during the phase in which we are still controlled by our form nature and by our environment. When the powers of the form are expressing themselves potently, the natural spiritual tendencies are inhibited (for Pisces is often a sign of inhibition and hindrances), thus the personality powers, particularly the emotional, are our obvious and visible qualities.

Later, the personality is brought into captivity by the soul, releasing us from the life of form. From the standpoint of the spirit, the soul itself is form, though far subtler than the personality. A dual renunciation occurs: the soul renounces the personality and later the spirit renounces the soul. This associates Pisces with will and sacrifice, for the act of redeeming matter releases its essence to a higher state of consciousness. World saviors are the manifested symbols of this process. Recognitions such as these contain the mainspring of the life of service.

Pisces energy is associated with service to humanity and ministering to its needs upon some level of consciousness. Thus the ancients prepared for the final sacrifice in Pisces. The life of service and the directed intention to serve constitutes a scientific mode of achieving release.

We must take care not to assume that Piscean energy is gentle and unassuming; in Pisces, under the influence of Pluto, we can find the power to further the ends of evolution through initially destroying old and useless social forms.

Pisces' Relationships With Rays and Constellations

Pisces forms a point of two constellational triangles that bring through the energies of Rays Two and Six from the Great Bear, Sirius, and the Pleiades (see the table on page 79). Pisces, Gemini, and Virgo form the Ray Two triangle of love-wisdom. Pisces, Virgo, and Sagittarius form the Ray Six triangle of devotion and idealism.

Through its planetary rulers, Pisces is associated with the energies of Rays Two, Six, and One. These ray energies relate Pisces to other signs that have planetary rulers on those rays: Taurus, Cancer, Leo, Virgo, Sagittarius, and Aquarius. The interplay of the dual potencies of these rays:

- Produces the duality of Pisces

- Brings about psychic sensitivity

- Causes the lure of the path of evolution

- Precipitates the process of transmutation and eventual escape through death

- Unfolds the significance, activity and beauty of death and the work of the destroyer[70]

Jupiter's Ray Two force relates soul and personality and brings the two together; this magnetic potency describes the activity of Pisces. Pisces and Taurus, through Pluto and Vulcan, are related to each other through Ray One, which transmutes desire into sacrifice and the individual will into the divine will.

Pisces and its polar opposite Virgo make up the vertical arm of the mutable cross. Gemini and its polar opposite Sagittarius make up the horizontal arm. In the cycle of consciousness-expansion and initiation, Pisces represents the culmination and synthesis of experience upon the mutable cross prior to moving on to the fixed cross. Indirectly, Pisces has access to the energies of the planets of the signs on the other arms of the mutable cross: Mercury, Moon/Vulcan, Jupiter, Venus, Earth, and Mars, which embody the energies of Rays Four, Four/One, Two, Five, Three, and Six, respectively. All the rays except Ray Seven manifest in Pisces.

Although the Tibetan assigns only Jupiter and Pluto as rulers in Pisces, Alan Leo and others suggest a Neptunian influence. The Tibetan explains that, in this regard, Alan Leo sensed and touched upon a mystery of initiation, where Neptune focuses the influence of Pisces as it concerns humanity as a whole and not just the individual;[71] this takes place when humanity achieves a certain state of evolution, which is happening now.

Personality Ruler—Jupiter

Jupiter, the exoteric or personality ruler of Pisces, is associated with the Ray Two energies of love-wisdom. In connection with a duality in every human being—those of head and heart, mind and love, and will and wisdom—the work of Jupiter is to develop both qualities of each duality and bring them into synthesis.

Jupiter relates Pisces to Sagittarius and Leo, where Jupiter (veiled by the Sun in Leo) also rules on the personality level.

Soul and Group Ruler—Neptune

Neptune's role of esoteric and group ruler of Pisces is to bring light and inspiration into the world to transform the consciousness of self into group-consciousness. Patrizia Noreli-Bachelet, a student of Sri Aurobindo, suggests that Neptune was not known as the co-ruler of Pisces during much of the Piscean age, which passed almost entirely under Jupiter's influence. She states that the "dark ages" were a result of Jupiter being no longer sufficient to express the sign Pisces, thus humanity was restricted and our spiritual experience became dogmatized. During the dark ages, Pisces/Jupiter represented the kingly or divine power of orthodox religion, the age of monarchies, and the expansion of exploration of the Earth as represented by the discovery of the new world. Then, when Neptune was discovered, people developed the need to experience the more subtle regions that science had relegated to superstition.[72]

Neptune relates Pisces to Cancer and Leo, where Neptune (veiled by the Sun in Leo) also rules on the soul level. Neptune rules on the group level in Cancer, as well.

Soul and Group Ruler—Pluto

Pluto, the esoteric or soul ruler of Pisces, is associated with the Ray One energies of will and power. Pluto is also the hierarchical or group ruler of Pisces. In Pisces, the energy of Pluto is transformative; we renounce all attachments and liberate our soul energy for service on a universal scale. Christ in Pisces exemplified the substitution of love for attachment.[73] The power of Pluto in Pisces shatters the materialist illusion of death and clears the way for the final transfiguration of the immortal spirit into the realm of light. Pluto delivers the spirit from the flesh, but does not annihilate consciousness.

According to the Tibetan in his writings on esoteric formulas: "Formula Six is sometimes called 'the word of death.' It negates the destructive effect of the death process which is going on all the time within the mechanism of the disciple or initiate. The death proceeds with its needed work, but it is not destructive in effect. This formula has never been given out before to disciples, but can now be known because the Piscean Age is one in which at last the power of physical death is definitely broken and the signature of the Resurrection is revealed."[74]

Exaltations, Falls, and Detriments

In Pisces, Venus is exalted, and the power of Mercury is lessened and finally falls. Venus is exalted through relationship to Gemini, where Venus is the esoteric ruler. Also, Venus is the Earth's alter ego, and thus closely related to the human kingdom.

The fishes in Pisces are bound together, a symbol of captivity of the soul in form before the experience upon the fixed cross. The twins in Gemini symbolize the same basic duality, but the experience of many changing incarnations has done its work and the band uniting the two fishes is dissolving, for part of the work of Pluto is to "cut the thread which binds the two opposing lives together." It is the task of Venus to "reunite the severed lives but with no binding thread."[75]

Therefore, Venus is exalted in Pisces and at the end of the greater cycle, the "Sons of God who are the Sons of Mind" are raised up into glory through experience and crucifixion because they have learned to love and truly reason.[76] In Monique Pommier's words, "The exaltation of Venus in Pisces illumined in Venus the grail stone of redemption, the sophianic jewel of sacrificial love, the saving force of beauty."[77]

The power of Mercury is lessened in Pisces and finally falls in Pisces, which means that, after we achieve a certain point in evolution, the power of the mind lessens and we come into a state of full soul-consciousness where we require no mediator but work directly with our emanating source. Thus, the illuminating aspects between soul and physical brain are no longer required.

Mercury illumines the mind and establishes relationship between the personality and the soul. Later, Mercury shifts to a still higher plane and no longer mediates between two different stages in consciousness but fuses life and consciousness itself, a very different matter, affecting higher understanding.[78]

Meditation Seed Thoughts

The keywords and phrases associated with Pisces are:

- Sensitivity to higher impression

- Renunciation or detachment

- Sacrifice and death

- Identification, governing liberation

- Sensation, mediumship, and fluidity, leading to world salvation and mediatorship

- Divine consciousness

- I and the Father are one

- "Father, not my will but Thine be done"

In Pisces, the soul and personality enter upon that process that will transmute:

- Lower nature into higher manifestation
- Lower psychical powers into the higher spiritual faculties:
  - Negativity into positive soul control
  - Mediumship into mediatorship
  - Clairvoyance into spiritual perception
  - Clairaudience into mental telepathy and finally inspiration
- Instinct into intellect
- Selfishness into divine selflessness
- Acquisitiveness into renunciation
- Self-preservation into selfless world service
- Self-pity into compassion, sympathy and divine understanding
- Spiritual and mental inhibition into soul expression and mental sensitivity
- Devotion to the needs of the self into developed devotion and response to the needs of humanity
- Attachment to environment and to personality conditions into detachment from form and ability to identify with the soul

When we achieve the objectives underlying these phrases, we can truthfully say: "I leave the Father's home and turning back, I save." The key phrase for the personality level during a Pisces cycle is: "And the Word said: Go forth into matter." This is the urge expressed by people during the earlier stages of evolution when it was necessary to develop the personality and live in the material world. Pisces cycles inspire the following trends of development:[79]

- Responsiveness to environment, leading to sensitivity to soul, leading to spiritual responsibility
- The medium, leading to the mediator, leading to the savior

Keynote on the Path: Pisces takes from all the signs

Chapter 7—
Solar and Planetary Energy

"The system will then be characterized by a 'blaze of refulgent glory,' and
by a radiation that will link it up with its cosmic centre, and thus effect the
liberation of the Son, and His return to the far distant source from whence
the primal impulse originated."—AAB[1]

Our Sun is a member of a constellation that the Tibetan teacher calls "The Seven Solar Systems of Which Ours is One." These seven solar systems comprise the centers in the body of a vast intelligence, and these centers work together to bring in the cosmic energies appropriate to that great Being and deflect other energies that are not needed. They then step these energies down, "modifying, qualifying, and adapting" them for all the lesser lives within their area of responsibility. This chain of energy flow goes on throughout the universe, with each level of life drawing upon and redistributing the energies. Universal mind permeates all of them.

The vast intelligence who embodies the seven solar systems is called the "One About Whom Naught May Be Said." This "One" is linked up astrologically with the Great Bear, Sirius, and the Pleiades, but the effect of their combined influence cannot as yet produce noticeable results upon humanity and the other kingdoms of nature.[2]

We are told that the focused energies of the six other systems in the seven solar systems reach our own solar system via Taurus, Scorpio, and Mars, but that the objective in evolution and basic purpose of this energy configuration cannot be revealed to us until we surpass the fifth initiation (the level of master). However, the configuration involving Taurus, Scorpio, and Mars is concerned with the higher octaves of the problem of desire and its transmutation into spiritual will and divine purpose. These entities are closely connected to Ray Four energy of harmony through conflict and have a special relationship to humanity, the fourth kingdom of nature on Earth.[3]

The seven solar systems correspond to the seven sacred planets in our own solar system, and the seven human chakras correspond on a much lesser scale to these greater centers.

The Sun

"...Unveil to us the face of the true spiritual sun,
Hidden by a disk of golden light,
That we may know the truth and do our whole duty
As we journey to Thy sacred feet."—Gayatri Mantram[4]

The Sun has long been thought of as the Father in Heaven as it is He who brings life. It is He who gives us light. It is He who crosses the sky daily, radiating us with warmth and making things grow. In ancient mythology, solar religions gradually took hold as we became crop growers rather than hunters and gatherers. We staged ceremonies of propitiation to ensure that the Sun would come back after dropping down over the horizon in the dead of winter. We feared eclipses, imagining large wolves and other creatures devouring the Sun.

Our calendars were measured in solar cycles and our astrology is based on the equinotical and solsticial points, the cardinal points of the seasons when the length of the days and the evenings are the same and when the Sun shines for the longest and the shortest times of the year. This is the whole foundation of tropical astrology, emphasizing the fact that our lives and much of our consciousness are based on the rhythms of the seasons within the realm of "He within whom we live and move and have our being."

The Sun is the mode of enterprise and the vehicle of expression for a great Life, called our Solar Logos. His purpose, which he achieves on indescribable cosmic levels, is:[5]

- Gaining experience
- Making contact
- Developing full self-knowledge
- Achieving full mastery or control
- Attaining "manhood" cosmically
- Expanding his consciousness

Our solar system is a system of love-wisdom, and these energies are manifested through the heart center. Accordingly, the Sun is very possibly a heart center of a greater system and Jupiter, the planet of love-wisdom, is most likely the heart center of our solar system. We will keep this in mind as we work with energies because our focus should always come from the heart. This is also our safeguard, inasmuch as good, heartfelt intentions evoke a certain amount of protection by the soul. There are two primary types of solar energies:[6]

- Pranic energies, emanating from the physical Sun, producing physical and vital effects upon us

- Soul energies, emanating from the "Heart of the Sun," sweeping through the planets in seven great streams, and producing the sensitivity that we call awareness

The "Heart of the Sun," as referred to by the Tibetan, is not the heart center of the Sun. Instead it represents the soul of the Sun, whereas the physical Sun represents the body and the "Central Spiritual Sun" represents the monad or spirit of this great triple being.

From the love-wisdom ray of the Sun, seven subrays of energy radiate. These subrays correspond to the seven major rays and produce the seven types of souls, giving us seven fields of expression and seven grades of consciousness. As we come under the influence of our soul ray, we then come under the influence of one of the seven solar systems and one of the seven sacred planets.[7] We note that:

- The Sun is exalted in Aries.

- The Sun acts on the exoteric, esoteric, and hierarchical levels with energies from Leo, where Jupiter represents the exoteric personality level (or the physical Sun), Neptune represents the esoteric soul level (the "Heart of the Sun"), and Uranus represents the hierarchical group level (the "Central Spiritual Sun").

Keynotes: Vitality, creativity, life force.

The Planets

"The goal for the evolution of man is group consciousness, as exemplified by a planetary Logos. The goal for the planetary Logos is God consciousness, as exemplified by the solar Logos."—AAB[8]

Seven planets were known to ancient humanity, who observed their motions in the sky against the backdrop of "fixed" stars. In mythology, the planets were the lesser gods who fought, loved, argued, and cooperated amongst themselves and who brought humanity various forms of knowledge and wisdom. These planetary lords, with their variety of characteristics and qualities as perceived by humanity, influenced the nuances of our culture.

Today, these planetary archetypes still influence us through these great thoughtforms of how men and women should behave. Because we all have the same expectations to a large degree, the thoughtforms of antiquity still persist in large measure. Certain planets are said to "rule" certain characteristics of life, which is where we get the concept of planetary rulers. These expectations largely hold true on our personality level, but as we evolve and begin to link in with the higher archetypes of the soul, the influence of the traditional planetary rulers is more elective and we control our own lives to a large degree.

In the ageless wisdom teachings, there are seven sacred planets— those whose Logoi have reached a high level of development and attained five of the major cosmic initiations.[9] These sacred planets are: Vulcan, Mercury, Venus, Jupiter, Saturn, Uranus, and Neptune. Earth, Mars, and Pluto are not sacred planets, nor are the Moon and the Sun considered sacred in their roles of veiling other hidden planets (though the hidden planets that they veil are sacred).

Logoi of sacred planets can transcend the knowledge, reactions, and responses that are purely of this solar system; they are conscious of and can respond to the life of Sirius. They are also in the first stages of being able to respond consciously to the vibratory influences of the Pleiades. Even though the Pleiades are regarded as embodying the matter aspect in manifestation, they are in reality the expression of the principle of life that we associate with vitality, or prana in all its aspects.

Logoi of non-sacred planets are becoming inclusive in their consciousness to everything within the boundaries of our solar system and are establishing relations with the Solar Logos.[10]

The influences of a sacred planet affect the fusion of soul and body, consciousness and form, whereas the influences of a non-sacred planet affect the life of the personality.

"Eventually, there will be twelve sacred planets, corresponding to the twelve constellations."[11] We must also remember that there are several undiscovered planets that are producing pulls and shifts and complicating our understanding still further.[12]

Planetary influences indicate the trend of circumstances in our outer life—our personality destiny. They condition and control people who have no conscious soul experience. The moment that we become aware of our soul and start taking charge of our destiny, the influence of the energies flowing through the planets lessens and the influence of the more subtle energies of the solar system and the twelve zodiacal constellations increases.[13] However, planetary configurations play an important role in helping us receive energies to elevate human consciousness, especially at the times of the full moon when the Sun, Moon, and Earth are aligned.

The outer planets, Uranus, Neptune, and Pluto, have a much stronger affect on soul and group life than individual personality life. Humanity today is rapidly responding to these higher spiritual influences and we can look for the discovery of increasingly subtle forces.

Planetary Triangles

As we discuss in Chapter 9, "Timing, Relationships, and Karmic Opportunity," the configuration of the triangle represents aspects of the three major energies in the universe, relates to spirit and synthesis, and is an expression of a fixed consciousness, focused in reality. This archetypal structure plays a significant part in all symbolism and is important in our investigation of the content of the universal mind.

Great interlocking triangles of force exist between the planets, and especially the seven sacred planets. A knowledge of these lines of force will assist us when the time comes that we have learned enough to cast the horoscope of Earth. The Tibetan teacher tells us that we will find that Earth's response to these lines of force will become known to be more significant than the influence of the zodiacal constellations upon the human being. This is because the planetary spirits have largely transcended the influence of the twelve constellations and are responding more to the higher vibrations of the Great Bear, Sirius, and the Pleiades. This is in correspondence to what the Tibetan has always said about initiates being able to offset the influence of the planets and that, in their lives, predictions of their activities and circumstances are no longer possible. The soul dominates, in the case of initiates and planets; it is their choice as to what vibrations they respond to.[14]

The seven Planetary Logoi who are in charge of the planets in our solar system are the seven centers in the body of the Solar Logos, bearing to him a relationship similar to that borne by the masters and their affiliated groups to a particular Planetary Logos. Kundalini in the solar system vivifies these centers and, at this stage of development, certain planetary centers are more closely allied than others. Following are some of the important planetary triangular configurations that the Tibetan specifically points out to us for our study:

- **Triangle of Saturn, Mercury, and Uranus**: This triangle relates to the evolution and destination of the human family and, after a certain stage of evolution, provides more specific energies to develop self- and spiritual-consciousness. These are the destination planets of two major triangular configurations of energy coming from the Great Bear, Sirius, and the Pleiades and through nine constellations in total; these configurations are depicted in two diagrams under "Triangles / Trines" in Chapter 9.

- **Triangle of Venus, Earth, and Saturn**: This triangle is currently undergoing vivification through the action of kundalini, increasing the vibratory capacity of the centers of the Solar Logos, which are slowly becoming fourth-dimensional. Venus corresponds to the heart center and Saturn corresponds to the throat center of the Solar Logos.[15] We are not told which center Earth corresponds to.

- **Triangle of Venus, Jupiter, and Saturn**: Three of the sacred planets are the home of the three major rays, the embodied forms of the three logoic aspects or principles. Other planets embody the four minor rays. Venus, Jupiter, and Saturn might be considered the vehicles of the three super-principles at this time.

- **Triangle of Earth, Mercury, and Mars**: In connection with the Planetary Logos of Earth, the three etheric planetary bodies of our chain, Earth, Mercury, and Mars, form an important triangle.

- **Triangle of the Sun, the Moon, and Neptune**: This esoteric triangle of force affects us in Leo and expresses Rays Two, Four, and Six; where these three are dominantly active, there is an "inner alignment and attitude which forces open the Door into the Holy Place." Neptune, through Ray Six, governs the astral plane of desire. When Neptune is active in Leo, we can transmute emotion-desire into love-aspiration and orient ourselves to the soul. This orientation is brought about by sublimating the influence of the Moon, the symbol of the form nature, and emphasizing the Sun, or will aspect.

- **Triangle of Vulcan, Neptune, and Uranus**: Vulcan, Neptune, and Uranus determine or condition physical, astral, and mental natures, creating the personality and forming a triangle of immense creative potency.

- **Triangle of Earth, Mars, and Pluto**:[16] These non-sacred planets indicates a relation and a possibility which can impel us onward in our evolution.

- **Triangle of Mars, Mercury and Uranus**: This triangle guides the work of Ray One energy from the divine prototype in the Great Bear, which is transmuted through Aries and the Planetary Logos of Ray One.

- **Triangle of Neptune, Venus, and Jupiter**: At the second initiation, the candidate comes under the influence of three planets—Neptune, Venus, and Jupiter. This triangle stimulates the activity of the solar plexus, heart, and throat centers.

- **Triangle of Saturn, Neptune, and Uranus**: Saturn, Neptune, and Uranus are considered to be the three synthesizing schemes and the focal point for the transmission of cosmic manas (mind) to all the seven sacred planets. Sirius influences our entire system psychically via these three synthesizers.[17]

- **Triangle of Sun, Uranus, and Neptune**: Conscious, integrated people can function with full occult knowledge and also with mystical perception when the influences focused through the Sun, Uranus, and Neptune are carried forward adequately in their lives.

The Process of Veiling

In his book, *Esoteric Astrology*, the Tibetan introduces a very mysterious process called "veiling" where the Sun and the Moon veil certain planets and are the "exoteric symbols for certain esoteric forces." He states that, at present, many of us have not developed the sensitivity to receive energies from Vulcan, Neptune, and Uranus, all sacred planets, embodying Rays One, Six, and Seven, respectively.[18] These planets "determine or condition the physical, astral and mental natures, thus creating the personality. They form a triangle of immense creative potency."[19] As evolution proceeds, these planets will not be veiled.[20]

The Sun is a star and not a planet, therefore, when it is listed among the planets, it is simply because it stands for or veils a hidden planet.[21] Nor is the Moon a planet. Whenever the Moon veils a planet, the Moon itself still influences us from the personality angle and also influences mass humanity, but the planet that is veiled influences the soul or spiritual level of those who can respond to its vibrations.

Following is a summary of veilings mentioned by the Tibetan, followed by the specific references:

Ref.	Veiled	Veiler	Constellation	Level of Veiling
1.	Neptune	Moon	Cancer	exoteric
2.	Vulcan	Sun	Cardinal Cross	—
3.	Neptune	Sun	Leo	esoteric
4.	Uranus	Sun	Leo	hierarchical
5.	Vulcan	Moon	Virgo	esoteric
6.	Uranus	Moon	Aquarius	hierarchical
7.	Vulcan	Moon	Taurus	exaltation
8.	Jupiter	Sun	Leo	exoteric

1. The Moon veils Neptune as the exoteric ruler in Cancer. The Moon's rulership represents the form nature which is dominant in the longest stage of human unfoldment. When Neptune takes over, we are exposed to emotional impacts from humanity and, thus, need a higher level of development in order to interpret them accurately and handle them constructively.[22]

2. The Sun is spoken of as veiling Vulcan as it transmits the Cardinal Cross energies of the Great Bear, Aries, and Libra.[23] In a later reference during a discussion of Taurus, the Tibetan says that Vulcan is a substitute for the Sun: "The light from the eye of the Bull which with ever increasing radiance has guided the struggling soul must give place eventually to the light of the Sun, for Vulcan is a substitute for the Sun: it is spoken of sometimes as being veiled by the Sun and at others it stands for the Sun itself."[24]

3/4. In the case of Leo, the Sun focuses its energies through Neptune and Uranus. Neptune is associated with the "Heart of the Sun" and Uranus with the "Central Spiritual Sun."[25] The Heart of the Sun represents the soul of the Sun, whereas the Central Spiritual Sun represents the spirit or monad of the Sun.

5. In Virgo, the Moon, in its own right of antiquity and of ancient thoughtform control, and also as veiling both Vulcan and Neptune, connects Virgo forces with those of Taurus, Cancer, and Aquarius. This relates the form-building aspect with the consciousness aspect.[26] As indicated on page 123, Virgo represents the form-building aspect of the Moon, which is the energy of Vulcan.

6. The Moon veils Uranus in Aquarius. This refers to the hierarchical rulership; that combined with Uranus ruling Aquarius exoterically gives us a double influence of Uranus in Aquarius. The Moon inclines us to create the conditions that lead to the transformation of instinct into intellect, and Uranus causes "the great transference in the human consciousness from intellectual perception to intuitive knowledge."[27]

7. The Tibetan speaks of the Moon veiling Vulcan on the Fixed Cross, which encompasses the signs of Aquarius, Leo, Taurus, and Scorpio. Aquarius is the only sign of these which has the Moon as ruler, and that is for the hierarchical level. But since Uranus is already given as the hierarchical ruler of Aquarius, this probably means that the influence of the Moon veiling Vulcan refers to Taurus, where the Moon is exalted; in this reference, Vulcan is specifically stated to be the hidden planet.[28] Accordingly, for a complete picture of the energies flowing through the crosses, we must also consider the planets that are exalted in the signs comprising the particular cross.

8. Although the Tibetan does not specifically state that Jupiter is veiled by the Sun on the exoteric level of Leo, we do know that the Sun is standing in for a planet and the following references strongly indicate that it is Jupiter. Conversely, the Tibetan definitely treats Jupiter differently from the other hidden planets, so its relationship with the Sun may be other than a veiling one. The references are: "Second ray influences and potencies are abidingly present and pour into our planetary sphere and life, via the Sun (veiling a hidden planet) and Jupiter. These sweep the forces of Leo, Sagittarius, Pisces, Aquarius and Virgo into and through our entire planet and all its kingdoms in nature."[29]

    These five constellations have the rulership of Jupiter in common, as follows:

- Jupiter is the exoteric ruler of Sagittarius and Pisces
- Jupiter is the esoteric ruler of Aquarius.
- Jupiter is the hierarchical ruler of Virgo.
- It seems that the Sun veils Jupiter in Leo as the exoteric ruler.

also:

> "In connection with the Mutable Cross, the rays of the Sun in a threefold form (combining the lowest energies of the threefold Sun) pour into and through the man, via Jupiter. Jupiter is the agent of the second ray which the Sun expresses—cosmically and systemically."[30]

Implications for Full Moon Meditation Work

What ramifications does the process of veiling hold for full moon (and new moon) meditations? In relation to the horoscope of an individual, the Tibetan states the following:

"If he will study the 'fluid area' where the planets, veiled by the Sun and Moon, come into play and will realise that he must decide (from a study of the chart of the subject and any knowledge he may have) what is the point in evolution reached and which of the three veiled planets [Vulcan, Neptune, and Uranus] is the ruler, he will get much intuitive understanding. He will find himself able to throw much light upon the problem of the probationary disciple when considering the exoteric rulers and upon the problems of disciples when dealing with the esoteric rulers."[31]

Accordingly, we learn that, in the chart of an individual, the Sun and the Moon veil either Vulcan, Neptune, or Uranus, and that, depending on the level of development of the individual, we can substitute the veiled planet most commensurate with the individual's development. Note that Jupiter (which might veil the Sun on the exoteric level of Leo) is not mentioned here, which implies that Jupiter's relationship with the Sun is special in some other sense than that of veiling.

Applying this to the chart of the time of the full moon, what can we infer? It seems that we can substitute one of the veiled planets for both the Sun and the Moon. (Interestingly enough, Vulcan, Neptune, and Uranus all veil both the Sun and the Moon, when we consider all the constellations.) Should we use Vulcan when we are attempting to invoke energies for mass humanity, Neptune for advanced humanity, and Uranus for initiated humanity and Hierarchy itself? Or should we approach this by drawing in Vulcan energies for the personality, Neptune for the soul, and Uranus for the spirit levels of all humanity? Or both? Or can we only access the veiled energies of Vulcan, Neptune, and Uranus whenever we are under the influence of constellations that contain their energies as veiled by the Sun and the Moon? We need to meditate upon these questions and develop the sensitivity and discrimination that will enable us to find the answers for ourselves.

In conclusion, here are two minor hints that might add a little more light on the veiling process:[32]

"At the third initiation, the Moon (veiling a hidden planet) and Mars bring about a fearful conflict, but at the end the man is released from personality control."

"All this time the energy of the sun (veiling a sacred planet, hitherto unknown) is steadily and persistently reaching the man via the solar angel."

Vulcan

Vulcan is not really known to science or humanity and is said to be a hidden planet close to the Sun in an astrological chart. The Sun and the Moon also veil Vulcan, which means that we might be able to substitute Vulcan's energies for those of the Sun and the Moon under special circumstances.

In a particular sense, the energy which streams from Vulcan is fundamentally the strength and potency which sets the world evolutionary process in motion.[33] Vulcan embodies the energy of Ray One,[34] that force which initiates or begins and that which also destroys, bringing about the death of the form in order that the soul may be set free.

Vulcan, the forger of metals, works in the densest, most concrete expression of the natural world, from the human angle. He goes down into the depths to find the material upon which to use his innate art to fashion that which is beautiful and useful. He stands for the soul, the individual, inner, spiritual man or woman, implementing the soul's task upon the wheel of life. Hercules upon the fixed cross had to fashion his own weapons before he succeeded in the struggle, which refers to the art of Vulcan who rules the inner person and guides our fashioning.[35]

Vulcan stands for the glorification and upliftment of matter through its purification and detachment.[36] As the god of the forge who created fine and beautiful artifacts, he symbolizes our ability to produce the instruments we need for constructive living.[37] Vulcan fashions his instruments of expression in the depths, grasping the divine purpose and bending the will of the little self to that of the greater Self.[38]

Vulcan reveals what is deeply hidden and brings it up into the light. Whenever we need crystallizing or destroying forces that reach into the very depths to ferret out forms that have outlived their usefulness, we can invoke Vulcan. Vulcan also plumbs the depths of aloneness until we can renounce desire and see the Plan as the only desirable objective.

Vulcan helps condition and build the personality from the physical, astral, and mental natures, thus forming a triangle of immense creative potency. Vulcan stimulates the flow of creative energy from the sacral center to the throat center because Vulcan governs a center in the front of the throat related to the parathyroids. This center acts as a mediator between the higher and lower creative centers and falls into disuse once the transformation to the throat center has been made.[39]

Vulcan brings in the endurance aspect of the will-to-be, which helps us persevere and achieve tangible results, carrying us through the processes of evolution. These processes necessitate persistence, endurance, and continuity of effort, all characteristics imparted or stimulated by energies pouring from Vulcan.[40] These are Ray One attributes, the reverse side of which are death or the activity of the destroyer aspect.

"Vulcan controls the anvil-like processes of time and strikes the blow which shapes the metal into that which is desired, and this is true today as never before." He is forging the way for the coming avatar who will at the right moment come forth, embodying the will of God which is the divine will-to-good, peace through understanding, and right relations between people and between nations.[41]

Vulcan rules nations at a certain stage of embryonic soul expression and governs their activities, fashioning instruments of war when war and conflict are the only means by which liberation can come.[42]

We note that:

- Vulcan is never an exoteric ruler, according to the Tibetan.[43]

- Vulcan acts on the esoteric level with energies from Taurus and Virgo (where Vulcan is veiled by the Moon).

- Vulcan acts on the hierarchical level with energies from Taurus.

Keynotes: Endurance, persistence, rhythmic effort.

Mercury

The Tibetan calls Mercury the star of the intuition and transmuted manas. In mythology, Mercury is known as the Messenger of the Gods, with winged heels to speed him upon his way. The winged feet, symbolizing aspiration, represent the wings of the soul upon which we travel as messengers of the gods. The wings also represent the fluidic, restless mind which becomes developed and begins its integrating control of the personality. According to the *Old Commentary*, a manuscript in the archives of the Hierarchy that the Tibetan often quotes from, Mercury the messenger brings bright gifts to man from the Pleiades, Capricorn, and Sirius—the Pleiades providing the light to shine upon the birth-giving mountain top of Capricorn, and Sirius giving accolades of love.[44]

In its role as messenger, Mercury (along with Saturn and Uranus) is part of two great triangles that transmit energies from the Great Bear, Pleiades, and Sirius. One triangle filters energies from Leo, Capricorn, and Pisces; through Saturn, Mercury, and Uranus; and eventually to the head, ajna, and heart centers of Earth and then of humanity. The other triangle filters energies from three pairs of polar opposites and the more spiritually advanced members of humanity are able to respond to them. Mercury's direct line of energy comes from the Pleiades and is then distributed through Gemini/Sagittarius. (See "Triangles / Trines" in Chapter 9.)

Mercury, the ruler of the antahkarana, as a "divine Intermediary, carries messages between the poles with speed and light."[45] This mediation falls into stages: the concrete mind as mediator within the personality, the illumined mind relating soul and personality, and the abstract mind relating soul and spirit. As the illuminating principle, Mercury helps us escape from illusion and enter into the light to become what we essentially are. In its messenger role, Mercury helps us find points of contact with others and acts as the mediating interpreter between the higher worlds and the three lower kingdoms in nature (animal, vegetable, and mineral).[46]

Mercury, a Ray Four planet, spreads the light of the soul—intuitive and illuminating—upon world situations to interpret for us, through our own illumined minds, the significance of events and to relate the old and the new, the past and the future through the light of the present. "Hence, the subjective usefulness of the present general trend towards meditation processes which bring about the capacity to be 'impressed from on high' (technically understood) and to be illumined by the light of the soul."[47]

Concerning illumination, the Tibetan adds: "...as far as the consciousness of the race is concerned, Mercury is becoming increasingly active. A steady illumination is taking place and light is being thrown on all problems—light on government and politics through experiments and the study of great and basic ideologies; light on the material nature of the world through all the many branches of science; light on humanity itself through education, philosophy and psychology. This light is spreading down to the very darkest places in our planet and its many forms of life."[48]

Mercury works upon the mutable cross and is concerned with the activities of humanity. Mercury indicates that the line of least resistance for humanity is harmony through conflict, for Mercury expresses Ray Four energy, which is buddhic and intuitional, to humanity, which is the fourth creative hierarchy.[49] This messenger in his true character is able to "comprehend extremes and relate them divinely to each other."[50] He helps us interpret experience, develop intuition, and to become aware of the divine plan.

We note that:

- Mercury is exalted in Virgo.

- Mercury acts on the exoteric level with energies from Gemini and Virgo.

- Mercury acts on the esoteric level with energies from Aries.

- Mercury acts on the hierarchical level with energies from Scorpio.

Keynotes: Intuition, conscious mind, communication, thinking, attitudes.

Venus

Venus brings through the Ray Five energies of mind and egoic-consciousness, representing the transmutation of desire to love-wisdom, and establishing relationships between people and nations. Venus reveals the nature of Ray Two, which is consciousness or intelligent love, and expresses the basic energy of Ray Three, active intelligence, in its aspect of intelligent love.[51] We can best "take advantage of the Venusian influence to use the mind as the reflector of soul purpose"[52]

At first, Venus stimulates desire and awakens the sense of duality. Venus has long been associated with the polarity between man and woman, and accordingly with the sex relationship. Desire is the underlying theme of the evolutionary and creative process. Later on the emphasis on sex is transmuted to a more widely based love principle under the direction of the mind. When this occurs, we are involved with the relationship of the lower nature to the higher self, lifted up to a union with spirit. This is the divine marriage, carried out and consummated upon the levels of soul awareness. "Sex is but the symbol of an inner duality which must be itself transcended and wrought into a unity. It is not transcended by physical means or rituals. It is a transcendence in consciousness."[53]

Venus places an emphasis upon intuition, wisdom, brotherhood, and spiritual will. Representing the union of heart and mind, Venus sees issues clearly and achieves the point of balance where love, mind and will meet.

Through the ages, Venus has been involved with the major human crises of individualized consciousness and initiation, achieved through the power of the mind and its purpose. During the Age of Aquarius, Venus will again influence an expansion in consciousness throughout all humanity, the consciousness of group responsibility. An interplay of energy from the triangle, Venus, Uranus, and Earth, combining the energies of Ray Five (concrete mind), Ray Seven (ceremonial order or magic), and Ray Three (active intelligence), will manifest this consciousness expansion.[54]

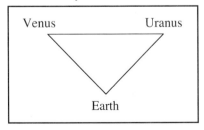
Venus
Uranus
Earth

The influence of Venus will usher in the long hoped for era of love-wisdom and peace on Earth. The four constellations that are ruled by Venus (Taurus, Gemini, Libra, and Capricorn) "constitute a potent quaternary of energies and between them produce those conditions and situations which will enable the initiate to demonstrate readiness and capacity for initiation.

They are called the 'Guardians of the Four Secrets.' "[55]

- Taurus guards the secret of light and confers illumination upon the initiate.

- Gemini guards the mystery or secret of duality and presents the initiate with a word which leads to the fusion of the greater pairs of opposites.

- Libra guards the secret of balance, of equilibrium, and finally speaks the word which releases the initiate from the power of the Lords of Karma.

- Capricorn guards the secret of the soul itself and reveals it to the initiate at the time of the third initiation. This is sometimes called the "secret of the hidden glory."

We note that:

- Venus is exalted in Pisces.

- Venus acts on the exoteric level with energies from Taurus and Libra.

- Venus acts on the esoteric level with energies from Gemini.

- Venus acts on the hierarchical level with energies from Capricorn.

Keynotes: Values, wisdom, relationship, intelligent love.

Mars

Mars, the God of War, produces conflicts that lead to purification. A Ray Six planet, Mars embodies the energies of fanaticism, struggle, strife, war, effort, idealism, and evolution. These forces, however, lead us from personal ambition to spiritual aspiration, where we seek to save the world. In Mars, idealism is the power to see the vision and to direct our course toward it.

Mars rules and controls the physical vehicle and personality and governs the five senses, which are the basis of our knowledge of what is tangible and objective. Therefore, Mars rules science, which is currently fundamental and material. This materiality is, however, lessening, as Mars nears the end of its present cycle of influence. Subtler senses will supersede the physical senses over which Mars has so long had control and, accordingly, again there will be more of an emphasis on the world of the psychic senses and the appearance of the subtler and more esoteric powers of clairvoyance and clairaudience.[56]

The color of Mars is red, which corresponds to the color of the blood stream, through which Mars vitalizes, purifies, and stimulates all aspects and organisms in the body. The color red also associates Mars with passion, anger, and a sense of general opposition. The sense of duality is powerful, producing conflict. This conflict, however, enables us to use the energy of Mars to uplift our physical nature, emotional nature, and mental processes.

Mars establishes relations between the opposites and is a beneficial and not a malefic influence. Mars is closely related to sex, an aspect of the pairs of opposites. The activity of Mars arouses the entire lower nature and brings about its final rebellion and the last stand of the personality against the soul. The "quarrel of the sexes" is resolved in its highest aspect through the battle between the highly developed personality and the soul which seeks to be the ultimate controlling factor.

In the early stages of evolution in Mars, materialism, the fight for the satisfaction of personal ambitions, and the conflict with higher spiritual tendencies goes steadily forward. This most material of all the planets becomes the battleground of the old established order and habits and the new and higher inclinations and tendencies. The tests involve the form nature, gross and subtle, integrated and potent. It is war to the death of the influences of our lower natures.

Then, the forceful and dynamic energy of Mars is focused toward devotion to an ideal. Throughout all this, Mars produces great struggles, but they lead to great revelations. The revelation in Aries is of the nature of knowledge and the purpose of incarnation. In Scorpio, the revelation is of the vision of liberation and service. In Sagittarius, the revelation is of the purpose of soul control over the lower kingdoms in nature via the human center of energy.

Christianity is governed by Mars through Ray Six. It is a religion of devotion, fanaticism, high courage, idealism, of the spiritual emphasis upon the individual and his or her worth and problems, of conflict and death.

Eventually, old identifications cease, new trends toward higher, subtler, and more spiritual identifications begin to appear, and Mars and Neptune begin to work together. Mars carries conflict into the very depth of circumstance, environment, and being, and confers at the same time such devotion to the envisioned objective—as seen at any particular point upon the path—that final failure is rendered impossible.

The tests and difficulties of our era portend the birth of the new era. "This will happen if—speaking esoterically—the sixth ray energy of Mars is transmuted into the sixth ray energy of Neptune, for the one is 'objective and full of blood' and the other is 'subjective and full of life.'"[57]

We note that:

- Mars is exalted in Capricorn.

- Mars acts on the exoteric level with energies from Aries and Scorpio.

- Mars acts on the esoteric level with energies from Scorpio.

- Mars acts on the hierarchical level with energies from Sagittarius.

Keynotes: Desire, will to act, drive, physical energy, purification.

Jupiter

Jupiter, the conveyor of expansion, gives an inherent tendency to fusion. This fusion, or unity, is the subjective purpose of manifestation. The achievement of the ultimate synthesis that Jupiter promotes is, accordingly, inevitable.

On the mutable cross, the rays of the Sun pour into and through us via Jupiter. Jupiter is the agent of Ray Two, which the Sun expresses, cosmically and systemically. The cardinal cross brings about certain great points of synthesis as a consequence of both change and crisis, and Jupiter focuses the energies at this point.

In its lower aspect, Jupiter fulfills desire and satisfies demand; in its higher aspect, Jupiter is the outgoing expression of love, which attracts magnetically to itself what is desired—this time, the good of the whole.

Through Jupiter, the force that brings everything together is applied to promote evolutionary development. The magnetic potency of Ray Two relates soul and form and brings them together. In connection with the other dualities found in all of us, that of head and heart, mind and love, and will and wisdom, Jupiter's work is to develop the two qualities and bring them into synthesis.

Jupiter helps us develop individual-consciousness into world-consciousness. Jupiter will eventually inaugurate a long cycle of beneficent development in which the conflict essential to the interplay between the dualities will be stabilized upon the mental plane and, with the help of Hierarchy and humanity working together, will entirely change world civilization.

The influences of Jupiter and Mercury, working together, can transmute material desire into divine love, and the conflict which is the distinguishing characteristic of the human family can be instrumental in resolving dissonance into harmony.

Will, love, and harmony through conflict are the controlling forces that make us what we are. These governing and directing energies use the mind (Mercury), the emotional nature, love (in Jupiter), and the physical body (the Moon, or esoteric will) for purposes of divine expression and manifestation.

Jupiter and Neptune, working together, develop and use the form aspect and engender psychic sensitivity both in the higher and the lower senses.

Jupiter and Uranus, working together, are considered to be planets of beneficent consummation and employ the fullest eventual cooperation through Ray Two and Ray Seven. When we reach a very high level of evolution, Jupiter and Uranus produce a "beneficent organization" of energies in our equipment which, when complete, enables us to "escape from off the wheel" and truly live.[58]

When we are fully awakened to spiritual and not simply material possibilities, the work of Jupiter will immediately intensify and this beneficent ruler will lead us into the ways of peace and progress.

Jupiter rules four signs and each of them represents a different element out of the four which are expressing themselves in the three worlds of human evolution.

We note that:

- Jupiter is exalted in Cancer.

- Jupiter acts on the exoteric level with energies from Sagittarius and Pisces, and possibly Leo.

- Jupiter acts on the esoteric level with energies from Aquarius.

- Jupiter acts on the hierarchical level with energies from Virgo.

Keynotes: Expansion, opportunity, faith, integration, synthesis.

Saturn

Saturn, the planet of opportunity, is exceedingly active today, giving us difficult situations and crises that involve free choice, discriminative pioneering, wise response, and correct decision.

We stand at the gateway of a new world, with its new civilizations, ideals, and culture. Saturn, having offered opportunity and a choice to bring about the needed changes and to reject that which holds back the free expression of the soul, eventually stands aside to let Mercury spread the light and intuition of the soul upon the situation, to interpret for us, through our own illumined minds, the significance of events, and to relate the old and the new, the past and the future through the light of the present.

Hence, the usefulness of meditation processes which give us the capacity to be "impressed from on high" and to be illumined by the light of the soul. When the task of Saturn and Mercury is accomplished, Venus, representing the union of heart and mind, ushers in the era of love-wisdom and brotherhood. The Tibetan says: "Opportunity— Illumination—Brotherhood: these are the gifts that Shamballa is planning to confer upon mankind during the Aquarian Age, if man will but prepare for them, accept them, and use them."[59]

Saturn provides stressful conditions and situations that lead us to struggle against wrong orientation. Saturn represents the conflict of the soul with its environment, which provides the conditions of suffering that the soul has willingly undertaken "when—with open eyes and clear vision—the soul chose the path of earth life with all its consequent sacrifices and pains, in order to salvage the lives with which it had an affinity."[60] Thus, through our suffering, we learn to discriminate, make correct choices, and decide upon higher values.

Saturn is one of the most potent of the four Lords of Karma and forces us to face up to the past, and in the present to prepare for the future. This is the intention and purpose of karmic opportunity. Saturn demands full payment of all debts, both from the form side and the soul side. When we finally free ourselves from karma, Saturn's power is completely ended and his work accomplished, for he cannot follow us onto the cardinal cross, according to the Tibetan.[61]

Saturn brings through Ray Three energies, encompassing the nature of intelligent substance. Saturn represents the path of choices, deliberately applied purificatory measures, and the turning point. At the point of balance, opportunity comes which makes choice and determination possible and inevitable. The choice offered by Saturn has to be made upon the physical plane, in our waking consciousness. Now that humanity has reached a point of general and widespread intelligence and can make responsible, intelligent choices, Saturn's work for humanity can reach a point of group usefulness.

We can accept or reject opportunity consciously and shoulder responsibility in a planned and ordered life. The *Old Commentary* describes this point in the evolutionary process in the following symbolic, mantric phrases:[62]

"Amid the whirling forces, I stand confused. I know them not, for, during all my past, they swept me up and down the land wherein I moved, blinded and unaware. From place to place and point to point, they drove me up and down the land and nowhere was there rest.

"I know them now and here I stand and will not move until I know the Law which governs all this movement up and down the land. I may revolve and turning face the many different ways; I face some wide horizons and yet today I stand.

"I will determine for myself the way to go. Then onward I will move. I will not travel up and down the land nor turn in space. But onward I will move."

Saturn (along with Mercury and Uranus) is part of two great triangles that transmit energies from the Great Bear, Pleiades, and Sirius. One triangle filters energies from Leo, Capricorn, and Pisces; through Saturn, Mercury, and Uranus; and eventually to the head, ajna, and heart centers of Earth and then of humanity. The other triangle filters energies from three pairs of polar opposites and the more spiritually advanced members of humanity are able to respond to them. Saturn's direct line of energy comes from Sirius and is then distributed through Cancer/Capricorn. (See "Triangles / Trines" in Chapter 9.)

We note that:

- Saturn is exalted in Libra.

- Saturn acts on the exoteric and esoteric levels with energies from Capricorn.

- Saturn acts on the hierarchical level with energies from Libra.

Keynotes: Choice, discrimination, discipline, structure, preservation.

Uranus

Uranus, connected with the Hierophant of the Mysteries of Initiation, rules the occult way. Occult-consciousness is an intelligent, fusing condition which produces a unification of our higher and lower selves through our intelligent use of mind. Trained occultists are mentally polarized and profoundly aware of the realities, forces, and energies of existence and, therefore, free from the ordinary glamours and illusions that color the reactions and lives of average people.

As the occult planet, Uranus stands for exoteric science which penetrates into the hidden side of form life and governs the period wherein we are not alert or conscious enough to seize opportunity and turn it to esoteric or soul ends, but can identify ourselves with more advanced aspects of form. Uranus then stimulates the will to be and to know simultaneously on all planes of manifestation and causes the great transference in human consciousness from intellectual perception to intuitive knowledge and then to inspiration. Uranus inspires spontaneous activity which produces evolutionary development, in both the natural and spiritual sense. This is the innate urge to improve conditions.

The Sun and the Moon both veil Uranus, which means that we might be able to substitute the energies of Uranus for those of the Sun and the Moon under special circumstances. Uranus, veiled by the Sun, symbolizes the effect of the soul upon the personality.[63]

Uranus embodies the Ray Seven consciousness of organization and directed manifestation, and its work is analogous to that of Mercury, for Ray Seven relates spirit and matter, producing manifestation. Uranus also has a Ray Three flavor due to energies which came from Alcyone and "impregnated the substance of the universe with the quality of mind."[64] This force, which the Tibetan associates with Ray Three, helped humanity individualize on Earth in eons long gone. He asks us to consider this information along with the teaching that humanity will eventually act as the mediating principle to all the lower kingdoms on Earth (that, as we know, haven't individualized their consciousnesses yet).

Under the direction of Uranus, we are true observers, detached from the material side of life, but using it as we please. Our spiritual consciousness is capable of great expression and we can be electric, dynamic leaders, pioneers in new fields of endeavor, and magnetic centers of groups, whether large or small. The more material aspects of life no longer greatly appeal to us.

Uranus initiates a new order of life and conditions, producing an understanding of the causes of things as they are, and the desire to change the old order and the old orientation into the new. This is happening today in connection with humanity and world processes.

Carried to its logical conclusion, this influence of Uranus produces an unfolded spiritual consciousness. Our will is focused and developed and we become leaders. We bring about the desired changes and produce new conditions that will liberate the soul of humanity. This coming process of planetary service is truly effective when Aquarius rules and when our Sun is passing through that sign of the zodiac. Hence the immense importance of the Age of Aquarius and the next 2000 years.[65] When we become group-conscious world servers, this new world order can come to life. This is beginning to happen now for the first time in planetary history. It is one of the first fruits of initiation and later we will better understand the significance of the process and the true nature of the energies to be released through the medium of humanity upon the planet.

The following lines of energy enhance the cosmic pull of Uranus:

- One of the stars of the Great Bear to the creative hierarchies upon Earth

- Sirius, through Pisces, to Uranus, and then to Hierarchy and humanity

- Alcyone, through Aquarius, to Jupiter and Uranus, and then to humanity

Uranus (along with Mercury and Saturn) is part of two great triangles that transmit energies from the Great Bear, Pleiades, and Sirius. One triangle filters energies from Leo, Capricorn, and Pisces; through Saturn, Mercury, and Uranus; and eventually to the head, ajna, and heart centers of Earth and then of humanity. The other triangle filters energies from three pairs of polar opposites and the more spiritually advanced members of humanity are able to respond to them. Uranus's direct line of energy comes from the Great Bear and is then distributed through Aries/Libra. (See "Triangles /Trines" in Chapter 9.)

We note that:

- Uranus is exalted in Scorpio.
- Uranus acts on the exoteric level with energies from Aquarius.
- Uranus acts on the esoteric level with energies from Libra.
- Uranus acts on the hierarchical level with energies from Aries and Leo (where it is veiled by the Sun).

Keynotes: Originality, freedom, change, spontaneity, revolution.

Neptune

Neptune, god of the waters, is the initiator during this world period. His trident signifies the trinity in manifestation. The term water covers several aspects of esoteric wisdom, including:[66]

- The whole concept of matter
- The "waters" of substance
- The ocean of life
- The world of astral glamour and reaction
- The astral plane as a whole
- The desire and the emotional nature
- The world of focused incarnation for the masses
- Mass existence, as in Cancer

Neptune uniquely represents consciousness: consciousness that flows and penetrates to all levels of existence, across all planes, and encompassing all states of mind. The mystical aspect of Neptune, with its innate sensitivity, can lead us to higher vision and transcendental love.

Neptune relates to the consciousness aspect of evolution: mass-consciousness, self-consciousness, and group-consciousness. A high form of consciousness we can work with here is group-consciousness and individual-consciousness combined together in the service of the Plan. Neptune helps expand our group-consciousness so that we emerge on the physical plane as world servers, decentralized workers who are governed by the need and sensitive to the reactions of humanity. An example of such a group is a master's group, which is a collection of people who are imbued with the group ideal and are learning increasingly to respond to it.

A Ray Six planet, Neptune is idealistic, one-pointed, and devoted to an objective. Ray Six, which governs the astral or emotional plane of desire, can give us intense devotion to material things as well as intense devotion to spiritual values. In Neptune, Ray Six is "subjective and full of life."[67] Neptune introduces the water of life into the ocean of substance, and thus brings light to the world. This demonstrates control of the fluidic astral plane.

The Sun and the Moon can both veil Neptune, which means that we might be able to substitute the energies of Neptune for those of the Sun and the Moon under special circumstances. The effect of the Sun veiling Neptune can produce a potent effect upon the personality, symbolized by the astral body. Then, as development advances, the emotion-desire forces are transmuted into love-aspiration, dedicated and oriented to the soul; the entire emotional or sensitive nature then responds to energies from the Heart of the Sun. Upon the fixed cross, the Heart of the Sun pours its energies through Neptune upon humanity. These stimulate and affect the heart, throat, and ajna centers.[68]

The Tibetan tells us that personality-oriented humanity is fortunate that Neptune is veiled by the Moon, which means that the form fails to register the impacts of Neptune, to which a soul-conscious person is sensitive. Many people are simply not ready for the high degree of sensitivity that Neptune would provide. One of the major problems along the line of esoteric development is an extreme sensitivity to impacts from every side and having to learn to respond to these contacts appropriately.[69]

When we become initiated, we do not react to what the Tibetan calls "ordinary feeling, sentiment, or personality relations as they express themselves in pleasure or pain. All these are surmounted and eventually the watery life of emotional reaction is superseded by the life of true and of inclusive love. Soul control esoterically 'obliterates' the Moon and all traces of Neptunian life. The initiate is no longer ruled by the Mother of Forms or by the God of the Waters. When the 'waters break and are carried away,' the Mother gives birth to the Son and that individual spiritual entity then stands free."[70]

We note that:

- Neptune is exalted in Cancer.

- Neptune (veiled by the Sun) acts on the exoteric level with energies from Cancer.

- Neptune acts on the esoteric level with energies from Cancer, Pisces, and Leo (where it is veiled by the Sun).

- Neptune acts on the hierarchical level with energies from Cancer.

Keynotes: Transcendence, dissolution of boundaries, inspiration.

Pluto

Pluto is the hierophant who cuts the thread of worldly desires. As the planet of metamorphoses, Pluto alters the shape and structure of all it touches with scant regard for the sentiments of those who have labored to fabricate dream castles.

Pluto's Ray One power shatters the materialist illusion of death which has held the world in thrall for millennia. Pluto precipitates the process of transmutation and eventual escape through death and unfolds the significance, activity, and beauty of death and the work of the destroyer. Pluto is not itself an agent of doom, but clears the way for the final transfiguration which ushers the immortal spirit into the realm of light.

Pluto stands for death, or the region of death, and drags to the surface and destroys all that hinders in these lower regions. To achieve the final liberation, we experience the destroying power of death: death of desire, death of the personality, and death of everything that holds us between the pairs of opposites.

Although Pluto delivers the spirit from the flesh, it does not annihilate consciousness. Evolved people do not fear temporary defeat by the forces of destruction because they know that they are, and always will be, immortal. Our victory over Pluto's realm is won, not through denial, but through complete acceptance of the power that transcends the ephemeral rhythms of nature (the Moon) and therefore knows no extinction.

Pluto, a non-sacred planet, functions in connection with the solar plexus. Pluto becomes active in our lives when we are "becoming alive in the higher sense." Our lower nature passes into the "smoke and darkness of Pluto" in order that we may "live in truth in the higher land of light." Humanity only experiences the positive aspect of Ray One potency as we near the level of evolution where we can become world servers.

The destructive power of Ray One, focused in Pluto, brings change and darkness. Death through the energy of Pluto is a transformation so vital and so basic that the "…Ancient One is no longer seen. He sinks to the depth of the ocean of life; he descends into hell, but the gates of hell hold him not. He, the new and living One leaves below that which has held him down throughout the ages and rises from the depths unto the heights, close to the throne of God."[71]

Pluto brings about the finish of the separative, instinctual nature, which is the factor that lies behind all dualism. This is what *The Secret Doctrine* calls the ahamkara principle, or the awareness of the separative, isolated ego. For eons, it hampers the aspiration of the soul when it is identified with the personality.

Toward the end of the evolutionary process, we begin to respond consciously to the indirect influence of Pluto, producing the end of the hindering factors and of all that prevents synthesis.

We note that:

- Pluto acts on the exoteric level with energies from Scorpio.

- Pluto acts on the esoteric and hierarchical levels with energies from Pisces and Scorpio.

Keynotes: Death and rebirth, transformation, power, regeneration.

The Moon

In esoteric astrology, the effect of the Moon is considered to be a thought effect, the result of a powerful and ancient thoughtform. The ancient teaching speaks of it as veiling either Vulcan, Neptune, or Uranus. Accordingly, the Tibetan suggests that we work with the energies of the veiled planets instead of those of the Moon. He tells us that Vulcan, Neptune, and Uranus determine or condition the physical, astral, and mental natures, thus creating the personality, and he leaves it to our intuition to determine which planet to use for any particular situation.[72]

The Moon is the mother of the form, and the form side of life exerts a powerful control over us. The Moon fashions and molds the form, "bringing in both the feminine and masculine aspects of form-building, the dual functions of Father-Mother."[73]

World mythology through the ages related the Moon to goddesses, including Cassiopea, Venus, Coma Berenice, Andromeda, as well as Virgo the Virgin.[74] In Egypt, she was Isis, Hathor, and Hecate; in Greece, she was Diana, Demeter, Proserpina, and Rhea. In these roles, the Moon represents the feminine principle, form, the subconscious, and the vehicle through which life expresses itself.

The Moon and the Sun have long represented the primary pair of opposites—female/male, night/day—to humanity on Earth. The receptivity of the female aspect contains the effulgence of the male aspect. The coolness of the night balances the heat of the day.

The Moon symbolizes the subconscious and the Sun symbolizes the conscious. Blending the subconscious with the conscious gives us the point of balance from which we can achieve superconsciousness. At the time of the full moon, when the Sun and the Moon are in opposition, we have an opportunity to balance this pair of opposites.

At this time, over a period of five days, the Moon and Earth receive more reflected light from the Sun than at any other time. This is the time when our Planetary Logos practices his intensest mediation. This is his cyclic point of contact, which brings through energies that can facilitate our work on the mental plane and enable us to meditate more successfully. We "share in the achievement of the Lord of Shamballa."[75]

The Moon is an ancient form through which the Planetary Logos sought expression in the far distant past. Although it is slowly disintegrating physically, it is intact astrally and is therefore still closely linked with the astral body of our Planetary Logos, and therefore with the astral bodies of all people. Its influence is consequently more potent at the time of the full moon upon all who are unbalanced. This lack of equilibrium also affects the etheric and physical bodies.

People who are spiritual and mental can profit by these full-moon cycles; those who are unbalanced, emotional, and frequently swept by uncontrolled desire are hindered, overstimulated, and psychically upset by these same cycles. Says the Tibetan: "The veil of illusion is lit up at that time with a consequent result of hallucination, astral visions, psychic urges, and those misinterpretations of life, of overemphasis upon aspects of life which we call phobias, lunacy, ..."[76]

We note that:

- The Moon is exalted in Taurus.

- The Moon acts on the exoteric level with energies from Cancer.

- The Moon acts on the esoteric level with energies from Virgo.

- The Moon acts on the hierarchical level with energies from Aquarius.

Keynotes: Emotions, habitual responses, unconscious memory, the subconscious.

Chapter 8—
Earth Energy

"The planetary wheel of life turns on its lesser scale the wheel of life of the little pilgrim we call man; as it turns, it sweeps the life of the evolving planetary Logos into ever new forms and experiences until the fire of Spirit burns up all lesser fires."—AAB[1]

Earth is the physical body of our Planetary Logos, the great being whose consciousness overshadows our evolution on this planet. The physical elements of Earth—fire, air, water, and earth—correspond to the etheric, mental, astral, and physical planes, respectively. It is apparent that these vehicles differ for the Planetary Logoi of other systems, just as the elements differ amongst planets. Yet the teachings tell us that each Planetary Logos has a threefold condition, a higher correspondence of the physical, astral, and mental bodies of humanity, and each logoic vehicle is acted upon directly from the corresponding cosmic plane—physical, astral, and mental. "The condition of the various physical planets will some day be found to be dependent upon this fact."[2]

The vital body of our Planetary Logos is composed of the total of all the human and deva units upon Earth. The devic or angelic kingdom is said to be a parallel evolution to humanity. Humans and devas represent the soul or consciousness aspect of the planet. The corporeal body of the Planetary Logos is composed of the units in the animal kingdom (which are evolutionary) and all the elemental material forms (which are involutionary). Animals and elementals represent the personality or body aspect of the planet. Accordingly, we are but cells in the body of the Planetary Logos. Our development depends upon the cyclic purpose of our Planetary Logos and upon the currents of force he receives from other planetary schemes.[3]

The vibration of a Planetary Logos has a specific effect upon the vibratory level of initiates, adepts, and masters. Our Planetary Logos transmits an energy that is primarily astral-buddhic. The buddhic (intuitional) energy affects our souls and the astral (emotional) energy has an impact on our personality lives in this particular cycle. Although the intuitional energy is steadily increasing, the astral energy accounts for our "wild hunt for pleasure" and many of our problems today.[4]

The evolution of the Planetary Logoi in our solar system is unequal,[5] and Earth is not considered to be a sacred planet. Instead, our Planetary Logos is "one of the four minor Logoi, or Lords of the Rays, and is specially concerned, therefore, with the development of one attribute of manas [mind]."[6] "Our Planetary Logos is one of the Lords spoken of as being a lesser lord, and more 'full of passion' than the higher three."[7] However, our planet is considered to be one of the most important in the system during this particular cycle because we now have an alignment that presents a special opportunity to our Planetary Logos. This alignment "results in the clearing of a channel direct from the heart of our scheme through every ring-pass-not to the cosmic correspondence, found outside the solar sphere."[8]

Humanity currently stands at the middle point of evolution and, therefore, is regarded as the most important of the evolutions because we provide a bridge between the superhuman and the subhuman. We, therefore, act as a mediator and through us can be worked out group methods and laws of a cosmic nature. Due to the experiments our Planetary Logos has been performing in this regard, he has been called the "experimenting divine Physicist." If these experiments are successful, they will result in a great expansion of his knowledge of the laws governing all bodies and masses.[9] This is perhaps why it is so vital that we work in groups and modify our desire impulses until they are refined for group activity. We incarnate in groups, which is the basis of collective and family karma. This is impulsed, on a higher level, by the Planetary Logos working through the groups in his centers.[10] The work of the Planetary Logos includes (in addition to vast projects that we cannot even imagine) the following:

- Bringing into physical manifestation upon Earth the purpose or will of the Solar Logos. Our Planetary Logos does this through meditation.[11]

- Cooperating intelligently in certain cosmic enterprises, bringing in the factor of extra-systemic force.[12]

- Providing schools for the development of subordinate Logoi and training them, giving them opportunity for wide experience. "Even the Logoi Themselves progress onward, and Their places must be taken."[13]

Earth, Venus, and Mercury are related to the personality of our Planetary Logos. Earth is uniquely a "planet of releasing sorrow and of purifying pain," with Mercury and Venus focusing the energies to provide the release.

- The Earth influences the planetary vital or etheric body.

- Venus influences the planetary astral or emotional vehicle.

- Mercury influences the planetary mind.

The Earth is also an intermediary or relating planet because it rules both Gemini and Sagittarius and is potent within the line of the dual relationship existing between this pair of opposites. In the Earth, a great balancing process is going forward between the two great streams of cosmic energy emanating from Sagittarius and Gemini. Mercury and Venus aid and influence this condition, producing what the Tibetan calls a "somewhat unusual situation in our planet."[14]

Our Planetary Logos has three major centers or kingdoms of manifestation on Earth, which we will discuss next: Shamballa, the Hierarchy, and Humanity. In addition, there are the devic kingdom, which is parallel to these three centers; the animal kingdom; the vegetable kingdom; the mineral kingdom; and the elementals. These other lives interact with us closely and are very important to our evolution, but a discussion of them is beyond the scope of this book.

The Mind of the World (Shamballa)

"Now, as the Shamballa force is beginning to pour into the world, man is seeking another interpretation of God's will which will not involve the hitherto blind acquiescence and unavoidable acceptance of the inscrutable dictates of a potent, inescapable Providence, but which will produce an understanding cooperation with the divine Plan and an enlightened fusion of the individual will with the great, divine will and this for the greater good of the whole."—AAB[15]

Shamballa, through Sanat Kumara, the Lord of the World, is the custodian for the purpose of the Planetary Logos. Sanat Kumara is the head of the Council Chamber of Shamballa, a group of mighty entities who guide our planetary Hierarchy and transmit to them the will of God. The highest members of Hierarchy are in the council chamber. This group could be said to represent the mind of God, the universal mind.

Although Shamballa is spoken of as existing in physical matter and occupying a definite location in space, the physical matter referred to is etheric; the Lord of the World and his assistants of the higher degrees occupy bodies formed of etheric matter.[16]

Shamballa is the head center for our planet, into which pour the energies from the cosmos after they have been transmuted by our Solar Logos and after specific energies have been conditioned by the other planets in our system. Shamballa, in turn, distributes these energies to Hierarchy and then to us. We can have direct access to Shamballa energies, apart from the mediatorship of Hierarchy, only if we use them with understanding and in groups. The Tibetan says, "May I repeat those two key words to the use of the Shamballa energy: Group Use and Understanding."[17] During the Aquarian age, Shamballa hopes to endow humanity with opportunity, illumination, and brotherhood; it is our free will whether we prepare for, accept, and use these gifts.[18]

Shamballa stands for spirit, life, will, identification, and synthesis; it is the focus of the Ray One energy of will and power. We can contact these energies only from the mental plane, thus only those who are working through the mind can begin to appropriate this energy. The three major expressions of the will aspect are:[19]

- The life aspect of will, which sets the pace for the evolution of forms and concerns the force and endurance of the life that manifests through these forms.

- The will that brings fulfillment, which is the basis of all relationships and underlies consciousness itself. This is a higher correspondence of our joy of achievement when undertaking creative effort.

- The will that conquers death, which is the principle of victory when the ultimate goal of life is achieved and is the final united success to a long foreseen purpose.

This is the gateway to higher evolution. Will energy involves the establishing of right human relations, incentive, and realized purpose. Will is invocative and works downward into form, whereas desire is evocative and works from the form upwards. "It is this will—aroused by invocation—which must be focused in the light of the soul, and dedicated to the purposes of light and for the purpose of establishing right human relations which must be used (in love) to destroy all that is hindering the free flow of human life and that is bringing death (spiritual and real) to humanity. This Will *must* be invoked and evoked."[20]

A misuse of Shamballa force is due to the sensitivity of the lower, rather than the higher, nature and, consequently, the selfish use of this energy. Another misuse is when we do not stand up for our convictions and thus allow wrong situations to continue. This perpetuates focused evil. The only way we can overcome this evil is through an equally focused spiritual will; by learning how to train ourselves to be sensitive to the Shamballa energy so that we can invoke it and use it to stop the forces of evil. This involves more than just kindness and good intention; it involves a focused will-to-good.[21]

Thus, to eliminate evil, we must actively and consciously use Shamballa force (with the help of the Hierarchy) once our will-to-good is strong enough to safeguard us and keep us from being deflected on to wrong and dangerous lines. When humanity and Hierarchy can "stand together with massed intent" this will be the mental plane correspondence of prayer. This involves the focused will of the world thinkers and intuitives "who will use their minds and brains in the affirmation of right."[22]

Shamballa force is particularly active in the world now, as we move past the millennium and progress into the Age of Aquarius. However, the current manifestation of this force will no longer involve blind acquiescence with an inescapable Providence, but will produce an understanding cooperation with the divine plan and an "enlightened fusion of the individual will with the great, divine will and this for the greater good of the whole."[23]

Our responsiveness to these forces is manifesting through a growing human understanding and the efforts of world workers who are actively making the necessary changes to uplift human conditions. The adverse side of Shamballa impact is that it stimulates the will-to-power in people and nations who are polarized in the desire life, and not in the soul.

Zodiacal energies pass through Shamballa, relate to the will and power of Ray One, and affect the monad or spirit. These energies include the following primary sources:[24]

- The cardinal cross, which rules and conditions Shamballa

- The triangle of the Great Bear, Leo, and Saturn

- The triangle of the Great Bear, Aries, and Pluto
- Leo, Aries, and Capricorn, the great Ray One triangle:
  - The will aspect governs through Aries, which opens the door into Shamballa at the appropriate time
  - Capricorn carries the will of Shamballa to the Hierarchy and to the world initiates, giving them the dynamic and enterprising spirit to enable them to fulfill their missions
- Leo, which marks the height of achievement for the human soul
- Polaris, the pole star, the "Star of Direction," which governs Shamballa
- Libra, the polar opposite of Aries, which admits the soul into Shamballa
- A direct line of will energy flowing through:
  1. The Pointer in the Great Bear furthest from Polaris, which is a focal point for divine energy (the Pointer nearest to Polaris expresses self-will)
  2. Aries, which represents the will to create or to manifest
  3. Vulcan and Pluto, which affect human response
  4. Shamballa, the custodian of the purpose and the plan for our planet

The influx of Shamballa force emphasizes an energy relationship between Taurus, Pluto, and Earth, which is producing much of our present world difficulty. "It produces in certain nations, races and individuals, a welling up of the self-will or of the will-to-power which is characteristic of the developed lower nature, the personality aspect of integrated selfhood. It produces—though less readily—a stimulation of the will to serve the plan as it is grasped by the world aspirants, the world disciples and initiates.

Thus are the purposes of Deity materialised."[25]

The Heart of the World (Hierarchy)

"A thought is given; a symbol described; an idea portrayed. Then, as the minds of men ponder upon it and the intuitives of the world pick up the thought, it serves as a seed thought which eventually comes to fruition with the presentation and the unfolding of a revelation which serves to lead the race of men nearer to their goal."—AAB[26]

For a vast period of time, the custodians of the ageless wisdom made their headquarters at Shamballa, an etheric location, but during the first subrace of the Atlantean root race, they decided that it was necessary for them to found an organization for the mysteries on the dense physical plane if the evolution of the race was to proceed according to plan. In this headquarters, a band of adepts and chohans would function in dense physical bodies and thus meet the need of the rapidly awakening humanity.

The first outpost was the original temple of Ibez, located in the center of South America. Much later, one of its branches was in the ancient Maya world, where the Sun was worshipped as the source of life in the hearts of all men. The nature of the Ibezhan work was different from now; their objective was "to stimulate mysticism and the stimulating of the kingdom of God within the human atom."[27] We cannot comprehend this type of work now, since the Ibezhans dealt with an infant humanity, whose polarization was unstable and whose coordination was very imperfect. Humanity was almost altogether astrally focused at that time; there was little mentality. Thus, these adepts, working under instruction from Shamballa, needed to develop the energy centers of the human unit, stimulate the brain, and make it self-conscious on the physical plane. Their methods of work were definitely more physical than permissible now, and the remnants of these earlier Temple practices "have come down to us in degraded phallic teaching, in Tantric magic and the practices of Hatha Yogis."[28]

Later, Himalayan and Southern Indian adepts founded a second branch of Hierarchy in Asia. Schools of the mysteries were also founded in Chaldea, Egypt, Greece, and many other locations. In these branches, the work was materially changed.

When the Ibezhan adepts, under instruction from Shamballa, began to withdraw into the Temples, "to make the mysteries more difficult of attainment and to work against abuses and distortions," a number of their followers, many of great power and knowledge, fought against them, thus resulting in the appearance of black magic.

In the future, we are promised, discoveries will be made, revealing ancient records and monuments, some above ground and many below ground. "As the mysteries of central Asia in the land stretching from Chaldea and Babylon through Turkestan to Manchuria, including the Gobi desert, are opened up, it is planned that much of the early history of the Ibezhan workers will be revealed."

The emphasis of the teaching is now to help humanity transcend the physical and astral vehicles and to become group-conscious. The path of mysticism must lead eventually to the occult path and the mysteries must be organized to reveal the nature of God in all that is seen. Humanity must be taught that, even though individual, we are but parts of a greater whole and that our interests must be made subservient to those of the group.[29]

Our planetary Hierarchy is the heart center of planet Earth, from which flows the love that energizes us and gives our lives meaning. For whether we work with Hierarchy consciously or not, their love to us is all pervasive and motivates us toward higher evolution, or as we may say, toward doing the best we can during life.

In the past, many of the masters had Oriental bodies because these bodies are the oldest racially and therefore the most experienced. Also, many of the masters were men, because men had more power. However, now, in the School of Trans-Himalayan Yoga, there are masters of all races and both sexes.

We might wonder why we do not have contact with our sages. We did, in fact, during the Atlantean era, until humanity forced Hierarchy to leave us alone. "Humanity has chosen to proceed by means of the "trial and error" method and it is in many ways a sound choice, but it is slow and leads to points of crisis and moments of almost intolerable difficulty in the history of the race."[30] However, Hierarchy now finds that, if we can make the right spiritual contact, "there can be re-established on earth the condition which was brought to an end in earlier days, when the Hierarchy (in order to further man's mental development) withdrew behind the scenes for a period."[31]

Hierarchy wants people to know the fact of their existence and love nature. The main reason for this is because the world is now filled with highly evolved people with highly integrated personalities who are evolving a lot of intellect without a co-measurement of love energy. Intellect and love energy must be balanced if we are to evolve to our best capacity and regain our freedom by ridding ourselves of the forces of evil. "...three modes whereby the forces of darkness seek to control humanity are hatred, aggression and separativeness. The three great spiritual counterparts are love, selfless sharing and synthesis."[32]

Concerning the interaction of Hierarchy with humanity, the Tibetan tells us: "Where world values and where group consciousness are involved, the indication of needed change, the cyclic bringing about of the presentation to the soul of the Ageless Wisdom and the training of the world disciples—such is the definite and ordained technique of the Hierarchy."[33]

We are often so preoccupied with Hierarchy's attitude and effort toward our welfare and guidance that we overlook the goals of Hierarchy, which do not always relate to us. Our best attitude toward them would be to seek to help them rather than to ask for help. Some of Hierarchy's specific objectives include the following:

- Standing as a wall between humanity and excessive evil. This protection extends to all the subhuman kingdoms of Earth. "The excessive evil, emanating from cosmic sources, requires the trained skill of the Hierarchy and the fiat of Shamballa to prevent it flooding over disastrously."

- Awakening the consciousness aspect in all forms, so that it is expanded and intelligently employed.

- Directing world events, as far as humanity will permit "for the free will and free decision of mankind may not be ignored," which purpose is so that we might develop adequate social, political, religious, and economic world forms.

- Impressing and inspiring those who are in contact with them through the flow of ideas and revelations.

- Directing the unfolding cyclic cultures and their resultant civilizations so that they might be useful for the emerging soul of humanity. "The format of cultures and civilisations receives special attention."

- Receiving and transmitting energies and consequent forces from Shamballa, affecting the soul of all things in all kingdoms.

- Helping Shamballa bring an end to cycles, ideologies, organizations, and civilizations when the due and right time comes, to make way for that which is better.

- Preparing us for initiation by receiving us into their ashrams, offering us opportunities to serve the Plan, and training us for initiation. "Each major cycle receives new forms of the same ancient, yet basic, teaching. This present one is such a cycle, and much of my own work is in connection with this," the Tibetan says.[34]

These activities are only a very small part of the total work of the Hierarchy. We are told that much of the work would be incomprehensible to us, however that if we can measure up to the current opportunities that are offered us, it should be possible for us to very soon act as co-creators in the Plan.

Energies from the solar system that pass through the great center of Hierarchy are related to Ray Two, love-wisdom, and affect the soul. These energies come from the following primary sources:[35]

- The fixed cross

- Sirius, the "Star of Sensitivity," which governs the Hierarchy and brings through cosmic soul energy

- The triangle of Sirius, Leo, and Jupiter

- The triangle of Sirius, Pisces, and Uranus

  - Pisces provides the energy of mediation, of right relationship

  - Uranus transmits knowledge of the "hidden mystery" and inaugurates a new world order based on full creative expression

- Gemini, Virgo, and Pisces, the great Ray Two triangle

- Taurus, which brings through the love aspect and governs the Hierarchy

- Capricorn, the sign of initiation, which admits the soul into conscious participation in the life of Hierarchy

- Scorpio, which affects the transition of humanity into a new and higher unity

- Cancer, Leo, Scorpio, Capricorn, and Pisces, which relate to the five continents, Europe, Africa, Asia, Australia, America (not necessarily in that order)

Today, as never before, the Hierarchy stands as a "mediating transmitter" between:[36]

1. Humanity and the will of God; "the revelation of the true significance and purpose of that will as it stands behind all world events is needed now as never before"

2. Humanity and its karma; it is "essential that the laws for the transmutation of karma into active present good are clearly grasped"

3. Humanity and cosmic evil

An ancient aphorism:

"He who faces the light and stands within its radiance is blinded to the issues of the world of men; he passes on the lighted way to the great Centre of Absorption. But he who feels the urge to pass that way, yet loves his brother on the darkened path, revolves upon the pedestal of light and turns the other way.

"He faces towards the dark and then the seven points of light within himself transmit the outward streaming light, and lo! the face of those upon the darkened way receives that light. For them, the way is not so dark. Behind the warriors—twixt the light and dark—blazes the light of Hierarchy."[37]

The Creative Center of the World (Humanity)

"When the sun progresses into the mansion of the serving man, the way of life takes the place of the way of work. Then the tree of life grows until its branches shelter all the sons of men. The building of the Temple and the carrying of the stones cease. The growing trees are seen; the buildings disappear. Let the sun pass into its appointed place, and in this day and generation attend ye to the roots of growth."—AAB[38]

Humanity is the planetary ajna center,[39] but we often work through the throat center, which is the center of creative work. Our goal is to develop intuition, inclusiveness, and to prepare ourselves for initiation into hierarchical work.

When we can control our physical, astral, and mental natures by the soul or the love aspect—not just in theory, but in deed and truth—

then we can use these three vehicles in service to the Earth and, accordingly, transcend the human kingdom and pass into the spiritual kingdom "there to have further lessons."[40] Whatever these further lessons might be, we can be assured that they will impart the joy of higher creativity.

Average humanity is focused upon learning how to use astral and mental energy, and then has to develop the will aspect of the soul. From there, we strive to contact the energies of the buddhic plane, learn the meaning of illumination, and progress to the level of pure reason— pure intuitive perception. In this process, we become initiated, and our main characteristics are intuitive perception, pure vision, direct knowledge, and an ability to work with the energies of the universal mind. The will of the soul is later superseded by the will of the whole and we become truly inclusive, or group-conscious, on a higher level.[41]

Planetary forces pass through humanity, are related to Ray Three energies of active intelligence, and affect the personality. These energies include the following primary sources:[42]

- The mutable cross, which conditions humanity

- An aggregation of seven energies from the Pleiades, connected with the active intelligence aspect of logoic expression, which influences the form side of all manifestation and is focused primarily through humanity

- The triangle of the Pleiades, Capricorn, and Mercury

- The triangle of the Pleiades, Cancer, and Venus

- Alcyone, the "Star of the Individual," which governs humanity

- Cancer, Libra, and Capricorn, the great Ray Three triangle

- Cancer, where the influence of humanity begins to make its presence felt, consummated in Virgo

- Capricorn, which opens the door into Hierarchy when the significance of Scorpio and Virgo are understood and we achieve initiation

Capricorn also manifests the intelligence aspect

Races and Types of Humanity

Three major root races are currently coexisting on the face of the Earth: the fifth, the fourth, and a small remnant of third root race aboriginal peoples. In addition there are seven subraces in each root race. Typical Occidental people are in the fifth subrace of the fifth root race, with the sixth subrace in process of development. Many Oriental people are in the seventh subrace of the fourth root race, and this seventh subrace is the epitome of their development and achievement. (As we mentioned earlier, their vehicles are "more experienced.") The fourth root race was the predominant one in Atlantean times and the fifth root race represents the present goal for humanity. H.P. Blavatsky's *Secret Doctrine* ascribes vast periods of time and enormous periods of overlapping for root races and subraces, which we may or may not believe. However, it is certain that there are different racial types on Earth and that this accounts for much of the conflict within humanity. This mingling of races, and inherent conflict, is undoubtedly part of the plan for our development.

The New Group of World Servers

Now, in the beginnings of the Age of Aquarius, this unstructured group of servers consists of highly evolved members of humanity who are working, mostly behind the scenes, for the development of their fellow humans and the betterment of life on Earth for all kingdoms of nature. All who work sincerely in this manner are members of this group, whether conscious of it or not. The New Group of World Servers includes people from all walks of life, all ages, all nationalities, all religions, and all organizations and their service is cultural, political, scientific, religious, philosophical, psychological, economic—in other words, a true cross-section of humanity and activities that promote planetary betterment.

This group represents a physical-plane nucleus of the work of Hierarchy and forms a bridge between Hierarchy and the rest of humanity. An essential condition imposed upon this group is that each member must be spiritually oriented (in the inclusive sense), mentally polarized, and able to work subjectively, thus using the intuition. They must be willing to work behind the scenes, without recognition, as do the Great Ones. This means they must be free from ambition and pride and be sensitive to the thoughts and conditions of others.

The word "spiritual" in the inclusive sense means "an inclusive endeavour towards human betterment, uplift and understanding ...tolerance, international synthetic communion, religious inclusiveness, and all trends of thought which concern the esoteric development of the human being."[43] This group embodies all the aspects of all the seven rays and fulfills three main requirements:[44]

1. A certain amount of alignment and activity between the soul, mind, and brain.

2. A telepathic sensitivity, in two directions and at will, facilitating awareness of the world of souls and also of the world of men.

3. A capacity for abstract thought and an ability to synthesize, enabling a leap over racial and religious barriers and also ensuring knowledge of the continuity of life after death.

Specific qualifications are: learn to practice harmlessness, desire nothing for the separated self, and look for the sign of divinity in all.[45]

In the past, much of the work of this group was done more or less unknowingly, but the current work of the group is now increasingly being done by those who are aware of the fact that they are working from the level of the soul. As the Tibetan puts it, "they look upon the mind, emotions and body nature as simply an equipment whereby human contacts can be established, and their work, as they see it, is to be carried forward through the medium of this equipment, acting under the direction of the soul. They are therefore living souls, working through personalities, and not personalities actuated by occasional soul impulses."[46]

Unlike the Beethovens and Shakespeares of the past, the new type of group workers are (or are in the process of becoming) well-rounded, with a capacity to do almost anything they attempt. This flexibility and experience is much needed in the diverse world we have today. Predominant features of these group members will include "a universal touch, an intense sensitivity, a highly organised mental apparatus, an astral equipment which is primarily responsive to the higher spiritual vibrations, a powerful and controlled energy body, and a sound physical body...[they] possess a full realisation of their own limitations, but are not handicapped thereby, but proceed to think through into objective manifestation that aspect of the vision which it is their mission to vivify into form. They are necessarily cultured and widely read, for in these difficult transitional times they have to cultivate a world grasp of conditions and possess a general idea of what is going on in the different countries. They possess in truth no nationality in the sense that they regard their country and their political affiliations as of paramount importance. They are equipped to organise, slowly and steadily, that public opinion which will eventually divorce man from religious sectarianism, national exclusiveness, and racial biases."[47]

We must remember that these words of the Tibetan describe the prototypical group member and not to despair if we do not quite measure up at this time. For the Tibetan said elsewhere that we must take ourselves the way we are, with our current equipment, and just strive to do the best that we can.

The functions and activities of the New Group of World Servers include:

- Elevating humanity and expanding the human consciousness

- Communicating the new ideals, with a constant emphasis upon the essential oneness of all humanity

- Acting as examples of pure living and creative activity, subordinated to the general purpose, beauty, and inclusiveness

- Upholding the ideals of individual and group freedom

- Practicing focused meditation

- Emphasizing the fundamentals of the ageless wisdom while lessening a focus on the nonessentials

- Working together with other members to accomplish these goals, without criticism and without imposing one's method of work upon another

Members of the new group recognize each other through the quality of the work they are doing in the outer world and the inclusiveness of the note they sound. Groups of members coordinate with other groups to accomplish what is needed in the world, recognizing which aspects of the work that each is equipped to do and keeping an attitude of sectarianism out of it. The Great Ones and the souls of its members inspire the groups of servers, and they are energized into activity by the need of humanity itself.

The Tibetan offers the following information about how the New Group of World Servers is viewed on the inner planes:

"It is composed of living conscious souls, working through coordinated personalities. Its symbol is a golden triangle enclosing an even-armed cross with one diamond at the apex of the triangle. This symbol is never reproduced in form at all. It shines above the heads of all who are in the group and cannot be seen by anyone (not even a clairvoyant) except a group member, and then only if—for purposes of work—his recognition needs stimulation. The motto of the group is The Glory Of The One."[48]

Plans for Humanity

The plans for humanity are not laid down by Hierarchy or Shamballa, for humanity determines its own destiny. However, according to the Tibetan, plans have been established to make possible a closer relationship between humanity and the Hierarchy. This relationship could inspire the needed changes in our civilization.

Humanity works from an organizational angle and, after we envision an idea, we begin to build the outer physical form to express it. Hierarchy, works "under the inspiration of the Divine Vision as it is embodied in the Plan, seeks to evoke a response to that Plan in every human heart, and by fostering and fanning that response, to evoke not only a mental understanding but also an aspirational desire."[49] Together, Hierarchy and humanity can help condition human affairs to manifest the divine plan upon Earth, and thus build a better civilization.

When a sufficient number of people are in conscious touch with their souls, the sheer weight of numbers, plus the clarity of intentions and widespread distribution over the face of the Earth, must necessarily become effective. We will then bring about changes of such far-reaching impact that our culture today will seem barbarian to the culture of the future.

"This then is the task of the Workers in the field of human affairs: to awaken the soul ray to potency in the life of each human being, beginning with those whose mental equipment and achieved integration would warrant the belief that—once awakened—they would use the new forces at their disposal with a measure of wisdom and planned constructive intention."[50]

Chapter 9—
Timing, Relationships, and Karmic Opportunity

"The "stars in their courses" will aid humanity or bring destruction,
according to human determinations. Men can achieve liberty and organise
for the New Age with its unique civilisation and constructive synthesis, or
they can commit suicide (…symbolically) and hand over their immediate
future to the forces of evil and of death. These work for the death of all the
true values and of all for which the human spirit has fought."—AAB[1]

Each world epoch is created and guided by a great being, according
to Agni Yoga. This spirit, by his own fiery tension, creates that
preordained age in time, or cosmic cycle, and establishes the blueprint
or archetypes of what can be manifested within this period. Cosmic
cycles comprise entire millennia and the Spirit of the Cycle outlines
these cycles in the "cementing of space. Each fiery striving can already
be a pledge of a new link in the affirmation of the Cycle."[2]

In essence, each time one of us strives for the benefit of evolution
and manifests higher levels of creativity, we form a link in the spatial
structure of these cycles that manifests in space and time what already
exists in the "eternal now."

Concerning cyclical influences, however, we need to keep in mind
that the influence of the constellations and planets work out upon three
descending levels of awareness—the mental plane, the astral plane,
and then the physical plane. Up to this point in time astrologers have
been mainly concerned about the physical plane and have emphasized
happenings and events, and not their conditioning causes. This has
led to much confusion and distortion in interpreting horoscopes; for
example, a horoscope which could be interpreted upon the mental plane
is given a physical interpretation, and thus events that are entirely
mental are portrayed as physical occurrences. The Tibetan's teachings
tell us that we should look to the relationship of the exoteric, esoteric,
and hierarchical planets and the rays that they express to obtain a clue
to the right interpretation of a given chart.[3]

Correct interpretations always depend upon the levels of evolution of the entities studied, whether it be individuals, groups, or nations, which gives us another clue when we look at the interpenetrating relationships of energies and forces depicted in an astrological chart.

Timing and Cycles

"The general law, which produces cyclic effect, is the Law of Attraction and Repulsion, of which the subsidiary law is the Law of Periodicity, and of Rebirth. Cyclic evolution is entirely the result of the activity of matter, and of the Will or Spirit. It is produced by the interaction of active matter and moulding Spirit. Every form holds hid a Life. Every life constantly reaches out after the similar life latent in other forms."—AAB[4]

The seven rays manifest in cycles and their cycles are of varying length according to their energies and the opportunities the universe needs at the time. For there is what can be called group karma, affecting entire eons and large groups of humanity. Humanity seems to have the task of manifesting karmic consequences on the physical plane, and we need better techniques to be more proactive in what we choose to bring about.

Major Ray One and Ray Four energies are in lesser manifestation at this time than energies from Rays Seven, Six, Five, Three, and Two, although Ray One energy flows in strongly at the end of a century and the end of a millennium. We know that a Ray Seven cycle of energy is beginning at this time and a Ray Six cycle of energy is diminishing (even though there is a more long-term cycle of Ray Six energy coming to us from another more foundational cycle). Ray Two energy is always prevalent because we are members of a Ray Two, love-wisdom solar system. Ray Five energy in the past 300 years has sparked many technological breakthroughs and scientific accomplishments, however Ray Five influence might be beginning to wane.[5]

Ray Seven and Ray Five energies work well together because Ray Seven plays an important role in the building of a thoughtform and Ray Five in the work of implementing it. Rays Three, Five, and Seven enhance creative work, making it much easier than when Rays Two, Four, and Six are dominant. Under the incoming energy flow of Ray Seven, the "work of the numerous unconscious magicians will be much facilitated,"[6] which will help thinking humanity to evolve world structures for the betterment of all of humanity and to build a new civilization. This civilization will be based upon love energy and the ideals we have received and are still receiving along Ray Two and Ray Six lines.

What all this means to us is that some cosmic energies are more accessible and in tune with the current cycles of time than others. If great beings, Ray Lords, and Spirits of Cycles have decided that the world needs an inflow of Ray Seven and a withdrawal of Ray Six, and perhaps Ray Five, and also that we should receive Ray Four and Ray One energies in the next 25 to 50 years, then it might behoove us to examine the characteristics of these energies and align ourselves with them in order that we might assist in the trends of evolution decided upon by beings with more global knowledge than ourselves. This may seem to have no immediate effect for our own lives, but it will have profound effects for our children, for all of humanity, and—yes—also for us when we reincarnate.

The main energy we invoke is the energy of the Sun in whichever of the twelve signs it happens to be. During each season of the year, the Sun provides unique energy opportunities that we can take advantage of. For example, the three signs of the spring season offer different energies than the three winter signs, and so on.

We then need to determine which energies are working together or, in other words, which planets are in configuration with each other. Conversely, we need to notice which planets are not in configuration with other planets and appear to be quiescent at the time. For example, at the time of the full moon, the Sun and the Moon are always in opposition. The two angles of the opposition complete the circle and are, thus, the first powerful pattern that we notice. Typically we then find one or more planets forming angles to the Sun and the Moon. We note these angles and the patterns they form, thus realizing what planets are working together at the time, in cooperation with the Sun and the Moon, to bring specialized energies to our Earth.

We first relate the aspects of the planets to the Sun and the Moon, and then secondarily we note which planets might be in aspect to each other that are not in aspect to the Sun or the Moon. We might want to take note of that and conjecture how we can use that particular energy as well.

Timing and cycles work with the Law of Karma. The Law of Karma ensures that we have multiple opportunities to evolve and carry out our work. As stated in the Agni Yoga teachings: "Each epoch has its own distinctions. Each peculiarity of time is an imprint of consciousness. These manifestations of peculiarities can be magnified by the will of humanity. The peculiarities of the epoch, in the same way as evocations, have their roots in the consciousness...In this evolutionary and incessant turn of the spiral, man will find the Truth...And though human darkening be prolonged, yet from under the dark strata will be exhumed the affirmations of the Light. Thus, that which is ordained enters in awesome immensity."[7]

Geometrical Forms and Aspects

"When, therefore, the esoteric side of astrology, and of mystical geometry, has been studied, and alliance has been made between these two sciences, a flood of light will be thrown upon this matter of the intelligent principle; when the inner workings of the Law of Cause and Effect...is better comprehended, then—and then only—will the sons of men be able to study with profit the place of manas in the evolutionary scheme."—AAB[8]

We can assume that planets in a geometrical configuration are having some type of effect on each other and that the results of these streams of energy are entering Earth and causing effects here. Several major geometrical forms or aspects are discussed in the ageless wisdom teachings and in various mystery traditions, and also in the work of Carl Jung. These forms or aspects are:

- The Circle / Wheel of the Zodiac
- Crosses / Squares
- Polarities / Oppositions
- Triangles / Trines
- The Five-Pointed Star
- The Six-Pointed Star

We are not stressing that any particular aspect is more profound than another because their importance for our work is relative to what we might want to accomplish at the time and upon which plane of consciousness we want to manifest. In a linear presentation, we would discuss oppositions after the circle, and then trines, squares, and stars, in that order. Our rather eclectic order discusses the circle and then squares (crosses), thus setting the stage for the two polar opposites that are inherent upon a particular cross. Also, since stars contain triangles, they are arranged together, in the order listed above.

The 360-degree circle is the purest form in our universal consideration of energy and is the basis for all the other angles we work with. An opposition contains two 180-degree angles, a triangle contains three 120-degree angles, a cross contains four 90-degree angles, a five-pointed star contains five 72-degree angles, and a six-pointed star contains six 60-degree angles.

The circle or mandala represents our realm, or ring-pass-not, of activity, a point in the center of the circle represents us (be it person or group), and the intersections of the energy patterns around the circle represent the points around which energy flows. If we consider our realm of activity to be humanity on Earth, we can then consider the point in the center to be our full-moon meditation group. The points around the circle would then represent the configuration of planets in the sky at the time of our full-moon meditation. We can cast a chart of where the planets happen to be located at that particular time and also note in which signs they are located. The planets and the signs represent the current cycles of energy that we are able to invoke.

Carl Jung described the "circle as a mandala, the psychological expression of the totality of the self." In his studies on the mandala, he indicated that it contains key motifs, including the cross and the divided upper and lower halves.[9] Jung gave mandalas a lot of attention because of their worldwide cultural use, which is because mandalas, and the patterns contained within them, are archetypal images in the collective mind of humanity. To Jung, mandalas symbolize what he called the process of individuation or of whole-making.

Within the circle, conjunctions represent unity and the divided circle or mandala represents polarity. The triangle represents the potentiality of spirit—possibility—and the square represents the potentiality of matter—process and points of crisis. Energies flow through triangles and manifest through crosses. The four angles or arms of the cross divide space into the four sections of the circle, or mandala.

According to Dane Rudhyar, the horizontal and vertical axis of the cross defines the orientation of the individual to the universe. The vertical axis of an astrological chart refers to power and the horizontal axis to consciousness. In our power lies our strength, responsibility, and creativity. In our consciousness lies our knowledge and wisdom. Rudhyar tells us that all human experience and values can be evaluated in terms of consciousness and power.[10] Eventually, the Tibetan tells us, the twelve arms of the three crosses will take the place of the twelve houses when the horoscope of the soul is cast.[11]

Two five-pointed stars equal ten, or the decad. Two six-pointed stars equal twelve, or the dodecad. The Tibetan says, "The triangle and the star are subjective expressions of a fixed consciousness, focused in reality, whilst the square and the cross are objective expressions of the man focused outwardly."[12] He indicates that an initiate consciously and effectively relates within himself the triangle of energy, the square, the cross, and the five-pointed star; within these symbolic forms lies the whole history of humanity, the fourth kingdom in nature.

"These stars, triangles and squares are found in all horoscopes—human, planetary, systemic and cosmic—and constitute the life pattern of the particular Being under investigation; they determine the time of manifestation and the nature of the emanations and influences."[13] Astrologers of the future will emphasize triangles and the three crosses (as well as the rising sign) in charting the life of the soul.[14]

The Circle / The Wheel of the Zodiac

The circle, or the mandala, represents the wheel of the zodiac and the cycles of astronomical ages through the eons of the existence of the universe. The circle is a symbol of unity, wholeness, and protection of integrity.

Contemplating the mandala enables us to translate the illusion of separative existence into a knowledge of universal unity and totality. Jung tells us that the mandala symbolizes, by its central point, the ultimate unity of all archetypes as well as the multiplicity of the phenomenal world. He further indicates that the individual plays a primary role in the unification of the psyche with the cosmos.[15]

The energy in the central point of the mandala relates everything and impels us to become "what we are." This center is surrounded by everything that belongs to us, the paired opposites that make up our total personality. This totality comprises our personal consciousness and our collective consciousness and contains the collective unconscious whose archetypes are common to us all.[16]

Mandalas are fundamentally similar, regardless of their origin in time and space. Some of the common elements of mandala symbolism include:[17]

- The circle elaborated into a flower (rose, lotus) or a wheel

- A center expressed by a sun, star, or cross, usually with four, eight, or twelve rays

- Circles, spheres, and cruciform figures represented in rotation (swastika)

- A circle represented by a coiled snake

- Squaring of the circle, with a circle in a square or vice versa

- Eye (pupil and iris)

Most mandalas are characterized by the circle and the quaternary, according to Jung. The mandala often depicts the rose or the lotus (the rose being the western symbol for the lotus) arranged in groups of four petals, which Jung says indicates the squaring of the circle or the unification of opposites. Jung considers the squaring of the circle to be an archetype of wholeness.[18]

Jung speaks of the three and four playing a great role in alchemy, involving a transformation process that is divided into four stages of three parts each, analogous to the twelve transformations of the zodiac and its division into four. He relates the significance of the twelve to the end of the Pisces era and the twelfth house of the zodiac.[19]

The Tibetan tells us that:[20]

- The circle itself stands for the ring-pass-not of undifferentiated matter.

- The circle with the point in the center represents the heart of matter—the first straining of the atom into the sphere of influence of another atom, which produces the first radiation, the first pull of attraction, and the consequent setting up of a repulsion.

- Repulsion produces the circle divided into two, which marks the active rotation and the beginning of the mobility of the atom of matter. This extends the influence of the point within the atom from the center to the periphery. When it reaches the periphery, it contacts the influence of other atoms in its environment, radiation is set up, and force begins to flow in and out.

- The circle divided into four is the true circle of matter, or the equal-armed cross. The energy penetrates in four directions. Each wedge between two arms represents a triangle of radiation.

Crosses / Squares

The symbol of the cross or square signifies a relationship between two oppositions. According to astrologer Ed Perrone, "...the square aspect concretizes the spiritual process indicated by the oppositions themselves. It joins the two influences of the oppositions into two aspects of the same process and manifests the result on the physical level."[21] Thus, the square impels the abstract idea to become a concrete reality.

The Tibetan states that the square configuration relates to material appearance or form expression and the relationships between the many quaternaries within the planetary interrelationships, involving four constellations in a square plus many human and divine quaternaries.[22]

The right angles of a cross constitute the configuration of the square. When dealing with planetary systems, we might find, at any particular full moon, planets at right angles to each other. For example, Uranus might be in Aquarius and Mars might be in Taurus or Scorpio, in which cases Uranus would be in square formation to Mars. Aquarius, Taurus, and Scorpio are all members of the fixed cross and, if Uranus is in Aquarius and Mars is in Scorpio, two arms of the fixed cross are represented in this energy pattern.

The mutable, fixed, and cardinal signs of the zodiac represent the arms of the mutable, fixed, and cardinal cosmic crosses. Their energies, flowing into our system, present us with experiences and changes, give us the responsibility of choice, and evoke the free-will, determination, and decision necessary to further develop ourselves and the world.

The energies from the zodiac (received from even higher sources) come into the outer parts of the four arms of the cross and meet at the midway point. We stand at this midway point and receive these energies from all the constellations constituting the particular cross we are currently working on. From this point, we use the vertical axis to communicate with spirit, or Hierarchy, and we use the horizontal axis to distribute energies to and receive feedback from humanity. The four streams of energy from the four arms within each cross combine and flow upon all forms, and synthesize the processes and goals of evolution.

These three crosses relate to the three basic energies that brought the solar system into being; they constitute a synthesis of the three major expressions of divine will, motivated by love, and expressed through activity. The theme of all three crosses is integration and fusion; the integration of the personality, the fusion of soul and personality, and the fusion of spirit, soul, and personality. These combinations produce transitions in consciousness that enable us to move to the next cross, though we continue to work with the previous cross in some capacity. In the blending of these energies, the lesser are always included in the greater, giving us the power to express both the vertical and horizontal life simultaneously, in time and space.[23]

The crosses also turn, being the spokes of the great wheel. When spiritually unawakened, we move around the wheel in one direction and then we reverse this order once we develop ourselves and step upon the path of progress. Crosses involve change, then direction, and finally initiation. We must bear in mind, however, that these associations of the crosses relate to the path of consciousness expansion and initiation; the signs that we are manifesting in our current incarnations are a separate matter and do not indicate our level of development. For example, an initiate can have a predominance of signs of the mutable cross in his or her horoscope and, conversely, a person on the probationary path can have a predominance of signs of the cardinal cross.

Mutable Cross—Gemini, Virgo, Sagittarius, and Pisces

The mutable cross represents personality (form), activity, and humanity.[24] This cross produces great periods of change and reorientation in our lives. It governs our personality lives and produces changes, the accumulation of experiences, action and reaction, karmic control, and our responses to impacts that lead to the awakening of consciousness.

The mutable cross impels change, fluidity, and constantly altering environments that drive us from one extreme of experience to another, so that our lives shuttle between the pairs of opposites. This cross develops our responsiveness so that we can eventually make conscious contact with our souls. It is the cross of the personality, of the steadily developing and finally integrating human being. This takes place at first in response to circumstance and later to soul inclination.

The mutable cross governs the form or body nature and controls the life cycle of the soul through the lower experiences until we become aligned to a higher vision and a wider horizontal and vertical grasp of reality. This cross governs the lower triad in manifestation and rules in the three worlds of human evolution.

The signs of the mutable cross are related to so many other of the signs because of the repeated incarnations, varied experiments, and periodic changes we must go through to provide adequate experiences for expansions of consciousness. The forces of the mutable cross provide the complete fusion of love and mind necessary for full manifestation and efficient functioning of soul-consciousness.

The Pleiades sends dynamic energies into the mutable cross through Gemini, Mercury, and Sagittarius. We feel them when we are upon the path of initiation. The lessons of the mutable cross bring about planetary awareness, influenced by Gemini and focused by Mercury.[25]

Gemini, Virgo, Sagittarius, and Pisces are the constellations of the mutable cross, and they occupy the positions on the axis as follows:

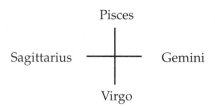

The energies of these four signs condition us for transformation:

1. Gemini produces changes needed for the evolution of soul-consciousness at any particular point in time and space.

2. Virgo, the nurturing force of substance itself, fosters and protects the embryonic life of the soul.

3. Sagittarius, the energetic activity of the life force, integrates the three aspects of the form nature with the three aspects of the soul.

4. Pisces embodies the life expression and active appearance of soul-consciousness in form.

All these signs mark points of change or are custodians of energies that help us reorient to new activities. The main objective of the four mutable energies is to produce a constant flux and periodic change in time and space that can provide adequate experience for the unfoldment of higher life and consciousness. This is true cosmically, and also from the standpoint of a solar system, planet, and human. The field of development for the lower three kingdoms depends upon the status and energy-distributing power of humanity as a whole.

The following planets and their rays condition the mutable cross:

Vulcan	Ray 1	Will and Power
Pluto	Ray 1	Will and Power
Jupiter	Ray 2	Love-Wisdom
Earth	Ray 3	Active Intelligence and Adaptability
Mercury	Ray 4	Harmony, Beauty, and Art
Moon	Ray 4	Harmony, Beauty, and Art
Venus	Ray 5	Concrete Knowledge and Science
Neptune	Ray 6	Devotion and Idealism
Mars	Ray 6	Devotion and Idealism

Fixed Cross—Leo, Scorpio, Aquarius, and Taurus

The fixed cross represents soul, consciousness, and Hierarchy. Its energies are most potent in our current world cycle. The fixed cross governs the conscious soul and controls the three human levels of activity (mental, emotional, and physical) and the two superhuman levels (the lower Trinity and the Spiritual Triad).[26] It integrates the soul and personality.

This cross presents opportunities and points of crisis. It transforms desire into aspiration and selfishness into group-consciousness. When we have fully tested ourselves and mastered our experiences, this cross brings about systemic awareness, that is, fuller awareness of the solar system in which we operate.

Many of the opportunities, points of crisis, and inner changes brought about upon the fixed cross are focused through the planet Saturn,[27] one of the most significant Lords of Karma to humanity today. Fixed-cross energies blend with and transmit the energies of the solar system itself. It can do this because, upon the fixed cross, we become increasingly sensitive to a larger whole and conscious of issues that are more dynamic than ourselves, more engrossing than our previous interests, and that concern humanity in its relation to the solar forces and not just to the planetary forces.

The fixed cross produces a vast experience of group life, group activity, and group awareness. We mount this cross when we have attained some measure of soul contact and have had some touch of illumination and spiritual intuition. Upon the fixed cross, we are increasingly aware of its influences and our direction upon the spiritual path.

It is called the "fixed" cross because it gives us fixed vision and immovable intent. We are stretched upon it by the directed choice of our soul, and from this decision there is no turning back. Upon this cross, we stand at the center where the four arms meet, at the point where the energy of all the four signs and their ruling planets can pour through us and evoke needed reactions, produce conditions that test us, and upgrade our life tendencies.

Taurus, Leo, Scorpio, and Aquarius are the constellations of the fixed cross. These signs are also the symbols associated with the Sphinx. They occupy the positions on the axis of the fixed cross as follows:

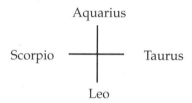

These signs bring humanity light and liberation:[28]

- Taurus—The Bull of Desire—The light of aspiration and knowledge
  "I seek illumination and am myself the light."

- Leo—The Lion of Self-assertion—The light of the soul
  "I know myself to be the one. I rule by Law."

- Scorpio—The Agent of Deception—The light of liberation
  "Illusion cannot hold me. I am the bird that flies with utter freedom."

- Aquarius—The Chalice of Self-service—The light of the world
  "I am the server, and I the dispenser am of living water."

Points of crisis we encounter on the fixed cross give us the opportunity (Saturn) to further our evolution. The cycle of the fixed cross presents those opportunities and makes it possible for us (individually and in groups) to take initiation:

1. In Taurus, we transmute desire into aspiration and darkness into light and illumination. We focus our attention upon spiritual attainment and tread the path of discipleship.

2. In Leo, we focus our life expression on the soul and the spiritual goal of selflessness. We prepare for and take the first initiation.

3. In Scorpio, we undergo tests that enable us to take the second initiation and thus demonstrate that we have subdued our desire nature. Our lower nature can now reach the goal for this world period, and our personality is fit for world service.

4. In Aquarius, we consummate the long effort of the soul and conclude our experience upon the fixed cross. We take the third initiation and become free from personality control. We take the next two initiations upon the cardinal cross.

The following planets and their rays condition the fixed cross:

Vulcan	Ray 1	Will and Power
Pluto	Ray 1	Will and Power
The Sun	Ray 2	Love-Wisdom
Jupiter	Ray 2	Love-Wisdom
Mercury	Ray 4	Harmony, Beauty, and Art
Moon	Ray 4	Harmony, Beauty, and Art
Venus	Ray 5	Concrete Knowledge and Science
Neptune	Ray 6	Devotion and Idealism
Mars	Ray 6	Devotion and Idealism
Uranus	Ray 7	Ceremonial Order, Magic, and Organization

Cardinal Cross—Aries, Cancer, Libra, and Capricorn

The cardinal cross represents spirit, will, and Shamballa.[29] This cross synthesizes the results of all our experience and initiates us into the realm of Hierarchy. This cross is the place of transcendence, where personality, form, and planetary life no longer control, and we stand free. This brings about cosmic awareness. According to the Tibetan, Jupiter focuses the energies at this point.

The cardinal cross is mysterious to most of us, as average humanity is working on the mutable cross and more advanced humanity is working on the fixed cross. We work upon the cardinal cross only after achieving continuity of consciousness, usually by the third initiation.

The cardinal cross governs the manifestation of the monad (or spirit) in all its glory and beauty, and this cycle of influence falls into two stages:

- One in which the monad expresses itself upon the six planes of manifestation in wisdom, strength, and beauty through the medium of the integrated soul and personality. This is a relatively brief stage.

- Then, no longer manifesting through the soul and personality, the monad "proceeds upon the higher Way and passes on to realms unknown e'en to the highest of the Sons of God upon our Earth."

The Tibetan calls this the cross of the "widespread arms, the open heart and the higher mind," because, when we can experience life upon the cardinal cross, we know and enjoy the significances of omnipresence and omniscience, and are in the process of unfolding the higher phases of being called omnipotence.[30]

The zodiacal influences of the signs of the cardinal cross express spirit or life more than soul or body, as they flow throughout the universe. These four energies, pouring through the four arms of this cross, produce a vortex of synthesizing force, a "pool of pure, fiery light," which purifies and cleanses each aspect of our lower threefold nature, preparatory to the higher initiations.

The energies of the cardinal cross blend with cosmic energy, carry the quality of the One About Whom Naught May be Said, and are "tinctured with the Light of the seven solar systems" of which our solar system is one.

The consummating influence of the cardinal cross, after one has achieved hierarchical standing, is illumined by the following passage from *Tibetan Yoga and Secret Doctrines*.

"All beauty, all goodness, all that makes for the eradication of sorrow and ignorance upon the Earth must be devoted to the Great Consummation. Then when the Lords of Compassion shall have spiritually civilised the Earth and made of it a Heaven, there shall be revealed to the Pilgrims the Endless Path which reaches to the Heart of the Universe. Man, then no longer man, will transcend nature and impersonally, yet consciously, in at-one-ment with all Enlightened Ones, help to fulfill the Law of the Higher Evolution, of which Nirvana is but the beginning."[31]

Aries, Cancer, Libra, and Capricorn are the constellations of the cardinal cross, and they occupy the positions on the axis as follows:

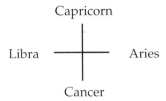

These four energies of the cardinal cross direct us as we move forward upon the path of initiation. Thus, we could say that it is the cross of initiation and of our beginnings upon the way of higher evolution and endless perfectionment. For this purpose, all of our previous stages of evolution have been only preparatory. The energies of the cardinal cross, as they affect our solar system, are:

- Aries—Creation—Originating purposeful work

- Cancer—Manifestation—Materializing the work

- Libra—Legislation—Working within spiritual and natural law

- Capricorn—Initiation—Using the gained consciousness and experience to consummate the work and to begin the cycle again, from a higher level

We become cooperators in the great creative process and purpose. We begin to create our own body of expression upon the cardinal cross and the impulse of Aries appears to us. We manifest consciously in the world what we intend to carry forward and Cancer then reveals to us its secret. We become our own legislator, ruling our conduct wisely, controlling our impulses intellectually, and then Libra enables us to balance the material and the spiritual law.

When we have done all this, we discover ourselves ready to enter into new and deeper experiments and experiences and, as participators in the divine plan and cooperators in the divine purpose, we become our own initiator and are thus ready to take initiation. The following planets and their rays condition the cardinal cross:

Saturn	Ray 3	Active Intelligence and Adaptability
Mercury	Ray 4	Harmony, Beauty, and Art
Moon	Ray 4	Harmony, Beauty, and Art
Venus	Ray 5	Concrete Knowledge and Science
Neptune	Ray 6	Devotion and Idealism
Mars	Ray 6	Devotion and Idealism
Uranus	Ray 7	Ceremonial Order, Magic, and Organization

Polarities / Oppositions

The relation of the opposites in the zodiacal circle express the interrelation of spirit and matter and the interplay of their energies. They bear witness to the fact that the "two are one and are simply the expression of great mutable, and yet fixed and initiated spiritual Lives."[32] Our solar system is itself energized by dual forces, those of love and wisdom. A specific task of humanity is to balance the dualities, or "pairs of opposites," that thread through our lives upon all the planes of manifestation through which we work. This involves much discrimination.

The energies of Gemini are particularly useful in balancing the pairs of opposites: "Gemini, therefore, forms with each of the pairs of opposites in the Zodiac a third factor, powerfully influencing the other two constellations, and thus forms, with them, certain great zodiacal triangles. These only become of importance when considering the horoscopes of advanced human beings or esoteric groups, but eventually when casting the horoscope of a disciple or an initiate, the esoteric astrologer will have to consider their potency."[33]

Pairs of opposites can gain and profit from each other, for there is a direct line of force and contact between them. "In terms of energy, polarity means a potential, and wherever a potential exists there is the possibility of a current, a flow of events, for the tension of opposites strives for balance," Jung says.[34] The pairs of opposites in the zodiac are, in effect, six great energies which we can use to express both personality and soul awareness, depending on the need at the time.

In the zodiacal circle, the opposites express the interrelation of spirit and matter plus the interplay of qualitative energies; they bear witness that the two are one and express great mutable, and yet fixed and initiated, spiritual Lives.

Oppositions are the basis for full-moon meditations, when "it is almost as if a door suddenly opened wide."[35] This gives us the opportunity to take these cyclical energies into our meditation groups, condition them with our love and goodwill, and then send them forth to humanity and places on the planet that particularly need them at the time.

On a more personal level, the Tibetan tells us that it would be interesting to analyze horoscopes of incarnations where the polar opposites appear opposite to each other, one as the Sun sign and the other as the ascendant for, he indicates, these lives usually express some degree of equilibrium or consummation and are not, in any case, passive lives or lacking in direction, event, or purpose.[36]

The following quotation from *The Old Commentary* describes polar affinity, the "Marriage in the Heavens." This is the transference of life from the attractive planet to the receptive one, and finally, at a later period, the absorption of the life of the two planets by a third planet, "the Son," which is the synthesizing planet that forms the apex of the solar triangle.

1. "The life pulsates, and the pole performs its function. The sphere revolves in many cycles. As it revolves it senses other spheres, and seeks to know their secret.

2. They meet each other. They seek a greater intimacy or reject with hatred any more approach. Some pass away; others return and marry. They know each other. They spiral through their courses hand in hand. Through union the fires blaze up, the two become the one, and live again in their Son, who is the Third."[37]

Polar Opposites of the Mutable Cross

Gemini/Sagittarius

- Focus and determination

- Activity and achievement

- One-pointed soul effort

- Spiritually directed activity

- Waning of the power of form and the waxing of the life of the soul

- Separativeness to unity

- Versatility yet directedness

Virgo/Pisces

- The attraction between matter and soul

- Revelation of the indwelling soul

- World saviorship

- Consummation of work for a cycle

- Sensitiveness and fluidity combined with mental introspection and critical analysis

Polar Opposites of the Fixed Cross

Taurus/Scorpio

- Victory over the lower nature

- Death and darkness become life and light

- Desire becomes spiritual aspiration

- Experience becomes illumination

- Disruptions and alterations in character, quality, and direction take place

- Aspiration gives place to intelligent activity, leading to cooperation with the Plan and the end of self-centeredness

- Self-indulgence gives way to selfless attitude

- Ambition gives place to the executive activity of the soul

- Attachment to personality desires, likes, and dislikes is transmuted into the tenacity of soul purpose

- Demonstration of creativity, inspired by aspiration and vision

- Expression of the beauty that all forms veil, revealing the underlying purpose that motivates all events and forms

Leo/Aquarius

- Personality interests submerged in the good of the whole

- Potential of reaching heights of noted service

- Expansion from self-consciousness into group awareness

- The height of achievement of the soul

- Shift of attention away from the individual to the environing group, from selfish interests to group requirements

- Universality and its sense of "general distribution"

Polar Opposites of the Cardinal Cross

Aries/Libra

- Transmutation of passion to love and desire into love-wisdom

- Balance of spirit and matter

- Achievement of equilibrium

- Mental impetus for soul control
- An intense interplay takes place, with attainment of equilibrium in Libra of what began in Aries

Cancer/Capricorn

- Pull of matter superseded by the free choice of the soul
- Form life becomes a conscious method of expression for service
- Growing emphasis upon soul life and a pull away from form experience

Equinotical Phases Represented by Pairs of Opposites

The cycle of equinox to equinox is considered by the western mystery tradition to be a Sun tide, just as a Moon tide is the phase between new moons.[38] The two Sun tides of the year represent a pair of opposites, with each tide containing and disseminating the energies of six astrological signs.

The vernal to autumnal equinotical tide includes the forces of the signs Aries through Virgo, which are considered by astrologers to be the personal signs of the zodiac, whereas the autumnal to vernal cycle includes the signs Libra through Pisces, considered to be the social signs. The first phase develops the personality and the second phase integrates the personality into the soul.

Within the equinotical tide, the major pair of opposites, the six zodiacal pairs of opposites interrelate in their own particular evolutionary phase and affect us according to our own phase of evolutionary development.

- Aries/Libra provides the beginnings and the foundation for further development
- Taurus/Scorpio represents the means to be used
- Gemini/Sagittarius defines the scope of awareness
- Cancer/Capricorn represents a concretion of effort
- Leo/Aquarius develops the consciousness and identity
- Virgo/Pisces synthesizes all the preceding phases and prepares us to move on to the next level

Triangles / Trines

Triangles relate to spirit and synthesis.[39] These archetypal structures play a significant part in all symbolism[40] and are important in our investigation of the content of the universal mind.

The Tibetan presents the Science of Triangles as a means of helping Earth achieve the status of "sacred planet." The etheric web around Earth is now a pattern of squares, but as the divine plan works out, the Earth's etheric web will be transformed into a network of intricate, constantly moving, interwoven series of triangles, "in rapid movement, revolving eternally in space and ceaselessly moving onward and in fourth and fifth dimensional existence."[41] These energies penetrate into the etheric body of humanity and result in the development of our consciousness and the precipitation of events on Earth. The seven sacred planets have already achieved this network of triangles and the etheric pattern around the Sun is now that of interlaced circles.[42]

In all the possible triads we can study in esoteric astrology, we find correspondences to the monad, the soul, and the personality of the individual. For a particular cycle, one line of the triangle embodies a determining and dominating force, and the other two lines are conditioned by this energy.[43]

This pair of triangles show a downflow of energy from an emanating center, merging into an evocative center of reception. The energy then flows toward a magnetic center and then into a center for distribution. The energy then returns to the evocative center, then to the magnetic center again, and finally to the source at the top. All together, this forms a figure 8, and represents an antahkarana of energy flow, invocative and evocative. The entities invoking and evoking can be a human, a planet, or a solar system: any

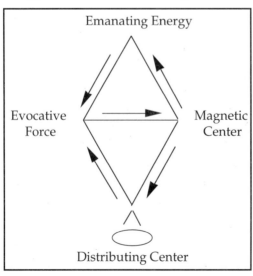

Emanating Energy

Evocative Force

Magnetic Center

Distributing Center

level, in conformity to the Law of Correspondences.

The triangle is the basic geometric form of the cosmos; it underlies the entire fabric of manifestation, whether of a macrocosm or a microcosm.[44] The Tibetan tells us that the Science of Triangles is "the science of the universal geometrical blue-print underlying the phenomenal worlds and is also closely related to Karma. It concerns the first precipitation of the interaction and the effect of the duality of manifestation, of spirit-matter, as they constitute one substance."[45]

The Triangles of The Great Bear, Sirius, and The Pleiades

The energies coming from the three major constellations, the Great Bear, Sirius, and the Pleiades, form the major triangle of potential influence in our solar system. These energies relate to humanity as follows:[46]

- Energies from the Great Bear influence the will and purpose of our Solar Logos (just as the energies of the monad influence the individual human). These energies pass through Shamballa and correspond to the monad.

- Energies from Sirius influence the love-wisdom aspect, or the attractive power, of our Solar Logos. These cosmic soul energies pass through Hierarchy.

- Energies from the Pleiades influence the active intelligent aspect of our Solar Logos and affect the form side of all manifestation in our solar system. These energies focus through humanity and correspond to the personality.

From this major triangle of energies, many different combinations and permutations of interlocking triangles form, which are discussed at length in *Esoteric Astrology* by Alice A. Bailey and the Tibetan.

The following diagram is a primary example of how streams of energy from the cosmos eventually reach and influence humankind. These particular energies relate to the evolution and destiny of the human family.[47]

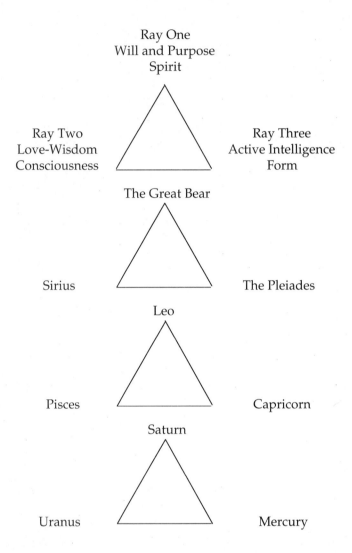

Note: Each point of the triangles in this diagram represents a descending stream of energy to the corresponding point beneath it.

Another cosmic configuration of the Great Bear, Sirius, and the Pleiades depicts energies flowing through other constellations before they arrive at the same destination planets of Saturn, Mercury, and Uranus, and eventually to Earth. After we achieve certain evolutionary goals and are on the path of return, these constellational influences assist us in the development of self-consciousness and then spiritual consciousness.[48]

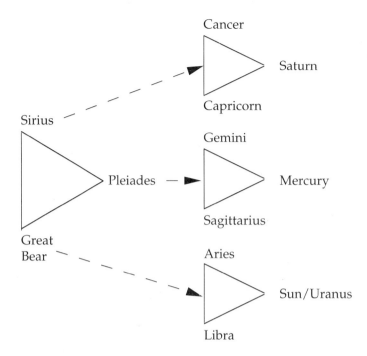

For an in-depth discussion of the cosmic configuration of the Great Bear, Sirius, and the Pleiades, refer to the chapter "Sirius, The Field of Energies, and the Prototypical Triangle" in M. Temple Richmond's valuable book, *Sirius* (see bibliography).

Ray, Constellational, and Planetary Triangles

As noted earlier, each of these seven rays, coming from the Great Bear, are transmitted into our solar system through the medium of three constellations and their ruling planet.[49]

The following table depicts the triangle of constellations that each of the rays transmits to. The planets listed are those that are associated with those particular constellations, so we can assume that a modified form of the ray energy, as directed through these triangles, is reaching these planets.

Constellational and Planetary Triangles

Ray	Constellation	Exoteric Planets	Esoteric Planets	Hierarchical Planets
1	Aries	Mars	Mercury	Uranus
	Leo	Sun (Jupiter)	Sun (Neptune)	Sun (Uranus)
	Capricorn	Saturn	Saturn	Venus
2	Gemini	Mercury	Venus	Earth
	Virgo	Mercury	Moon (Vulcan)	Jupiter
	Pisces	Jupiter	Pluto / Neptune	Pluto
3	Cancer	Moon (Neptune)	Neptune	Neptune
	Libra	Venus	Uranus	Saturn
	Capricorn	Saturn	Saturn	Venus
4	Taurus	Venus	Vulcan	Vulcan
	Scorpio	Mars / Pluto	Mars / Pluto	Mercury
	Sagittarius	Jupiter	Earth	Mars
5	Leo	Sun (Jupiter)	Sun (Neptune)	Sun (Uranus)
	Sagittarius	Jupiter	Earth	Mars
	Aquarius	Uranus	Jupiter	Moon (Uranus)
6	Virgo	Mercury	Moon (Vulcan)	Jupiter
	Sagittarius	Jupiter	Earth	Mars
	Pisces	Jupiter	Pluto / Neptune	Pluto
7	Aries	Mars	Mercury	Uranus
	Cancer	Moon (Neptune)	Neptune	Neptune
	Capricorn	Saturn	Saturn	Venus

The Triangle of Shamballa, Hierarchy, and Humanity

Through the great triangle of Shamballa, the Hierarchy and Humanity, cosmic, zodiacal and systemic force is focused and these three become, in their turn, a macrocosmic triangle of energies in relation to the individual human being upon the planet.[50]

Each point of the triangles in this diagram represents a descending stream of energy to the corresponding point beneath it.

The sacral center is omitted in this diagram because it is primarily related to the physical body and its expression of life perpetuation, rather than to the energies of will, love-wisdom, and active intelligence. For esoteric purposes, sacral energies are transmuted to the throat center.

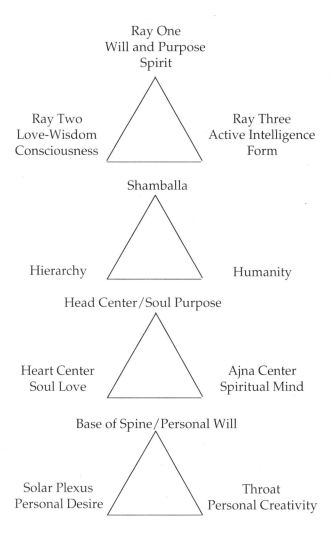

Ray One
Will and Purpose
Spirit

Ray Two
Love-Wisdom
Consciousness

Ray Three
Active Intelligence
Form

Shamballa

Hierarchy

Humanity

Head Center/Soul Purpose

Heart Center
Soul Love

Ajna Center
Spiritual Mind

Base of Spine/Personal Will

Solar Plexus
Personal Desire

Throat
Personal Creativity

The Triangle of Spirit, Soul, and Personality

The energy from the spirit comes from our monad and also from our master and his ashram. Soul energy comes from our own solar angels and the solar angels of those in our spiritual group. Personality energies come from the matter and elemental lives which comprise our subtle bodies and also the pranic energy from the atmosphere and the Sun. The macrocosmic planetary and astrological entities also work with the energies of spirit, soul, and personality on their own levels. Their physical energies are the ones that inspire and enlighten our spirits; spiritual energy is always that which comes from a higher source than us. Soul energy is the highest energy that we normally use in our daily lives, and the personality energy is the ordinary waking consciousness of humanity.

Stars

According to the Tibetan, the star configuration relates to states of consciousness.[51] A pentagon, or five-pointed star, is five streams of energy from five sources acting together. Pentagons can be related to quintile aspects in a horoscope. A hexagon, or six-pointed star, is six streams of energy from six sources acting together. Hexagons can be related to sextile and grand sextile aspects in a horoscope.

The Five-Pointed Star

The five-pointed star has often been called the "star of man" because our body consists of a trunk with five appendages, four limbs and the head. This pentagram, giving the same value to arms, legs, and head, symbolizes the instinctual, unconscious, corporeal human.[52]

This fivefold nature of the physical body represents the fact that only five centers are dominant in the body up to the third initiation, and the fivefold shape symbolizes the fivefold direction of force currents from the five centers. When the other two centers (of seven centers, altogether) function actively, the person is then qualified to distribute higher levels of energy.

This pentagon represents the fifth principle of mind and the five planes of human evolution. On the mental plane, the five-pointed star signifies the evolution of the principle of mind, the attainment of self-consciousness. On the buddhic plane of intuition, this star represents group-consciousness. Five letters of the sacred Word, sounded forth on the right note, give the key to the true inwardness of matter and also to its control.[53]

One of the major configurations of five entities that are working together is the one comprising Aries, Gemini, Virgo, Scorpio, and Earth. These entities are connected through the expression of Mercury in its following roles:[54]

- The esoteric ruler of Aries, which "leads into the mysteries."

- The exoteric ruler of Gemini, the sign of the major opposites of humanity, signifying soul and personality, consciousness and form.

- The exoteric ruler of Virgo, which represents the form and which indwells the form.

- The hierarchical ruler of Scorpio, the sign of discipleship.

- The expression of Ray Four energy, which relates to the fourth kingdom in nature on Earth, humanity.

Here is a symbol that we should visualize in rapid revolution. Through this five-pointed star, Mercury, Messenger of the Gods, carries a certain type of force to humanity, which precipitates a point of crisis that will bring about a revolution in human thought and experience and reveal the nature of divinity.

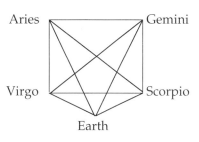

The Six-Pointed Star

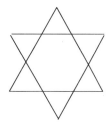

The six-pointed star conditions our consciousness, but not events, except insofar as our consciousness assumes control at a certain point in our evolution.[55] The six-pointed star contains six 60-degree angles and each one of these angles is called a sextile. A 60-degree angle also represents a part of a triangle. If the energy configuration contains six sextiles, it is a complete six-pointed star, or two triangles—a very potent energy configuration.

The six-pointed star portrays symbolically the process of involution and evolution, carried to a point of balance. The interlaced triangles of the Seal of Solomon, which form the six-pointed star, represent the relationship of the individual to the group, or to humanity.[56] Jung asserts that the number six means creation and evolution and points out that the hexad shows that the mandala consists of two triads, demonstrating that the personality needs to be extended both upwards and downwards.[57]

It is the job of humanity to be the planetary light bearer and to transmit the light of knowledge, wisdom, and understanding through the world soul, the soul in all forms, and to the three lower kingdoms—animal, vegetable, and mineral. The downpouring spiritual triangle of knowledge, wisdom, and understanding combines with the upraising matter triangle of matter from the three lower kingdoms to attain a balance point in humanity.[58] Thus, it is our duty to protect and save the world.

Geometry in the Wisdom Teachings

Below are some wonderful quotations from the ageless wisdom traditions relating to geometry and evolution.

Geometry in Three Solar Systems

STANZA IX of the *Stanzas of Dzyan*:

"The thirty thousand million Watchers refused to heed the call. 'We enter not the forms,' they said, 'until the seventh aeon.' The twice thirty thousand million hearkened to the call and took the forms designed.

"The rebellious ones laughed within themselves, and sought pralayic peace until the seventh aeon. But the seven great Lords called to the greater Chohans, and with the eternal Lhas of the third cosmic heaven entered into debate.

"The dictum then went forth. The laggards in the highest sphere heard it echo through the scheme. 'Not till the seventh aeon, but at the fourteenth seventh will the chance again come round. The first shall be the last and time be lost for aeons.'

"The obedient Sons of Mind connected with the Sons of Heart, and evolution spiralled on its way. The Sons of Power stayed in their appointed place, though cosmic karma forced a handful to join the Sons of Heart.

"At the fourteenth seventh aeon, the Sons of Mind and Heart, absorbed by endless flame, will join the Sons of Will, in manvantaric manifestation. Three times the wheel will turn.

"At the centre stand the buddhas of activity, helped by the lords of love, and following their twofold work will come the radiant lords of power.

"The buddhas of creation from out the past have come. The buddhas of love are gathering now. The buddhas of will at the final turn of the third major wheel will flash into being. The end will then be consummated."

The above stanza from the *Stanzas of Dzyan*, found in *The Secret Doctrine* and *A Treatise on Cosmic Fire*,[59] is a portion of an ancient scripture. This Stanza IX refers to the three solar systems; it associates the first solar system with the Sons of Mind, the second with the Sons of Heart, and the third and future solar system with the Sons of Will.

These three solar systems, according to the ageless wisdom teachings, contain the evolution of our Solar Logos, and all his associated vehicles of manifestation, through three incarnations; we are currently in the second of these three solar systems.

The first solar system led to a perfection of Ray Three energy of mind and material manifestation. In that system, the square represented the desirable way for energy to flow and the culmination of effort at the close of that system. This energy is represented as a grid or network of squares around the planet.

In this, the second solar system of Ray Two energy, we are building from the materials left over to us from the first solar system, working with the products of mind and merging them with the qualities of love. The triangle represents the desired pattern for energy in this system, and we are transforming the energy grid of squares around the Earth into triangles, halving the squares from the first system.

In the third and future Ray One solar system, we will merge the combined qualities of mind and love with the energy of will—a quality of will such as we have never experienced and cannot imagine. When this task is completed, energy will flow around a network of concentric circles, representing the perfectionment of energy for our Solar Logos in this threefold evolution. Our job then will be to transform the grid of triangles into a network of interlaced circles.

The below quotation from Alice Bailey and the Tibetan gives us an elegant picture of what the energy web surrounding our planet might look like:

"The inner web of light which is called the etheric body of the planet is essentially a web of triangles and when the evolutionary process is completed, it will have been organised. At present a pattern of squares is the major construction of the web but this is slowly changing as the divine plan works out. The etheric webs of the sacred planets are largely triangles whilst that of the Sun is that of interlaced circles. The effort on Earth today (as seen by the planetary Logos) is to bring about a transformation of the web of the planet and thus slowly change the existing squares into triangles. This is done by the creation of division, by the application of the Law of Separation, but also by the recognition, in consciousness, of duality, the application of directed motion and the appearance of two triangles in the place of one square. When this has taken place, the perceiving consciousness recognises identity and the rule of the square is ended. These words were once spoken to me by an ancient seer who bisected the square esoterically, thus forming two triangles and united them in a fresh manifestation to form a Star of Life. Ponder on this."[60]

Geometry in the Charts of Initiates

The Tibetan tells us:

"In the archives of the esoteric astrologers connected with the Hierarchy, charts are kept of those members of the human family who have achieved adeptship and upwards. They are composed of superimposed squares, stars and triangles, contained within the zodiacal wheel and mounted upon the symbol of the cardinal cross. The squares, having each of their four angles and points in one or other of four zodiacal constellations, are depicted in black; the five-pointed star is depicted yellow or golden colour and its five points are in contact with five of the constellations on the great wheel; the triangles are in blue and have, above each point of the triangle, an esoteric symbol, standing for the constellations of the Great Bear, Sirius and the Pleiades. These symbols may not here be revealed but indicate the point of spiritual consciousness achieved and the responsiveness of the initiate to these major cosmic influences. A glance at these geometrical charts will indicate in a moment the status of the initiate, and also the point towards which he is striving. These charts are fourth dimensional in nature and not flat surfaces as are our charts. This is an interesting piece of information but of no value, except in so far that it indicates synthesis, the fusion of spirit, soul and body, and the point of development. It proves also the fact that 'God geometrises' where the soul is concerned."[61]

Karmic Opportunities

"Every Cause has its Effect; every Effect has its Cause; everything happens according to Law; Chance is but a name for Law not recognized; there are many planes of causation, but nothing escapes the Law."—The Kybalion[62]

The concepts of reincarnation and karma are inherent in the eastern traditions and implicit in the western mystery teachings including the Pythagorean and Platonic traditions, as well as esoteric Judaism and Qabalah. The complex interaction of human lives between birth and death and between death and a new birth gives an expanded meaning to individual lives lived on Earth in community with others and also to human history and evolution as a whole.[63]

According to Dane Rudhyar, karma operates in and through the fourth ether of the human etheric body,[64] and from there precipitates into physical existence by the power of thought. Karma acts through the concrete mind, which forms desires that result in the actions we take to fulfill these desires. Later, as the concrete mind is able to contact the higher mind, the level of desire is transformed upward. As we develop spiritual will and discover more about our purpose in life, we take action—called dharma—to fulfill our destiny and, accordingly, work off our karma in a proactive manner. A great sage once said "it is essential that the laws for the transmutation of karma into active present good are clearly grasped,"[65] and this is so that we might live according to our destinies or the highest archetypes of our existence that we can reach. We also need to remember that karma includes "good" effects as well as "bad."

We are karmically obligated to develop and use the abilities we came into incarnation with, lest we set our development back in future lives. We could say that this is the true meaning of responsibility: "response-ability." Concerning responsibility, the Tibetan tells us that, "In the olden days in the East, the Master exacted from His disciple that implicit obedience which actually made the Master responsible and placed upon His shoulders the destiny or the karma of the disciple. That condition no longer holds good. The intellectual principle in the individual is now too much developed to warrant this type of expectancy…In the coming New Age, the Master is responsible for the offering of opportunity and for the right enunciation of the truth but for no more than that. In these more enlightened days, no such position is assumed by the teacher as in the past, and I do not assume it."[66]

Group Karma

A great deal of our karma is group karma, shared with other people, which is an impelling reason for working in groups. We incarnate in groups and all our lives we are associated with groups: our families, our friends, our co-workers, our special-interest groups, our communities, and our nations. As we interact with our group members, over time we fulfill our group destiny. Some of the possible ways of fulfilling our destinies through group interaction include the following points that the Tibetan teacher related in his talks to his disciples:

"First of all, a disciple may be called to work off certain karmic relationships, to fulfill certain obligations of very ancient origin and thus 'clear the decks' for more complete and uninterrupted service to humanity at a later date. This occurs quite frequently between the first and second initiations. Sometimes a disciple may be doing effective service upon the inner planes and on a large scale and yet there may be no evidence of this upon the physical plane, except in the beauty of a life lived. Others may be learning certain techniques of psychological relationships and of energy distribution and may have dedicated some particular life to the acquiring of these esoteric sciences. One life is but a short moment in the long cycle of the soul. The true disciple will never fall back on the reasons given above as alibis for lack of effort. I would remind you that world influence alone does not always imply discipleship. There are many groups—well known and magnetic—which have at their centre some dominant personality who is not necessarily a disciple."[67] Later on in the same work, we learn that a disciple:

- Works off unavoidable karma as intelligently and consciously as possible.

- Takes on some karma which would ordinarily be precipitated in some later life.

- Consciously takes part in and shoulders a part of the karma of his or her group, thus setting up a veritable vortex of force in the group aura which attracts hierarchical attention.

- Begins to shoulder some of the general karma of humanity, thus increasing her or his own load of karma.

- Begins to comprehend and work with planetary karma, though she or he cannot take responsibility in this connection until the third initiation.[68]

"This egoic [soul] impulse in any group or any group unit makes itself felt as a pulsation, or access of energy, emanating from the central point. This central activity is produced by the action of the planetary Logos working through the groups in His centres, and according to the centre under stimulation so will the groups concerned be affected."[69]

We can also choose to work in groups with whom we do not have a karmic relationship, but to whom we are drawn by other reasons of the individual and group mind. Every link that we make on Earth does not necessarily involve the past or the influence of the soul, for we also make fresh links and start new lines of karma and dharma. We can only use our best judgment and work with intelligence.

World conditions today, caused by human greed and ignorance, are nevertheless basically conditioned by the will-to-good, which is the primary quality of the energies and forces coming from the great cosmic lives that encompass us all. The Law of the Universe, which works out the purposes of those lives, is for the good of the whole and the impact of these energies is inevitable.

However, this does not mean that we can assume a fatalistic attitude and simply wait for karma and destiny to fulfill itself. For karma fulfills itself in relation to our attitudes. Where there is a quiescent attitude, the process moves slowly and we fail to experience a needed, forceful awakening. Thus we have to repeat the process until we finally respond. This finally leads to our resistance to the karmic situation, which leads to our liberation from it. In other words, we finally get so fed up we do something about it.

Only through resistance to evil can karma be brought to an end, which means that we must do what we can to improve the world, as well as our own personal lives.[70]

The Tibetan states: "Those who refuse to share in the world karma and pain will find their entire progress inevitably slowed down, for they will have put themselves outside the great tide of spiritual force now sweeping in regenerating streams throughout the world of men."[71]

Planetary and Cosmic Karma

Shifts in the Earth's axis cause upheaval, confusion, and cataclysm, which leads to reconstruction, stabilization, and relative quiet. Corresponding to these macrocosmic events, similar events occur in the lives of people. Although our present world situation has been precipitated by the group karma of humanity, this is basically the result of much greater combinations of forces on a macrocosmic scale, according to our Tibetan teacher. He gives the following causes for our present world difficulties:[72]

1. A welling up of magnetic force on Sirius, which produces effects upon our solar system and particularly upon Earth.

2. A shift in the Earth's polarity, due to the pull of a great cosmic center. This affects the Earth's orientation and is responsible for earthquakes and volcanic eruptions.

3. The completion of a cycle of 250,000 years, which came to an end when the Age of Pisces began over 2,000 years ago.

4. The passing from the Age of Pisces to the Age of Aquarius. This transition period is 500 years.

We can assume that these mammoth combinations of forces relate to the dharma of the stupendous entities involved, as they are carrying forth the processes of evolution for all the myriad lives that they are responsible for.

The following subsections summarize various statements by the Tibetan about the karmic activities of great entities in our universe as they particularly pertain to Earth evolution.

The Lord of Karma on Sirius

The Lords of Karma of our system are under the rule of a greater Lord of Karma on Sirius, by which we are governed.[73] In her book, *Sirius*, M. Temple Richmond associates karma with the cosmic mental plane, which impels the advancement of consciousness, and she presents information that links this dimension with Sirius. In her work, Richmond also connects the Law of Karma with the Law of Attraction, which in turn is closely related to Sirius and is the basis of cyclicity or periodicity. "These ponderous forces and energies," she tells us, "are great spiritual principles exerting enormous influence over the conditions in which evolution proceeds."[74]

An example of how these evolutionary processes occur, according to Richmond, is that "forces from Sirius set in motion the latent Karma carried over from the previous solar system at the beginning of the current one, therefore initiating our system into activity. Sirius also functions as a point of reabsorption and karmic adjustment for at least certain units of consciousness associated with our planet, if not for the entirety of the solar system."[75]

The Seventh Ray

Ray Seven, the ray of organization and manifestation, has a special role in working with world forces to precipitate karma. It is invoking demand upon the world thinkers from the masses for direction and guidance. It is helping us to regroup and rearrange our attitudes and thought and is bringing about the structure of a new civilization. It impels us into full awareness and intentional conscious purpose so that we can understand the implications of our choices, and it organizes our spirit of freedom in its revolt against slavery.[76]

The Mutable and Fixed Crosses

On the mutable cross and on the fixed cross the so-called green ray (of Ray Three and Saturn) controls the daily life of karmic liability upon the path of evolution and the experiences and processes of evolution. The reason for this is that Capricorn is an earth sign and because Rays Three and Five work pre-eminently through this sign, embodying the third major aspect of divinity, active intelligence, plus that of its subsidiary power, the fifth ray of mind. These rays pour through Capricorn to Saturn and Venus and thus reach Earth.[77]

Many of the energies coming into the fixed cross are focused through the planet Saturn, one of the most significant Lords of Karma to humanity today. Fixed-cross energies blend with and transmit the energies of the solar system itself. They can do this because, upon the fixed cross, we become increasingly sensitive to a greater whole and conscious of issues that are larger than ourselves, more engrossing than our previous interests, and that concern humanity in its relation to the solar forces and not just to the planetary forces.

The mutable cross, the cross "of changing and absorbed experience," is the place of action and reaction, karmic control, and response to impacts "leading to the awakening of consciousness to the nature of the goal ahead."[78]

Libra

Libra guards the secret of equilibrium and "finally speaks the word which releases the initiate from the power of the Lords of Karma."[79] Libra represents the point of balance where opportunity comes and we stage a situation that makes choice and determination inevitable. We have to make this choice intelligently and upon the physical plane, in the waking brain-consciousness.

Only in our current era can the full purpose and work of Saturn for humanity reach a point of group usefulness, for only now has humanity reached a point of general and widespread intelligence that can make any choice a definite conscious act, entailing responsibility. Libra governs and controls this path of choice, "of deliberately applied purificatory measures."[80]

Capricorn

When crystallization reaches a certain degree of density and hardness, it is easily shattered and destroyed. In this case, it is the destruction of our materialistic nature. Thus we meet with the "blows of fate" dealt to us by the Law of Karma.

Capricorn, which connotes density, firm foundations, and concretion, represents the mountain of karma that holds us down and the mountain of initiation that we must eventually climb. Thus, in our current world cycle, Capricorn symbolizes the great force of liberation which both drives human experience and brings experience to an end.[81]

The Planets

The karma of the seven sacred planets is working out in our solar system and will be revealed when the cosmic triangle formed by the following three groups—and the subsidiary triangles within this cosmic triangle—are understood:[82]

1. The Great Bear
2. The Pleiades
3. The cosmic triangle formed by the seven Rishis of the Great Bear, the seven Planetary Logoi of our solar system, and the seven Pleiades or Sisters.

All twelve planets, in their relation to our physical plane expression and personality lives, work with inherited karmic conditions to produce the environments and circumstances necessary to give us the opportunities to develop, and eventually control, the form side of life.

Saturn

Saturn controls the experiences and processes of evolution, which path is built as we work out karma on a daily basis. As one of the most potent of the four Lords of Karma, Saturn forces us to face up to the past and, in the present, find and use available opportunities to prepare for the future. This is the intention and purpose of karmic opportunity. Saturn demands full payment of all debts, both from the form side and the soul side. When we finally free ourselves from karma, Saturn's power is completely ended and his work accomplished.

In Leo, Saturn's power is lessened when we are not conditioned by our surroundings or life events, but rule them with deliberation, bringing what we require out of our circumstances and environment. Saturn's influence exhausts itself when we achieve initiation in Capricorn.

Saturn is the synthesizing scheme for the four planets that embody manas purely and simply. These are the four planets with Planetary Logoi on Rays Four, Five, Six, and Seven, the rays of attribute. The four rays of attribute are eventually (on the path of return) absorbed into Ray Three.

Moses, the Lawgiver on Mount Sinai, is Saturn in Capricorn imposing the Law of Karma upon the people.[83]

Driving Our Own Karma

Humorist Steve Bhaerman wrote a delightful book in 1989 about karma entitled, *Driving Your Own Karma: Swami Beyondananda's Tour Guide to Enlightenment*, which emphasizes that we control our own destiny and gives us a sense of perspective. For example:

"The past would be okay if it would just stay back there in our old photo albums where it belongs. But unfortunately, it follows us. For each of the positive photos we've kept, there's a negative which we've held on to as well. And since most of us hate to throw anything away, we still take these negatives with us wherever we go—even when we no longer need them to develop."[84]

Chapter 10—
What Energies Are Available Now?

"…astrology is essentially the purest presentation of occult truth in the world at this time, because it is the science which deals with those conditioning and governing energies and forces which play through and upon the whole field of space and all that is found within that field."—AAB[1]

The combination of planetary influences at any given moment of time represents the archetypal patterns which, at that moment, pervade our psyches and lives. These patterns affect the lives of individuals, groups, cultures, and civilizations, as well as the characteristics of events and other situations. As Carl Jung said, whatever happens at any given moment of time shares the qualities of that moment.

To determine the energies available during any particular cycle, and the opportunities that we can discover or create therein, we can begin by examining the placement of planets in the signs and the relationships of planets to each other.

Following is a summary of the various configurations that are commonly examined in an astrological chart:

Configuration	Angle	Type of Energy
conjunction	0°	emphasis
opposition	180°	striving for balance, awareness
trine	120° or 1/3	creative flow, synthesis
square	90° or 1/4	trigger of action
sextile	60° or 1/6	mental and creative integration
star	combination	consciousness

In our chart interpretations in this chapter, we use the term "sign" rather than "constellation" to carry on the expression of the symbol used in the astrological chart, still bearing in mind, however, that energies are directed into the signs through the constellations of the same name (as discussed earlier in this book).

Planetary and Zodiacal Influences

"We will endeavour to work from the universal to the particular and from the general to the specific, but our emphasis will always be on the universal and the general, and not upon the particular and specific."—AAB[2]

As we study the attributes of the rays, constellations, and planets, we realize that the energies of these great entities blend in many combinations of ways. Some of these great energies flow smoothly together while others present more of a challenge. However, it is our resistance to challenging energies that gives us stress, more than the inherent nature of the energies themselves.

Ray	Type of Energy	Constellations	Planets
I	Will and Power: leadership, focus, courage, action, detachment, death and rebirth	Aries, Leo, and Capricorn	Vulcan, Pluto
II	Love-Wisdom: understanding, receptivity, intuition, inclusiveness, patience	Gemini, Virgo, and Pisces	Jupiter, Sun
III	Active Intelligence and Adaptability: abstract thinking, mental fertility, creativity	Cancer, Libra, and Capricorn	Saturn, Earth
IV	Harmony, Beauty, and Art: conflict, mediation, aesthetics, mathematical exactitude, bridging	Taurus, Scorpio, and Sagittarius	Mercury, Moon
V	Concrete Knowledge and Science: focused intellect, discrimination, truth, analysis, research	Leo, Sagittarius, and Aquarius	Venus
VI	Devotion and Idealism: faith, optimism, sincerity, purity, persuasiveness, persistence	Virgo, Sagittarius, and Pisces	Neptune, Mars
VII	Ceremonial Magic and Organization: ritualism, order, management, synthesis, law	Aries, Cancer, and Capricorn	Uranus

Our response to planetary influences depends a lot upon which of the seven rays are most prominent in our soul and personality bodies. For example, people who resonate with Ray One will respond more readily to the Shamballa influence transmitted from Leo and Saturn, and people who resonate with Ray Two energies will respond more to the Hierarchy, which transmits energies from Pisces and Uranus.[3]

Nevertheless, through the guidance of our soul and assuming the position of spiritual observer, we can learn to invoke the influences of the constellations and planets for spiritual purposes and goals that can benefit humanity as a whole.

Following is a list of the zodiacal constellations and some of the energetic principles associated with them:

Aries	Beginnings, creativity, identity, activity, pioneering
Taurus	Values, refinement, resources, building, illumination
Gemini	Communication, understanding, versatility, truth
Cancer	Nurturance, sensitivity, mass-consciousness
Leo	Individuality, self-consciousness, creativity, magnanimity
Virgo	Analysis, discrimination, service, germination
Libra	Balance, choice, relationship, justice, judgment
Scorpio	Intensity, transformation, power, testing, triumph
Sagittarius	Direction, intuition, idealism, aspiration, achievement
Capricorn	Authority, accomplishment, crystallization, synthesis, initiation
Aquarius	Group-consciousness, idealism, inventiveness, humanitarianism
Pisces	Inspiration, spirituality, sacrifice, release, liberation

Following is a list of the various planets and some of the energetic principles associated with them:

Sun	Vitality, creativity, life force
Moon	Emotions, habitual responses, unconscious memory
Vulcan	Endurance, persistence, rhythmic effort
Mercury	Intuition, conscious mind, communication, thinking, attitudes
Venus	Values, wisdom, relationship, intelligent love
Mars	Desire, will to act, drive, physical energy, purification
Jupiter	Expansion, opportunity, faith, integration, synthesis
Saturn	Choice, discrimination, discipline, structure, preservation
Uranus	Originality, freedom, change, spontaneity, revolution
Neptune	Transcendence, dissolution of boundaries, inspiration
Pluto	Death and rebirth, transformation, power, regeneration

Conjunctions, A Symbolic Union

The alchemical adepts were ultimately concerned with a union of substances, or conjunctions, through which "they hoped to attain the goal of the work: the production of the gold or a symbolical equivalent of it."[4] For example, the symbolic union of Mars and Venus, that famous pair of opposites, points to a love relationship on the personality level and to an implementation of values on a higher level.

When we consider the conjunctions of planets, we note that conjunctions with outer planets, Uranus, Neptune, and Pluto, have a more global and transformative effect and that inner planets are more temporary or personal in their effect. The energies of the outer planets may have been speculated on but were not actually sensed by average humanity until their relatively recent discoveries. Consciously or unconsciously, we have been working with the basic energies of Mercury, Venus, and Mars for long historical ages, as evidenced in mythology, and we have been using the energies of Jupiter and Saturn in our personal and group lives for almost as long.

Recent outer planet conjunctions are listed below, along with some dates of their contact and some suggestions on how their combined energies could affect our global consciousness. We might remember that these years indicate when the energies come in, but that it could take a period of time for their manifestation on the physical plane.

- Uranus and Neptune are conjunct every 172 years: 1992. Changes in ideals and consciousness. Opportunity for a unified, one-world point of view and redistribution of the resources of the planet.

- Saturn and Uranus are conjunct every 45 to 46 years: 1988-1989. Clashes between status-quo leadership and progressive urges.[5] Opportunity to break apart structures that are no longer serving our purposes and to choose freedom and social change.

- Saturn and Neptune are conjunct every 35 to 36 years: 1989 and 2025. Focus on structures relating to ideals. Opportunity to transcend our limitations.

- Jupiter and Saturn are conjunct every 20 years: 1980-81, 2000, and 2020. Development of new social structures and a conflict between expansive and contractive tendencies.[6] Opportunity to synthesize and preserve the best aspects of our social order while expanding our options and making wise choices for the future.

- Jupiter and Uranus are conjunct about every 14 years: 1997 and 2011. Expansion, invention, entrepreneurism, and rebellion against the status quo.[7] Opportunity to invent ways of improving the world and to have the faith to know that we can.

- Jupiter and Neptune are conjunct about every 13 years: 1997 and 2010. Focus on idealism, humanitarianism, and the unfoldment of social activity and spiritual beliefs.[8] Opportunity for inspiration and an expansion of consciousness.

- Jupiter and Pluto are conjunct about every 12 years: 1994-95 and 2006-07. Expansion of political power, wealth, and spiritual ideology.[9] Opportunity to expand our options for the healing and regeneration of the world.

The planets cycle through the system on a regular basis, taking a specified average amount of time to return to their starting places. The Moon, of course, has the fastest cycle of only one month, or approximately 29.5 days between conjunctions of the Moon and the Sun as observed from the Earth.

Mercury and Venus each average about a year before they return to their starting points and, since they are so close to the Sun, they are usually found in the same sign or signs adjacent to the Sun. Accordingly, their energies are always linked to a season of the year.

The Mars cycles is almost two years long, making it possible for Mars to form trines and squares to the Sun, whereas Mercury and Venus cannot range outside of a sextile configuration to the Sun.

The length of cycles change dramatically when we reach the outer planets, starting with Jupiter which has a 12-year cycle. Saturn's cycle is 28 to 30 years, Uranus's is 84 years, Neptune's is 164 years, and Pluto's is 248 years.

Lunar Nodes

The nodes of the Moon are points of collective or world-wide energy and when planets are conjunct to these nodes, the particular planetary energies are strengthened and underlie the world's activities for the duration, according to Maya del Mar, who writes a monthly column for *The Mountain Astrologer* and who focuses on world scenarios from a conventional astrological standpoint.

The nodes are represented on a chart by the symbols ☊ and ☋ depicting the north and south nodes, respectively. Thus, when we see a conjunction involving these nodes, we can theorize that the energies involved might be strengthened.

Retrograde Planetary Movement

Whether a planet is called "retrograde" is relative to our position here on Earth and our observation of the direction of the planet in the skies. Entire books have been written on the topic of retrograde planets, stating the differences in the qualities of the planetary energies when the planet appears to reverse its direction.

The outer planets are retrograde for a significant proportion of the year: Pluto is retrograde 44% of the time, Neptune 43%, Uranus 41%, Saturn 36%, and Jupiter 30% (these percentages are approximate). Of the inner planets, Venus is retrograde 7% and Mars 9% of the time. In contrast, though, Mercury is retrograde 20% of the time.[10]

It seems to be the consensus in astrological circles that the energies of retrograde planets are more subjective to us and that these times give us a chance to review, repeat, and work again with the energies of the planet involved; to recapitulate or process information that we have already learned. An awareness of this process can add more sophistication to our analysis of the energies available at a given time.

Exaltations, Detriments, and Falls

As mentioned in Chapter 6, the powers of planets in particular signs—their exaltations, detriments, and falls—are symbolic of the effects of energy upon form and can modify our use of planetary energies at a given time. The exalting sign elicits the planet's purpose and gives insights into its energy, and the falls and detriments indicate where the planetary energy is less effective.[11]

The Tibetan recommends that we carefully investigate these qualifications of power that take place within a zodiacal sign. He tells us that we must view the whole problem in a large manner and relate the planets rightly to the rays that they are expressing.[12]

The emphasis that the Tibetan places on exaltations, falls, and detriments throughout the book, *Esoteric Astrology*, can surely indicate that if these planets are involved in a pattern we are working with, it might be appropriate to assign them almost the same significance that we would give to a planetary ruler involved in the same pattern.

Sacred vs. Non-Sacred Planets

As we note in Chapter 7, the influences of a sacred planet affect the fusion of soul and body, consciousness and form, whereas the influences of a non-sacred planet affect the life of the personality.

Thus, in a chart which we are using as a focus for meditations to elevate consciousness, we want to be aware of the sacredness of the energies involved. At a given time, a personality focus might be just as valid in the solution of the problems we are presented with, but we still always work from a point of soul-consciousness.

Sidereal vs. Tropical?

"In the great evolutionary process and owing to certain shifts and astronomical-astrological discrepancies, the Sun is not in the constellation to which a particular sign refers at any given moment."—AAB[13]

In our study, based on the Tibetan's *Esoteric Astrology*, we have been referring to the "influences of the constellations as they are represented by the signs," and not to where the constellations actually are in the sky. The Tibetan also says that we should not consider the margin of contact between two signs of the zodiac to have set boundary lines; it is not the case because there are no rigid lines of demarcation separating two entirely different areas of experience and consciousness upon the solar path.[14]

Tropical astrology is based on the relationship between the Sun and the Earth and the Sun's apparent path projected on the Earth's surface, called the ecliptic. The Sun crosses the equator twice a year, at the vernal equinox in the spring and the autumnal equinox in the fall. Tropical astrology defines these positions as 0 degrees Aries and 0 degrees Libra, respectively. When the Sun moves to its maximum position northward in the summer, this summer solstice point is called 0 degrees Cancer, and the winter solstice point is called 0 degrees Capricorn. These are the cardinal degrees and are consistent with the change of seasons that we experience here on Earth.

Sidereal astrology is star-based; 0 degrees Aries is associated with the beginning of the Aries constellation in the heavens, regardless of the season here on Earth. Because of the wobbling of the Earth on its axis, we have a phenomenon called the precession of the equinoxes by which, over a period of about 26,000 years, the sidereal and the tropical points shift farther and farther away until they meet again. Right now, their alignment is off by almost one month, meaning that it will take around 24,000 years from now for the points to meet again.

This is where we derive the astrological ages of Pisces, Aquarius, and so on, all of which last for around 2200 years. As we cycle through these ages, we not only experience all the combinations and permutations of the various signs within an age, but we experience as well the influence of the spatial differences between the tropical and sidereal zodiacs, of which influences we can only speculate at this time.

After much research and consideration, I finally ended up using the tropical system because the Sun's relations to the seasons on Earth are probably most applicable to our current stage of development. The Tibetan's system seems to support this by referring repeatedly in his writings to the influences of the constellations as represented by the signs and to the fact that the signs transmit the energies of the constellations to us. However, it can be argued that the sidereal zodiac may well affect large groups of people and also initiates, just as the hierarchical rulerships we have been studying affect these same groups of people. Also, eastern systems of astrology use the sidereal zodiac.

Accordingly, I leave it up to you. If you want to use the sidereal zodiac, give both systems some study first and then go for it. A sidereal ephemeris and a computer program with several sidereal options are easy to find, as well as several books on the subject. The examples included here are based on the tropical system, but the relationships of the planets to each other are the same for sidereal-based astrology; it is just that the constellations in the tropical system are later by approximately 24 to 28 degrees (depending upon which sidereal system you use).

What to Look For at the Full Moon

"We are told that God geometrises…and that a subtle geometrical form lies behind the exoteric manifestation. These forms convey to the occult student the symbolism of the world of meaning. Behind the mathematics and the geometrical designs, and behind the numerology which attempts…to convey the truth, but which in a mysterious manner conditions the creative work, are certain formulas which…express significance, intention, meaning."
—AAB[15]

The first configuration to look for in a chart is the placement of the Sun and the Moon; in which constellations are the Sun and Moon in opposition? Are there planets that are conjunct with the Sun and the Moon?

We have discussed earlier in the book that energies flow through triangles and manifest through crosses. Accordingly, we could next observe the various triangles in a full-moon chart to determine the inflow of energies.

An ordinary trine between two planets would apply to a certain extent, but a "complete triangle" involving three planets, all in aspect to each other, would definitely show a significant flow of energies, around each of the three points. The complete triangle, then, is the first configuration to look for after noting the signs of the Sun and the Moon and any planets that might be conjunct with them. (The complete triangle does not have to be equilateral.)

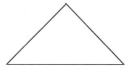

Jung tells us that the three (triangle) is masculine and the four (square) is feminine, and that fourness is a symbol of wholeness, whereas threeness is not. In the polarity of the male and female energies, there is a current or flow of events as the tension of opposites strives for balance.[16] If we divide the square diagonally into two equal halves, we get two opposing triangles. Also, if we place two equal triangles together at their bases, we have a square. Therefore, the wholeness symbolized by the square consists of two opposing triads.

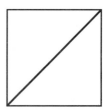

The circle divided into four represents the even-armed cross. The Sun and the Moon at opposition during the time of the full moon divides the wheel of the zodiac in two which, as we discussed in Chapter 9, sets up the situation for force to flow in and out.[17] This is the vertical arm of the cross. We provide the horizontal arm when we modify, qualify, and adapt these energies and transmit them to the world. Accordingly, it seems likely that if the vertical axis points to a Leo Sun and Aquarius Moon opposition, we would be distributing the energies into the world along a Taurus/Scorpio axis.

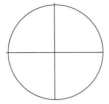

The symbol of the cardinal cross depicts a triangle superimposed on a cross with three circles at the points of the triangle. This symbolizes three cycles of four energies, focused and blended in unity, with the line of the evolution of consciousness going down deep into and becoming inclusive of matter, while also reaching out into the "spaces of divinity."[18] This creative symbol of the highest form of manifestation known on our planet clearly depicts energies flowing from a triangle into a cross or square. Accordingly, we can look at the flow of energy through a triangle into the angles of a cross or square as the basis of our interpretation.

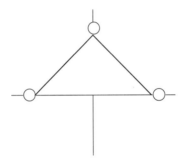

Next, we can examine connections with other planets, first from the standpoint of the Sun and the Moon, then in their relationships to each other. We can also determine the locations of the rulers of the constellations in which the Sun and Moon are placed and determine if they are in any special configurations of their own. This can get quite complex because there are three rulers assigned to each constellation. However, after we take note of all these relationships, we can look for prominent and recurrent energy patterns only, to simplify things to the degree that we want to handle. An advantage of this system is that we can selectively use the energies that we determine to be particularly warranted at the time and, thus, avoid further analysis. Or, if we want, we can analyze these energies to the hilt.

In the examples that follow, I have not considered the ascendant or houses because my focus is to bring through energies for the use of the world at large. Full moons occur at the same time around the globe, no matter what time it may happen to be in any particular time zone. These example charts use GMT because it is a standard for ephemerides and most people know where they are in relation to Greenwich Mean Time. These charts are also called "natural," meaning that the ascendant is always in the first sign of the zodiac, Aries.

When we are concerned with bringing in energy to a particular locale on Earth, we would cast the chart according to the coordinates of that locale and consider the energy coming in to the ascendant and the meridians, as discussed in traditional astrology texts.

Finally, we are not considering fixed stars at all, although astrologers and esotericists are beginning to use them in their calculations. We have provided an appendix of fixed-star locations just as a matter of general interest, but do not recommend that you use it without a thorough research of fixed stars in astrology. The bibliography lists some relevant books.

Example Configurations

We now discuss the energy relationships of four full-moon charts, applying what we have learned in the chapters that discuss the energies of the rays, constellations, and planets plus the studies of relationships discussed above and in Chapter 9. Chapter 11 gives meditations that we can use to apply the energies for the upliftment of consciousness.

These examples should be used as guidelines only in a possible interpretation of the energies available at a particular time. In actual use, we need to look at our individual spiritual goals to get an in-depth mental and intuitive sense as to how to apply the energies. Without the application, which can only be provided in a real-life situation, the interpretation of these examples shows only the mechanical aspect of identifying the energies. Accordingly, we need to add the understanding and the heart energy to this strictly mental process, using the meditations provided in the next chapter.

Here is a list and brief description of the four example full-moon charts:

- **Leo/Aquarius**: On August 8, 1998, the Sun is in Leo and the Moon is in Aquarius at 15 degrees. Leo and Aquarius are polar opposites of the fixed cross.

- **Taurus/Scorpio**: On April 30, 1999, the Sun is in Taurus and the Moon is in Scorpio at nine degrees. Taurus and Scorpio are polar opposites of the fixed cross.

- **Capricorn/Cancer**: On December 22, 1999, the Sun is in Capricorn and the Moon is in Cancer at 0 degrees. Cancer and Capricorn are polar opposites of the cardinal cross.

- **Sagittarius/Gemini**: On December 11, 2000, the Sun is in Sagittarius and the Moon is in Gemini at 19 degrees. Sagittarius and Gemini are polar opposites of the mutable cross.

Leo/Aquarius

This chart for August 8, 1998 shows the Sun in Leo and the Moon in Aquarius at 15 degrees. This combination of solar and lunar energies gives us vital, creative, and inventive forces. The energies from two primary rays flow through the Sun into this solar/lunar axis: Ray One, will and power, and Ray Five, concrete knowledge and science.

The Moon, veiling Uranus, is the group or hierarchical ruler of Aquarius and the Sun rules all three aspects of Leo, veiling Jupiter, Neptune, and Uranus for the personality, soul, and group levels respectively. Thus the opposition of the Sun and the Moon in these signs at this full moon is particularly dynamic because it involves rulerships as well.

Neptune, Uranus, and the Moon are all in Aquarius; all opposite the Sun in Leo. Neptune and Uranus, the soul and group rulers of Leo, placed in Aquarius, the polar opposite of Leo, signifies a cooperative balance of these planetary energies that can be used for the unification of consciousness symbolized by Aquarius and Leo. Uranus, also the personality ruler of Aquarius, gives us an added urge toward transformation and improvement.

The single complete triangle in this chart shows Venus at 23° Cancer, Neptune at 0° Aquarius, and Jupiter at 27° Pisces, a combination of two emotional water signs and the mental air sign of Aquarius. (As introduced on page 248, a "complete triangle" is a representation of three planets in a chart that are in some type of relationship to each other. See the following chart for a good visual example of this pattern.)

Venus brings values, wisdom, relationship, and intelligent love to the nurturing, sensitive, mass-conscious sign of Cancer. The conjunction of Mars with Venus adds a dynamism and an active impetus to the Venusian energies, which can elevate our emotional sensitivity to a more mental level.

Neptune lends inspiration to the group-conscious, humanitarian ideals of Aquarius, and can help us dissolve the boundaries that hold us back from unity and a transcendent consciousness. Neptune is strengthened because it is the esoteric or soul ruler of Leo.

Jupiter, the planet of expansion, integration, and synthesis, gives us an opportunity to use the energies of Pisces to promote world service.

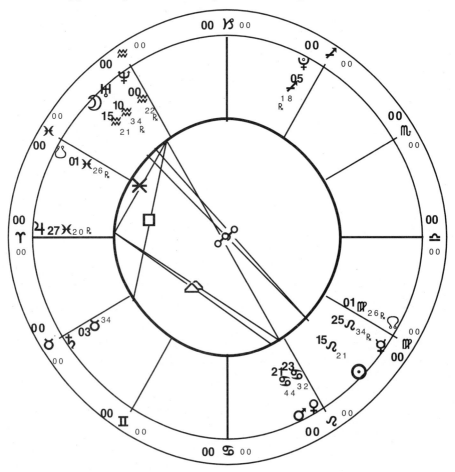

Jupiter is strengthened because it is the soul or esoteric ruler of Aquarius and the veiled personality ruler of Leo.

Thus, the energies that circulate around the triangle of Venus, Neptune, and Jupiter can easily be used in an elevation of consciousness that can be manifested through the arms of the fixed cross, flowing in through the Leo/Aquarius axis and out the Taurus/Scorpio axis.

Taurus/Scorpio

This chart for April 30, 1999 shows the Sun in Taurus and the Moon in Scorpio at nine degrees. This combination of solar and lunar energies can lend vitality and creativity to transforming trying situations into a use of our resources to build and refine human values. These are the signs that test and, later, illumine us. The energies from one primary ray flows through the Sun into this solar/lunar axis: Ray Four, harmony through conflict, beauty, and art.

The Sun and Saturn are conjunct in Taurus and both oppose the conjunction of the Moon and Mars in Scorpio. Mars is the personality ruler of Scorpio, which gives it extra force in this sign. One effect of these two conjunctions could be to vitalize the lunar energies while putting restrictions and parameters upon the solar energies, thus emphasizing the testing situations that Scorpio and Taurus are noted for.

Of the six complete triangles in this chart, four of them focus on the Sun, Moon, Mars, and Saturn configurations, with the added energy of Neptune, which is placed on the Aquarian arm of the fixed cross. These triangles lend the transcendence and inspiration of Neptune and the group-consciousness of Aquarius to the testing, building, refining, and illumination process of Taurus/Scorpio.

Two additional complete triangles involve Venus/Jupiter/Uranus and Venus/Mercury/Uranus. Venus is 20° in Gemini; Jupiter and Mercury are 18° and 16° Aries, respectively; and Uranus is 16° Aquarius. Mercury and Uranus have a special relationship since they are on the same 16th degree of two signs that are in sextile—Aries and Aquarius.

The conjunction of Mercury and Jupiter stands at the midpoint of the energies flowing between Venus and Uranus. Because of the Mercury/Jupiter conjunction, we can consider these two complete triangles to be one configuration.

Mercury in Aries gives intuition, communication, and conscious thought to the active and pioneering sign of Aries. Mercury is also the soul ruler of Aries, which adds an extra impact. Jupiter in Aries adds the energies of expansion, faith, opportunity, integration, and synthesis.

Venus in Gemini lends values, wisdom, intelligent love, and a sense of relationship in the goals of communication, understanding, and truth. Venus is also the soul ruler of Gemini.

Uranus in Aquarius provides strong energies of originality, freedom, change, and spontaneity to the Aquarian goals of group-consciousness. Uranus is also the personality ruler of Aquarius and the hierarchical ruler of Aquarius (veiled by the Moon), which gives emphasis and dynamism to Uranian energies in this chart. Its conjunction to the south lunar node further augments the energy of Uranus in Aquarius.

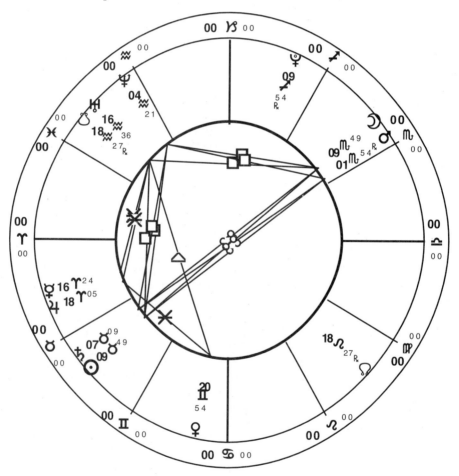

Three arms of the fixed cross dominate in this chart. Because Uranus and Neptune are in a vital placement on this cross, all of the energies from the aspects of this chart can be manifested through the arms of the fixed cross, flowing in through the Taurus/Scorpio axis and out through the Leo/Aquarius axis.

Pluto stands alone at the ninth degree of Sagittarius without major aspect, but on the exact degree as the Sun and the Moon. Thus, we can possibly invoke Pluto through numerical resonance.

Capricorn/Cancer

This chart for December 22, 1999 shows the Sun in Capricorn and the Moon in Cancer at 0 degrees, which are the solsticial points. This combination of solar and lunar energies can lend vitality and creativity to the transformation of an emotionally sensitive mass-consciousness into accomplishing the goals that can lead humanity to the gateway of initiation. The energies from three primary rays flow through the Sun into this solar/lunar axis: Ray One, will and power; Ray Three, active intelligence and adaptability; and Ray Seven, ceremonial magic and organization.

A single complete triangle between the Sun in Capricorn, Moon in Cancer, and Jupiter in Aries is focused upon three arms of the cardinal cross. The energy of the Sun lends vitality, creativity, and life force to the authority of Capricorn, with its goals of accomplishment, synthesis, and initiation. The Moon, which is the personality ruler of Cancer, gives a course of least resistance to emotional sensitivity, nurturance, and mass-consciousness. Jupiter lends expansiveness and opportunity to the active, pioneering sign of Aries, thus giving an impetus toward new beginnings and creativity.

Uniquely, Aries, Cancer, and Capricorn are also the three signs that form the Ray Seven constellational triangle; Ray Seven energy is especially dominant as we enter the Age of Aquarius. We can use the energies of this triangle to propel us toward greater accomplishment, authority, and synthesis in Capricorn, and thus initiate new ideals, forms of life and consciousness, preparing the way for future opportunities upon the cardinal cross of initiation. Four planets—Mars, Uranus, and Neptune—and the south node in Aquarius emphasize the opportunities for synthesis and group-consciousness.

Other aspects of this chart include:

- A square between Uranus in Aquarius and Saturn in Taurus
- A square between Venus in Scorpio and Mars in Aquarius
- A square between Venus in Scorpio and Uranus in Aquarius
- A sextile between Pluto in Sagittarius and Uranus in Aquarius
- A sextile between Mercury in Sagittarius and Uranus in Aquarius
- A sextile between Mercury in Sagittarius and Mars in Aquarius

These aspects involve the fixed and mutable crosses, but are linked to the cardinal cross through the following rulerships: Saturn and Venus, the rulers of Capricorn; and Mars, Mercury, and Uranus, the rulers of Aries. Because these square and sextile aspects are dynamic and action-oriented, we can use them to further our objectives.

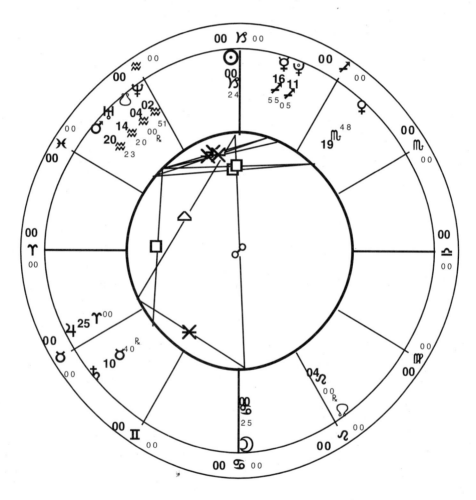

However, we can emphasize a consideration of the dominant cardinal cross of this chart, with the energies from the Sun, Moon, and Jupiter triangle flowing through its main axis of Capricorn/Cancer and out through the Aries/Libra axis.

Sagittarius/Gemini

This chart for December 11, 2000 shows the Sun in Sagittarius and the Moon in Gemini at 19 degrees. This combination of solar and lunar energies can lend vitality and creativity to a search for truth and an increased consciousness and communication of spiritual goals. The energies from three rays flow through the Sun into this solar/lunar axis: Ray Four, harmony through conflict, beauty, and art; Ray Five, concrete knowledge and science; and Ray Six, devotion and idealism.

Conjunctions and oppositions along the Gemini/Sagittarius axis increase the effects of the Sun and Moon energy. Conjunctions are Sun/ Pluto, Sun/Mercury, and Pluto/Mercury in Sagittarius. Oppositions are Moon/Pluto, Moon/Mercury, and Jupiter/Mercury in Gemini/ Sagittarius. Mercury and Jupiter are strengthened due to their rulerships of Gemini and Sagittarius, respectively. This combination of energies, balanced properly, enhances the qualities of thinking, communication, higher consciousness, opportunity, expansion, and synthesis. Pluto adds a quality of power and transformation to this.

Four complete triangles in this chart embody the energies of the Sun in Sagittarius, the Moon in Gemini, Uranus in Aquarius, and Mars in Libra. One of these triangles is an equilateral triangle (a grand trine) of the air signs, Gemini, Libra, and Aquarius, with Sagittarius anchoring the energies in a kite configuration.

The positions of the Sun and the Moon in these triangles add extra force to the energies of the Sun and Moon: the energy of the Sun lends vitality, creativity, and life force to the intuitive, idealistic, achievement-oriented sign of Sagittarius; and the Moon in Gemini enables ease of communication and understanding and provides versatility.

Uranus in Aquarius (where it also rules on the exoteric and hierarchical levels) enhances change, originality, and inventiveness and gives an impulse to idealism and group-consciousness.

Mars in Libra gives energy to the desire to make free choices and form balanced relationships.

Jupiter in Gemini is in close trine to Venus in Aquarius and in exact trine to Neptune in Aquarius; Venus and Neptune are conjunct within one degree. This configuration can represent transcendental, expansive, love.

Saturn, the ruler of an earth sign, situated in Taurus, another earth sign, would give extra power to the earth energies, but Saturn is the only planet that is not aspected in this chart of mainly fire and air signs. The element of water is totally absent.

The mutable cross and air signs dominate, which gives us a great deal of flexibility with a full spectrum of active planetary energies. This chart could easily provide opportunity for significant expansions of consciousness.

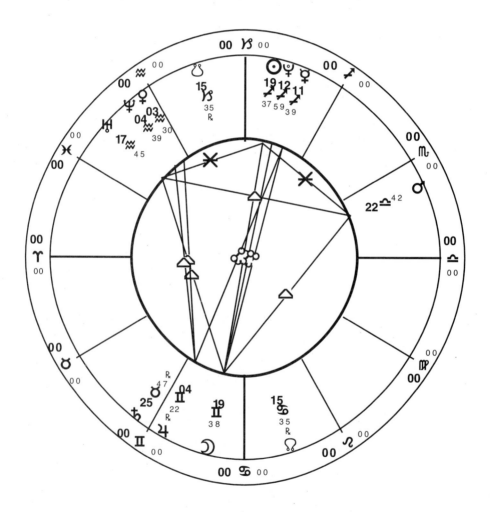

For general interest, astrologer and esotericist David Kesten has kindly provided us with the following two charts of significant events in the first quarter of the twenty-first century.

The chart on this page is for the full moon on December 28, 2012: 5:20:35 AM EST, New York, Geocentric, Tropical, Placidus, and True Node.

This is the date of the end of the Mayan calendar and is also the time of the New Group of World Servers festival, which is between December 21 and December 28 every seven years.

One of the key features of this chart is two clusters of planets in opposition to each other.

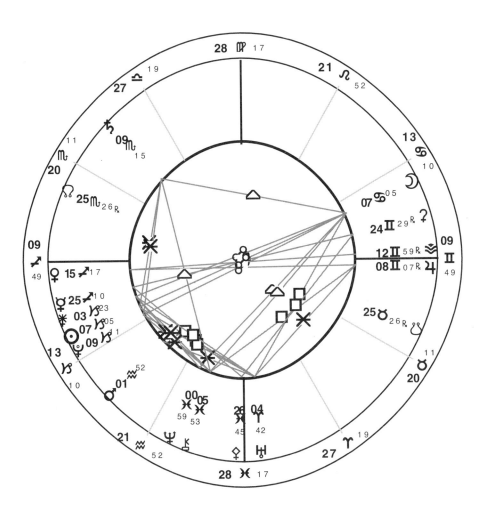

The following chart is for the new moon on March 29, 2025: 5:56:31 AM EST, New York, Geocentric, Tropical, Placidus, and True Node.

This chart is in the year when Ray Four is expected to come into manifestation. It is also the beginning of a one-hundred-year Sapta Rishi cycle, which is a Great Bear Ray One cycle. Throughout his books, the Tibetan indicates events of spiritual significance that are expected to occur around the year 2025; this is a very significant year in the ageless wisdom tradition.

The energies from the cluster of planets in Aries and Pisces is likely to be felt by all.

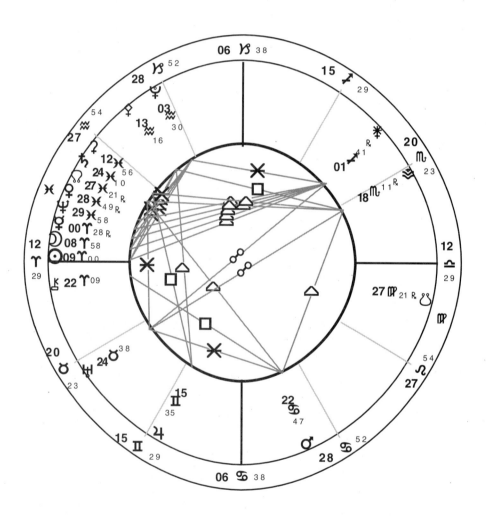

Table of Glyphs

Signs	
♈	Aries
♉	Taurus
♊	Gemini
♋	Cancer
♌	Leo
♍	Virgo
♎	Libra
♏	Scorpio
♐	Sagittarius
♑	Capricorn
♒	Aquarius
♓	Pisces

Aspects	
♂	Conjunctions
☍	Oppositions
△	Trines
□	Squares
⅋	Semi Sextiles
✶	Sextiles
⊼	Inconjuncts
∠	Semi Squares
⊡	Sesquiquadrates
Q	Quintiles
//	Parallel
⫫	Contra-Parallel

Planets					
☉	Sun	☽	Moon	☿	Mercury
♀	Venus	♂	Mars	♃	Jupiter
♄	Saturn	♅	Uranus	♆	Neptune
♇	Pluto	☊	North Node	☋	South Node
⚷	Chiron	⚴	Pallas	✳	Juno
⚳	Ceres	⚶	Vesta	⊕	Earth

Chapter 11—
Meditation

"This makes factual and clear that, at this time, the signs of balance and of initiation can be intelligently used to produce effects on our Earth and this they will immutably do…Initiation—characterised by self-initiation—is the demand of man today. The stars declare it and decree it. The Hierarchy therefore intentionally collaborates. The crying demand and aspirations of man indicate appreciation of the opportunity and recognised understanding of the proved necessity. The Spirit of Life enforces this."—AAB[1]

Meditation, to be effective, is done under the guidance of the soul, in alignment with our spiritual natures and often through affiliation with a group of others working for the same objectives. Our groups of coworkers are not necessarily present with us, but we should seek to work with others subjectively, if not physically. We can use energies safely, consciously, and creatively by following two conditions:[2]

1. Orienting ourselves consciously toward the soul and toward the Hierarchy

2. Sensing a deep love for humanity, based on mental perception and intuitive understanding and not on emotional reaction

Our focus should come from the heart. This is our loving responsibility and also our safeguard inasmuch as good, heartfelt intentions evoke a certain amount of protection from our soul. Through intuitive understanding, based on logic, experience, and inner knowing, we comprehend whole truths rather than fragments of truth. Spirituality gives us the power to create and the power to experience meaning.

The Tibetan told his disciples: "As the Hierarchy stands as a centre of light and strength to humanity, so do your souls stand to you, and—as your Master—I blend my light with yours and thus increase the efficiency of your service; I blend my love with the love which pours forth from the soul towards each of you, and thus I deepen the relation of love between each and all of you. It is not often that I speak to you in this manner, but in the process of freeing you for increased service I have drawn nearer to you and my love surrounds you. Learn, my brothers, the meaning of words, their transmitting potency and their spiritual significance."[3]

The method and procedure of Hierarchy is to "try out the personalities of Their intended and indicated disciples and—should these measure up with adequacy—then to proceed with the work of esoteric training. It is the same with groups; these are tested and tried in connection with the group personality, and upon the response depends the future activity of both the group and its Master and Teacher. But it is the group, as you see, which decides procedure."[4]

The Tibetan suggested that we study the following "Rules of the Road," for they have helped many people.[5] The mantric flow of this old commentary effectively sets the stage for a meditation session.

1. The Road is trodden in the full light of day, thrown upon the Path by Those Who know and lead. Naught can then be hidden, and at each turn upon that Road a man must face himself.

2. Upon the Road the hidden stands revealed. Each sees and knows the villainy of each. And yet there is, with that great revelation, no turning back, no spurning of each other, no shakiness upon the Road. The Road goes forward into day.

3. Upon that Road one wanders not alone. There is no rush, no hurry. And yet there is no time to lose. Each pilgrim, knowing this, presses his footsteps forward, and finds himself surrounded by his fellowmen. Some move ahead; he follows after. Some move behind; he sets the pace. He travels not alone.

4. Three things the Pilgrim must avoid. The wearing of a hood, a veil which hides his face from others; the carrying of a water pot which only holds enough for his own wants; the shouldering of a staff without a crook to hold.

5. Each Pilgrim on the Road must carry with him what he needs: a pot of fire, to warm his fellowmen; a lamp, to cast its rays upon his heart and shew his fellowmen the nature of his hidden life; a purse of gold, which he scatters not upon the Road, but shares with others; a sealed vase, wherein he carries all his aspiration to cast before the feet of Him Who waits to greet him at the gate.

6. The Pilgrim, as he walks upon the Road, must have the open ear, the giving hand, the silent tongue, the chastened heart, the golden voice, the rapid foot, and the open eye which sees the light. He knows he travels not alone.

Group Telepathic Alignment

"The Universal Mind is tapped by some member of the planetary Hierarchy according to His mental bias and equipment, and the immediate needs sensed by the working adepts. He then presents the new idea, new discovery, or the new revelation to the group of adepts."—AAB[6]

Before we can work together in a group telepathically, we need to align our individual souls, minds, and brains and simultaneously relate each aspect of this alignment to those of the other members of our group. It is quite common for world workers to already have soul and mind alignment with each other, but so far we have not succeeded too well in bringing it down into the brain. In other words, we work together on the subtle levels, but are largely unable to remember this work in our waking consciousness.

In *A Treatise on White Magic*, the Tibetan tells us how we can perfect the mechanism of the brain so that it can correctly register and transmit the soul impressions and the group purposes and recognitions. This involves:[7]

1. Awakening the ajna center

2. Subordinating the activity of the awakened ajna center to the head center so that the two vibrate in unison, causing
   a. Direct conscious alignment between soul, mind, and brain
   b. Development of a magnetic field which embraces both the head centers and thus affects the pineal gland and the pituitary body
   c. Recognition of this field of dual activity as a dynamic center of energy through which the will or purpose aspect of the soul can be felt

3. Developing a facility which enables us to:
   a. Use the mind in any direction we choose, either externally toward the material world or internally toward the spiritual world
   b. Produce consciously and at will a corresponding responsiveness in the physical brain so that it can register accurately any information coming from the physical world and the emotional world
   c. Discriminate intelligently between all these spheres of sentient activity

Meditations

"Mastery consists not in abnormal dreams, visions and fantastic imaginings or living, but in using the higher forces against the lower—escaping the pains of the lower planes by vibrating on the higher. Transmutation, not presumptuous denial, is the weapon of the Master."
—*The Kybalion*[8]

Meditation opens a channel in consciousness through which energies are invoked, received, and consciously directed.[9]

The Tibetan says: "The goal of meditation is to bring about the free play of all the incoming forces so that there is no impediment offered at any point to the incoming energy of the soul; so that no obstruction and congestion is permitted and no lack of power—physical, psychic, mental and spiritual—is to be found in any part of the body. This will mean not only good health and the full and free use of all the faculties (higher and lower) but direct contact with the soul. It will produce that constant renewing of the body which is characteristic of the life expression of the initiate and the Master, as well as of the disciple, only in a lesser degree. It will produce rhythmic expression of the divine life in form."[10]

Meditation is successful when, through effort and attention, we succeed in touching fields of consciousness that are of a quality rarer than usual for us. Eventually, we contact the energies of the buddhic plane, the plane of intuition. If we persist over time, we can contact the energies of the atmic plane, the plane of spiritual will. The masters work on these planes.

In their books, the Tibetan and Alice Bailey have given us a wealth of information about meditation, as well as many practical exercises we can use. In particular, refer to *Rays and Initiations, Letters on Occult Meditation, Discipleship in the New Age, Vol. I and II*, and *Esoteric Psychology, Vol. II.*

These meditations can be practiced at any time. However, many people (including us) have noticed excellent results from a regular practice of the meditation "Inspiration and Spiritual Impression." In addition, we heartily recommend the Rainbow Bridge meditation, which is discussed at length in the books, *Bridge to Superconsciousness*, by Rick Prater and *Rainbow Bridge, A Link With the Soul*, by Two Disciples.

The Five Stages of Meditation

The five stages of meditation—concentration, meditation, contemplation, illumination and inspiration—taught to us over the ages by the eastern adepts, are paralleled in five signs of the zodiac:[11]

1. Leo represents concentration, soul life focused in form, individualization, self-consciousness, undeveloped and average humanity, and human experience.

2. Virgo represents meditation, soul life as sensed in the individual, the gestation period, the stage of the hidden Christ, intelligent humanity, and personality, as hiding the Christ life.

3. Libra represents contemplation, soul and form balanced, equilibrium, an interlude wherein the soul organizes itself for battle and the personality waits, the probationary path, and duality known.

4. Scorpio represents illumination, soul triumph, experience in Taurus consummated, astral glamour dissipated, soul light pouring in, the path of discipleship, and the disciple.

5. Sagittarius represents inspiration, preparation for initiation, soul-inspired personality life, soul expressing itself through personality, and the initiate.

Inspiration and Spiritual Impression[12]

This meditation involves bringing through inspiration and impression consciously by determined contact with our sources. It will give us a growing sense of planetary relationship and a conscious realization of a living world of intelligences linked together, making the world of phenomena recede into the background of consciousness while the world of meaning becomes more vital and real. This world, in its turn, is the antechamber to the world of causes, where conscious relationship can be established with our spiritual leaders.

The second purpose of this meditation is to bring to light the fact that we must be oriented to humanity in a more definite manner. The purpose of this orientation is to germinate ideas and enhance our civilization and culture. Through the resulting expansion of our consciousness and the greater scope of our vision, we distribute ideas, life, and potential into the world.

We receive these from:

- Our own soul, as our intuition awakens
- The groups we are linked to and working with on the inner levels

The meditation, done correctly and consistently, increases our realization, service, and understanding and helps us cooperate in the task of furthering the work of the spiritual Hierarchy, thus helping to bring in the new civilization, new attitudes, and the new world religion.

Holding the consciousness steadily in the mind, and not in the head, we enter:

The Stage of Recognition

1. Recognition of our pledged discipleship.
2. Recognition of our equipment, gratefully rendered.
3. Recognition of our achieved alignment.
4. Recognition of the soul, the source of love-wisdom.
5. Recognition of the Hierarchy.

The Stage of Consideration

1. Of the Ashram as a whole, of the Hierarchy as the Ashram of Sanat Kumara. We see, through the use of the creative imagination, all the Ashrams in close contact with Shamballa as:
   a. Responsive to the Purpose, implemented by the Ashrams of the Chohans.
   b. Impressed by the energy of Will as the great Ashram energizes its component parts—the various Ashrams within its periphery of influence.
   c. Vitalizing the initiates and disciples who are affiliated with the Masters and working in their Ashrams.
   d. Reaching out, through the accepted and pledged disciples, into the world of humanity.

We then say, with purpose and determination:

I strive towards comprehension.
Thy will, not mine, be done.

2. Of the world of souls, which is the Hierarchy in relation to the world of humanity. This involves:
   a. A study of the nature of the hierarchical effort, as it is expressed through love.

b. A conscious identification with the Plan.

c. Dedication to the work originating in the Ashram with which we know ourselves to be in touch, seeing it all as an integral part of the hierarchical work.

We then say, with love and aspiration:

I strive towards understanding.
Let wisdom take the place of knowledge in my life.

3. Of ourselves as a unit in our Master's Ashram. This involves:

a. Recognizing which aspect of our Master's planned work we are equipped to do.

b. Determining how to do it.

c. Considering the factor of preparation for eventual initiation as a means of increasing our capacity for hierarchical cooperation.

d. Energizing by light, faith, love, and power the spiritual center within which we serve and the ashramic projects for which we accept responsibility.

We then say:

I strive towards cooperation.
Let the Master of my life, the soul,
and likewise the One I seek to serve,
throw light through me on others.

The Stage of Fixed Determination

1. A reflection upon the distinction between Purpose, Will, and Intention.

2. A period of complete focused silence as we seek to present an unobstructed channel for the inflow of light, love, and strength from the Hierarchy.

A statement made by us, the soul, the disciple to the personality:

In the center of the will of God I stand.
Naught shall deflect my will from His.
I implement that will by love.
I turn towards the field of service.
I, the Triangle divine, work out that will
Within the square and serve my fellowmen.

Twelve Words / Twelve Months Work[13]

As an aid to concentration and receptivity, use twelve words as a theme for twelve month's work. As we gain the power to concentrate, meditate, relate, receive, and transmit, we can use these words as seed thoughts for longer or shorter periods of time.

As we use these words to open the door to a month's realization and inspiration, we think of them as living things, possessing form, soul, spirit, and life. The words are:

1. Recipient
2. Impression
3. Recognition
4. Relationship
5. Source
6. Ashram
7. Transmitter
8. Expression
9. Determination
10. Seed
11. Idea
12. Attachment

Stage One—Preliminary

Pass rapidly through the steps of recognition, consideration, and fixed determination (see previous meditation). These will bring us to the point at which this new meditation starts. Then proceed as follows:

Stage Two—The Center of Focused Thought

1. Polarization—Polarize and focus ourselves consciously upon the mental plane, tuning out all lower vibrations and reactions.

2. Orientation—Orient ourselves to the Spiritual Triad, through an act of the will and the imaginative use of the antahkarana.

3. Meditation on theme word—Take our theme word under consideration and ponder deeply upon it for at least five minutes. Endeavor to extract its quality and life, thus lifting it and our thought to as high a plane as possible.

4. OM, Pause—Sound the OM and wait silently, holding the mind steady. This is the pause of reception.

Stage Three—The Recipient of Impression

1. Statement of highest idea received—Assuming an attitude of the highest expectancy, express in our own words the highest truth of the monthly word-theme that we have been able to reach.

2. Relation of theme to present world opportunity—Relate that theme to the present world opportunity, thus universalizing the concept, seeing its relationship to world affairs, its usefulness and spiritual value to humanity as a whole.

3. Write down first thought received—Holding the mind in the light, write down the first thought that enters into our waiting mind in connection with the theme of our meditation. The ability to do this grows with practice and eventually evokes the intuition and thus fertilizes our mind.

4. OM, Refocus on the mental plane—Again, sound the OM, with the intent of refocusing ourselves upon the mental plane. If our work is successful, our original focus will have shifted to intuitional levels or to the levels of the higher, abstract mind, via the antahkarana.

Stage Four—The Analyzer of Ideas

1. Period of analytic thought—Now analyze or think over with clarity the work we have done and the ideas now in our mind, seeing them in a true perspective in relation to the whole problem of the day.

2. Summarize conclusions practically—Choosing one of the ideas which our theme-word has evoked, think about it, analyze it, and relate it to life, getting all we can out of it. This evoked idea may and should vary from day to day but will always remain related to the monthly theme.

3. Breathe out the idea into the world of thought—Study the idea in connection with ourselves, the disciple, active in service and the Master's work, but not in connection with the personality. Make the idea practical, enabling it to enrich us.

4. OM—Again, sound the OM with the intent of making the sensed idea a part of our very nature.

Stage Five—The Transmitter of Ideas

1. As the disciple, realize that a knowledge of truth and the reception of ideas places upon us the responsibility to be a transmitter to others.

2. Take the idea that the theme has engendered, or take the theme-word itself if no ideas have come, and in imagination formulate it in such a way that it can be presented to others, to our friends, to those we seek to help, and to humanity, when opportunity offers. Think the idea through mentally, emotionally, and practically, thus precipitating it outwards into the world of thought.

3. Using the creative imagination and seeing ourselves as responsible transmitters, doing the work of the Ashram, breathe out the idea as a formulated living thoughtform into the great stream of mental substance which is ever playing upon the human consciousness.

4. Sound the OM, thus closing the meditation with a daily dedication of ourselves to the service of humanity and to the Ashram.

Rainbow Bridge

The Rainbow Bridge (antahkarana) meditation builds a central energy channel through our bodies, along which spiritual energies can flow. This purifies the substance of our energy fields, increases our vibratory levels, and enables us to send refined energies back into the world to help others. The completed central channel, or Rainbow Bridge, extends from the Earth below our feet into the universe above our head.

The Rainbow Bridge concept is based on the premise that the substance of our energy fields mingles with the substance of the Earth's energy field. This is why we are sensitive to each other; why we are all one. The Rainbow Bridge visualization exercises recognize that "energy follows thought."

Our first step is to align our personality with our soul. To link in to the soul, we visualize our soul star and focus our attention on it. Located approximately six inches above our head, the soul star symbolizes the portion of our soul that is closest to matter—the abstract mind. To further the process of linking in to our soul, we say the Soul Mantram. These phrases of affirmation strengthen the connection and make the meditation techniques effective by turning them over to our higher self.

We mentally move our soul star through our body to build and expand our central energy channel, and to clear away thoughtforms that are clogging it. After that, we use the spiritual vortex to sweep away the debris of the loosened thoughtforms.

About thoughtforms: we create them, we accumulate them from our environment, and we are born with them. These thoughtforms are the result of individual and collective wishes and desires that are not empowered with enough energy to be sent from our fields into manifestation. Instead they linger in our fields and filter our awareness, prejudicing our impressions and experiences.

We build, clear, and add on to our energy channel a segment at a time, so as not to overload our energy field. Using our imagination and will, we move our soul star upward through a portion of our central channel each day until, after a few weeks, we can clear our entire central channel during one process.

The spiritual vortex then sweeps away everything we cleared from our energy field. We visualize a vortex or whirlwind of white light 30 feet above our head, coming down and whirling about us in a clockwise direction, clearing our field, unloading the impurities from our field deep into the ground, and then dissipating. Then we visualize another vortex, and another, and so on, for several minutes, until our field is cleared.

After we become familiar with it, we are able to do the clearing process in just a few minutes, and wherever we happen to be at the time. We can also just use the vortex whenever we happen to be in a crowd or in a situation that is disturbing us—we often find that situations "lighten up" as we vortex.

As we use the Mantram of Unification, the Great Invocation, and the Mantram of the Disciple, we can be assured that we are joining thousands of other people around the world in bringing in higher energies to help humanity. Memorizing these mantrams and saying them whenever we can lends a beauty and a serenity to our lives as well.

The Use of Mantrams

The Rainbow Bridge meditations make use of mantrams, all derived from the books of Alice A. Bailey and the Tibetan. The following quotation from *A Treatise on Cosmic Fire* gives us information about mantrams:

"Mantric Sounds. A mantram is a combination of sounds, of words, and of phrases that through virtue of certain rhythmic effects, achieve results that would not be possible apart from them. The most sacred of all the Eastern mantrams given out as yet to the public is the one embodied in the words, 'Om mani padme hum.' Every syllable of this phrase has a secret potency, and its totality has seven meanings and can bring about seven different results.

"There are various mantric forms, based upon this formula and upon the Sacred Word, which, sounded rhythmically and in different keys, accomplish certain desired ends, such as the invoking of protective angels or devas, and definite work, either constructive or destructive upon the planes.

"The potency of a mantram depends upon the point in evolution of the man who employs it. Uttered by an ordinary man it serves to stimulate the good within his bodies, to protect him, and it will also prove of beneficent influence upon his environment. Uttered by an adept or initiate its possibilities for good are infinite and far-reaching.

"Mantrams are of many kinds, and generally speaking might be enumerated as follows:

1. Some very esoteric mantrams, existing in the original Sensa, in the custody of the Great White Lodge.

2. Some Sanskrit mantrams employed by initiates and adepts.

3. Mantrams connected with the different rays.

4. Mantrams used in healing.

5. Mantrams used in the departments of either the Manu, the Bodhisattva, or the Mahachohan.

6. Mantrams used in connection with the devas and the elemental kingdoms.

7. Special mantrams connected with fire.

"All these mantrams depend for their potency upon the sound and rhythm and upon the syllabic emphasis imparted to them when enunciating and intoning. They depend too upon the capacity of the man who uses them to visualize and to will the desired effect."[14]

Basic Rainbow Bridge Meditation Steps

1. Take a few deep breaths and feel centered. Visualize your soul star shining brightly about six inches above your head.

2. Link in with your soul and say the soul mantram:

   I am the soul
   I am the light divine
   I am love
   I am will
   I am fixed design

3. Link in with other individuals and groups using similar processes. To do this, visualize lines of light connecting your soul star to theirs. This reinforces the energies of the people doing this type of work.

4. Say the Mantram of Unification, pausing afterwards to feel the energies:

   The sons of men are one, and I am one with them
   I seek to love, not hate
   I seek to serve and not exact due service
   I seek to heal, not hurt

   Let pain bring due reward of light and love
   Let the soul control the outer form, and life and all events
   And bring to light the love
   which underlies the happenings of the time

   Let vision come, and insight
   Let the future stand revealed
   Let inner union demonstrate, and outer cleavages be gone
   Let love prevail, let all men love

5. Clear your central channel. To do this, take the soul star from above
    your head and move it diagonally out in front of your body to the
    location you are currently working with. Points (a) through (d)
    below describe the locations to use, pictured on the Triangulation
    diagram, and indicate their timing:

    a. The first several meditation sessions, move the soul star
        diagonally, out and downward, to a point in front of your
        forehead, between your eyes. Then move it straight inward,
        into the center of your head. From there, move it up through
        your head, slowly, until the soul star returns to its original place
        above your head. Repeat this five times.

    b. The next few sessions, follow the process in (a), above, but do
        it once rather than five times. Then move the soul star
        diagonally out and downward, to a point in front of your throat.
        Move it inward into the center of your throat, and then upward
        to its original place above your head. Repeat five times from
        the throat level.

    c. Thereafter, move the soul star to a lower level, a few sessions
        for each level, after taking the soul star through each of the
        preceding upper levels one time (forehead first, throat second,
        and so on). Repeat the process five times from the lower level.
        The lower levels are: the heart, the solar plexus, the sacral area
        below your navel, the base of your spine, the knees, and the
        feet.

    d. After you complete the foot level, you are ready to clear the
        entire channel at once:

        Move the soul star to a location six inches beneath your feet.
        Spin the soul star while moving it up through the entire central
        channel. Spinning the soul star widens the channel so that more
        energy can flow through.

    e. Follow process (d) only from now on in your meditation
        sessions.

The Triangulation diagram depicts the movement of the soul star to points in front of the body and then inward and up to its original position. (We recommend spending at least three to seven days on each center before moving to the next lower level. The solar plexus and sacral center may require more time.)

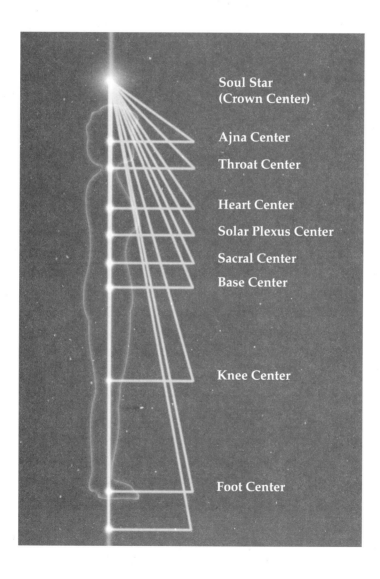

Soul Star
(Crown Center)

Ajna Center

Throat Center

Heart Center

Solar Plexus Center

Sacral Center

Base Center

Knee Center

Foot Center

6. Invoke the spiritual vortex after each clearing session. The spiritual vortex is a whirlwind of white light that sweeps your energy field clear. Say:

   In the wisdom of the soul, I invoke the spiritual vortex.

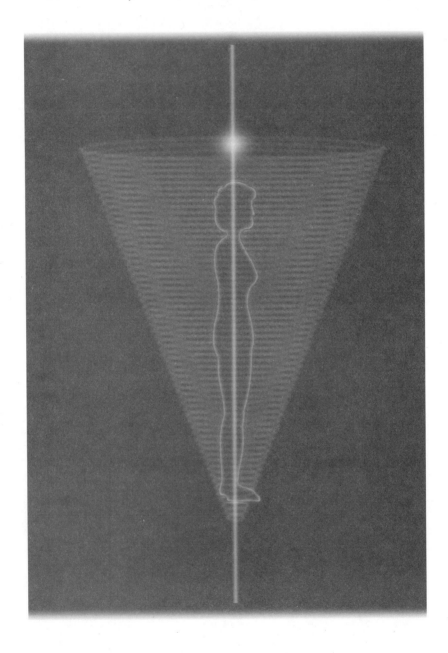

7. Visualize a vortex of white light 30 feet above your head. See it coming down and whirling around you in a clockwise direction, clearing your energy field. Visualize the vortex unloading the impurities from your energy field to at least three feet into the ground, and then dissipating.

   Visualize another vortex, then another, and another, for five minutes or until you sense that your field is clear.

8. Invoke the group spiritual vortex. Say:

   In the wisdom of the soul, we invoke the group spiritual vortex.

9. Invoke the One. Say:

   As the soul-infused personal self, the personal self infused by the soul, as the unified group, we invoke the One.

10. Next, say the Great Invocation with love and meaning. Pause in a positive meditative state for several minutes afterwards to visualize the higher energies flowing through you and out into the universe.

    From the point of light within the mind of God
    Let light stream forth into the minds of men
    Let light descend on Earth

    From the point of love within the heart of God
    Let love stream forth into the hearts of men
    May Christ return to Earth

    From the center where the will of God is known
    Let purpose guide the little wills of men
    The purpose which the masters know and serve

    From the center which we call the race of men
    Let the plan of love and light work out
    And may it seal the door where evil dwells

    Let light and love and power restore the plan on Earth

11. As a way of asking for guidance in your daily activities, say the following and pause a few minutes to let the energies come in:

    In the wisdom of the soul, and to serve hierarchical or soul purpose,
    I draw that which I need from the central reservoir

12. Send out healing energies from your group or individual soul star to the soul stars of other groups, individuals, or situations by saying:

    In the wisdom of the soul,
    we send healing energy from the group soul star
    to individuals, groups, or situations named out loud or silently.

13. Say the Mantram of the Disciple with a sense of purpose and dedication:

    I am a point of light, within a greater light
    I am a strand of loving energy within the stream of love divine
    I am a point of sacrificial fire, focused within the fiery will of God
    And thus I stand

    I am a way by which men may achieve
    I am a source of strength enabling them to stand
    I am a beam of light shining upon their way
    And thus I stand

    And standing thus revolve
    And tread this way the ways of men
    And know the ways of God
    And thus I stand

14. Pause a few moments before closing to silently give thanks to our souls, the group soul, and to our inner-world teachers for the benefits of the meditation.

15. Sound the OM three times:

    OM   OM   OM

16. Say the closing affirmations:

    May reality govern my every thought, and truth be the master of my life.

    We affirm that Earth is a sacred planet, and there is peace on Earth.

The Group Antahkarana

Following these steps will help us build the group antahkarana, which is constructed of the antahkaranas of each group member. This process enables an inflow of light from the spiritual triad via the group antahkarana.[15]

1. View the interior interrelation of the seven centers in the body as the objective of the meditation, basing the work upon the occult maxim that "energy follows thought."

2. Consider the subsequent relation of the centers in any one individual to the remainder of the group members, regarding the seven centers as radiating transmitters of energy to the centers of the other group members. This results in the forming of seven great centers of energy that will constitute the group centers. Recognize that these seven great centers are fed and enlightened by the energy transmitted by each individual.

3. Recognize the fusion of the individual soul with the group soul, and consequently a conscious rapport with the Hierarchy, which is inherently the kingdom of souls.

This figure shows a Rainbow Bridge group with linked soul stars.

Meditation for Recognizing and Solving Problems

We can work with this triangle of master, soul, and personality to call down a stream of pure white light and pour it through our lower vehicles to cleanse away everything that hinders us. In this way, we can use a strong mental body to get rid of our fears and use the love aspect to flood ourselves with love and light.[16]

1. Quiet the physical body.

2. Quiet, by temporary inhibition, the astral body.

3. Link up with the soul and reason out the proper method of procedure in meeting the difficulty. Having exhausted all the higher rational methods and having clearly seen our course of action,

4. Raise our vibration as high as possible and call down, from intuitional levels, added light on the difficulty.

Resources for Hierarchical Work[17]

The goal of this meditation is to attract money for hierarchical purposes. If we could practice it simultaneously, and on Sunday mornings (joining those who are currently using this meditation on Sunday mornings), it could generate funds for uplifting life on Earth.

Stage I

After achieving a link with the soul and the members in our group, formulate clearly to ourselves the answers to the following questions:

1. If money is one of the most important things needed today for spiritual work, what is the factor which is at present deflecting it away from the work of the Hierarchy?

2. What is our personal attitude toward money? Do we regard it as a great and possible spiritual asset, or do we think of it in material terms?

3. What is our personal responsibility in regard to money which passes through our hands? Are we handling it as a disciple of the masters should handle it?

Stage II

1. Ponder on the redemption of humanity through the right use of money. Visualize the money in the world today as:

   a. Concretized energy, at present largely used for purely material purposes and for the satisfaction of personal desires.

   b. A great stream of flowing, golden substance, passing out of the control of the forces of materialism into the control of the forces of light.

2. Then say the following invocative prayer, with focused mental concentration and from a heartfelt desire to meet spiritual demands:

   O Thou in Whom we live and move and have our being, the Power that can make all things new, turn to spiritual purposes the money in the world; touch the hearts of men everywhere so that they may give to the work of the Hierarchy that which has hitherto been given to material satisfaction. The New Group of World Servers needs money in large quantities. We ask that the needed vast sums may be made available. May this potent energy of Thine be in the hands of the Forces of Light.

3. Visualize the work to be done by those groups that claim our present allegiance. Then, through the creative imagination and by an act of the will, see untold and unlimited sums of money pouring into the hands of those who seek to do the masters' work.

4. Then say aloud, with conviction and emphasis:

   He for Whom the whole world waits has said that whatsoever shall be asked in His Name and with faith in the response will see it accomplished.

   Remember at the same time that "faith is the substance of things hoped for and the evidence of things not seen." Then add:

   We ask for the needed money for . . . . . and can demand it because
   'From the Center which we call the race of men
   Let the Plan of Love and Light work out.
   And may it seal the door where evil dwells.'

5. Close with a careful consideration of our own responsibility to the Plan, being practical, realistic, and knowing that if we do not give, we may not ask, for we have no right to evoke that which we do not share.

Full Moon Approaches

"At the time of the full moon, it is almost as if a door suddenly opened wide, which at other times stands closed. Through that door, ingress is possible; through that door or opening, energies can be contacted which are otherwise shut off; and through that door approaches can be made to the planetary Hierarchy and to reality which are at other times not possible."—AAB[18]

We plan our full-moon meditations as close as possible to the hour of the full moon, and before that hour rather than after. During the five-day period around each full moon, we have a special opportunity to deepen our inner spiritual contacts. Two days before the full moon, we cultivate an inner attitude of poise, introspection, and stepped-up state of consciousness, while at the same time proceeding with our normal lives. Then, two days afterwards, we hold the focus of the full-moon energies as they are consolidated into our waking consciousness. We approach the work with clear vision and loving understanding of the needs of the world as we:

1. Seek to draw near to our teacher and sense his vibration.

2. Try to realize at the same time the vibration of his other students.

3. Register any phenomena, if present.[19]

Most of the Trans-Himalayan Masters now work with groups rather than individuals because of the needs of the world during these times of rapid evolution. Group format also protects us from over-stimulation. Thus, full-moon meditations are group events. As a result, the group becomes closely integrated and can, therefore, achieve spiritual objectives in the world. As individuals, we become more closely aligned with our soul and become more and more fully able to achieve higher levels of intuition and inspiration—and, eventually, initiation.

"This Full Moon work involves the use of the creative imagination, the cultivation of the power to visualise, the intensification of the magnetic vibration of the ajna centre, and consequently of the pituitary body. This establishes a magnetic field for the interplay of the currents and energies which are brought into action by the activity of the head centre and of the pineal gland. These higher forces are brought in and utilised in the meditation processes followed by all the group."[20]

As mentioned in our discussion on the Moon in Chapter 7, the cycle of the full moon facilitates meditation for those who are doing spiritual work or are mentally polarized, whereas the lunar energies can upset those of us who are emotional. Since our goal is to elevate human consciousness, practicing meditation at the time of the full moon for this purpose might be of great practical value in helping to dispel some of the astral energies that are hampering people.

The Tibetan Master suggested that we review his teachings for information on:[21]

- The importance of the full moon.

- What should be done and what should happen at the time of the full moon.

- Any information we can find about the causes behind the spiritual opportunites.

Invocation and Evocation

"Under the law, we draw forth from others what is actually present within ourselves, and to this law, races and nations are no exception."[22] In the future, we are told, the process of invocation and evocation will form the basis for the religions of the world. When we attune ourselves to the life of the soul, we will become dissatisfied with some of the old religious forms, and we will turn to invocation. The process of invocation consists of two stages:[23]

1. The stage of aspiration, where we gradually want a better way.

2. The stage of mysticism, merging into occultism (the study of that which is hidden). We recognize the higher way and contact the spiritual vision.

The above applies to the individual and to humanity as a whole. These two stages are taking place today as we are realizing the value of the good of the whole and are evoking the will-to-good in others. The mass of human consciousness is now being organized and focused on the ideal of the general welfare of humanity.

A united call from the different levels of the human consciousness can invoke the help of higher forces to save us, but we have to make that appeal because Hierarchy cannot help us without our requesting their assistance. It is ultimately the responsibility of humanity to inaugurate a new world cycle. For this reason, the Tibetan gave us the

Great Invocation "for the use of those men and women whose aim is the will-to-good, who think in terms of world service and who are oriented towards light—the light of knowledge, the light of wisdom and understanding and the light of life itself."[24]

At the time of the full moon each month, we can invoke energies from higher spiritual groups, mainly the Hierarchy. Hierarchy, in turn, invokes energies from Shamballa, and Shamballa from the Planetary Logoi. Members of Hierarchy study timing and cycles in order to know which energies are most available at the time and which invocations would create the least resistance; in effect, using the aspects mentioned earlier and, thus, obeying the Law of Economy. Our invocative process can be along the following lines:

1. We, in our training for eventual membership in Hierarchy, link in with the members of our spiritual group and members of Hierarchy, sending lines of light to these groups and other spiritual groups working for the evolution of humanity at the time of the full moon.

2. Consider what energies are available to us at this time:

    Recognize that the Sun and the Moon are in opposition, which creates a gateway of light for the solar energies to illuminate humankind. The more immediate effect of such energies is the transmission of illumination from the members of Hierarchy to ourselves, though it may be a couple of days before such illumination might penetrate through to our waking consciousness.

    Recognize the planetary energies involved in their relationships to each other, knowing that these great entities are working together for a cause. We understand that Hierarchy is more knowledgeable than we are of what these causes might be, so we align our energies with hierarchical energies for the purpose of salvaging and evolving our planet Earth.

3. Recognize our task of mediatorship, which is the major task of the Hierarchy, mediating between Shamballa and Humanity.

4. Resolve to carry forward the dual task of invocation and evocation simultaneously—the evocation (through right invocation) of the will-to-good of the world thinkers and aspirants, and also the will-to-save of the Shamballa Lords, via the Hierarchy.[25]

5.   From this point of alignment, say the Great Invocation, thus making invocative appeal to all the higher forces to let light, and love, and power flow forth on Earth:

From the point of Light within the Mind of God
Let Light stream forth into the minds of men,
Let Light descend on Earth.

From the point of Love within the Heart of God
Let Love stream forth into the hearts of men,
May Christ return to Earth.

From the centre where the Will of God is known
Let purpose guide the little wills of men—
The purpose which the Masters know and serve.

From the centre which we call the race of men
Let the Plan of Love and Light work out
And may it seal the door where evil dwells.

Let Light and Love and Power restore the plan on Earth.

6.   Visualize the energy web surrounding the Earth as a network of triangles, representing groups and centers of human activity; visualize light circulating around the points of these triangles and pouring into them. As we do this, think of the planetary energies that are most prominent in the Earth's energy field, and absorb these energies into our group field.

7.   After we have achieved a group relationship and rapport with these energies, visualize ourselves, still in group formation, transmitting these energies to humanity. Think of the group good that can be done with these energies and imagine those effects occurring in the energy field of humanity and the planet. This is the evocation part of the work—where our love for humanity is evocative and thus causes us to want to promote its evolution. In the same manner, we evoke energy from Hierarchy, and so on up the line.

8.   Pause a few moments before closing to silently give thanks to our souls, the group soul, and to our inner-world teachers for the benefits of the meditation.

9.   Sound the OM three times:

OM   OM   OM

The Tibetan tells us: "The etheric body is the organ whereby personality or soul expression becomes evidenced upon the physical plane. Its potency is that which evokes the physical form. Most of the vehicles have a dual capacity—invocation and evocation. They also have a third function: they *ground or focus energy, thus producing a point of tension, of crisis and an interlude, prior to a process of transmission.* Ponder on these words. The physical body can be evoked into manifestation and subsequent activity, but it has no power of invocation...The etheric body invokes and evokes; but it also, in relation to the physical plane, precipitates energy through a process of appropriation."[26]

Approach to the Master's Ashram

At the hour of the full moon, or as close before the hour as possible, follow the procedure outlined below, using the creative activity of the imagination to visualize the steps:[27]

1. Center our consciousness in the head.

2. Imagine ourselves as retreating even more consciously within, toward that point of contact where personality/soul and the teacher in the world of souls can meet and become as one.

3. Hold ourselves as poised and steady as possible, preserving that detached poise as fully as possible during the following process.

   a. Imagine or visualize ourselves as standing before a golden or ivory door.

   b. See that door slowly open, revealing a long low room with three windows—one looking east, one looking west, and one looking north. Seated before the eastern window on a low carved chair, looking toward us and sitting with his back to the window, we visualize our Tibetan brother, in deep meditation, seeking to contact us and all for whom he is responsible.

   c. Picture ourselves as advancing slowly up the long room (which is his study and work room) and then standing before him. We see our group brothers and sisters standing with us.

   d. Then each of us can constitute ourselves, in imagination, as spokesperson for our group and offer the group in service and deep consecration to the service of the Plan.

e. Now imagine that we see our Tibetan brother rising from his chair. Then as a group, with him, we face the east and say together the Great Invocation, endeavoring consciously to follow the Tibetan's lead as we say the words, listenong with care and using the creative imagination. This involves intense concentration.

4. We now say the Great Invocation:

From the point of Light within the Mind of God
Let Light stream forth into the minds of men,
Let Light descend on Earth.

From the point of Love within the Heart of God
Let Love stream forth into the hearts of men,
May Christ return to Earth.

From the centre where the Will of God is known
Let purpose guide the little wills of men—
The purpose which the Masters know and serve.

From the centre which we call the race of men
Let the Plan of Love and Light work out
And may it seal the door where evil dwells.

Let Light and Love and Power restore the plan on Earth.

5. As a special tribute to our Solar Logos, the Great Being Who manifests through our Sun, we now say the Gayatri Mantram:

O Thou, Who givest sustenance to the Universe,
From Whom all things proceed,
To Whom all things return
Unveil to us the face of the True Spiritual Sun,
Hidden by a disk of golden light,
That we may know the Truth,
And do our whole duty,
As we journey to Thy sacred feet.

6. Pause a few moments before closing to silently give thanks to our souls, the group soul, and to our inner-world teachers for the benefits of the meditation.

7. Sound the OM three times:

OM   OM   OM

Another meditation we can use to approach the Master's Ashram at the time of the full moon is given as follows:[28]

1. Link up mentally and raise our consciousness as high as possible, holding it steady in the light, letting the brain consciousness drop below the level of consciousness.

2. Realize that our Master is also standing steady, pouring out to us his love and strength, and endeavoring to lift us to a higher state of consciousness.

3. Visualize a disk or sphere of indigo blue, a deep electric blue. In the center of that disk imagine that our Master is standing.

    His appearance and personality do not matter.

4. When we have visualized him standing, waiting, then endeavor to see a band of golden light stretching between us, the group and the Master, knowing this to be the symbol of the path that we are all treading. See this path gradually shortening, thus bringing us closer together, slowly and steadily, until we enter into the heart of the blue disk.

5. We now say the Great Invocation:

    From the point of Light within the Mind of God
    Let Light stream forth into the minds of men,
    Let Light descend on Earth.

    From the point of Love within the Heart of God
    Let Love stream forth into the hearts of men,
    May Christ return to Earth.

    From the centre where the Will of God is known
    Let purpose guide the little wills of men—
    The purpose which the Masters know and serve.

    From the centre which we call the race of men
    Let the Plan of Love and Light work out
    And may it seal the door where evil dwells.

    Let Light and Love and Power restore the plan on Earth.

6. In closing, sound the OM three times:

    OM   OM   OM

Spiritual Festivals

"Each of the months of the year will later be dedicated (through accurate astrological and astronomical knowledge) to whichever constellation in the heavens governs a particular month, as Sirius governs Leo."—AAB[29]

Three major spiritual festivals are currently being observed widely and form the high point in the annual cycle. These festivals establish a relationship between the work of the Christ and the Buddha, thus demonstrating to the world a linking of eastern and western religion.

These three festivals are:

- The Easter Festival at the Aries full moon
- The Wesak Festival at the Taurus full moon
- The Festival of Goodwill at the Gemini full moon

Eventually there will be others, including one at the time of the full moon of August and the festival of the New Group of World Servers in December every seven years.

Through the steady, persistent meditation work of many individuals and groups in all parts of the world, these festivals are now achieving a subjective anchorage in the consciousness of humanity. Their basic divine purpose will begin to manifest as various groups and religious institutions simultaneously acknowledge and observe, each in its own way, the approach of humanity to the inner kingdom of souls and to God.

We should also consider the purpose and effect of each full moon throughout the year. These nine lesser festivals build the "divine attributes" into human consciousness, while the three major festivals establish the "divine aspects." The aspects are associated with Rays One, Two, and Three and the attributes are associated with Rays Four, Five, Six, and Seven. All these qualities are equally divine; we can use all twelve festival opportunities to stimulate the evolutionary spiritual growth in all kingdoms of nature.

In the future, all people of spiritual inclination will keep the same holy days. This will bring about a pooling of spiritual resources and a united spiritual effort, plus a simultaneous invocation. The potency of this will be apparent. The three major festivals each year are concentrated in three consecutive months and lead to a prolonged annual spiritual effort that affects the remainder of the year.[30]

The Easter Festival

This great western and Christian festival celebrates the risen, living Christ, the teacher of all humanity and the head of the spiritual Hierarchy. Christ is the expression of the love of God. On this day, we recognize Christ and the spiritual Hierarchy that Christ guides and directs, and we emphasize the nature of God's love.

The date of Easter is always determined by the date of the full moon of spring. This season of the year, which is also the beginning of the astrological year, symbolizes renewal and resurrection after a time of quiescence, giving us new hope, new life, inspiring us to new activities and invigorating all forms of nature.

The Easter festival engages the forces of the Spirit of Resurrection, which can restore livingness to humanity's spiritual aims and add life to our planning. This spirit of resurrection can provide the vitality needed to implement the trends of a coming new civilization, guiding humanity out of separativeness and selfishness into an age of group-consciousness and unification.

On a planetary scale, we are told, the Spirit of Resurrection is the opponent and the antagonist of the Spirit of Death.[31] We are aware that the processes of death are necessary, in destroying old, worn-out forms. After death does its job, the Spirit of Resurrection restores us to new life.

At the full moon of March, we can invoke this life-giving spirit with such intensity that the Hierarchy will be called into active response to release the potency of this spirit into the hearts of humanity.

Under the guidance of the Christ, all of these spiritual forces are working and their activities are closely synchronized. This can happen because members of the human family are at all stages of responsiveness. As our will to live and will to good are strengthened, we will feel an immediate effect on a larger scale, for the forces of resurrection will intensify. This will show up in more practical attitudes, clear thinking, fixed determination, and better laid plans by all of us.

The Wesak Festival

This great eastern festival celebrates the Buddha, the spiritual intermediary between the highest spiritual center, Shamballa, and the Hierarchy. The Buddha is the expression of the wisdom of God, the embodiment of light, and the indicator of divine purpose. The Wesak festival is fixed annually in relation to the full moon of May. Over the centuries, it has been held in the Wesak valley of the Himalayas in order to:[32]

- Substantiate the fact of Christ's physical existence among us.

- Prove on the physical plane the factual solidarity of the eastern and western approaches to God. Both the Christ and the Buddha are then present.

- Form a rallying point and a meeting place for those who annually, in synthesis and symbolically, link up and represent the Kingdom of God and humanity.

- Demonstrate the nature of Christ's work as he stands as the representative of the spiritual Hierarchy and as the leader of the New Group of World Servers. In person, Christ voices our demand for the recognition of the Kingdom of God, here and now.

Historically, this festival has been five days in length. The first two days are preparatory days of alignment, dedication, and upward-striving. The day of the festival itself is the day of safe-guarding and we hold ourselves "steady in the light." The two days after the full moon are the days of distribution. During this process, we keep in mind the needs of the world and the necessity of providing a group channel by which spiritual forces can be poured through the body of humanity under the guidance of members of Hierarchy. This Wesak energy flows through the following entities:[33]

1. The Forces of Light and the Spirit of Peace
2. The Planetary Hierarchy
3. The Buddha
4. The Christ
5. The New Group of World Servers
6. Humanity

The Wesak festival is one of the best times to invoke beneficent extraplanetary forces of light, inspiration, and spiritual revelation.[34] The Buddha focuses the downpouring forces and the Christ focuses the outgoing demand and spiritual aspiration of the entire planet, making a planetary alignment of great potency. The result can be a flood of power that can make definite changes in the human consciousness and uplift conditions in the world. This depends largely upon the mediatory work of the New Group of World Servers to inspire the thinking public and to give them faith, hope, and a sense of confidence that we, humanity, can make the needed changes in the world.

The Festival of Goodwill

This is the festival of the spirit of humanity aspiring toward God, seeking conformity with the will of God and dedicated to the expression of right human relations. This festival is always at the full moon of June. It is a day on which the spiritual and divine nature of humankind is recognized. At this festival, for 2,000 years, the Christ has represented humanity and has stood before the Hierarchy and in the sight of Shamballa as the God-man, the leader of his people, and "the eldest in a great family of brothers."[35]

Each year at this time, Christ preaches the last sermon of the Buddha before the assembled Hierarchy. This is, therefore, a festival of deep invocation and appeal, of a basic aspiration toward fellowship, and of human and spiritual unity. It represents the effect in human consciousness of the work of the Buddha and of the Christ. This festival is also observed as World Invocation Day.

Humanity is related uniquely to Gemini through the influences of Venus, the esoteric ruler of Gemini and also the hierarchical ruler of Capricorn. This shows the power of the mind and its place and purpose in connection with individualization and initiation. During the process of individualization, Venus actively helped to produce the relationship of the fifth kingdom of souls with the third kingdom of animals, leading to a great approach between soul and form, resulting in the fourth kingdom of humanity.

During the month of June in the coming world religion when the influences of Gemini are particularly strong, we will note this fact to bring ourselves nearer to the spiritual realities and make appeal to the forces which can use this planetary potency to work out the divine plan upon Earth.[36]

Full Moon of August[37]

Special energies come to us at the full moon of August which, in the future when the mystery schools are externalized, will be comparable to the three spiritual festivals in the spring and early summer.

Pluto focuses a potent stream of force from Leo and Aquarius through the three aspects of the Sun, through Uranus and Neptune and then to Earth during the month of August, as shown in the following diagram.

LEO and AQUARIUS

Physical Sun	Heart of the Sun	Central Spiritual Sun

Pluto
Uranus and Neptune
Humanity
The animal kingdom

There are many such cosmic lines of directed forces such as this, but this one in particular is of major importance to humanity at this time.

August, which is the month of Sirius and is ruled by Leo, brings Sirius into close relation to Leo. Leo, in the cosmic sense (apart from our solar system) is ruled by Sirius, the home of that greater Lodge to which the fifth initiation admits a master. When the new world religion is manifesting, the full-moon festival in August will be dedicated to making contact, via the Hierarchy, with Sirian force.

Also involved is an esoteric quaternary—Sirius, Leo, Mercury, Saturn—which has a powerful effect upon the human quaternary of spirit, soul, mind, and brain. This energy brings about an interrelation and an inner awakening which prepares us for initiation. The following table gives us a hint as to the basic reality and necessity of meditation.

Sirius	Leo	Mercury	Saturn
Spirit	Soul	Mind	Brain
Life	Quality	Illumination	Appearance
Inhalation	Interlude	Exhalation	Interlude

The influence of Sirius is not consciously felt until after the third initiation when the true nature of the spirit aspect begins to dawn upon the liberated, intuitive perception of the initiate. For the advanced initiate in Leo, Sirius becomes a major life factor because the advanced initiate rules the energies of the Sun and the Moon, controlling what those two planets represent. At that stage, Sirius, Leo, the Sun, the Moon, and Mercury are the influences with which the initiate is concerned. The influences of Sirius, three in number, are focused in Regulus, a star of the first magnitude, frequently called "the heart of the Lion."

Festival of the New Group of World Servers

Since 1942, there has been a planetary inflow of energy for which we are asked to prepare and avail ourselves. The source of this energy is a great constellation which is to our zodiac what our zodiac is to the Earth. The week during which this energy enters the Earth occurs every seven years and lasts from December 21 through December 28, during the beginning of the Capricorn cycle. If the full moon should happen to fall within this period, the opportunity is most significant and this possibility should be watched for.[38]

Counting from 1942, these seven-year periods culminate in 1949, 1956, 1963, 1970, 1977, 1984, 1991, 1998, 2005, 2012, 2019, and 2026.

This week is the festival week of the New Group of World Servers. These new groups are appearing everywhere around the world. Whenever there are three or more members of the New Group of World Servers in any one exoteric group, it then becomes "linked by a triple thread of golden light to the New Group of World Servers, and can in some measure be used."[39]

Members of the New Group of World Servers are rather loosely linked on the physical plane, whereas the linking is stronger on the astral plane and is based upon love of humanity. The major linking is on the mental plane, which also consolidates the efforts of the physical and astral planes.

The New Group of World Servers is "the principal group at this time definitely working under the Law of Group Progress."[40] This Law of Group Progress embodies one of the energies which have gradually been released over the past two centuries, and is connected with producing a coherence of units in a group, forming them into one living organism.

The expressions of this law are group affinity, group objective, and group goal. It is similar to that type of consciousness that demonstrates as tribal, national, or racial unity, but in this case there is no physical connotation nor a physical-plane basis. Instead, the basis is a group idealism that can only become consciously registered when the units in the group are beginning to function on the mental plane and are developing the capacity to think things through, or register in the brain what the soul has imparted to the mind.

As the Tibetan says: "When we come to study the astrological implications in connection with these laws, we shall discover that the energies of the zodiacal signs have a specific effect upon the energy of a Being, Whose purpose works out into manifestation through these laws, which are regarded by us as great and inevitable natural laws and also spiritual laws. This effect produces a blending of energies which is both balancing and, at the same time, impelling."[41]

Meditation on the Symbol of World Servers

The symbol of the New Group of World Servers is a golden triangle enclosing an even-armed cross with one diamond at the apex of the triangle. This symbol is never reproduced in form at all. It shines above the heads of all who are in the group and cannot be seen by anyone (not even a clairvoyant) except a group member and then only if, for purposes of work, his recognition needs stimulation.

The motto of the group is "The Glory Of The One."[42]

Chapter 12—
The Living Commitment

"The possession of Knowledge, unless accompanied by a manifestation and expression in Action, is like the hoarding of precious metals—a vain and foolish thing. Knowledge, like Wealth, is intended for Use. The Law of Use is Universal, and he who violates it suffers by reason of his conflict with natural forces."—The Kybalion[1]

Keeping in mind the archetypes of our own best possibilities, we can make a commitment to ourselves and to the world to live each day according to our highest aspirations and greatest potential, building the daily events of our lives into new ideas, thoughts, and actions leading toward our goals.

We have found that there are many helpful forces we can draw upon. Through our link with our sages and spiritual guides—the link of humanity with the planetary Hierarchy—we have access to the energies of the universe, though they are appropriately transformed for our use as they flow through various levels of life. We can interrelate with these tremendous energies through meditation by the methods of invocation and evocation, which are expressions of the focused will.

We have discussed the concepts of initiatory teachings and working with groups but, on a practical level, these are concerns that are best left to the individual. We are, or should become, the best judge of what teaching is appropriate for our own needs, and we need to exercise our power of choice in determining what we will study.

In the meantime, we can recognize that, throughout the course of our development, our family groups, friends, and work groups have proven to be good teachers for us, since the interactions and communications that are demanded in life develop the personality and soul growth of both individuals and groups. The polarities of our contemporary male/female relationships embody a major opportunity for us. The next big step away from self-consciousness for many people is family-consciousness; being forced in family situations to grow by having to take other people's needs into consideration (thus learning to be less self-centered) is giving people an opportunity to push their evolution to the next level. For many in the world, the next stage of group-consciousness on a spiritual level is already becoming a fact.

We need to exercise caution and discrimination as to which spiritual teachers we select. When we find people we can learn from, we still need to maintain our own sense of integrity and constantly evaluate whether the situation is still effective for us and for the group involved. Often what is appropriate for one stage of development is not appropriate for another, and it is a wise teacher that can let the student go. The appendix of resources at the end of this book lists various reputable groups that one can possibly link with for spiritual study and work in the world. There are many others.

It is important for all of us to allocate time for our own creative pursuits, and the world will often not invest us with this time unless we find a means of taking it for ourselves. I believe that time for personal creativity for all people is the birthright of our future progress.

We can be creative about how we meditate using the material in this book. For example, at the time of the full moon, we can cut out the symbols of the planets and signs from construction paper, and associate various colors with them. Then, each group member can hold forth a symbol while reciting the keywords and characteristics of the entity involved. After meditation upon the energy of this entity, we can position the symbol in its appropriate place on a chart, which can be laid out on a table with a candle burning in the center. Candle flames and incense have long been used to purify and consecrate the space for ceremonial rituals.

We may have the best of intentions when we attempt to transmit healing energies to other people, groups, and situations in the world, but we need to honor the free will of those concerned, just as Hierarchy does not impose upon the free will of humanity. To respect the free will of others while yet meditating to help them is possible if we are always sure to invoke the will of the soul or souls concerned. For example, in the Rainbow Bridge meditation work, we ask this permission to send healing energies by saying beforehand: "In the wisdom of the soul…" All souls are linked in the kingdom of souls, so "the soul" as invoked will only act within the wisdom of all the souls affected.

As individuals, it is helpful to keep a spiritual diary in which we record the results of our meditations or even just the fact that we have meditated. My current version of this diary is a simple shorthand tablet that I always carry with me. I also use it to jot down ideas, dreams, important events, and sometimes simply to record quickly what is going on in my life. I find this notepad valuable for marking my progress on the "path."

This leads into some speculations as to what the "path" might be for any individual or group of us. In this day and age, I am convinced that the quickest path to spiritual development is being actively involved and participating in the outer world, while we are attempting to develop ourselves in the inner world.

We need balance and versatility to not only develop ourselves but to help in the development of humanity as a whole. Any time any one of us achieves an insight or lifts oneself a little higher, the whole world receives the capacity to act on that insight and is uplifted accordingly.

Working in the world gives us contact with public opinion and changes in human consciousness that result from world affairs. Thus, we can gauge when humanity is ready for new teachings and assist the spiritual Hierarchy in making changes in the techniques or curriculum whenever humanity needs a new presentation of the ageless truths.

If, as I think, the divine plan and purpose for humanity is the ability for everyone to be creative and to have the means to create beauty and truth in life, then how do we create? The ability and opportunity to create and add beauty to life sounds simple, but indeed is not. First of all, the ability to create has to be developed. Then we must create the opportunity itself. For this empowerment of humanity to happen on a universal level would be very profound. Just for all of us in our own groups to be empowered at the same time would be quite an achievement.

To create, we use our energy to formulate thoughtforms that are to be impressed upon the substance of the level of consciousness we are working on. Our energies then combine with other energies in a reservoir of similar energy, and we and other people who are working with these energies project them to their destination where they will do their creative work.

For every word we speak, multitudes of deva lives respond and build corresponding forms from deva substance, manifesting the intent of what was sounded forth and initiating action upon the physical plane. The consequences of speech affect the plane on which the speaker dwells and all the planes below it, thus the more highly evolved the speaker is, the higher the planes on which manifestation occurs and the greater the effect on surrounding lives.

Many people build unconsciously and the forms created depend upon the underlying motive or purpose of the person. However, as our awareness increases, we need to understand the significance of what we speak, be aware of the creative consequences on all planes, and only speak words that will further our purposes of uplifting humanity and the lower kingdoms of nature. Our own evolution also depends upon it: we cannot be permitted access to higher planes until we demonstrate that we can use our speech wisely and harmlessly.

We need to be pure in thought, accurate in word, and skillful in action, especially when creating in mental matter and producing potent results in astral or physical manifestation. Purity of thought includes good intention, but also implies a primary focus and a lack of extraneous mentalizing. Focused, purposeful thought leads to accurate speech which results in skillful action. It is a matter of being precise about what we want to create, and taking responsibility for the effects it has on other lives (human and other kingdoms).

Using the "silence of the high places" to bring about our desired effects involves meditating upon our purposes and planning the details of our creations (just like the Solar Logos does on his own vast scale). The high places represent the levels we reach in our meditations. As we learn more fully how to reach these high places and bring back higher ideas, we increase our effectiveness in our powers of creation and manifest only what we intend.

The more focused the thinking, the greater the energy that moves toward what is being thought about. For those upon the path, focused thinking invokes soul energy from the heart, which streams into the brain via the etheric body and conditions our type of living, our expression, and our influence upon the physical plane. This is useful in getting the job done for the sake of the world.

Practical manifestation is our job (with help from our sages) because we are close to the need. Through developing our skills and using them, we achieve mastery and evolve. Because of the free will of humanity, no one knows for sure how we will get to the eventual goal, but Hierarchy does know that humanity will eventually achieve the goal and, based on the past, they can make reasonable predictions as to the general directions humanity will go. However on the detail level, it can change, so we have to keep abreast of daily changes and modify our own ideas, actions, and recommendations accordingly.

Once we know our purpose, our thoughts and activities become directed automatically toward expressing that purpose. The universal mind stages events, or vortices in the currents of thought, called synchronicities, that help develop and express our purposes and further our goals. In other words, if we are aware always in the back of our minds as to what we need to accomplish, that underlying purpose in our existence will prompt us to be alert for means of furthering our goals. In addition, the workers on the inner planes will help magnetize those situations needed.

Thus, our basic underlying focus can be to express our purpose as well as we can in this lifetime and to magnetize opportunities and abilities for future lifetimes and inner-plane work. This is alignment with the Plan and correct orientation, expressed briefly. The goal is to stay mindful of Purpose and Plan, to keep in alignment as much as possible, and be prepared to adapt when energies shift.

One way of checking our alignment is to meditate upon what we would do if, suddenly, all the resources we could ever need were made available. This effectively removes all the limitations and excuses that the concrete mind can offer as to why something is not possible and gives us a chance to see just what our priorities really are. It would be informative to practice this exercise repeatedly over a period of time, note the results in our spiritual diary, and then check for changes.

Our most difficult chore, then, remains as to how to select the teachings and teachers that are best for us, out of a multitude of possibilities available. After practice, we usually find that certain teachings can be trusted over time and that certain organizations have high values and hold a point of integrity. After we develop experience with teachings that we have discovered for ourselves to be sound, we can then venture out to explore new ideas, intuit their value, and perhaps incorporate portions of them into our field of thought.

During this process, we can reserve judgment and, instead, develop working hypotheses until we reach the point where we recognize intuitively that for which we are seeking.

Eventually, we find that, in our own way, we become teachers ourselves.

In closing, I would like to share a passage from *Agni Yoga*:

Someone will come to you and speak of his desire to approach Agni Yoga.
Ask him what prompted him to this decision.
He will answer, "I seek proofs."
You will think, "He is not one of us."
Or he will speak of his sad fate.
You will think, "He is not one of us."
Or he will speak of his intention to conquer his enemies.
You will think, "He is not one of us."
Or he will speak of his desire for riches.
You will think, "He is not one of us."
Or he will speak of earthly privileges.
You will think, "He is not one of us."
Or he will speak of his desire for rest.
You will think, "He is not one of us."
But one will say, "I wish to perfect myself."
Ask, "What reward dost thou expect?"
He will say, "The approach to the Teaching."
You will rejoice, as his spirit has knocked correctly.
He can begin to watch himself.
He can painlessly eject useless attributes.
He will understand that not suffering is needed, but liberation.
He will understand that not the manifestation of a miracle is needed, but
straight-knowledge.
He will understand that not intellectual learning is valuable, but
realization and application.
Exultant the first day, he will not droop on the morrow.
He will walk like an elephant of happiness, pushing aside the brush.
He will accept success as the smile of the sun.
He will drive away the scorpion of fear.
He will accept the gift as the light on the path.
He will understand the realization and development of the fires as an
attracting magnet.
And he will understand that fires grow like plants, unnoticeably.
He will understand that the fire burns away the past and illumines the
future.
And he will understand what attainment means![2]

Appendix A—
Full Moon Ephemeris

These tables show the relationships among the Sun, Moon, and planets at the time of the full moons during the years 1998 through 2007. The first column shows the GMT date and time—you will need to convert GMT for your own locale to determine the time of the full moon where you live. Or, you can simply look at the weather page in a local newspaper to obtain the time of the full moon.

The other columns show the abbreviations for the constellations and the degrees. Degrees begin at 0° and go through 30°. For example, on the full moon of January 12, 1998, the Sun is at the 21st degree of Capricorn. The Moon is directly opposite at 21° Cancer.

You can use these tables anywhere in the world because, for our purposes, precision is not necessary. Mercury, Venus, and Mars might be up to 1 degree off. If you want greater accuracy, consult a detailed ephemeris, available at bookstores, or use an astrology computer program.

1998	☉	☽	☿	♀	♂	♃	♄	♅	♆	♇
1/12 17:27	Cp 21	Cn 21	Sg 29	Cp 28	Aq 19	Aq 24	Ar 14	Aq 7	Cp 29	Sg 7
2/11 10:23	Aq 22	Le 22	Aq 13	Cp 18	Pi 13	Pi 1	Ar 16	Aq 9	Aq 0	Sg 7
3/13 4:35	Pi 22	Vi 22	Ar 8	Aq 6	Ar 6	Pi 8	Ar 19	Aq 11	Aq 1	Sg 8
4/11 22:24	Ar 20	Li 20	Ar 13	Pi 5	Ar 28	Pi 15	Ar 23	Aq 12	Aq 2	Sg 7
5/11 14:30	Ta 20	Sc 20	Ar 24	Ar 8	Ta 20	Pi 21	Ar 26	Aq 12	Aq 2	Sg 7
6/10 4:19	Ge 18	Sg 18	Ge 18	Ta 12	Ge 11	Pi 25	Ta 0	Aq 12	Aq 1	Sg 6
7/9 16:02	Cn 16	Cp 16	Le 11	Ge 17	Cn 1	Pi 27	Ta 2	Aq 11	Aq 1	Sg 5
8/8 E 2:11	Le 15	Aq 15	Le 25	Cn 23	Cn 21	Pi 27	Ta 3	Aq 10	Aq 0	Sg 5
9/6 11:22	Vi 13	Pi 13	Le 26	Le 29	Le 10	Pi 24	Ta 3	Aq 9	Cp 29	Sg 5
10/5 20:13	Li 11	Ar 11	Li 18	Li 5	Le 28	Pi 20	Ta 1	Aq 8	Cp 29	Sg 5
11/4 5:19	Sc 11	Ta 11	Sg 3	Sc 12	Vi 16	Pi 18	Ar 29	Aq 8	Cp 29	Sg 6
12/3 15:20	Sg 10	Ge 10	Sg 7	Sg 18	Li 3	Pi 18	Ar 27	Aq 9	Aq 0	Sg 8

1999	☉	☽	☿	♀	♂	♃	♄	♅	♆	♇
1/2 2:51	Cp 11	Cn 11	Sg 22	Cp 26	Li 18	Pi 22	Ar 26	Aq 11	Aq 1	Sg 9
1/31 16:08	Aq 10	Le 10	Aq 7	Pi 2	Sc 1	Pi 27	Ar 27	Aq 12	Aq 2	Sg 10
3/2 7:00	Pi 10	Vi 10	Pi 28	Ar 10	Sc 10	Ar 3	Ta 0	Aq 14	Aq 3	Sg 10
3/31 22:50	Ar 9	Li 9	Pi 21	Ta 15	Sc 11	Ar 10	Ta 3	Aq 15	Aq 4	Sg 10
4/30 14:56	Ta 9	Sc 9	Ar 15	Ge 20	Sc 2	Ar 17	Ta 7	Aq 16	Aq 4	Sg 9
5/30 6:41	Fe 8	Sg 8	Fe 13	Cn 23	Li 24	Ar 24	Ta 10	Aq 16	Aq 4	Sg 9
6/28 21:38	Cn 5	Cp 5	Le 1	Le 20	Li 27	Ar 29	Ta 13	Aq 16	Aq 3	Sg 8
7/28 11:26	Le 4	Aq 4	Le 2	Vi 5	Sc 9	Ta 3	Ta 16	Aq 15	Aq 2	Sg 7
8/26 23:49	Vi 2	Pi 2	Le 19	Le 23	Sc 25	Ta 4	Ta 17	Aq 14	Aq 2	Sg 7
9/25 10:52	Li 1	Pi 1	Li 14	Le 22	Sg 14	Ta 3	Ta 16	Aq 13	Aq 1	Sg 8
10/24 21:04	Sc 0	Ta 0	Sc 24	Vi 13	Cp 5	Ar 29	Ta 14	Aq 12	Aq 1	Sg 8
11/23 7:05	Sg 0	Ge 0	Sc 16	Li 15	Cp 27	Ar 26	Ta 12	Aq 13	Aq 2	Sg 9
12/22 17:32	Sg 29	Ge 29	Sg 15	Sc 18	Aq 19	Ar 25	Ta 10	Aq 14	Aq 2	Sg 11

2000	☉	☽	☿	♀	♂	♃	♄	♅	♆	♇
1/21 E 4:42	Aq 0	Le 0	Aq 3	Sg 25	Pi 13	Ar 26	Ta 10	Aq 15	Aq 3	Sg 12
2/19 16:28	Aq 29	Le 29	Pi 16	Aq 0	Ar 5	Ta 0	Ta 11	Aq 17	Aq 5	Sg 12
3/20 4:46	Pi 29	Vi 29	Pi 4	Pi 8	Ar 27	Ta 6	Ta 14	Aq 19	Aq 5	Sg 12
4/18 17:43	Ar 28	Li 28	Ar 7	Ar 13	Ta 18	Ta 13	Ta 17	Aq 20	Aq 6	Sg 12
5/18 7:35	Ta 27	Sc 27	Ge 7	Ta 20	Ge 9	Ta 20	Ta 21	Aq 20	Aq 6	Sg 11
6/16 22:28	Ge 25	Sg 25	Cn 17	Ge 26	Ge 29	Ta 26	Ta 24	Aq 20	Aq 6	Sg 11
7/16 E 13:56	Cn 23	Cp 23	Cn 10	Le 3	Cn 19	Ge 3	Ta 28	Aq 19	Aq 5	Sg 10
8/15 5:14	Le 22	Aq 22	Le 15	Vi 10	Le 8	Ge 8	Ge 0	Aq 18	Aq 4	Sg 10
9/13 19:38	Vi 20	Pi 20	Li 8	Li 15	Le 27	Ge 10	Ge 0	Aq 17	Aq 4	Sg 10
10/13 8:54	Li 19	Ar 19	Sc 14	Sc 22	Vi 16	Ge 10	Ge 0	Aq 16	Aq 3	Sg 10
11/11 21:16	Sc 18	Ta 18	Sc 0	Sg 27	Li 4	Ge 8	Ta 28	Aq 17	Aq 3	Sg 11
12/11 9:04	Sg 19	Ge 19	Sg 11	Aq 3	Li 22	Ge 4	Ta 25	Aq 17	Aq 4	Sg 13

2001	☉	☽	☿	♀	♂	♃	♄	♅	♆	♇
1/9 20:25	Cp 19	Cn 19	Cp 27	Pi 5	Sc 9	Ge 1	Ta 24	Aq 19	Aq 5	Sg 14
2/8 7:13	Aq 19	Le 19	Aq 29	Ar 4	Sc 26	Ge 1	Ta 24	Aq 20	Aq 6	Sg 14
3/9 17:24	Pi 19	Vi 19	Aq 21	Ar 17	Sg 11	Ge 4	Ta 25	Aq 22	Aq 7	Sg 15
4/8 3:23	Ar 18	Li 18	Ar 2	Ar 4	Sg 23	Ge 8	Ta 28	Aq 23	Aq 8	Sg 15
5/7 13:54	Ta 17	Sc 17	Ge 1	Ar 6	Sg 28	Ge 14	Ge 1	Aq 24	Aq 8	Sg 14
6/6 1:40	Ge 15	Sg 15	Ge 29	Ar 29	Sg 25	Ge 21	Ge 5	Aq 24	Aq 8	Sg 13
7/5 15:05	Cn 13	Cp 13	Ge 23	Ta 29	Sg 16	Ge 28	Ge 9	Aq 24	Aq 8	Sg 13
8/4 5:57	Le 11	Aq 11	Le 9	Cn 2	Sg 16	Cn 4	Ge 12	Aq 23	Aq 7	Sg 12
9/2 21:44	Vi 10	Pi 10	Li 1	Le 6	Sg 26	Cn 10	Ge 14	Aq 22	Aq 6	Sg 12
10/2 13:50	Li 9	Ar 9	Li 29	Vi 13	Cp 13	Cn 14	Ge 14	Aq 21	Aq 6	Sg 12
11/1 5:42	Sc 8	Ta 8	Li 20	Li 20	Aq 2	Cn 15	Ge 13	Aq 20	Aq 6	Sg 13
11/30 20:50	Sg 8	Ge 8	Sg 5	Sc 26	Aq 23	Cn 14	Ge 11	Aq 21	Aq 6	Sg 14
12/30 10:42	Cp 8	Cn 8	Cp 22	Cp 4	Pi 15	Cn 10	Ge 9	Aq 22	Aq 7	Sg 15

2002	☉	☽	☿	♀	♂	♃	♄	♅	♆	♇
1/28	Aq	Le	Aq	Aq	Ar	Cn	Ge	Aq	Aq	Sg
22:52	8	8	7	11	6	7	8	23	8	16
2/27	Pi	Vi	Aq	Pi	Ar	Cn	Ge	Aq	Aq	Sg
9:18	8	8	12	18	28	5	8	25	9	17
3/28	Ar	Li	Pi	Ar	Ta	Cn	Ge	Aq	Aq	Sg
18:26	7	7	26	24	18	6	10	27	10	17
4/27	Ta	Sc	Ta	Ge	Ge	Cn	Ge	Aq	Aq	Sg
3:01	6	6	25	1	9	10	13	28	10	17
5/26	Ge	Sg	Ge	Cn	Ge	Cn	Ge	Aq	Aq	Sg
11:52	5	5	6	6	28	15	16	28	10	16
6/24	Cn	Cp	Ge	Le	Cn	Cn	Ge	Aq	Aq	Sg
21:43	3	3	9	10	17	21	20	28	10	16
7/24	Le	Aq	Le	Vi	Le	Cn	Ge	Aq	Aq	Sg
9:08	0	0	4	14	6	28	23	27	9	15
8/22	Le	Aq	Vi	Li	Le	Le	Ge	Aq	Aq	Sg
22:30	29	29	23	14	25	4	26	26	9	14
9/21	Vi	Pi	Li	Sc	Vi	Le	Ge	Aq	Aq	Sg
14:00	28	28	11	9	14	10	28	25	8	15
10/21	Li	Ar	Li	Sc	Li	Le	Ge	Aq	Aq	Sg
7:21	27	27	12	13	3	15	29	24	8	15
11/20	Sc	Ta	Sg	Sc	Li	Le	Ge	Aq	Aq	Sg
1:35	27	27	0	0	22	17	27	25	8	16
12/19	Sg	Ge	Cp	Sc	Sc	Le	Ge	Aq	Aq	Sg
19:11	27	27	15	12	11	17	25	25	9	17

2003	☉	☽	☿	♀	♂	♃	♄	♅	♆	♇
1/18 10:49	Cp 27	Cn 27	Cp 14	Sg 10	Sg 0	Le 15	Ge 23	Aq 27	Aq 10	Sg 18
2/16 23:52	Aq 27	Le 27	Aq 3	Cp 13	Sg 19	Le 11	Ge 22	Aq 28	Aq 11	Sg 19
3/18 10:36	Pi 27	Vi 27	Pi 23	Aq 18	Cp 8	Le 8	Ge 22	Pi 0	Aq 12	Sg 19
4/16 19:37	Ar 26	Li 26	Ta 15	Pi 23	Cp 26	Le 8	Ge 24	Pi 1	Aq 12	Sg 19
5/16 3:37	Ta 24	Sc 24	Ta 11	Ar 29	Aq 13	Le 10	Ge 27	Pi 2	Aq 13	Sg 19
6/14 11:17	Ge 23	Sg 23	Ge 1	Ge 4	Aq 28	Le 14	Cn 1	Pi 2	Aq 12	Sg 18
7/13 19:22	Cn 20	Cp 20	Cn 28	Cn 10	Pi 8	Le 20	Cn 5	Pi 2	Aq 12	Sg 17
8/12 4:49	Le 19	Aq 19	Vi 16	Le 17	Pi 8	Le 26	Cn 8	Pi 1	Aq 11	Sg 17
9/10 16:37	Vi 17	Pi 17	Vi 19	Vi 22	Pi 2	Vi 2	Cn 11	Pi 0	Aq 10	Sg 17
10/10 7:29	Li 16	Ar 16	Li 5	Sc 0	Pi 1	Vi 9	Cn 13	Aq 29	Aq 10	Sg 17
11/9 1:14	Sc 16	Ta 16	Sc 24	Sg 7	Pi 10	Vi 14	Cn 13	Aq 28	Aq 10	Sg 18
12/8 20:38	Sg 16	Ge 16	Cp 6	Cp 13	Pi 25	Vi 17	Cn 11	Aq 29	Aq 10	Sg 19

2004	☉	☽	☿	♀	♂	♃	♄	♅	♆	♇
1/7 15:41	Cp 16	Cn 16	Sg 26	Aq 20	Ar 12	Vi 18	Cn 9	Pi 0	Aq 11	Sg 20
2/6 8:48	Aq 16	Le 16	Cp 28	Pi 26	Ta 1	Vi 17	Cn 7	Pi 1	Aq 13	Sg 21
3/6 23:15	Pi 16	Vi 16	Pi 17	Ta 0	Ta 20	Vi 13	Cn 6	Pi 3	Aq 14	Sg 22
4/5 11:04	Ar 15	Li 15	Ta 1	Ge 1	Ge 9	Vi 10	Cn 7	Pi 5	Aq 14	Sg 22
5/4 20:34	Ta 14	Sc 14	Ar 21	Ge 22	Ge 27	Vi 8	Cn 9	Pi 6	Aq 15	Sg 21
6/3 4:21	Ge 12	Sg 12	Ta 25	Ge 21	Cn 16	Vi 10	Cn 12	Pi 6	Aq 15	Sg 21
7/2 11:10	Cn 10	Cp 10	Cn 25	Ge 9	Le 5	Vi 13	Cn 15	Pi 6	Aq 14	Sg 20
7/31 18:06	Le 8	Aq 8	Vi 4	Ge 23	Le 23	Vi 18	Cn 19	Pi 5	Aq 14	Sg 19
8/30 2:23	Vi 7	Pi 7	Le 26	Cn 21	Vi 12	Vi 24	Cn 23	Pi 4	Aq 13	Sg 19
9/28 13:10	Li 5	Ar 5	Vi 28	Le 23	Li 1	Li 0	Cn 25	Pi 3	Aq 12	Sg 19
10/28 3:08	Sc 5	Ta 5	Sc 18	Vi 28	Li 20	Li 6	Cn 27	Pi 2	Aq 12	Sg 20
11/26 20:08	Sg 4	Ge 4	Sg 25	Sc 4	Sc 9	Li 12	Cn 27	Pi 2	Aq 12	Sg 21
12/26 15:05	Cp 5	Cn 5	Sg 12	Sg 11	Sg 0	Li 16	Cn 25	Pi 3	Aq 13	Sg 22

2005	☉	☽	☿	♀	♂	♃	♄	♅	♆	♇
1/25 10:33	Aq 5	Le 5	Cp 21	Cp 19	Sg 21	Li 18	Cn 22	Pi 5	Aq 14	Sg 23
2/24 4:55	Pi 5	Vi 5	Pi 13	Aq 26	Cp 12	Li 18	Cn 21	Pi 6	Aq 15	Sg 24
3/25 21:00	Ar 5	Li 5	Ar 12	Ar 2	Aq 3	Li 15	Cn 20	Pi 8	Aq 16	Sg 24
4/24 10:07	Ta 4	Sc 4	Ar 7	Ar 10	Aq 24	Li 11	Cn 21	Pi 9	Aq 17	Sg 24
5/23 20:19	Ge 2	Sg 2	Ta 18	Ge 15	Pi 15	Li 9	Cn 23	Pi 10	Aq 17	Sg 23
6/22 4:15	Cn 0	Cp 0	Cn 20	Cn 22	Ar 6	Li 9	Cn 26	Pi 10	Aq 17	Sg 22
7/21 11:01	Cn 28	Cp 28	Le 20	Le 27	Ar 25	Li 11	Le 0	Pi 10	Aq 16	Sg 22
8/19 17:54	Le 26	Aq 26	Le 9	Li 2	Ta 11	Li 16	Le 4	Pi 9	Aq 15	Sg 21
9/18 2:02	Vi 25	Pi 25	Vi 25	Sc 7	Ta 21	Li 21	Le 7	Pi 8	Aq 15	Sg 21
10/17 12:15	Li 24	Ar 24	Sc 12	Sg 9	Ta 21	Li 28	Le 10	Pi 7	Aq 14	Sg 22
11/16 0:59	Sc 23	Ta 23	Sg 10	Cp 10	Ta 12	Sc 4	Le 11	Pi 6	Aq 14	Sg 23
12/15 16:17	Sg 23	Ge 23	Sg 2	Cp 29	Ta 8	Sc 10	Le 10	Pi 7	Aq 15	Sg 24

2006	☉	☽	☿	♀	♂	♃	♄	♅	♆	♇
1/14 9:49	Cp 24	Cn 24	Cp 15	Cp 23	Ta 14	Sc 15	Le 8	Pi 8	Aq 16	Sg 25
2/13 4:45	Aq 24	Le 24	Pi 7	Cp 17	Ta 27	Sc 18	Le 6	Pi 9	Aq 17	Sg 26
3/14 23:37	Pi 24	Vi 24	Pi 19	Aq 7	Ge 12	Sc 18	Le 4	Pi 11	Aq 18	Sg 26
4/13 16:41	Ar 23	Li 23	Pi 25	Pi 7	Ge 29	Sc 16	Le 4	Pi 13	Aq 19	Sg 26
5/13 6:52	Ta 22	Sc 22	Ta 15	Ar 10	Cn 16	Sc 12	Le 5	Pi 14	Aq 19	Sg 26
6/11 18:04	Ge 20	Sg 20	Cn 12	Ta 14	Le 4	Sc 9	Le 8	Pi 14	Aq 19	Sg 25
7/11 3:03	Cn 18	Cp 18	Cn 29	Ge 20	Le 22	Sc 9	Le 11	Pi 14	Aq 19	Sg 24
8/9 10:55	Le 16	Aq 16	Cn 27	Cn 25	Vi 10	Sc 10	Le 15	Pi 13	Aq 18	Sg 24
9/7 18:43	Vi 15	Pi 15	Vi 19	Vi 0	Vi 29	Sc 14	Le 18	Pi 12	Aq 17	Sg 24
10/7 3:14	Li 13	Ar 13	Sc 6	Li 8	Li 18	Sc 19	Le 21	Pi 11	Aq 17	Sg 24
11/5 12:59	Sc 12	Ta 12	Sc 21	Sc 14	Sc 8	Sc 25	Le 24	Pi 10	Aq 17	Sg 25
12/5 0:26	Sg 12	Ge 12	Sc 25	Sg 22	Sc 29	Sg 2	Le 25	Pi 10	Aq 17	Sg 26

2007	☉	☽	☿	♀	♂	♃	♄	♅	♆	♇
1/3 13:59	Cp 12	Cn 12	Cp 9	Cp 28	Sg 19	Sg 8	Le 24	Pi 11	Aq 18	Sg 27
2/2 5:46	Aq 12	Le 12	Aq 29	Pi 6	Cp 11	Sg 14	Le 22	Pi 12	Aq 19	Sg 28
3/3 23:18	Pi 12	Vi 12	Aq 26	Ar 11	Aq 3	Sg 18	Le 20	Pi 14	Aq 20	Sg 28
4/2 17:16	Ar 12	Li 12	Pi 16	Ta 18	Aq 26	Sg 19	Le 18	Pi 16	Aq 21	Sg 28
5/2 10:10	Ta 11	Sc 11	Ta 9	Ge 22	Pi 19	Sg 18	Le 18	Pi 17	Aq 21	Sg 28
6/1 1:05	Ge 10	Sg 10	Cn 3	Cn 25	Ar 12	Sg 15	Le 19	Pi 18	Aq 22	Sg 28
6/30 13:50	Cn 8	Cp 8	Cn 5	Le 21	Ta 3	Sg 12	Le 22	Pi 18	Aq 21	Sg 27
7/30 0:49	Le 6	Aq 6	Cn 19	Vi 2	Ta 24	Sg 10	Le 25	Pi 18	Aq 21	Sg 26
8/28 10:36	Vi 4	Pi 4	Vi 15	Le 19	Ge 12	Sg 10	Le 29	Pi 17	Aq 20	Sg 26
9/26 19:46	Li 3	Ar 3	Li 28	Le 21	Ge 28	Sg 13	Vi 2	Pi 16	Aq 19	Sg 26
10/26 4:53	Sc 2	Ta 2	Li 27	Vi 15	Cn 9	Sg 18	Vi 5	Pi 15	Aq 19	Sg 26
11/24 14:31	Sg 1	Ge 1	Sc 18	Li 16	Cn 11	Sg 24	Vi 7	Pi 14	Aq 19	Sg 27
12/24 1:17	Cp 1	Cn 1	Cp 5	Sc 21	Cn 2	Cp 1	Vi 8	Pi 15	Aq 20	Sg 28

Appendix B— Fixed Star Locations

For the stars in the three great constellations we have been discussing in this book—Sirius, the Great Bear, and the Pleiades—this appendix gives their locations in the tropical zodiac for Epoch 2000 and some suggestions for their rays.

Sirius is located at 14° 05′ Cancer.

The following locations and rays of the stars of the Great Bear are suggested by David Kesten:

Merak	10° 26′ Leo	Ray 6
Dubhe	15° 59′ Leo	Ray 5
Phecda	0° 29′ Virgo	Ray 7
Megrez	1° 04′ Virgo	Ray 4
Alioth	8° 56′ Virgo	Ray 3
Mizar	15° 42′ Virgo	Ray 2
Alcor	15° 52′ Virgo	Ray 1
Alkaid (Benetnasch)	26° 56′ Virgo	Ray 1

The following placements of the seven sisters of the Pleiades are suggested by Niklas Nihlen and David Kesten:

Electra	29° 24′ Taurus	Ray 2
Celaeno	29° 25′ Taurus	Ray 1
Taygeta	29° 33′ Taurus	Ray 7
Maia	29° 40′ Taurus	Ray 4
Merope	29° 41′ Taurus	Ray 6
Asterope	29° 44′ Taurus	Ray 5
Alcyone	29° 59′ Taurus	Ray 3

Please note that these fixed stars are not on the zodiacal ecliptic, thus they are not really conjunct any of these points; only their position relative to our ecliptic is conjunct.

I do not imply that you can do any work with the information in this appendix; it is here only for your interest and speculation.

Glossary

adept. A master, or human being who, having traversed the path of evolution and entered upon the final stage of the path, the path of initiation, has taken five of the initiations, and has therefore passed into the fifth, or spiritual kingdom, leaving but two more initiations to take.

Age of Aquarius. A period of time encompassing approximately 2000 to 2160 years during which the vernal equinox point is seen against the backdrop of the constellation Aquarius. Because of uncertainties regarding the measurements necessary to determine this period, the actual dates for the beginning and ending of the Age of Aquarius are highly controversial. Evidence that the Aquarian age began during the first decade of the twentieth century was found by Charles Jayne, an astrological authority of the mid to late twentieth century. Conversely, a letter to Alice A. Bailey from the Tibetan in February 1940 indicates the year 2117, according to David Kesten.

ageless wisdom. A spiritual teaching and tradition which has existed since the dawn of evolution upon our planet. It is presented in the works of H.P. Blavatsky, Alice A. Bailey, Helena Roerich, and others.

Agni Yoga. A body of spiritual literature penned in the early twentieth century by Russian esotericist Helena Roerich, who wrote under the spiritual inspiration of the Master Morya.

antahkarana. A fusion of two Sanskrit words, antara (between) and karana (cause), this word signifies the channel of subtle matter connecting the ephemeral personality with the soul, the spiritual triad, and the monad.

Aryan Race. A period of human evolution in which the emphasis is upon the development of the mind principle, and in which human evolution currently finds itself. The word Aryan comes from the name for an ancient race of people who inhabited what is now India, and who were likely the early manifestation of the Aryan period. The term Aryan Race as encountered in esotericism has nothing whatsoever to do with the similar term used by the Nazi Third Reich to signify a group of supposedly superior Germanic peoples.

ashram. An affiliation of disciples and initiates of various degrees who assemble in shared intention, love, and dedication for the purpose of carrying forward specific work within the Plan and under the impression of the Master. Such affiliation takes place on the inner planes, for every ashram is "essentially a reservoir of thought." (*Discipleship in the New Age I*, p. 697).

aspect. A term used by astrologers to indicate the distance between two or more celestial bodies or astrological factors, expressed in degrees of arc and often named for the geometrical forms associated. Aspect analysis is one of the main tools used by traditional astrologers to delineate the content or meaning of any astrological chart.

aspirant. An individual who has glimpsed the world of higher truths and who has dedicated his or her life to the eventual perfection of the self through practice of high ideals and right activity.

Atlantean Race. A period of human evolution in which the emphasis was upon the development of astral and psychic sensitivity. This period drew to a close at approximately the time of the sinking of Atlantis.

atma-buddhi-manas. Spiritual will, intuition, and higher mind, the three components of the spiritual triad. This triad is that part of consciousness which makes it possible to intuit the purposes of Deity and to form the resulting impression into intelligible thoughtforms. Atma-buddhi-manas is the correspondence in the individual to will, wisdom, and intelligent activity.

atmic plane. The third cosmic and third systemic plane of consciousness, the plane of intelligent will.

avatar. An incarnation of a highly liberated Being.

Buddhas of Activity. Three advanced consciousnesses who stand closest to Sanat Kumara, the representative of our Planetary Logos.

buddhic plane. The fourth cosmic and fourth systemic plane. It is the plane of universal or spiritual love and of the true intuition.

buddhic vehicle. The body or vehicle of consciousness operative on the buddhic plane and constituted of the matter of that plane.

cardinal cross. In astrology, the four signs Aries, Cancer, Libra, and Capricorn. In esotericism, the cardinal cross is a level of consciousness concerned with cosmic energies and with the fusion of the personality and the soul with the monad. This does not mean, however, that persons influenced by the signs of the cardinal cross are necessarily of this type of awareness.

causal body. The matter in which the soul exists upon its own level, the third subplane of the mental plane.

chain. A grouping of planetary globes, usually seven in number, which manifest over time, through space, and in different grades of matter, and which function as the force centers for a Planetary Logos.

chakra. A Sanskrit word meaning wheel and having reference to the force centers in the etheric and other bodies. Can also mean circle or cycle.

conjunction. A term used by astrologers to indicate the close proximity of celestial bodies or astrological factors within the circle of the zodiac. Considered to be a difference of 10 degrees of arc or less. A precise conjunction is zero degrees of difference. The precise conjunction is thought to be more powerful than an approximate one.

Cosmic Paths, the Seven. Also called the Ways of Higher Evolution, these are avenues of spiritual progress which become relevant after the fifth and sixth initiations. They are said to begin where nirvana leaves off.

Council Chamber at Shamballa. The conclave of intelligences gathered
   around Sanat Kumara, the representative of our Planetary Logos,
   at the planetary head center (Shamballa).

creative hierarchy. The archetypal life waves that are connected with
   the twelve signs of the zodiac. A group of lives that seeds the
   archetypes of the universe. There are twelve creative hierarchies,
   five of which have moved on to higher realms. The seven creative
   hierarchies that are currently active in our system are each
   associated with one of the seven rays, a constellation, a planet, and
   a plane of manifestation.

deva. A terrestrial, celestial, and/or angelic being which may be of
   any of numerous orders and levels of consciousness. They are
   frequently the agency by which energy and force are transmitted
   to various kingdoms.

disciple. An individual pledged to serve humanity, to cooperate with
   the Plan and the masters of the planetary Hierarchy, and to develop
   the powers of the soul.

egoic lotus. The causal body, said to have the appearance of a lotus
   with twelve petals, the three innermost of which remain concealed
   for long ages. Spiritual development causes the egoic lotus to open
   or express fully, a fact visible to spiritual clairvoyance. At the fourth
   initiation, the light contained in the egoic lotus becomes so brilliant
   and intense that the lotus undergoes conflagration, releasing its
   contained light matter to higher planes.

energy and force. An important distinction made by the Tibetan in
   which he says the word energy connotes the living activity of the
   spiritual realms, while the word force connotes the activity of the
   form nature.

esoteric occultism. The study of energies, forces, planes of
   consciousness, and the overall process of evolution as taught by
   Djwhal Khul, the Tibetan, through Alice A. Bailey.

etheric. Pertaining to the four higher subplanes of the systemic physical plane and the four higher planes of the cosmic physical plane. It is a relative term, meaning a grade of matter and a state of consciousness of a more refined character than the grades and states just below it.

etheric body. The physical body of a human being is, according to occult teaching, formed of two parts, the dense physical body, and the etheric body. The dense physical body is formed of matter of the lowest three subplanes of the physical plane. The etheric body is formed of the four highest or etheric subplanes of the physical plane.

fixed cross. In astrology, the signs Taurus, Leo, Scorpio, and Aquarius. In esotericism, it is a state of consciousness characterized by awareness of issues larger than the self and concerning humanity (group consciousness), the taking on of appropriate responsibility, and the recognition of the task of the planetary Hierarchy. This notion, however, does not indicate that persons influenced by the signs of the astrological fixed cross are necessarily of this consciousness.

Heart of the Sun. The "Heart of the Sun," as referred to by Djwhal Khul and Alice Bailey, is not the heart center of the Sun. Instead it represents the soul of the Sun, whereas the physical Sun represents the body and the Central Spiritual Sun represents the monad of this great triple being.

Hierarchy, planetary. The entire group of advanced intelligences who work for the unfoldment of the divine plan. Composed of masters and initiates of various degrees, this group is also known as the Great White Lodge. Such groups exist on every planet. They represent the Law of Love and work with the spiritual liberation of the consciousness within the form.

initiation. An expansion of consciousness. The Tibetan has formally described a series of nine such expansions which span from the first stirrings of spiritual awareness to states of great transcendence.

The nine are as follows:

1) Birth
2) Baptism
3) Transfiguration
4) Renunciation or Crucifixion
5) Revelation
6) Decision
7) Resurrection
8) Transition
9) Refusal

intuition. The aspect of consciousness which grasps spiritual truths. The intuition is responsible for the recognitions which flower as group consciousness and as the awareness of the existence of divine or impersonal love.

karma. Physical action. Metaphysically, the law of retribution: the law of cause and effect, or ethical causation. There is the karma of merit and the karma of demerit. It is the power that controls all things, the resultant of moral action, or the moral effect of an act committed for the attainment of something which gratifies a personal desire.

kundalini. The power of Life: one of the forces of nature, typically originating from the base-of-spine chakra, and usually experienced only by those engaged in intense spiritual practices.

Logos (pl. Logoi). A Being endowed with consciousness and inhabiting some form; a Planetary Logos (which manifests through seven planetary chains), a Solar Logos (which manifests through seven planetary schemes or a solar system), or a Cosmic Logos (which manifests through seven solar systems).

lunar nodes. The points at which the orbit of the Moon intersects the ecliptic, arising because the plane of the Moon's orbit is inclined (or angled) to the plane of the solar system.

macrocosm. A greater unit within which there exist smaller units which are a reflection of the more inclusive unit.

The lesser unit is called the microcosm.

manas. A Sanskrit term meaning the mind, or that which makes humans intelligent and moral beings, distinguished from the animal. It is the individualizing principle; that which enables humanity to know that it exists, feels, and knows. It is divided in some schools into two parts, higher or abstract mind, and lower or concrete mind.

mantrams. A form of words or syllables rhythmically arranged, so that when sounded certain vibrations are generated.

manvantara. A compound of the Sanskrit terms manu (one who oversees a long period of race evolution) and antara (between). Literally meaning "between manus," this word signifies a very long period of manifestation.

master. An initiate of the fifth degree or above.

mental unit. A point of concentrated light within the egoic lotus or causal body which acts as a positive nucleus, containing the energy of divine purpose.

monad. The point of absolute synthesis for the human unit.

monadic ray. That one of the seven rays which primarily conditions the monad of any given human unit.

mutable cross. In astrology, the signs Gemini, Virgo, Sagittarius, and Pisces. In esotericism, a state of consciousness in which the individual viewpoint blocks out the greater frame of reference, forces beyond one's control are blamed for life conditions, and much diverse experience is required and sought as a basis for spiritual growth. This notion, however, does not indicate that persons influenced by the signs of the mutable cross are necessarily in such a frame of consciousness.

New Group of World Servers. A worldwide group of individuals linked subjectively in the effort to serve humanity and the Plan.

non-sacred planet. A planet of which the Logos has taken less than five cosmic initiations.

occult. That which is hidden or is not commonly known.

One About Whom Naught May Be Said. The entity who manifests through seven solar systems; also called the Cosmic Logos.

Paths of Probation, Discipleship, and Initiation. Segments of the path of progressive unfoldment of consciousness. Probation deals with preliminary spiritual purification and the attaining of right habits. Discipleship involves greater commitment and a demonstrated stability upon which the masters can depend when the disciple is needed. Initiation connotes progress into greater positions of insight and responsibility within Hierarchy.

Plan (divine plan). The ultimate expression of Divinity to be attained by any globe, chain, scheme, or system, and all the intermediate stages leading to that consummation. The Plan is precipitated into the universal mind by the great beings who are responsible for the evolution of our solar system and planet. The Plan always works within the laws of nature and of cause and effect. The Plan to humanity represents however much of the divine purpose we can grasp and align with.

plane. A dimension or state of consciousness with its corresponding type of matter.

planetary chain. A number of globes (usually seven) manifesting in a purposeful sequence over vast spans of time and acting as one of the force centers in the body of manifestation of a Planetary Logos.

Planetary Logos. This term is generally applied to the seven highest spirits corresponding to the seven archangels of Christianity. They have all passed through the human stage and are now manifesting through a planet and its evolutions, in the same way that man manifests through his physical body. The highest planetary spirit working through any particular globe is, in reality, the personal God of the planet.

planetary schemes. A number of chains (usually seven) manifesting in a purposeful sequence over vast spans of time and acting as one of the force centers in the body of manifestation of a Solar Logos.

pralaya. A compound Sanskrit word made from pra (away) and laya (from a verb root meaning "to dissolve"). This word literally means a period of dissolution, and signifies a very long phase of cosmic rest between periods of active manifestation. A period of obscuration.

precession of the equinoxes. The slow movement against the backdrop of the stars made by the imaginary axis drawn between the spring and autumn equinox points. May be caused by the slow rotation of the entire solar system upon its own axis.

Qabalah. An esoteric aspect of the Hebrew tradition which deals with cosmology and spheres of consciousness.

race. A long period of human evolution. There are said to have been five races upon our globe so far—two ancient, the Lemurian, the Atlantean, and the Aryan.

ray. One of seven energy qualities, or rates of vibration, upon which the manifested creation is built. The seven streams of force of the Logos; the seven great lights; streams of divine cosmic consciousness. Each ray is the embodiment of a great cosmic entity. The seven rays can be divided into three rays of aspect and four rays of attribute, as follows: Rays of aspect: Ray One, Will and Power; Ray Two, Love-Wisdom; and Ray Three, Active Intelligence and Adaptability. Rays of attribute: Ray Four, Harmony, Beauty, and Art; Ray Five, Concrete Knowledge and Science; Ray Six, Devotion and Idealism; and Ray Seven, Ceremonial Order, Magic and Organization. These names are simply some chosen from among many, and embody the different aspects of force by means of which the Logos manifests.

Renunciation Initiation. The Fourth Initiation. The complete relinquishment of the personality realm, a shift to intuitive functioning, and noticeably greater integration into hierarchical activity.

ring-pass-not. This is at the circumference of the manifested solar system, and is the periphery of the influence of the Sun, both esoterically and exoterically understood. The limit of the field of activity of the central life force.

root race. One of the seven races of man which evolve upon a planet during the great cycle of planetary existence. This cycle is called a world period. The Aryan root race, to which the Hindu, European, and modern American races belong, is the fifth, the Chinese and Japanese belonging to the fourth race.

round. A period of evolution comprised of the time required to complete the full course of seven races on forty-nine globes, or the totality of a planetary scheme. In other words, races one through seven on globe one, races one through seven on globe two, etc.

ruler, planetary. A planet that has a special rapport with a zodiacal sign and acts as a ruler, or carrier, for the sign's qualities and energies.

sacred planet. A planet of which the Logos has taken five or more cosmic initiations.

Sanat Kumara. The representative on Earth of the Planetary Logos of the scheme to which our planet belongs.

Seven Cosmic Paths. Also called the Seven Ways of Higher Evolution. These are seven directions for further spiritual progress open to initiates beyond the fifth degree.

Shamballa. The point on our planet which functions as the head center of our globe. Existing in matter beyond the level of human perception, Shamballa is the retreat of Sanat Kumara, the Ancient of Days.

Solar Logos. The Entity whose body of manifestation is the solar system in entirety.

solar angel. These are the Sons of Mind, the individual principle in man, the Ego (soul), in his own body on the abstract levels of the mental plane. (*A Treatise on Cosmic Fire*) Solar angels are dual in Nature. "Manas is dual—Lunar in the lower, Solar in its upper portion." (*Secret Doctrine*) The solar angels form the "soul" or second aspect. (*A Treatise on Cosmic Fire*) Entities of a high spiritual order—with a refined consciousness that corresponds to the material substance in which they are clothed. In previous incarnations, they spent long periods in toil for the sake of rearing wisdom in the world, and hence they eventually emerged as angels under their karmic impulse. (*Some Thoughts on the Gita,* p. 137)

This is a very abstract concept. A solar angel is not specifically the human soul, but in a sense is the guiding principle of the soul.

soul ray. That one of the seven rays which primarily conditions the soul nature of a human individual.

spiritual triad. The germinal spirit containing the potentialities of divinity. A blending of energies which bridge from the soul to the monad. Constituted of atma (spiritual will), buddhi (wisdom as intuition), and manas (higher mind), representing the planes they are named after. These potentialities are unfolded during the course of evolution. Every life—macrocosmic and microcosmic—has its own spiritual triad, the influence of which affects its incarnation, evolution, and progress.

Transfiguration Initiation. The Third Initiation. The complete submergence of personal concerns into the good of the whole, the demonstrated mastery of the mind nature, and the capacity to consciously direct energies in accord with the Plan.

veil, veiling. Terms used to indicate the obscuring of one factor by another. Certain esoteric information is thought to have been intentionally veiled, or masked, to prevent recognition by the unready or untried seeker. Veiling also occurs when a lower principle or rate of vibration obscures a higher principle or rate of vibration and prevents it from being accurately known. In this sense, the personality veils the soul, and the soul veils the monad. This kind of veiling is inevitable in the process of manifestation, but is removed by the process of spiritual discipline.

Wesak. A festival which takes place in the Himalayas at the full moon of May. It is said that at this festival, at which all the members of the Hierarchy are present, the Buddha, for a brief period, renews his touch and association with the work of our planet.

Yoga. (1) One of the six schools of India, said to be founded by Patanjali, but really of much earlier origin. (2) The practice of meditation as a means of leading to spiritual liberation.

Most of these definitions were graciously provided by M. Temple Richmond from her book, **Sirius**.

Notes and References

Chapter 1—Life in the Universe

[1] W. Y. Evans-Wentz, *Tibetan Yoga and Secret Doctrines*, p. 12.

[2] Three Initiates, *The Kybalion, A Study of the Hermetic Philosophy of Ancient Egypt and Greece*, p. 28.

[3] Alice A. Bailey, *A Treatise on Cosmic Fire*, pp. 1059-60.

[4] Ken Wilber, *Quantum Questions*, p. 14-15.

[5] Richard M. Restak, M.D., *The Brain, The Last Frontier*, p. 16.

[6] Carl G. Jung, *The Archetypes and the Collective Unconscious*, p. 308.

[7] Alice A. Bailey, *Esoteric Astrology*, p. 415.

[8] Manly P. Hall, *Invisible Records of Thought and Action*, pp. 74-75.

[9] Alice A. Bailey, *A Treatise on Cosmic Fire*, Stanzas of Dzyan, Stanza VIII.

[10] Alice A. Bailey, *A Treatise on Cosmic Fire*, p. 42.

[11] *Ibid.*, p. 1034.

[12] *Ibid.*, p. 102.

[13] Alice A. Bailey, *A Treatise on Cosmic Fire*, pp. 1058-1059; *Esoteric Astrology*, p. 641.

[14] Alice A. Bailey, *A Treatise on Cosmic Fire*, p. 143.

[15] *Ibid.*, p. 235.

[16] *Ibid.*, p. 1056-7.

[17] *Ibid.*, pp. 1036, 274, 1040, 1034, 46.

[18] Agni Yoga Society, *Fiery World III*, Verses 283-284.

[19] Alice A. Bailey, *A Treatise on Cosmic Fire*, p. 1184.

[20] Three Initiates, *The Kybalion*, p 53.

[21] Alice A. Bailey, *Discipleship in the New Age, Volume II*, pp. 234-235.

[22] Alice A. Bailey, *A Treatise on White Magic*, p. 11.

[23] See also Huston Smith's *The Illustrated World's Religions: A Guide to Our Wisdom Traditions*, and Manly P. Hall's *The Secret Teachings of All Ages*.

[24] Willis Harman, "A Re-examination of the Metaphysical Foundations of Modern Science," p. 71.

[25] *Ibid.*, p. 72.

[26] Fritjof Capra, "The Unity of All Things" in *The Tao of Physics*, p. 138.

[27] Curtis Smith, *Jung's Quest for Wholeness*, p. 113.

[28] Carl G. Jung, *Archetypes and the Collective Unconscious*, p. 313.

[29] Lama Anagarika Govinda, *Foundations of Tibetan Mysticism*, p. 93.

[30] Alice A. Bailey, *A Treatise on White Magic*, p. 553.

[31] *Ibid.*, pp. 554-555.

[32] *Ibid.*, p. 365.

[33] *Ibid.*, pp. 366-368.

[34] *Ibid.*, p. 369.

Chapter 2—Levels of Consciousness

[1] Three Initiates, *The Kybalion, A Study of the Hermetic Philosophy of Ancient Egypt and Greece*, p. 35.

[2] Note that this is a major stream of energy, but not the only stream. According to *Esoteric Astrology*, another stream of energy flows through the "Seven Solar Systems of Which Ours Is One." References on these solar systems are in *Esoteric Astrology*, pp. 29, 33, 50, 466-467, but they do not give us a lot of information; page 467 states that "their peculiar nature, objective in evolution and basic purpose is only revealed to initiates above the fifth initiation." This information is summarized in Chapter 7 of this book. The fifth initiation is that of master and, as far as we know, that is the level achieved by the Tibetan, Djwhal Khul.

[3] Alice A. Bailey, *Esoteric Astrology*, p. 563.

[4] *Ibid.*, p. 23.

[5] *Ibid.*, p. 299.

[6] Alice A. Bailey, *A Treatise on Cosmic Fire*, p. 212.

[7] Alice A. Bailey, *A Treatise on White Magic*, p. 364.

[8] Annie Besant, *Study in Consciousness*, pp. 16-17.

[9] Alice A. Bailey, *A Treatise on White Magic*, p. 113.

[10] *Ibid.*, p. 56.

[11] Dion Fortune, *The Mystical Qabalah*, p. 17.

[12] Alice A. Bailey, *Esoteric Astrology*, p. 42.

[13] *Ibid.*, p. 613.

[14] *Ibid.*, pp. 240-241.

[15] *Ibid.*, pp. 307-308.

[16] *Ibid.*, p. 131.

[17] *Ibid.*, p. 304.

[18] *Ibid.*, p. 477.

[19] *Ibid.*, pp. 264-265, 475.

[20] *Ibid.*, pp. 29, 55, 31, 269, 382, 511.

21 *Ibid.*, p. 331.
22 *Ibid.*, pp. 161-162.
23 *Ibid.*, p. 141.

Chapter 3—Mind and Telepathy

1 Alice A. Bailey, *A Treatise on Cosmic Fire*, p. 80.
2 Gregory Bateson, *Mind and Nature: A Necessary Unity*, quoted in: *A Reexamination of the Metaphysical Foundations of Modern Science*, p. 97.
3 Alice A. Bailey, *Telepathy and the Etheric Vehicle*, pp. 101-102.
4 Curtis Smith, *Jung's Quest for Wholeness*, p. 66.
5 *Ibid.*, p. 55.
6 *Ibid.*, p. 66.
7 Carl G. Jung, *Archetypes and the Collective Unconscious*, pp. 308-310.
8 *Ibid.*, p. 384.
9 *Ibid.*, p. 38.
10 F. David Peat, *Synchronicity: The Bridge Between Matter and Mind*, p. 106.
11 *Ibid.*, pp. 108, 106.
12 *Ibid.*, p. 110.
13 Barker, *The Mahatma Letters*, No. XXII from KH to Hume, pp. 137-138.
14 Satprem, *Sri Aurobindo or the Adventure of Consciousness*, pp. 167-168.
15 *Ibid.*, p. 168, quoting Aurobindo from *Letters on Yoga*.
16 Satprem, *Sri Aurobindo or the Adventure of Consciousness*, pp. 168-169.
17 Three Initiates, *The Kybalion*, p. 65.
18 Willis Harman, "A Re-examination of the Metaphysical Foundations of Modern Science," pp. 82-83.
19 *Ibid.*, p. 83.
20 Ernest Holmes, *The Science of Mind*, p. 40.
21 *Ibid.*, pp. 350-351.
22 *Ibid.*, p. 113.
23 *Ibid.*, p. 95.
24 Manly P. Hall, *Invisible Records of Thought and Action*, pp. 9-10.
25 *Ibid.*, p. 33.
26 *Ibid.*, p. 77.
27 *Ibid.*, pp. 10-11.
28 Dion Fortune, *Esoteric Orders and Their Work*, p. 21.
29 *Ibid.*, p. 85.

[30] Marilyn Ferguson, "Karl Pribram's Changing Reality," from Wilber, *The Holographic Paradigm and Other Paradoxes: Exploring the Leading Edge of Science*, p. 25.

[31] Jeanne Achterberg, "Consciousness in Dialogue: Responses to Ken Wilber: Humanity's Common Consciousness." *Noetic Sciences Review*, Winter 1996, p. 19.

[32] Willis Harman, "A Re-examination of the Metaphysical Foundations of Modern Science," p. 73.

[33] Ken Wilber, *The Holographic Paradigm and Other Paradoxes: Exploring the Leading Edge of Science*, p. 3.

[34] Ken Dychtwald, Ph.D., "Commentaries on the Holographic Theory: Reflections on the Holographic Paradigm," from Wilber, *The Holographic Paradigm and Other Paradoxes: Exploring the Leading Edge of Science*, pp. 109-111.

[35] F. David Peat, *Synchronicity: The Bridge Between Matter and Mind*, p. 173.

[36] Renée Weber, "The Enfolding-Unfolding Universe: A Conversation With David Bohm," from Wilber, *The Holographic Paradigm and Other Paradoxes: Exploring the Leading Edge of Science*, p. 78.

[37] *Ibid.*, p. 79.

[38] F. David Peat, *Synchronicity: The Bridge Between Matter and Mind*, p. 173.

[39] Russell Targ, "Remarkable Distant Viewing," *Noetic Sciences Review* Summer 1996, p. 22.

[40] *Ibid.*, p. 22.

[41] *Ibid.*, p. 21. Their complete article is published in the *Journal of Scientific Exploration* and is available from the Society for Scientific Exploration, PO Box 5848, Stanford, CA. Additional references of works by Targ, Puthoff, and J. Bamford are listed at the end of the Noetic Sciences article, referenced here.

[42] Rupert Sheldrake, *A New Science of Life: The Hypothesis of Morphic Resonance*, p. 13.

[43] Carl G. Jung, *The Archetypes and the Collective Unconscious*, p. 43.

[44] F. David Peat, *Synchronicity: The Bridge Between Matter and Mind*, p. 162.

[45] *Ibid.*, p. 163.

[46] *Ibid.*, p. 166.

[47] Carl G. Jung, *Synchronicity: An Acausal Connecting Principle*, quotation on back cover by *The Journal of Religious Thought*.

[48] F. David Peat, *Synchronicity: The Bridge Between Matter and Mind*, p. 16.

[49] *Ibid.,* p. 17.

[50] *Ibid.,* p. 94.

[51] *Ibid.,* p. 97.

[52] *Ibid.,* p. 99.

[53] *Ibid.,* p. 198.

[54] Marilyn Ferguson, "A New Perspective on Reality: The Special Updated Issue of The Brain/Mind Bulletin," from Wilber, *The Holographic Paradigm and Other Paradoxes: Exploring the Leading Edge of Science,* p. 10.

[55] Willis Harman, "A Re-examination of the Metaphysical Foundations of Modern Science," p. 101.

[56] Arne A. Wyller, *The Planetary Mind,* pp. 217-218.

[57] *Ibid.,* p. 218.

[58] *Ibid.,* p. 218.

[59] Satprem, *Sri Aurobindo or the Adventure of Consciousness,* p. 226.

[60] *Ibid.,* p. 227, fn.

[61] Arne A. Wyller, *The Planetary Mind,* pp. 218-219.

[62] Bohm and Hiley, *The Undivided Universe,* pp. 31-38, as quoted in *The Planetary Mind,* by Arne A. Wyller, p. 222.

[63] Arne A. Wyller, *The Planetary Mind,* p. 222.

[64] *Ibid.,* p. 232.

[65] *Ibid.,* p. 237.

[66] Alice A. Bailey, *Telepathy and the Etheric Vehicle,* p. 1.

[67] *Ibid.,* pp. 5-6.

[68] *Ibid.,* p. 19.

[69] *Ibid.,* p. 19.

[70] *Ibid.,* p. 12.

[71] *Ibid.,* pp. 18-19.

[72] *Ibid.,* pp. 8-9, 13-14.

[73] Alice A. Bailey, *Esoteric Psychology, Volume II,* p. 191.

[74] Alice A. Bailey, *Telepathy and the Etheric Vehicle,* p. 1.

[75] *Ibid.,* p. 4.

[76] Alice A. Bailey, *A Treatise on White Magic,* pp. 430-431.

[77] Alice A. Bailey, *Telepathy and the Etheric Vehicle,* p. 1.

[78] Alice A. Bailey, *A Treatise on White Magic,* p. 608.

[79] Alice A. Bailey, *Esoteric Psychology, Volume II,* pp. 572-576.

[80] *Ibid.,* pp. 573-574.

[81] Alice A. Bailey, *Discipleship in the New Age, Volume I,* pp. 49-50.

Chapter 4—Astrology, The Science of Relations

[1] H. P. Blavatsky, *The Secret Doctrine, Volume I*, p. 709, as referenced in *Esoteric Astrology*, p. 636.

[2] Betz, *Greek Magical Papyri*, p. 147, as quoted by David Ulansey in *The Origins of the Mithraic Mysteries*, pp. 85-86.

[3] *A Catholic Dictionary of Theology, Vol. I* (Nelson) 1962 as quoted in John Addey's, *Selected Writings*, p. 119.

[4] Interview with Will Keepin on "Astrology as a Sacred Science, the Holographic Universe, and the Deeper Reality," *The Mountain Astrologer*, Feb/Mar 1997, pp. 24-25.

[5] Bradley E. Schaefer, "Sunspots that Changed the World," *Sky & Telescope*, April 1997, p. 37.

[6] *Ibid.*, p. 38; Sallie Baliunas and Willie Soon, "The Sun-Climate Connection," *Sky & Telescope*, December 1996, pp. 38-41.

[7] Bradley E. Schaefer, "Sunspots that Changed the World," *Sky & Telescope*, April 1997, pp. 34-38.

[8] Sallie Baliunas and Willie Soon, "The Sun-Climate Connection," *Sky & Telescope*, December 1996, p. 39.

[9] *Ibid.*, p. 40-41.

[10] Bradley E. Schaefer, "Sunspots that Changed the World," *Sky & Telescope*, April 1997, p. 38.

[11] Kenneth R. Lang, "Unsolved Mysteries of the Sun—Part I," *Sky & Telescope*, August 1996, p. 42.

[12] Sun Kwok, "A Modern View of Planetary Nebulae," *Sky & Telescope*, July 1996, pp. 39, 43.

[13] "News Notes," *Sky & Telescope*, November 1996, p. 12.

[14] Jeff Kanipe, "Dark Matter and the Fate of the Universe," *Astronomy*, October 1996, p. 35.

[15] "News Notes," *Sky & Telescope*, June 1996, p. 12-13.

[16] Agni Yoga Society, *Agni Yoga*, Verses 666-667.

[17] Bo Rotan graduated from the University of California with a Summa cum Laude degree in Comparative Religion. He is a long time student of esotericism and also a dedicated amateur astronomer. Bo is one of the founding members of the LaHonda Study Group.

[18] Bo Rotan, "The Resonance Triad of Gravity, Magnetism and Plasma" in *The Journal of Esoteric Psychology*, Vol. XI, No. 1, Spring/Summer 1997, p. 56.

[19] *Ibid.*, pp. 65-66.

[20] *Ibid.*, p. 72.

[21] *Ibid.*, p. 66.

[22] *Ibid.*, pp. 73-74.

[23] *Ibid.*, p. 74.

[24] Dean Inge's discussion of Plotinus's teaching about free will as quoted in John Addey's, *Selected Writings*, p. 100.

[25] Alice A. Bailey, *A Treatise on White Magic*, p. 436.

[26] Alice A. Bailey, *Esoteric Astrology*, pp. 464-465.

[27] *Ibid.*, p. 500.

[28] The Tibetan lists nine points on page 513 of *Esoteric Astrology* and then asks us to add to them three points that he made earlier. I have taken some liberties to find points that he would consider relevant and to combine others that seemed to be duplicated somewhat. Thus, you should not consider these points that I have chosen to be all-inclusive; more research would likely uncover other points that are equally valuable.

[29] Alice A. Bailey, *Esoteric Astrology*, p. 513.

[30] Alice A. Bailey, *The Destiny of the Nations*, p. 93.

[31] Alice A. Bailey, *Esoteric Astrology*, p. 513.

[32] *Ibid.*, p. 513.

[33] *Ibid.*, p. 513.

[34] *Ibid.*, p. 513.

[35] *Ibid.*, pp. 513-514.

[36] *Ibid.*, pp. 16-17, 514.

[37] *Ibid.*, p. 109.

[38] *Ibid.*, p. 480.

[39] *Ibid.*, pp. 513-514.

[40] *Ibid.*, p. 514.

[41] *Ibid.*, pp. 98, 480.

[42] *Ibid.*, p. 413.

Chapter 5—The Seven Rays

[1] Alice A. Bailey, *Esoteric Psychology, Volume I*, p. 49.

[2] Alice A. Bailey, *A Treatise on Cosmic Fire*, p. 1058.

[3] Alice A. Bailey, *Esoteric Astrology*, pp. 348-349.

[4] Alice A. Bailey, *A Treatise on Cosmic Fire*, p. 1052.

[5] *Ibid.*, p. 177. For introductory information on the concept of the Seven Rays, refer to *Esoteric Psychology I*, particularly the "Introductory

Remarks" section of that book. Page 7 refers to the 49 groups of forces. In his first two volumes of *Tapestry of the Gods*, Michael Robbins discusses these energies in great detail from the standpoint of the psychology of the individual.

[6] Alice A. Bailey, *Esoteric Astrology*, p. 589.

[7] *Ibid.*, p. 590; adapted and modified.

[8] Alice A. Bailey, *Esoteric Psychology, Volume I*, p. 334.

[9] Alice A. Bailey, *A Treatise on Cosmic Fire*, p. 102.

[10] Alice A. Bailey, *Esoteric Astrology*, pp. 66-68.

[11] Alice A. Bailey, *Esoteric Psychology, Volume I*, pp. 320-321, 343.

[12] *Ibid.*, p. 391.

[13] *Ibid.*, pp. 352-353.

[14] *Ibid.*, p. 358.

[15] *Ibid.*, pp. 201-212, 411, 415-416.

[16] Alice A. Bailey, *The Rays and The Initiations*, pp. 501-518.

[17] Alice A. Bailey, *Esoteric Psychology, Volume I*, p. 48.

[18] Alice A. Bailey, *Esoteric Astrology*, p. 605.

[19] *Ibid.*, p. 490.

[20] *Ibid.*, pp. 66-68.

[21] Alice A. Bailey, *Esoteric Psychology, Volume I*, p. 48.

[22] Alice A. Bailey, *Esoteric Astrology*, p. 605.

[23] *Ibid.*, p. 490.

[24] Alice A. Bailey, *Esoteric Psychology, Volume I*, p. 48.

[25] Alice A. Bailey, *Esoteric Astrology*, p. 606.

[26] *Ibid.*, p. 490.

[27] *Ibid.*, pp. 66-68.

[28] *Ibid.*, p. 606.

[29] *Ibid.*, p. 490.

[30] *Ibid.*, p. 219.

[31] *Ibid.*, pp. 66-68.

[32] *Ibid.*, p. 606.

[33] *Ibid.*, p. 490.

[34] *Ibid.*, p. 66-68.

[35] Alice A. Bailey, *A Treatise on White Magic*, p. 511.

[36] Alice A. Bailey, *Esoteric Astrology*, p. 490.

[37] *Ibid.*, p. 606.

[38] *Ibid.*, pp. 66-68.

[39] *Ibid.*, p. 490.

[40] *Ibid.*, p. 606.

[41] *Ibid.*, pp. 66-68, 296, 299, 306, 139.

[42] Charles DeMotte, *The Inner Side of History*, p. 234.

[43] *Ibid.*, p. 234.

[44] Alice A. Bailey, *The Destiny of the Nations*, pp. 142-143.

Chapter 6—The Zodiacal Constellations

[1] Alice A. Bailey, *Esoteric Astrology*, pp. 621-2.

[2] *Ibid.*, p. 223.

[3] *Ibid.*, pp. 120-121, 144, 150.

[4] *Ibid.*, p. 216.

[5] *Ibid.*, pp. 140-141.

[6] Monique Pommier, "Exaltations of the Planets," *The Journal of Esoteric Psychology* 1995-1997.

[7] See reference 8 under "The Process of Veiling" in Chapter 7 for my rationale as to why the Sun might veil Jupiter on the personality level.

[8] Alice A. Bailey, *Esoteric Astrology*, p. 63.

[9] Marcia Moore and Mark Douglas, *Astrology, the Divine Science.*

[10] Alice A. Bailey, *Esoteric Astrology*, pp. 557-558.

[11] Monique Pommier, "Exaltations of the Planets," *The Journal of Esoteric Psychology* 1995-1997.

[12] Alice A. Bailey, *Esoteric Astrology*, p. 105.

[13] *Ibid.*, p. 332.

[14] *Ibid.*, p. 375.

[15] *Ibid.*, p. 401.

[16] *Ibid.*, p. 387.

[17] *Ibid.*, p. 383.

[18] Monique Pommier, "Exaltations of the Planets," *The Journal of Esoteric Psychology* 1995-1997.

[19] Alice A. Bailey, *Esoteric Astrology*, p. 399.

[20] *Ibid.*, p. 401.

[21] *Ibid.*, p. 403.

[22] *Ibid.*, p. 332.

[23] *Ibid.*, p. 347.

[24] *Ibid.*, p. 352.

[25] *Ibid.*, p. 355.

[26] *Ibid.*, p. 357.

[27] *Ibid.*, p. 332.

[28] Marcia Moore and Mark Douglas, *Astrology, the Divine Science.*

[29] Alice A. Bailey, *Esoteric Astrology*, p. 220.

[30] *Ibid.*, p. 342.

[31] *Ibid.*, p. 332.

[32] *Ibid.*, pp. 154, 288.

[33] See reference 8 under "The Process of Veiling" in Chapter 7 for my rationale as to why the Sun might veil Jupiter on the personality level.

[34] Alice A. Bailey, *Esoteric Astrology*, p. 297.

[35] *Ibid.*, p. 310.

[36] *Ibid.*, p. 332.

[37] *Ibid.*, pp. 253, 260.

[38] *Ibid.*, p. 279.

[39] Marcia Moore and Mark Douglas, *Astrology, the Divine Science.*

[40] Alice A. Bailey, *Esoteric Astrology*, p. 263.

[41] Monique Pommier, "Exaltations of the Planets," *The Journal of Esoteric Psychology* 1995-1997.

[42] Alice A. Bailey, *Esoteric Astrology*, pp. 281-282.

[43] *Ibid.*, p. 332.

[44] *Ibid.*, p. 238.

[45] *Ibid.*, p. 183.

[46] Marcia Moore and Mark Douglas, *Astrology, the Divine Science.*

[47] Alice A. Bailey, *Esoteric Astrology*, p. 245.

[48] *Ibid.*, pp. 244-245.

[49] *Ibid.*, p. 249.

[50] *Ibid.*, p. 250. The *Old Commentary* is quoted from frequently in the Alice A. Bailey books. I can only speculate that it is an ancient commentary to an even more ancient scripture. It is possible that the Tibetan Buddhists might yet have access to it.

[51] Alice A. Bailey, *Esoteric Astrology*, p. 333.

[52] *Ibid.*, p. 509.

[53] *Ibid.*, p. 333.

[54] *Ibid.*, pp. 188-189.

[55] *Ibid.*, pp. 176, 211.

[56] *Ibid.*, p. 191.

[57] *Ibid.*, p. 333.

[58] Patrizia Norelli-Bachelet, *The Gnostic Circle: A Synthesis in the Harmonies of the Cosmos.*

[59] Alice A. Bailey, *A Treatise on Cosmic Fire*, pp. 63, 101, 727. Also, refer to *A Treatise on Cosmic Fire* for information on schemes, rounds, and chains.

[60] Alice A. Bailey, *Esoteric Astrology*, p. 167.

[61] *Ibid.*, p. 170.

[62] Monique Pommier, "Exaltations of the Planets," *The Journal of Esoteric Psychology* 1995-1997.

[63] Alice A. Bailey, *Esoteric Astrology*, p. 171.

[64] *Ibid.*, p. 333.

[65] *Ibid.*, p. 137.

[66] *Ibid.*, p. 200.

[67] Marcia Moore and Mark Douglas, *Astrology, the Divine Science*.

[68] Alice A. Bailey, *A Treatise on White Magic*, p. 548.

[69] Alice A. Bailey, *Esoteric Astrology*, p. 333.

[70] *Ibid.*, p. 125.

[71] *Ibid.*, p. 129.

[72] Patrizia Noreli-Bachelet, *The Gnostic Circle: A Synthesis in the Harmonies of the Cosmos*, pp. 79-80.

[73] Alice A. Bailey, *Esoteric Astrology*, p. 215.

[74] Alice A. Bailey, *Discipleship in the New Age, Volume II*, p. 249.

[75] Alice A. Bailey, *Esoteric Astrology*, p. 130.

[76] *Ibid.*, p. 130.

[77] Monique Pommier, "Exaltations of the Planets," *The Journal of Esoteric Psychology* 1995-1997.

[78] Alice A. Bailey, *Esoteric Astrology*, pp. 131-132.

[79] *Ibid.*, p. 333.

Chapter 7—Solar and Planetary Energy

[1] Alice A. Bailey, *A Treatise on Cosmic Fire*, p. 229.

[2] Alice A. Bailey, *Esoteric Astrology*, p. 29.

[3] *Ibid.*, pp. 466-467.

[4] Excerpt from the *Gayatri*, an ancient mantram. (See Taimni in Bibliography.)

[5] Alice A. Bailey, *A Treatise on Cosmic Fire*, pp. 230-231.

[6] Alice A. Bailey, *A Treatise on White Magic*, p. 433.

[7] *Ibid.*, pp. 437-438.

[8] Alice A. Bailey, *A Treatise on Cosmic Fire*, p. 7.

[9] Alice A. Bailey, *Esoteric Astrology*, p. 503.

[10] *Ibid.,* p. 504.

[11] Alice A. Bailey, *A Treatise on White Magic,* p. 438.

[12] *Ibid.,* p. 439.

[13] Alice A. Bailey, *Esoteric Astrology,* p. 16.

[14] *Ibid.,* p. 31-32.

[15] Alice A. Bailey, *A Treatise on Cosmic Fire,* p. 181.

[16] Alice A. Bailey, *Esoteric Astrology,* pp. 507-508.

[17] Alice A. Bailey, *A Treatise on Cosmic Fire,* p. 369.

[18] Alice A. Bailey, *Esoteric Astrology,* p. 509.

[19] *Ibid.,* p. 219.

[20] *Ibid.,* p. 509.

[21] *Ibid.,* p. 669.

[22] *Ibid.,* pp. 321-322.

[23] *Ibid.,* p. 49.

[24] *Ibid.,* p. 393.

[25] *Ibid.,* pp. 296-297.

[26] *Ibid.,* p. 273.

[27] *Ibid.,* pp. 138-139.

[28] *Ibid.,* pp. 395, 399.

[29] *Ibid.,* p. 167.

[30] *Ibid.,* p. 297.

[31] *Ibid.,* p. 510.

[32] *Ibid.,* pp. 70-71.

[33] *Ibid.,* p. 392.

[34] *Ibid.,* pp. 195, 280.

[35] *Ibid.,* pp. 385-386.

[36] *Ibid.,* p. 126.

[37] Marcia Moore and Mark Douglas, *Astrology, the Divine Science.*

[38] Alice A. Bailey, *Esoteric Astrology,* p. 393.

[39] *Ibid.,* p. 78.

[40] *Ibid.,* p. 274.

[41] *Ibid.,* p. 274.

[42] *Ibid.,* p. 386.

[43] *Ibid.,* p. 509.

[44] *Ibid.,* p. 432.

[45] *Ibid.,* p. 353.

[46] *Ibid.,* pp. 353-354, 364.

[47] *Ibid.,* p. 149.

[48] *Ibid.*, p. 172.
[49] *Ibid.*, p. 127.
[50] *Ibid.*, p. 354.
[51] *Ibid.*, pp. 173, 402.
[52] *Ibid.*, p. 543.
[53] *Ibid.*, p. 385.
[54] *Ibid.*, p. 447.
[55] *Ibid.*, pp. 164-165.
[56] *Ibid.*, pp. 215-216.
[57] *Ibid.*, p. 217.
[58] *Ibid.*, p. 71.
[59] *Ibid.*, pp. 148-149.
[60] *Ibid.*, p. 342.
[61] *Ibid.*, p. 164.
[62] *Ibid.*, p. 20.
[63] *Ibid.*, p. 300.
[64] *Ibid.*, p. 200.
[65] *Ibid.*, pp. 200-201.
[66] *Ibid.*, pp. 219-220, 275.
[67] *Ibid.*, p. 217.
[68] *Ibid.*, p. 297.
[69] *Ibid.*, p. 322.
[70] *Ibid.*, p. 323.
[71] *Ibid.*, p. 214.
[72] *Ibid.*, pp. 13, 219.
[73] *Ibid.*, p. 399.
[74] *Ibid.*, p. 400.
[75] Alice A. Bailey, *Esoteric Healing*, p. 341.
[76] *Ibid.*, pp. 339-342.

Chapter 8—Earth Energy

[1] Alice A. Bailey, *A Treatise on Cosmic Fire*, p. 367.
[2] *Ibid.*, p. 674.
[3] *Ibid.*, pp. 281, 301-302, 1069; *A Treatise on White Magic*, p. 432.
[4] Alice A. Bailey, *A Treatise on Cosmic Fire*, pp. 432, 464.
[5] *Ibid.*, p. 291.
[6] *Ibid.*, p. 361.
[7] *Ibid.*, p. 673.

[8] *Ibid.*, pp. 361-362.

[9] *Ibid.*, p. 1212.

[10] *Ibid.*, pp. 770-771.

[11] *Ibid.*, p. 1043.

[12] *Ibid.*, p. 882.

[13] *Ibid.*, p. 1255.

[14] Alice A. Bailey, *Esoteric Astrology*, p. 362.

[15] *Ibid.*, pp. 371-372.

[16] Alice A. Bailey, *A Treatise on White Magic*, p. 378.

[17] Alice A. Bailey, *Esoteric Astrology*, p. 581.

[18] *Ibid.*, p. 149.

[19] *Ibid.*, pp. 585, 590-593.

[20] *Ibid.*, pp. 582-583.

[21] *Ibid.*, pp. 583-585.

[22] *Ibid.*, p. 587.

[23] *Ibid.*, p. 372.

[24] *Ibid.*, p. 411, 558, 427, 415, 156, 158, 633-634, 446, 197, 168, 195-196.

[25] *Ibid.*, pp. 376-377.

[26] Alice A. Bailey, *Esoteric Astrology*, p. 589.

[27] Alice A. Bailey, *A Treatise on White Magic*, p. 380.

[28] *Ibid.*, p. 390.

[29] *Ibid.*, pp. 378-382.

[30] Alice A. Bailey, *Esoteric Psychology, Volume II*, p. 598.

[31] Alice A. Bailey, *The Externalisation of the Hierarchy*, p. 20.

[32] Alice A. Bailey, *Esoteric Psychology, Volume II*, p. 577.

[33] Alice A. Bailey, *Discipleship in the New Age, Volume II*, pp. 5-6.

[34] Alice A. Bailey, *The Externalisation of the Hierarchy*, p. 520.

[35] Alice A. Bailey, *Esoteric Astrology*, p. 411, 558, 198, 416, 427, 445, 438, 590, 156, 168, 319, 426.

[36] *Ibid.*, p. 445.

[37] Alice A. Bailey, *Discipleship in the New Age, Volume II*, p. 15.

[38] Alice A. Bailey, *A Treatise on White Magic*, p. 426.

[39] Alice A. Bailey, *Esoteric Astrology*, p. 427.

[40] Alice A. Bailey, *A Treatise on White Magic*, p. 382.

[41] *Ibid.*, p. 383.

[42] Alice A. Bailey, *Esoteric Astrology*, p. 558, 416, 427, 415, 198, 590, 319, 158, 168, 156.

[43] Alice A. Bailey, *A Treatise on White Magic*, p. 414.

[44] *Ibid.*, pp. 414-415.

[45] *Ibid.*, p. 430.

[46] *Ibid.*, p. 415.

[47] *Ibid.*, pp. 416-417.

[48] *Ibid.*, p. 431.

[49] Alice A. Bailey, *Esoteric Psychology, Volume II*, p. 705.

[50] *Ibid.*, p. 705.

Chapter 9—Timing, Relationships, and Karmic Opportunity

[1] Alice A. Bailey, *Esoteric Astrology*, p. 541.

[2] Agni Yoga Society, *Fiery World III*, p. 157, v. 215.

[3] Alice A. Bailey, *Esoteric Astrology*, p. 216.

[4] Alice A. Bailey, *A Treatise on Cosmic Fire*, p. 275.

[5] Alice A. Bailey, *A Treatise on White Magic*, p. 511.

[6] Alice A. Bailey, *A Treatise on Cosmic Fire*, p. 1022.

[7] Agni Yoga Society, *Fiery World III*, Verse 184.

[8] Alice A. Bailey, *A Treatise on Cosmic Fire*, p. 396.

[9] Carl G. Jung, *The Archetypes and the Collective Unconscious*, pp. 299, 304.

[10] Dane Rudhyar, *The Astrological Houses*.

[11] Alice A. Bailey, *Esoteric Astrology*, p. 480.

[12] *Ibid.*, p. 382.

[13] *Ibid.*, p. 305.

[14] *Ibid.*, p. 480.

[15] Curtis Smith, *Jung's Quest for Wholeness*, pp. 114, 120.

[16] Carl G. Jung, *The Archetypes and the Collective Unconscious*, p. 357.

[17] *Ibid.*, p. 361.

[18] *Ibid.*, pp. 361, 389, 363, 388.

[19] *Ibid.*, pp. 65-68.

[20] Alice A. Bailey, *A Treatise on Cosmic Fire*, p. 159.

[21] Ed Perrone, *Astrology: A New Age Guide*, p. 214.

[22] Alice A. Bailey, *Esoteric Astrology*, p. 305.

[23] *Ibid.*, pp. 559, 563.

[24] *Ibid.*, p. 382.

[25] *Ibid.*, p. 357.

[26] *Ibid.*, pp. 382, 557.

[27] *Ibid.*, p. 350.

[28] Alice A. Bailey, *A Treatise on White Magic*, p. 548.

29 Alice A. Bailey, *Esoteric Astrology*, p. 382.

30 *Ibid.*, p. 556.

31 W. Y. Evans-Wentz, *Tibetan Yoga and Secret Doctrines*, p. 12.

32 Alice A. Bailey, *Esoteric Astrology*, p. 183.

33 *Ibid.*, pp. 346-347.

34 Carl G. Jung, *The Archetypes and the Collective Unconscious*, p. 235.

35 Alice A. Bailey, *Discipleship in the New Age, Volume II*, p. 25.

36 Alice A. Bailey, *Esoteric Astrology*, pp. 183-184.

37 Alice A. Bailey, *A Treatise on Cosmic Fire*, p. 1044.

38 Dion Fortune, *Moon Magic*, pp. 106, 125.

39 Alice A. Bailey, *Esoteric Astrology*, p. 305.

40 Carl G. Jung, *The Archetypes and the Collective Unconscious*, p. 243.

41 Alice A. Bailey, *Esoteric Astrology*, p. 416.

42 *Ibid.*, p. 479.

43 *Ibid.*, pp. 415, 460.

44 *Ibid.*, pp. 429-430.

45 *Ibid.*, p. 468.

46 *Ibid.*, p. 415.

47 *Ibid.*, pp. 426-427, 537.

48 *Ibid.*, pp. 465-466.

49 *Ibid.*, p. 589.

50 *Ibid.*, pp. 426-427.

51 *Ibid.*, p. 305.

52 Carl G. Jung, *The Archetypes and the Collective Unconscious*, pp. 373, 379.

53 Alice A. Bailey, *A Treatise on Cosmic Fire*, pp. 217-218, 696.

54 Alice A. Bailey, *Esoteric Astrology*, pp. 548-549.

55 *Ibid.*, p. 304.

56 *Ibid.*, pp. 256, 275-276.

57 Carl G. Jung, *The Archetypes and the Collective Unconscious*, p. 372.

58 Alice A. Bailey, *A Treatise on White Magic*, p. 100.

59 Alice A. Bailey, *A Treatise on Cosmic Fire*, pp. 26-27.

60 Alice A. Bailey, *Esoteric Astrology*, p. 479. (The ancient seer referred to is probably Pythagoras.)

61 *Ibid.*, pp. 305-306.

62 Three Initiates, *The Kybalion*, p. 171.

63 René Querido, *A Western Approach to Reincarnation and Karma: Selected Lectures & Writings by Rudolf Steiner*.

[64] Dane Rudhyar, *Rhythm of Wholeness*, pp. 174-174.

[65] Alice A. Bailey, *Esoteric Astrology*, p. 445.

[66] Alice A. Bailey, *Discipleship in the New Age, Volume I*, p. 5.

[67] *Ibid.*, pp. 96-97.

[68] *Ibid.*, pp. 714, 726.

[69] Alice A. Bailey, *A Treatise on Cosmic Fire*, pp. 770-771.

[70] Alice A. Bailey, *Esoteric Astrology*, p. 444.

[71] Alice A. Bailey, *Discipleship in the New Age, Volume I*, p. 772.

[72] Alice A. Bailey, *Esoteric Astrology*, p. 408.

[73] Alice A. Bailey, *A Treatise on Cosmic Fire*, p. 570.

[74] M. Temple Richmond, *Sirius*, p. 277.

[75] *Ibid.*, p. 280.

[76] Alice A. Bailey, *Esoteric Astrology*, p. 138.

[77] *Ibid.*, p. 164.

[78] *Ibid.*, p. 144.

[79] *Ibid.*, p. 165.

[80] *Ibid.*, p. 249.

[81] *Ibid.*, pp. 158, 434-436.

[82] Alice A. Bailey, *A Treatise on Cosmic Fire*, p. 801.

[83] Alice A. Bailey, *Esoteric Astrology*, pp. 164, 310-311, 167.

[84] Steve Bhaerman, *Driving Your Own Karma: Swami Beyondananda's Tour Guide to Enlightenment*, p. 65.

Chapter 10—What Energies Are Available Now?

[1] Alice A. Bailey, *Esoteric Astrology*, p. 5.

[2] *Ibid.*, p. 9.

[3] *Ibid.*, p. 449.

[4] Carl G. Jung, *Mysterium Coniunctionis: An Inquiry into the Separation and Synthesis of Psychic Opposites in Alchemy*, p. 457.

[5] Vivian B. Martin, *Astrocycles*, p. 297.

[6] *Ibid.*, p. 297.

[7] *Ibid.*, p. 297.

[8] *Ibid.*, p. 297.

[9] *Ibid.*, p. 297.

[10] Sullivan, *Retrograde Planets: Traversing the Inner Landscape*, pp. 15-16, 56.

[11] Monique Pommier, "Exaltations of the Planets," *The Journal of Esoteric Psychology* 1995-1997.

[12] Alice A. Bailey, *Esoteric Astrology*, p. 282.

[13] *Ibid.*, p. 409.

[14] *Ibid.*, p. 137.

[15] Alice A. Bailey, *Discipleship in the New Age, Volume II*, p. 304.

[16] Carl G. Jung, *The Archetypes and the Collective Unconscious*, p. 235.

[17] See discussion in Chapter 9 under "The Circle / The Wheel of the Zodiac," which references Alice A. Bailey, *A Treatise on Cosmic Fire*, p. 159 for this particular piece of information.

[18] Alice A. Bailey, *Esoteric Astrology*, p. 561.

Chapter 11—Meditation

[1] Alice A. Bailey, *Esoteric Astrology*, p. 550.

[2] *Ibid.*, pp. 450-451.

[3] Alice A. Bailey, *Discipleship in the New Age, Volume II*, p. 15.

[4] *Ibid.*, pp. 5-6.

[5] Alice A. Bailey, *Discipleship in the New Age, Volume I*, pp. 583-584.

[6] Alice A. Bailey, *Telepathy and the Etheric Vehicle*, p. 4.

[7] Alice A. Bailey, *A Treatise on White Magic*, pp. 422-423.

[8] Three Initiates, *The Kybalion*, p. 77.

[9] World Goodwill, "Three Spiritual Festivals" flyer.

[10] Alice A. Bailey, *Esoteric Psychology, Volume II*, p. 593.

[11] Alice A. Bailey, *Esoteric Astrology*, pp. 228-229.

[12] Alice A. Bailey, *Discipleship in the New Age, Volume II*, pp. 139-142.

[13] *Ibid.*, pp. 144-147.

[14] Alice A. Bailey, *A Treatise on Cosmic Fire*, p. 926.

[15] Alice A. Bailey, *Discipleship in the New Age, Volume II*, pp. 18-19.

[16] Alice A. Bailey, *A Treatise on White Magic*, pp. 345-346.

[17] Alice A. Bailey, *Discipleship in the New Age, Volume II*, pp. 228-231.

[18] *Ibid.*, p. 25.

[19] Alice A. Bailey, *Discipleship in the New Age, Volume I*, p. 632.

[20] *Ibid.*, p. 664.

[21] *Ibid.*, p. 467.

[22] Alice A. Bailey, *Esoteric Psychology, Volume II*, p. 580.

[23] Alice A. Bailey, *Esoteric Astrology*, pp. 569-570.

[24] *Ibid.*, p. 573.

[25] *Ibid.*, p. 574.

[26] Alice A. Bailey, *Discipleship in the New Age, Volume II*, p. 20.

[27] *Ibid.*, p. 26.

[28] *Ibid.*, p. 16.

[29] Alice A. Bailey, *Esoteric Astrology*, p. 299.

[30] World Goodwill, a worldwide organization of groups around the world "works to establish right human relations through the use of the power of goodwill." They hold meditations at the times of the spiritual festivals, discussed here. (See "Resources" for information on how to contact them.) This information is adapted from their leaflet, "Three Spiritual Festivals."

[31] Alice A. Bailey, *The Externalisation of the Hierarchy*, p. 458.

[32] *Ibid.*, p. 599.

[33] Alice A. Bailey, *Esoteric Psychology, Volume II*, pp. 687-688, 698-699.

[34] *Ibid.*, p. 698.

[35] *The Holy Bible*, Romans VIII:29.

[36] Alice A. Bailey, *Esoteric Astrology*, p. 355.

[37] *Ibid.*, p. 299.

[38] Alice A. Bailey, *Esoteric Psychology, Volume II*, p. 196.

[39] *Ibid.*, pp. 196-197.

[40] *Ibid.*, p. 197.

[41] *Ibid.*, pp. 194-195.

[42] Alice A. Bailey, *A Treatise on White Magic*, p. 431.

Chapter 12—The Living Commitment

[1] Three Initiates, *The Kybalion*, p. 213.

[2] Agni Yoga Society, *Agni Yoga*, Verse 527.

Bibliography

Achterberg, Jeanne. "Consciousness in Dialogue: Responses to Ken Wilber: Humanity's Common Consciousness." *Noetic Sciences Review*, Winter 1996.

Addey, John. *Selected Writings*. Tempe, AZ: American Federation of Astrologers, Inc., 1976.

Agni Yoga Society. *Agni Yoga*. New York: Agni Yoga Society, Inc.

——*Fiery World, Volume III*. New York: Agni Yoga Society, Inc., 1948.

Allen, Richard Hinckley. *Star Names: Their Lore and Meaning*. New York: Dover Publications, Inc., 1963.

Astronomy. Waukesha, WI: Kalmbach Publishing Co., October 1996, June 1997.

Bailey, Alice A. *A Treatise on Cosmic Fire*. New York: Lucis Trust, 1962.

——*A Treatise on White Magic*. New York: Lucis Trust, 1979.

——*Discipleship in the New Age, Volume I*. New York: Lucis Trust, 1972.

——*Discipleship in the New Age, Volume II*. New York: Lucis Trust, 1955.

——*Esoteric Astrology*. New York: Lucis Trust, 1951.

——*Esoteric Healing*. New York: Lucis Trust, 1953.

——*Esoteric Psychology, Volume I*. New York: Lucis Trust, 1962.

——*Esoteric Psychology, Volume II*. New York: Lucis Trust, 1970.

——*Initiation, Human and Solar*. New York: Lucis Trust, 1951.

——*Telepathy and the Etheric Vehicle*. New York: Lucis Trust, 1950.

——*The Destiny of the Nations*. New York: Lucis Trust, 1949.

——*The Externalisation of the Hierarchy*. New York: Lucis Trust, 1957.

——*The Rays and The Initiations*. New York: Lucis Trust, 1960.

Barker, A. T., compiler. *The Mahatma Letters to A. P. Sinnett*. Facsimile Edition. Pasadena: Theosophical University Press, 1975.

Bateson, Gregory. *Mind and Nature: A Necessary Unity*. New York: Bantam Books, 1980.

Besant, Annie. *Study in Consciousness*. Los Angeles: Theosophical Publishing House, 1918.

Bhaerman, Steve. *Driving Your Own Karma: Swami Beyondananda's Tour Guide to Enlightenment*. Rochester, Vermont: Destiny Books, 1989.

Blavatsky, Helena P. *The Secret Doctrine, Volume I*. London: The Theosophical Publishing Company, Ltd., 1888.

Bohm, David. *Wholeness and the Implicate Order*. London and New York: Routledge, 1983.

Bohm, David and B. J. Hiley. *The Undivided Universe*. London and New York: Routledge, 1993.

Capra, Fritjof. *The Tao of Physics*. Boulder: Shambhala, 1975.

Capt, E. Raymond. *The Glory of the Stars*. Thousand Oaks, California: Archaeological Institute of America, 1976.

DeMotte, Charles. *The Inner Side of History*. Mariposa, California: Source Publications, 1997.

Evans-Wentz, W. Y., ed. *Tibetan Yoga and Secret Doctrines*. London: Oxford University Press, 1935.

Fagan, Cyril. *Primer of Sidereal Astrology*. Tempe, AZ: American Federation of Astrologers, Inc., 1971

Fortune, Dion. *Esoteric Orders and Their Work*. London: The Aquarian Press, 1987.

——*Moon Magic*. York Beach, Maine: Samuel Weiser, Inc., 1988.

——*The Cosmic Doctrine*. Great Britain: Helios Book Service Ltd., 1966.

——*The Training and Work of an Initiate*. London: The Aquarian Press, 1987.

Govinda, Lama Anagarika. *Foundations of Tibetan Mysticism*. London: Rider & Company, 1959.

Hall, Manly P. *Invisible Records of Thought and Action*. Los Angeles: The Philosophical Research Society, Inc., 1990.

——*The Secret Teachings of All Ages*. Los Angeles: The Philosophical Research Society, Inc., 1988.

Harman, Willis W. *A Re-examination of the Metaphysical Foundations of Modern Science*: Research Report, Causality Project. Sausalito, California: Institute of Noetic Sciences, 1991.

Holmes, Ernest. *The Science of Mind*. New York: Jeremy P. Tarcher/Putnam Edition, 1997.

Holy Bible. *Book of Romans*.

Jung, C. G. *The Collected Works of C.G.Jung, Volume 8: Synchronicity: An Acausal Connecting Principle*. Translated by R. F. C. Hull, Bollinger Series XX, Second Edition. Princeton: Princeton University Press, 1973.

——*The Collected Works of C. G. Jung, Volume 9: The Archetypes and the Collective Unconscious*. Translated by R. F. C. Hull, Bollinger Series XX, Second Edition. Princeton: Princeton University Press, 1968.

——*The Collected Works of C.G.Jung, Volume 14: Mysterium Coniunctionis: An Inquiry into the Separation and Synthesis of Psychic Opposites in*

Alchemy. Translated by R. F. C. Hull, Bollinger Series XX, Second Edition. Princeton: Princeton University Press, 1963.

Keepin, Will. "Astrology as a Sacred Science, the Holographic Universe, and the Deeper Reality." Cedar Ridge, California: *The Mountain Astrologer*, Feb/Mar 1997.

Martin, Vivian B. *Astrocycles*. New York: Ballantine Books, 1990.

Moore, Marcia and Mark Douglas. *Astrology, the Divine Science*. York Harbor, Maine: Arcane Publications, 1971.

Norelli-Bachelet, Patrizia. *The Gnostic Circle: A Synthesis in the Harmonies of the Cosmos*. New York: Æon Books, 1975.

Parker, Ann E. *Galactic Astrology*. Skokie, Illinois: Ann E. Parker (847-674-4506), 1996.

Peat, F. David. *Synchronicity: The Bridge Between Matter and Mind*. New York: Bantam Books, 1987.

Perrone, Ed. *Astrology: A New Age Guide*. Wheaton, Illinois: The Theosophical Publishing House, 1983.

Pommier, Monique. "Exaltations of the Planets." *The Journal of Esoteric Psychology*. Mariposa, California: University of the Seven Rays Publishing, 1995-1997.

Prater, Richard B. *Bridge to Superconsciousness*. Mariposa, California: Source Publications, in process of publication.

Querido, René. *A Western Approach to Reincarnation and Karma: Selected Lectures & Writings by Rudolf Steiner*. Anthroposophic Press, 1997.

Restak, Richard M., M.D. *The Brain, The Last Frontier*. New York: Warner Books, 1979.

Rhine, J. B. *New World of the Mind*. New York: William Sloane Associates, Apollo Editions, 1953.

Richmond, M. Temple. *Sirius*. Mariposa, California: Source Publications, 1997.

Rigor, Joseph E. *The Power of Fixed Stars*. Hammond, Indiana: Astrology and Spiritual Publishers, Inc., 1979.

Robbins, Michael D. *Tapestry of the Gods*. Mariposa, California: University of the Seven Rays Publishing, 1996.

Rotan, Bo. "The Resonance Triad of Gravity, Magnetism and Plasma," *The Journal of Esoteric Psychology*, Vol. XI, No. 1. Mariposa, CA: University of the Seven Rays Publishing, 1997.

Rudhyar, Dane. *Rhythm of Wholeness*. Wheaton, Illinois: The Theosophical Publishing House, 1983.

——*The Astrological Houses*. New York: Doubleday & Company, Inc., 1972.

Satprem, *Sri Aurobindo or the Adventure of Consciousness*. Translated by Luc Venet. Mt. Vernon, Washington: Institute for Evolutionary Research, 1993.

Seymour, Percy. *Astrology: The Evidence of Science*. London: Arkana, 1988.

Sheldrake, Rupert. *A New Science of Life: The Hypothesis of Morphic Resonance*. Rochester, Vermont: Park Street Press, 1995.

Sky & Telescope. Cambridge, MA: Sky Publishing Corporation, March, April, June, July, August, November, and December 1996.

Smith, Curtis D. *Jung's Quest for Wholeness: A Religious and Historical Perspective*. Albany: State University of New York Press, 1990.

Smith, Huston. *The Illustrated World's Religions: A Guide to Our Wisdom Traditions*. San Francisco: Harper Collins, 1991.

Sullivan, Erin. *Retrograde Planets: Traversing the Inner Landscape*. New York: Penguin Books, 1992.

Taimni, I. K. *Gayatri*. Adyar, India: The Theosophical Publishing House, 1974.

Targ, Russell. "Remarkable Distant Viewing." *Noetic Sciences Review*, Summer 1996.

Three Initiates, *The Kybalion, A Study of the Hermetic Philosophy of Ancient Egypt and Greece*. Chicago: The Yogi Publication Society Masonic Temple.

Ulansey, David. *The Origins of the Mithraic Mysteries*. Oxford: Oxford University Press, 1989.

Wilber, Ken, ed. *Quantum Questions*. Boston: Shambhala, 1984.

——*The Holographic Paradigm and Other Paradoxes: Exploring the Leading Edge of Science*. Boston and London: Shambhala, 1985.

World Goodwill. "Three Spiritual Festivals."

Wyller, Arne A. *The Planetary Mind*. Aspen, Colorado: MacMurray & Beck, Inc., 1996.

Resources

The **School for Esoteric Astrology (S.E.A.)** was founded in 1997 to further the study of the esoteric astrology of Alice A. Bailey and the Tibetan. Course work is offered by correspondence to seekers whether or not they intend to be counseling astrologers. Studies cover the foundations of esoteric occultism, esoteric astrology, meditation, self-discipline, topics in astronomy, healing, and mystical geometry. No fees are charged. You can reach the S.E.A. care of Maureen Richmond, Director, P.O. Box 97187, Raleigh, NC 27624-7187, voice 919-846-8554, fax 919-870-5397.

The **University of the Seven Rays Publishing House** publishes the *Journal of Esoteric Psychology*, the purpose of which is to present articles by students of the ageless wisdom on topics such as esoteric philosophy, psychology, healing, cosmology, astrology, discipleship and initiation, meditation, spiritual politics and economics. For more information, contact P.O. Box 1160, Mariposa, CA 95338, voice 209-966-5379, fax 209-966-6811, or send email to source@yosemite.net. Their web site is located at http://www.yosemite.net/sources/

The **University of the Seven Rays** is an alternative institution of higher education that grants degrees in the esoteric sciences. For information on its programs of study, contact them at 128 Manhattan Ave, Jersey City Heights, NJ 07307, voice 201-798-7777, fax 201-659-3263.

World Goodwill, a worldwide organization of groups around the world "works to establish right human relations through the use of the power of goodwill." They hold meditations at the times of the spiritual festivals discussed in this book. For more information on the special meditations they hold for the spiritual festivals and about their work in general, contact them at 120 Wall Street, 24th Floor, New York, NY 10005. There are many of these goodwill organizations around the world; you can request a list of them.

Sydney Goodwill Unit of Service, Ltd. is one of the World Goodwill organizations. They also distribute esoteric books in the South Pacific. You can contact them at: Suite 2, Rear 34 President Ave, (P.O. Box 627), Caringbah, NSW 2229 Australia.

You can contact the **Arcane School**, a correspondence school founded by Alice A. Bailey, and **Lucis Trust**, the publishers of the books by Alice A. Bailey and the Tibetan, at 120 Wall Street, 24th Floor, New York, NY 10005. They publish a bi-monthly magazine called *The Beacon*.

The **School For Esoteric Studies** has correspondence courses on the ageless wisdom teachings, with an emphasis on the work of Alice A. Bailey and the Tibetan. You can contact them at 58 Oak Terrace, Asheville, NC 28704-2820, phone 704-654-9989.

The **Agni Yoga Society** is the custodian of the teachings given to humanity by Helena Roerich in the Agni Yoga series of books. They also have a fine museum of the paintings of Nicholas Roerich. You can contact them at 319 West 107th Street, New York, NY 10025-2799, which is also the location of the museum.

To embark on a correspondence course of study of the ageless wisdom in the western tradition, including the principles and practices of Tarot, Qabalah, Alchemy, Astrology, and the esoteric meaning and use of Sound and Color, you can contact **Builders of the Adytum**, (B.O.T.A.), 5101-05 No. Figueroa St., Los Angeles, CA 90042, voice 800-255-0041, fax 213-255-4166. The B.O.T.A. teachings were generated from the research of Paul Foster Case and Ann Davies. They have a web site at: http://ns. atanda.com/bota/

The **Center For Visionary Leadership** combines spirituality with practical considerations, such as leadership training and consulting, governance, and economics. You can contact them at 3408 Wisconsin Avenue, Suite 200, Washington, DC 20016, voice 202-237-2800, fax 202-237-1399, http://visionarylead.org/

The **School of Natural Science** offers correspondence courses in values and principles of living. Write them at 25355 Spanish Ranch Road, Los Gatos, CA 95030.

The **International Foundation for Integral Psychology** is engaged in the development of the theory and practice of Integral Psychology as an integration of American, European, and Eastern approaches to psychospiritual growth, combining esoteric meditation with counseling and psychotherapy. You can reach them care of Robert Gerard, President, 12021 Wilshire Blvd., Suite 537, Los Angeles, CA 90025-1200.

Meditation Mount offers periodic meditations and courses by correspondence. You can reach them at P.O. Box 566, Ojai, CA 93024, voice 805-646-5508, fax 805-646-3303, http://www.meditation.com/

Pathways To Peace holds that by acting in concert we can make a difference in the quality of our lives, our institutions, and our environment. You can contact them at P.O. Box 1057, Larkspur, CA 94977, voice 415-461-0500, fax 415-925-0330 (San Francisco area).

There are 29 **Robert Muller Schools**, based on Dr. Robert Muller's world core curriculum. You can contact their International Coordinating Center at 6005 Royaloak Dr., Arlington, TX 76016-1035, voice 817-654-1018, fax 817-654-1028.

The **Theosophical Association Scandinavia** offers an extensive esoteric study curriculum. They were featured in the Fall 1996 issue of the *Journal of Esoteric Psychology* under Focus on World Servers. You can contact them at Åarestrupsvej 17, 2500 Valby, Copenhagen, Denmark, tel. 45-36-46-60-70, and send them email in care of Niels Brønsted (bronsted@post4.tele.dk). They have a web site at http://www.teosofia.dk.

Another **Theosophical** contact in Denmark for those interested in research library facilities and an esoteric bookstore is Paul Birkholm, **Teosofisk Boghandel**, Tove Lund Ansvang, Sankt Knuds Vej 39, 1903 Frederiksberg C, Denmark, telephone 31-23-27-21, or send email care of: ansvang@post1.tele.dk.

The **Agnischool** is another spiritual school in Europe and was featured in the Fall/Winter 1997-98 issue of the *Journal of Esoteric Psychology* under Focus on World Servers. You can contact them at Eggholzliweg 2, CH-3074 Muri, Bern, Switzerland.

Light on the Bay and **Starfire Servers** are two San Francisco Bay Area organizations that hold full-moon meditations, coordinate study groups, and publish newsletters. You can contact Light on the Bay at P.O. Box 14771, Berkeley CA 94712 and Starfire Servers at their internet address, http://www.spircom.org/

Arcana Workshops offers classes and meditations on the ageless wisdom. You can reach them at Box 506, Manhattan Beach, CA 90267-0506, voice 310-379-9990, email: WebDisciple@meditationtraining.org.

Psychologist Roberto Assagioli, a student of the Tibetan's, founded Psychosynthesis, which has had profound impact on the human potential movement. There are many psychosynthesis organizations around the world. A starting contact is the **Association for the Advancement of Psychosynthesis (AAP)**, which has a web site at http://www.aap-psychosynthesis.org/. Their mailing address is AAP, P.O. Box 597, Amherst, MA 01004.

For good foundational information on the ageless wisdom teachings of the Trans-Himalayan School of Yoga, contact **The Theosophical Society**, P.O. Box 270, Wheaton, IL 60189. Their **Krotona** center holds classes and seminars and has an extensive bookstore and library. Krotona is located at 32 Krotona Hill, Ojai, CA 93023.

The **T.S.G. Publishing Foundation, Inc**. holds classes and seminars on the ageless wisdom and publishes the many books of Torkum Saraydarian. One of their current emphases is on their valuable leadership training series. You can contact them at P.O. Box 7068, Cave Creek, AZ 85327, voice 602-502-1909, fax 602-502-0713.

The **Center for World Servers**, is a spiritual study group that sponsors speakers, offers classes on the work of the Tibetan, and holds full-moon meditations throughout the year. You can contact them at 1875 Hendersonville Rd., Ashville, NC 28803, phone 704-687-0044.

The **Esoteric Sciences and Creative Education Foundation (ESCEF)** is an educational and spiritual service organization promoting esoteric arts and sciences and encouraging their practical and intelligent application in the world. They publish a newsletter and hold conferences in Australia. Contact them at 23 Everard Terrace, Forestville SA 5035, Australia, voice (08) 8371-1880, fax (08) 8371-1260.

The **White Mountain Education Association**'s web site at http://www.primenet.com/~wtmtn/ has a wealth of information on various aspects of the ageless wisdom teachings. They are in Prescott, AZ.

The **Other Dimensions Training Center** offers information or courses on esoteric topics. You can reach them at P.O. Box 2269, Salmon Arm, British Columbia, Canada VIE 3E4, 604-832-8483 or send email to: ods@jetstream.net.

Many political and new paradigm groups are listed in the book, *Spiritual Politics,* by Corinne McLaughlin and Gordon Davidson.

Wisdom Publications is a non-profit publisher of books on Buddhism, Tibet, and related East-West themes, with an appreciation of Buddhism as a living philosophy and the commitment of preserving and transmitting important works from all the major Buddhist traditions. You can reach them at 361 Newbury Street, Boston, MA 02115, voice 617-536-1897, fax 617-536-1897. Many of the ageless wisdom teachings have been preserved through the Tibetan Buddhist tradition.

To order new, used, and hard-to-find books on the ageless wisdom teachings, you can contact **Sunrise Books**, 3054 Telegraph Avenue, Berkeley, CA, telephone 510-841-6372.

Index

Source Publications

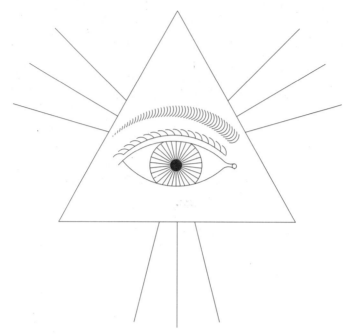

Source Publications is dedicated to providing carefully researched, clearly written, and thoroughly documented books on the Ageless Wisdom Teachings.

We specialize in books that empower people spiritually and yet offer practical techniques for living in today's world. Our books are unique— they contain many ideas and concepts that are only now beginning to emerge.

We welcome your questions and comments.

For information on our selections, please contact us:

Source Publications
P.O. Box 1160
Mariposa, CA 95338
source@yosemite.net